Michael Slote Encountering Chinese Philosophy

Fudan Studies in Encountering Chinese Philosophy

Series Editor:
Yong Huang, Chinese University of Hong Kong, Hong Kong

A gap exists between scholars doing Chinese philosophy and scholars in the mainstream Western philosophy, each working in their own tradition without knowing much, if at all, of what is going on in the other tradition. This series tackles the problem head on by promoting dialogues between philosophers specializing in Chinese philosophy and mainstream Western philosophers.

Each volume features one prominent living philosopher in the Western tradition, who may or may not know anything about Chinese philosophy. Around a dozen or so leading scholars in Chinese philosophy are invited to critically engage various aspects of the Western philosopher's work from Chinese philosophical perspectives. The featured Western philosopher is then asked to respond to the challenges brought to his/her philosophy by scholars in Chinese philosophy.

Michael Slote Encountering Chinese Philosophy

A Cross-Cultural Approach to Ethics and Moral Philosophy

Edited by Yong Huang

BLOOMSBURY ACADEMIC
LONDON • NEW YORK • OXFORD • NEW DELHI • SYDNEY

BLOOMSBURY ACADEMIC
Bloomsbury Publishing Plc
50 Bedford Square, London, WC1B 3DP, UK
1385 Broadway, New York, NY 10018, USA
29 Earlsfort Terrace, Dublin 2, Ireland

BLOOMSBURY, BLOOMSBURY ACADEMIC and the Diana logo are trademarks of
Bloomsbury Publishing Plc

First published in Great Britain 2020
This paperback edition published in 2022

Copyright © Yong Huang and Contributors, 2020

Yong Huang has asserted his right under the Copyright, Designs and Patents Act, 1988,
to be identified as Editor of this work.

Cover design by Rebecca Heselton
Cover image © Unsplash / @umby

All rights reserved. No part of this publication may be reproduced or transmitted
in any form or by any means, electronic or mechanical, including photocopying,
recording, or any information storage or retrieval system, without prior permission
in writing from the publishers.

Bloomsbury Publishing Plc does not have any control over, or responsibility for, any
third-party websites referred to or in this book. All internet addresses given in this
book were correct at the time of going to press. The author and publisher regret
any inconvenience caused if addresses have changed or sites have ceased to exist,
but can accept no responsibility for any such changes.

A catalogue record for this book is available from the British Library.

Library of Congress Cataloging-in-Publication Data

Names: Huang, Yong, editor.
Title: Michael Slote encountering Chinese philosophy: a cross-cultural
approach to ethics and moral philosophy/edited by Yong Huang.
Description: London; New York: Bloomsbury Academic, 2020. |
Series: Fudan studies in encountering Chinese philosophy |
Includes bibliographical references and index.
Identifiers: LCCN 2020026785 (print) | LCCN 2020026786 (ebook) |
ISBN 9781350129849 (hb) | ISBN 9781350184008 | ISBN 9781350129856 (ePDF) |
ISBN 9781350129863 (eBook)
Subjects: LCSH: Slote, Michael, 1941- | Ethics. | Philosophy, Chinese.
Classification: LCC BJ354.S583 M53 2020 (print) | LCC BJ354.S583 (ebook) |
DDC 190–dc23
LC record available at https://lccn.loc.gov/2020026785
LC ebook record available at https://lccn.loc.gov/2020026786

ISBN: HB: 978-1-3501-2984-9
PB: 978-1-3501-8400-8
ePDF: 978-1-3501-2985-6
eBook: 978-1-3501-2986-3

Series: Fudan Studies in Encountering Chinese Philosophy

Typeset by RefineCatch Limited, Bungay, Suffolk

To find out more about our authors and books, visit www.bloomsbury.com
and sign up for our newsletters.

Contents

Notes on Contributors		vi
1	Michael Slote Encounters Chinese Philosophy: An Introduction *Yong Huang*	1
2	Receptivity, Reason, and Responsiveness: From Feeling and Thinking to Action *Karyn Lai*	19
3	Michael Slote on *Yin/Yang* and Chinese Philosophy *Vincent Shen*	33
4	Slote's Sentimentalist Theory of the Mind versus A Neo-Confucian Unified Theory of the Mind *JeeLoo Liu*	47
5	Two Paths to One Goal: The Unity of the Heart-Mind in Michael Slote and Wang Yangming *Xinzhong Yao and Yan Zhang*	63
6	Belief, Desire, and Besire: Slote and Wang Yangming on Moral Motivation *Yong Huang*	81
7	The Value of Receptivity and *Yin/Yang* Clusters for Philosophy *Robin R. Wang*	99
8	Empathy, Meaning, and Approval in the *Mencius* and Michael Slote *R.A.H. King*	115
9	Moral Therapy and the Imperative of Empathy: Mencius Encountering Slote *Tao Jiang*	133
10	Slote's Moral Sentimentalism and Confucian *Qing*-ism *On-cho Ng*	155
11	Striving for the Impossible: Early Confucians on Perfect Virtue in an Imperfect World *Aaron Stalnaker*	179
12	Virtue Ethics, Symmetry, and Confucian Harmonious Appropriation of Self with Others *Qingjie James Wang*	199
13	Replies to Commentators *Michael Slote*	213
Index		243

Notes on Contributors

Yong Huang is Professor of Philosophy at The Chinese University of Hong Kong, China. He served as the President of Association of Chinese Philosophers in America, co-chair of University Seminar on Neo-Confucian Studies at Columbia University, and co-chair of the Confucian Tradition Group of American Academy of Religion. He is the founding editor of *Dao: A Journal of Comparative Philosophy* and *Dao Companions to Chinese Philosophy*.

Tao Jiang is associate professor of Chinese and Buddhist philosophy at Rutgers University in New Brunswick, New Jersey, US. He is the author of *Contexts and Dialogue: Yogācāra Buddhism and Modern Psychology on the Subliminal Mind* and co-editor of *The Reception and Rendition of Freud in China: China's Freudian Slip*.

R.A.H.King teaches the history of philosophy in Berne, Switzerland. He works mainly on Plato, Aristotle, Plotinus and the comparison of ancient Greek and early Chinese ethics.

Karyn Lai is Associate Professor of Philosophy at the University of New South Wales, Australia. She specialises in pre-Qin Chinese philosophy, and in comparative Chinese-Anglo research in moral philosophy, environmental ethics, reasoning, and epistemology. She is editor of the Chinese Comparative Philosophy section, *Philosophy Compass* (Wiley-Blackwell), Co-editor of the Chinese philosophy section, *Stanford Encyclopedia of Philosophy*, and Associate Editor of the *Australasian Journal of Philosophy*.

JeeLoo Liu is Professor of Philosophy at California State University, Fullerton. She was named 2019 Carnegie Fellow for her research project: Confucian Robotic Ethics. She has authored *Neo-Confucianism: Metaphysics, Mind, and Morality* (Wiley-Blackwell 2017), *An Introduction to Chinese Philosophy: from Ancient Philosophy to Chinese Buddhism* (Blackwell 2006).

On-cho Ng is Professor of History, Asian Studies, and Philosophy, and Head of the Asian Studies Department at the Pennsylvania State University. Primarily a specialist in late imperial Chinese intellectual history, he has published extensively on a wide range of topics, including Confucian hermeneutics, religiosity, ethics, and historiography.

Vincent Shen (passed away in 2018) was the Lee Chair in Chinese Thought and Culture at the University of Toronto, appointed to both the Department of East Asian Studies and the Department of Philosophy. His large number of publications ranges from Chinese philosophy, comparative philosophy, phenomenology, and philosophy of technology among others.

Michael Slote is UST Professor of Ethics at the University of Miami. A member of the Royal Irish Academy and former Tanner, Feng Qi, and Tang Chun-I lecturer, he has published widely in ethics and related fields. Most recently he has been seeking to integrate Chinese and Western philosophical thinking under the aegis of updated yin and yang.

Aaron Stalnaker is professor of Religious Studies at Indiana University. He has written two book-length studies in comparative religious ethics: *Mastery, Dependence, and the Ethics of Authority* (Oxford University Press, 2020) and *Overcoming Our Evil: Human Nature and Spiritual Exercises in Xunzi and Augustine* (Georgetown University Press, 2006).

Qingjie James Wang is currently Distinguished Professor of the Department of Philosophy and Religious Studies at University of Macau. Wang's recent publications include *Virtue, Law and Their Traditions in China: From a Comparative Perspective* and *Moral Affection and The Confucian Exemplary-Formative Ethics of Virtue*.

Robin R. Wang is the Robert H. Taylor Chair Professor in Philosophy at Loyola Marymount University, Los Angeles. A Berggruen fellow (2016-17) at The Center for Advanced Study in the Behavioral Sciences, Stanford University, she is the author of *Yinyang: The Way of Heaven and Earth in Chinese Thought and Culture* (Cambridge University Press, 2012).

Xinzhong Yao is Professor of Ethics at Renmin University and Professor Emeritus of King's College London. Among his publications are *Reconceptualizing Confucian Philosophy in the 20th Century* (ed., Springer 2017), *Wisdom in Early Confucian and Israelite Traditions* (Ashgate 2006, Routledge 2016), and *An Introduction to Confucianism* (CUP 2000).

Yan Zhang is currently Lecturer in Philosophy at Ocean University of China. She obtained her Ph.D from Renmin University of China and specializes in Western philosophy. She has published articles on sentimentalism and Humean ethics.

1

Michael Slote Encounters Chinese Philosophy

An Introduction

Yong Huang
The Chinese University of Hong Kong

1 Introduction

This is the first volume in our series of *Fudan Studies in Encountering Chinese Philosophy*. The series aims to promote dialogues between contemporary Western philosophy and traditional Chinese philosophy. Each volume, as well as each conference in preparation for the volume, features one prominent contemporary Western philosopher, who may or may not previously have known anything about Chinese philosophy. A dozen or so scholars in Chinese philosophy are invited to critically and constructively engage aspects of the work of the featured Western philosopher from Chinese philosophical perspectives, with responses from the Western philosopher. While clearly of a comparative nature, the primary purpose of each volume in this series is not merely to identify similarities and differences between a contemporary Western philosopher and some Chinese philosophical perspectives. Rather it attempts to see how insights from Chinese philosophical traditions may shed some new light on the philosophical issues dealt with by both the Western and traditional Chinese thinkers. In short, the project is primarily not historical but philosophical; not interpretive but constructive.

2 Slote as a Philosophical Sentimentalist

Michael Slote, the featured philosopher of this volume, is UST Professor of Ethics in the University of Miami. Having gained an A.B. and Ph. D. from Harvard University, he has taught at Columbia University, Trinity College Dublin, SUNY Stony Brook, and the University of Maryland, where he served as the department chair for many years. A member of the Royal Irish Academy, he served as the chairman of National Committee for Philosophy of the Academy, was President of the American Society for Value Inquiry, and a holder of the prestigious Tanner Lectureship in 1984–5.

Slote is widely recognized as a leading figure in the impressive revival of virtue ethics in the English-speaking world during the last few decades, and his contribution to this revival is unique in at least two respects. The first is his emphasis on the pure or radical or genuine form of virtue ethics, which is related to our very conception of virtue ethics. Virtue ethics is not just any type of ethics that has room for virtues, as otherwise deontology and consequentialism could also be classified as virtue ethics, since they both allow virtues to play important roles in their systems, just as virtue ethics can also allow moral rules and consequences to play some important roles in its system. What makes an ethics system *virtue* ethics is, to use Gary Watson's term, the primacy of character or virtue in the system. While virtue ethics can talk about rules and consequence, they are both derived from virtues, which are not derived from anything else. This is the primacy of virtue in virtue ethics. It is similar to deontology, which can talk about virtue, but virtue is derived from moral rules or principles, which are not derived from anything else. This is the primacy of moral principles in deontology. It is also similar to consequentialism, especially utilitarianism, which also allow virtue, but the virtue here is derived from consequence, which is not derived from anything else. This is the primacy of consequence in consequentialism.

Thus measured, however, Aristotelian ethics, original or neo, are not virtue ethics, or at least not a pure or genuine form thereof. It goes without saying that virtues do play an important role in Aristotle's ethics, but are they *primary* in Aristotle's ethics? Apparently not. Slote believes that there can be two plausible ways to interpret Aristotle. According to one interpretation, while Aristotle "characterizes the virtuous individual as someone who *sees* or *perceives* what is good or fine or right to do in any given situation.... In that case, if the virtuous individual is the measure of what is fine or right, that may simply mean that she is in the *best possible position to know/perceive* what is fine or right" (Slote 2001: 5). Here virtue is not primary but is subservient to "what is fine or right." The second interpretation, the one adopted by Rosalind Hursthouse, defends "Aristotle as deriving all evaluations of action from independent judgments about what a virtuous person would characteristically choose and about what counts as a virtue, but basing these latter, in turn, in judgment about, a conception of, *eudaimonia*" (Slote 2001:6). Here virtue is not primary either but is subservient to eudaimonia. It is in this sense that Gerasimos Santas claims that "the widespread belief that Aristotle had a virtue ethics is false" (see Santas 1997: 281). Thomas Hurka asks "the question of how distinctively virtue-ethical a theory is whose central explanatory property is in fact flourishing [eudaimonia].... This ethics would not be at all distinctive if it took the virtues to contribute causally to flourishing, as productive means to a separately existing state of flourishing" (Hurka 2001: 233).

In contrast, Slote aims to develop a virtue ethics, which he regards as agent-based in contrast to agent-prior (an example of which is Aristotle's ethics in the second interpretation above) and agent-focused (an example of which is Aristotle's ethics in the first interpretation above). Such an ethics, Slote claims, "is more radical and in some sense purer than other, more familiar forms of virtue ethics," in the sense that it "treats the moral or ethical status of acts as entirely derivative from independent and fundamental aretaic (as opposed to deontic) ethical characterizations of motives, character traits, or individuals" (Slote 2011: 4–5). Using Gary Watson's terms, Slote's ethics is one in which virtue is primary, i.e., everything else in it is derived from or based in virtue but virtue is not derived from or based in anything else.[1]

To explain Slote's radical, pure, or genuine virtue ethics—agent-based virtue ethics, as he would call it—leads our discussion to the second unique feature of Slote's virtue ethics. While most virtual ethicists in the revival of virtue ethics have been following the lead of Aristotle, Slote develops the sentimentalist theme in Hume. He claims that there are two types of agent-based virtue ethics, one cool and one warm. The cool type derives any sort of altruism and human concern for other people from the inner strength which is treated as ultimately admirable. Plato and Nietzsche are mentioned as virtue ethicists of this type. Slote argues that this version of virtue ethics is problematic, however, as it "treats sentiments or motives like benevolence, compassion, kindness, and the like as only *derivatively* admirable and morally good" (Slote 2001: 23; emphasis in the original). He prefers the warm type of agent-based virtue ethics, which treats the above-mentioned sentiments or motives themselves as ultimately admirable and morally good. Slote regards this version as sentimentalist agent-based virtue ethics "because such views are more (directly) influenced by British moral sentimentalism than by any other historical movements in ethics" (Slote 2001: 20).

The warm type of virtue ethics itself can be divided into two, that of universal benevolence and that of partial care. In the former, universal benevolence (i.e., universally directed or *impartial* benevolence is chosen as supremely regulative (Slote 2001: 24). In the latter, the agent-based ethical theory is grounded "in an ideal of *partial* benevolence, of caring *more* for some people than for others" (Slote 2001: 29). It is in this sense that Slote gives great attention to empathy, since it is partial: We tend to have empathy with our nearest and dearest, i.e., feel what they feel, more easily, more strongly, and more accurately than with strangers. Out of these two warm types of sentimentalist virtue ethics, Slote prefers the ethics of partial care. His main reason is that "We think highly of love and tend to think less well of someone who doesn't love, say, her own children or spouse. But if loving and loving concern are morally called for in regard to people who are near and dear to one, then morality as universal benevolence has a problem, because of the way it mandates equal concern for everyone" (Slote 2001: 136). Slote here is somehow presenting such a scenario: love and empathy are by their nature partial. So either we live in a world with loving and empathic people, who care for their loved ones more than they do strangers, or we live in a world of people who are impartial when it comes to helping others but who have no love and empathy. Slote's view is that the former is much preferable to the latter.

As we can see, Slote's sentimentalism is originally developed as a normative ethics: the warm and partialistic agent-based virtue ethics. However, Slote quickly expands it to other areas. The first area of expansion naturally is metaethics. Slote argues that empathy, or more precisely what he calls second-order empathy, is "core or basis of moral approval and disapproval" (Slote 2010a: 34). Seeing someone in pain, an empathic agent feels that person's pain and is motivated to help relieve it. This is first-order empathy. Now a third person who sees the empathic person "will feel warmly or tenderly toward" the agent (Slote 2010a: 35). Slote claims that this reflective feeling toward the empathic agent constitutes moral approval of the agent. Similarly, when seeing someone in pain, a non-empathic person exhibits a basic lack of empathy. Now a third person, empathic in the first-order sense himself/herself, "will tend to be chilled (or at least 'left cold')" toward the non-empathic person (Slote 2010a: 35). What the third person experiences here is second-order empathy. Slote claims that the reflective feelings the third person feels toward the non-empathic person constitutes moral disapproval of them.[2] In both cases, what the third person embodies is second-order empathy.

Slote's next area of expansion in his sentimentalism is political philosophy, which is also natural but significant. Part of the reason that virtue ethics was eclipsed by consequentialism and deontology in modern philosophy is that it apparently lacks its rivals' ability to develop a corresponding political philosophy. Virtue ethics is concerned about the character traits of individual persons, while political philosophy is focused on the social level of justice. Even if everyone in a society has the virtue of justice, this still does not guarantee that the society itself is just. Slote proposes a way of understanding the justice of laws, institutions, and social customs on the model of the justice of individuals' actions. Just as an individual's action is morally right or wrong if it expresses, exhibits, or reflects the empathically caring motivation (or not) of the individual, the laws, institutions, and customs of a given society are just or unjust if they express, exhibit, or reflect the empathically caring motivations (or not) of the social group making such laws, institutions, and customs. Similarly, just as an empathic person is partial and tends to care for loved ones more than strangers, a caring group of lawmakers tends to make laws that are more concerned with their compatriots than people in foreign countries (Slote 2007: Chapter 6).

Next, Slote expands his sentimentalism to epistemology to establish a sentimentalist virtue epistemology. First, open-mindedness, fair-mindedness, and objectivity regarding evidence are regarded as epistemic virtues, but Slote argues that such virtues involve some emotional states: "being emotionally open or receptive and to some degree *sympathetic* to views and arguments one initially disagrees with" (Slote 2014: 18). Second, belief itself contains an element of emotion or is "even nothing more than a certain sort of emotional/affective attitude toward (the content of) a proposition" (Slote 2014: 18). This is because for Slote "to believe something is to favor a certain way of seeing things over others, and favoring in general involves at least mild affect" (Slote 2016: 32). Third, Slote argues that epistemic justification in general requires receptivity, a feature of empathy. Rationalism requires us to subject everything to rational scrutiny: an unexamined life is not worthy living. However, from Slote's sentimentalism, "the person who seriously doubts the value of their own interests and emotions shows a lack of receptivity and trust toward (the contents of) their own life" (Slote 2014: 39).

Finally, Slote expands his sentimentalism to philosophy of mind. Although moral sentimentalism and sentimentalist epistemology already involve the function of mind, in his *A Sentimentalist Theory of Mind*, Slote aims to provide a "more general sentimentalist treatment of the mind" (Slote 2014: 1) against the rationalist theory of mind, according to which "our unity as persons depends on the rational conditions of the unity of our mind" and that "emotions and sense perceptions can be understood in cognitive/computational or more generally in cognitive/rational terms" (Slote 2014: 2). In this general sentimentalist theory of mind, Slote aims to show not only that emotion, contra rationalism, is an irreducible and distinctive part of the mind but also that emotion is involved in all those apparently non-emotional modes of thinking such as conceptual, mathematical, and scientific/empirical thinking and that certain emotions such as love, sympathy, anger, and gratitude are pervasive of human life and the human mind.[3]

3 Slote's Encounters with Chinese Philosophy

There is a good reason for Michael Slote to be the first philosopher featured in this series of Encountering Chinese Philosophy: he has considerable experience of it. I am not sure when Slote first encountered Chinese philosophy but certainly it was not later than the beginning of 2000, when he directed a Ph.D. dissertation, entitled "Early Confucian Ethics and Moral Sentimentalism" by Dr. Shirong Luo, in which the ethical ideas of three early Confucian philosophers—Confucius, Mencius, and Xunzi—are compared with Slote's own moral sentimentalism. In 2008, he co-directed the National Endowment for the Humanities' (NEH) Summer Seminar on Confucianism and Western Virtue Ethics, when he "began to learn more about the Chinese roots of the idea of empathy" (Slote 2010b: 305).

In the meantime, Slote started to make references to Chinese philosophy, particularly Confucianism, in his writings. However, the first publication in which he specifically discusses Chinese philosophy is a paper he published in the journal I edit, *Dao: A Journal of Comparative Philosophy*. The paper is entitled "Comments on Bryan van Norden's *Virtue Ethics and Consequentialism in Early Chinese Philosophy*." Van Norden regards Confucius and Mencius as virtue ethicists of the Aristotelian type and Mozi as a consequentialist. Slote agrees with van Norden on his treatment of Confucius but argues that Mencius is better considered to be a virtue ethicist of the sentimentalist type. Since van Norden says that the central concept of Mencius, *ren*, more frequently means benevolence and compassion,

Slote believes that Mencius's "ideas appear to resemble Hume's to a certain extent more than Aristotle", as "[t]hese warm sentiments just are not central for Aristotle" (Slote 2009: 291). Slote argues that, while there are passages in *Mozi* that commit him to consequentialism, he claims that "none of Van Norden's characterizations of Moism in his book and none of the quotations he offers entail Moism as a consequentialist doctrine. They are all neutral between that doctrine and the virtue ethics of impartial caring/ universal benevolence" (Slote 2009: 295).

This turns out to be the first of a series of papers on Chinese and comparative philosophy that Slote has published in our journal. In the second paper, entitled "The Mandate of Empathy," he claims that "ideals of compassion, sympathy, and, yes, empathy had taken hold or at least been articulated in China long before they became prominent in Western philosophy," where it appeared much later, in the British moral sentimentalists, especially Hume (Slote 2010b: 303–04). Slote first identifies the sixteenth-century Ming dynasty philosopher Wang Yangming as one who forms a clear idea of empathy. He thinks Wang's idea of forming one body with others is "similar to what we speak of (in the West) when we say that someone identifies with the problems of others or, *à la* Bill Clinton, feels their pain" (Slote 2010b: 304). Since this idea of Wang's originates from the Song dynasty philosopher Cheng Hao in the eleventh century, who claims that a person of *ren*, the cardinal virtue in Confucianism, is to be able to feel the itch and pain of oneself and everyone else with whom one forms one body, and both Wang and Cheng were really paraphrasing a passage in the pre-qin text *Mencius*, to the effect that everything in the world is part of myself, Slote claims that "Chinese philosophers were calling attention to the phenomenon of empathy more than 2,000 years before this was done in the West" (Slote 2010b: 304), although, as we can see in his replies in this volume, Slote now tends to think that Mencius's idea falls short of empathy. Thus, at the end of the paper, he calls for Chinese philosophers "to join in present efforts to revive interest in empathy and show its centrality to altruism and the moral life more generally" (Slote 2010b: 306).

The third paper that Slote published in *Dao* is "Updating Yin and Yang," which anticipates many ideas he later more fully develops in his book, *The Philosophy of Yin and Yang* (Slote 2018), a manuscript version of which was circulated among the conference participants who have contributed to this volume. In this paper, Slote calls for both Western and Chinese philosophers to recognize the long-neglected potential of the complementarity between *yin* and *yang* for ethical illumination. To illustrate it, he retells us the conclusion he draws in his (then) newly published book, *From Enlightenment to Receptivity* (Slote 2013a), that "Western thought has placed altogether too much emphasis, too much value, on rational control to the almost total neglect of the countervailing virtue and value of receptivity" (Slote 2013b: 272). What is needed is a balance and fusion between these two values, and Slote argues that "the *yin/yang* complementarity to a large extent anticipates what one can say in contemporary ethical terms about receptivity and rational control" (Slote 2013b: 272). The reason Slote thinks there is a need to update *yin/yang* for that purpose is that, for him, traditional ways of thinking *yin* and *yang* in the history of Chinese philosophy do not provide everything we need for our purpose and place emphasis on some aspects of *yin* and *yang* that are now outdated from modern scientific and egalitarian political points of view. We can see this theme will arise multiple times in several contributions to this volume as well as Slote's responses to them.

In 2014, Slote published two more papers related to Chinese philosophy in *Dao*. In one of the papers, "Virtue's Turn and Return," Slote argues that modern Western philosophy can be regarded as the medieval period in terms of virtue. In the ancient Western world, virtue ethics was flourishing, but thereafter virtue ethics became lifeless; today, however, virtue ethics is experiencing a powerful revival. Slote provides two arguments for his belief that this revival will be long lasting. The first is that "most ethics outside the West [particularly in Buddhism and Confucianism] has arguably been virtue-ethical in character (sic) and that non-virtue-ethical thinking has largely been confined to Western philosophy" (Slote 2014b). The second is that the revival of virtue ethics is coupled with the revival of virtue epistemology, and the two reinforce each other. The other paper is entitled "The Philosophical Reset Button: A Manifesto." Interestingly, the main title of the paper refers to Western philosophy (to reset the Western philosophical button), while the subtitle is for Chinese philosophers (a manifesto for Chinese philosophers). Slote claims that Western thought has been exceedingly intellectualistic and rationalistic, neglecting or downplaying the importance of body, feelings, and emotion. In his view, these deeply one-sided tendencies need to be corrected or rebalanced; in other words, the philosophical button for Western philosophy needs to be reset. However, "Thomas Kuhn has taught us that we are reluctant, and more than reluctant, to give up a theory in the absence of a new and better theory to grab onto" (Slote 2014a: 2). In Slote's view, we do have a new and better theory to grab onto, which is nothing but non-Western philosophy—and more precisely Chinese philosophy. This is because "the Chinese, especially the Confucian, tradition of philosophical thought contains ideas and perspectives that are arguably well-geared toward the kind of philosophical reset I have been arguing for" (Slote 2014a: 8).

Then, in 2018, just before our conference on "Slote Encountering Chinese Philosophy," Slote published yet another paper related to Chinese philosophy in *Dao*, "Yin-Yang and the Heart-Mind." In this paper, he argues that the Chinese term *xin,* as well as the Japanese term *kokoro* and the Korea term *maum,* characterize our psychology better than the Western "mind." The reason is that all these East Asian terms express the notion of a heart-mind, indicating the rational and the emotional are inseparable, while the Western term "mind" implies the possibility of being rational without being emotional. However, the main purpose Slote has in this paper is to do something for such a notion of heart-mind that Kant does for time, space, causality, etc.: a transcendental argument. In Slote's view, to capture the central feature of the psychology of the heart-mind, one needs to appeal to the Chinese notion of *yin-yang* in its philosophical rather than physical (as has been traditionally understood in Chinese history) sense. In this sense, *yin* is understood to be receptivity, and *yang* directed active purpose, and the two are mutually complementary. In the analytic tradition, mind has been thought to consist of two basic contents, desire and belief, and Slote argues that both belief and desire involve emotion and both *yin* and *yang* are involved in all the functioning mind's emotional states. One example he uses to illustrate this is empathy. An empathic person is receptive (*yin*) to what others are feeling, which necessarily entails the motivation to help (*yang*) in such a way that *yin* and *yang* are not merely both present but mutually inseparable in empathy.

Slote continues to contribute to *Dao*, even after the official encounter with Chinese philosophy recorded in this volume. His most recent paper, the seventh in the journal, entitled "Natural Autonomy, Dual Virtue, and *Yin-Yang*," appears in the first issue of 2020. In this paper, Slots aims to show that "*yin* and *yang* have the potential to explain and/or justify our thinking over a vast range of topics and in a way that no Western concepts have yet shown themselves capable of doing" (Slote 2020a: 10). First, he argues that virtues, both moral and epistemic, can be enriched by the idea of *yin-yang*. One example he uses to show this is the virtue of autonomy, which has two inseparable aspects, the epistemic and the practical, and he concludes that the epistemic aspect is *yin*, while the practical aspect is *yang*. Second, he argues that the notion of *yin-yang* can also enrich our understanding of rationality. We often distinguish between theoretical rationality and practical rationality as if these are two separate kinds of rationality. However, Slote argues that every case of rationality has both the theoretical aspect (*yin*) and the practical aspect (*yang*). Finally, toward the end of the essay, Slote indicates that his updated *yin* and *yang* could play a deep clarificatory role of even "chemical processes like oxidation and all physical processes involving action and equal and opposite reaction" (Slote 2020a: 9).

Many of the ideas of comparative nature initially developed in the papers discussed above have been subsequently systematized in his book, *The Philosophy of Yin and Yang*. It aims to show that "the age-old *yin/yang* complementarity offers us an answer to the most central and fundamental questions we (Western, but also Eastern) philosophers face and have historically faced in ethics, epistemology, and the philosophy of mind," as well as philosophy of science, and Slote even claims that "*Yin/yang* is arguably the 'philosopher's stone' for ongoing work in some of the most significant areas/parts of philosophy" (Slote 2018: Preface). Here, while praising Chinese philosophical tradition for its being able to "help reset the enterprise of philosophy in a vital way and on an international scale or basis" (Slote 2018: Preface), Slote also emphasize the need to provide a unique interpretation of the Chinese tradition, an interpretation even Chinese scholars and scholars of Chinese philosophy have failed to provide. What he means is the importance of understanding *yin-yang* primarily in terms of their complementarity, in which *yin* represents receptivity and *yang* rational control or decisiveness.[4]

4 Looking Forward

This volume includes eleven critical and constructive engagements with aspects of Slote's philosophy, with Slote's responses to them as the last chapter. In Chapter 2, Karyn Lai develops the idea of responsiveness, largely from the Daoist text of the *Zhuangzi*, in her words, to complement the idea of receptivity and reason (or directed purpose) in Slote's philosophy of *yin/yang*. Lai identifies what (to her) seems to be the missing link between motivation and action in Slote's internally-scaffolded account of motivation. Lai complains that what comes under scrutiny in Slote's account is intention and not action, since intention to act is not action itself, and a person with intention or motivation to act does not necessarily act. In contrast, his idea of responsiveness is action-oriented and not merely intention-oriented. Moreover, even if Slote's receptivity and directed purpose may ideally produce right or appropriate action, Lai emphasizes the fitting action.

In his response, Slote agrees that responsiveness is related to his philosophy of *yin* and *yang* but disagrees that the latter is inadequate without the former. The key issue here is the relationship between motivation to act and actual action. Slote believes that motivation explains action but only along with some other factors, including other motivations outweighing it. While motivation to act does normally result in action, when it is undercut by other motivations, the action it is supposed to bring out may not occur. Regarding Lai's complaint about not paying enough attention to inter-relationality, Slote responds that "even if most moral virtue is instantiated in the context of our inter-relations or interactions with others, what counts as virtuous action doesn't essentially depend on what others do in interactive response to such action." For example, Slote points out that one's morally appropriate caring responsiveness to a person may not be met with a morally equally appropriate response (say gratefulness) from the person being cared for, but the caring action is no less morally good despite this undesirable inter-relationship between the two persons, the care-giver and the person being cared for.

In Chapter 3, Vincent Shen states that Slote's philosophy of *yin* and *yang* emphasizes their complementary aspects rather than their differences. The former is structural, while the latter is dynamic, historical, or process-oriented. He uses the *Book of Change* and *Daodejing* to show this dynamic nature of *yin* and *yang*. Shen explains that, "in its act of creativity, the Great Ultimate launches a dynamic process of interaction between movement and tranquility, thus brings forth the dialectics of *yin* and *yang*, in the process of which is produced five material forces, which upon further complications and combinations give rise to myriad of things." In relation to this, Shen also complains that, in Slote's account, *yin* and *yang* become the ultimate category, while in Chinese philosophy, they are finite, with the finitude of their metaphysical status. The ultimate concept in Chinese philosophy is the great ultimate, *taiji*.

In his response, Slote claims that his interpretation avoids viewing *yin* and *yang* as causally interacting contraries in a process that the traditional interpretation highlights. However, he argues that, despite this limitation, his interpretation does not lose anything important about *yin/yang*, since science today has replaced *yin* and *yang*, providing a better explanation of natural phenomena. In contrast, his own interpretation allows them to provide a "metaphysically structural account of what is involved in moral and intellectual virtue in the mind's basic functionality. For example, the intellectual virtue of curiosity is metaphysically constituted of *yin* (receptivity to what is going on around one) but also *yang* (attentiveness to one's surroundings). So *yin* and *yang* here help constitute curiosity but don't causally explain why humans are curious. They do philosophical and not scientific work." Slote accepts Shen's criticism of wrongly regarding *yin* and *yang* as metaphysically ultimate, and agrees that we need to go deeper, which he says he is doing with concepts of *qi* and *taiji* in his forthcoming book, *The Large Philosophy of Yin and Yang*. At the same time, however, he still calls for a halt on using these deeper concepts in competition with modern science, as Shen suggests.

Jeeloo Liu, in Chapter 4, focuses on Slote's claim that there has not been effort toward unifying intellect and emotion in Chinese tradition since there has never been a separation between the two and presents a neo-Confucian "unified theory of the mind", largely based on Zhang Zai and Zhu Xi. One unique feature of this theory is that such a unification is both ontological (descriptive) and regulative (normative), which she argues is different from and superior to Slote's sentimentalist account of mind. If this account is supposed to be also normative, then Slote needs to show, which he does not, why one ought to follow one's emotion in cognition; and if it is supposed to be purely descriptive, then he needs to provide empirical evidence. Another important feature of the neo-Confucian theory of mind is that it continues the Mencian tradition and holds an innatist theory of the goodness of the human mind, which again is different from and superior to Slote's empiricist account of the mind, regarding our emotions as cultivated after birth and are the sheer results of familial and social grooming.

In response to Liu's complaint that his account of mind focuses only on how the mind actually functions, yet without empirical backup, and not how it ought to function, on the one hand, Slote states that his argument is entirely a priori and thus needs no empirical back-up and so any disagreement Liu might have with him on this issue should also be based on a priori arguments; on the other hand, Slote states that in his later book, *The Philosophy of Yin and Yang*, he tackles precisely the issue of normativity of his sentimentalist account of mind, asking why the *yin/yang* functioning the mind must exemplify is desirable and constitutes both moral and epistemic virtues. So Slote believes that the real disagreement that Liu has with him is his unwillingness to posit goodness of human beings, which he thinks lacks empirical evidence anyway despite its popularity in the Confucian tradition.

In Chapter 5, Yao and Zhang argue that, in his criticism of the rationalist account of mind, Slote goes to another extreme by providing a sentimentalist account. In their view, Slote's "attempt to revoke the dominant position of rationalist philosophy of the mind leads to the dissolving of reason in emotion."

Correspondingly, since Slote uses *yang* to explain the rational element of the mind and *yin* the sentimentalist element, "in a similar way as dissolving belief in sentiment, he may have, willingly or unwillingly, dissolved *yang* in *yin*." While they do see Slote acknowledging that receptivity and decisiveness each contains both *yin* attributes and *yang* attributes, they complain that "in the end, both receptivity and decisiveness are in the category of emotion: receptivity is an emotional trust of what we have perceived, while decisiveness is an emotional tendency to satisfying our desire." As an alternative, Yao and Zhang present a Confucian view of unity of mind, which is unique in the sense that it is not unified in reason as in traditional Western philosophy nor in emotion as in Slote. Rather, both reason and emotion are unified in the mind, or, rather, *xin*.

In his response, Slote denies that he dissolves reason in emotion. He states that he is providing a reductive account of reason and belief in terms of emotion, "and this in no way entails *eliminating* these categories or the entities they apply to." Similarly, Slote denies that his account may end up dissolving *yang* in *yin*, saying that his view is that "when we have emotions we are both receptive in a *yin* way and motivated in *yang* fashion to act." Overall, Slote argues that he pays attention to both reason and emotion, and both *yin* and *yang*. In other words, for him they are equally important, and he does not prioritize one over another.

In Chapter 6, Yong Huang examines Slote's view as a third anti-Humean position regarding moral motivation, as a contrast to the rationalist anti-Humean view represented by Thomas Nagel and Thomas Scanlon and the emotivist anti-Humean view represented by Ayer and Altham. This third anti-Humean position is unique in its embracing the idea of "besire," a single, unitary mental state that is both belief-like and desire-like, and which motivates a person to act. To do so, Huang focuses on Slote's *A Sentimentalist Theory of Mind*, in which alone Slote explicitly develops the idea of besire. While defending this third anti-Humean position, Huang argues that Slote's notion of besire is both unnecessarily too radical (as he claims that all beliefs are besires) and not sufficiently radical (as he needs an independent desire to explain the motivation of human action). He then argues that these two limitations of Slote's besire can both be overcome in the neo-Confucian philosopher Wang Yangming's notion of *liangzhi*, which, as a besire, applies only to the realm of morality or normativity and can motivate a person to act without the need for an independent desire. He further argues that Wang's *liangzhi* as a besire can adequately respond to the Humean criticism of it as bizarre or incoherent due to the perceived opposite directions of fit of the belief-like element and the desire-like element of besire.

In his response, Slote complains that Huang's comments focus almost exclusively on his 2014 book, *A Sentimentalist Theory of Mind*, while his thinking, especially about *yin* and *yang*, has advanced beyond that earlier book. He acknowledges that some of the questions raised by Huang regarding his idea of besire and other related ideas are insightful, which explains why he has now moved on from that work and focuses his philosophical efforts on *yin/yang*, which avoids the problems

Huang identifies in the 2014 publication. For example, Huang argues that Slote's view that all beliefs are besires is implausible, but Slote says that his philosophy of *yin* and *yang* can rob such a view of its initial implausibility. Since all beliefs involve emotions, and emotions involve desires, all beliefs involve desires, and thus all beliefs are besires.

In Chapter 7, Robin Wang proposes to complicate Slote's *yin/yang* complementarity by introducing the *yin/yang* clusters. The main point she makes is that *yin/yang* is a multilevel structure that cannot be reduced to a single string of complementarity or balance as is the case with Slote. To explain, Wang shows that the *yin/yang* clusters include such relationships between *yin* and *yang* as contradiction and opposition, interdependence, mutual inclusion, interaction or resonance, complementary or mutual support, and change and transformation. She argues that the *yin/yang clusters* show a more faithful and responsible way to the classical Chinese theory and practice of *yin/yang* and bring out a new perspective on a wide range of philosophical problems and justifications, including the one based on a process cosmology developed by Roger Ames.

In his response, Slote acknowledges that there are other dimensions of *yin* and *yang* in the Chinese philosophical tradition. However, he makes three points. First, some dimensions in Wang's *yin/yang Clusters* are out of date. For example, the opposition of *yin* and *yang* was historically used to causally explain various natural phenomena, but today science can do a better job in this respect. Second, his view of *yin* and *yang* as mutually complementary and friendly is valid, as it is visible in the standard diagram of *yin* and *yang* as curvy half-circles that each contains an element of the other. Third, his *yin/yang* model gives us interesting or plausible results regarding virtue, reason, and the nature of the mind of *xin* as shown in his *A Philosophy of Yin and Yang*, and "nothing comparable has been forthcoming from the tradition that sees *yin and yang* as dynamically interrelated opposites."

Richard King's chapter, Chapter 8, engages Slote's discussion of empathy, especially in his *Moral Sentimentalism*, in relation to the *Mencius*, since Slote says there that Mencius also has the idea of *empathy*. On the one hand, although Mencius's *ren*, when translated as "benevolence," can be regarded as empathy, King focuses on another term of Mencius's, *buren*, not being able to bear something. One of the meanings of *buren* is to take in the situation of the other humans. However, King states that "it is not clear if the agent is affected *exactly* as the sufferer is. Thus it may not count as empathy in Slote's sense." On the other hand, King states that the first function of empathy for Slote is to constitute moral approval and disapproval; and he raises the question: "does empathy constitute our understanding of morality, or is it prior to it?" The point he tries to make is that approval requires a proposition to be positive about: you can only yes to a proposition. So he makes a contrast between Slote and Mencius, favoring the latter: "for Slote, approval or disapproval are prior to moral judgement. And in the *Mencius*, the sense of approval and disapproval (saying yes and no) is the beginning of knowledge."

In his response, Slote takes back his early claim that Mencius has the idea of empathy, so he now agrees with King that while there is something like the concept of empathy operative in the *Mencius*, it may not be tantamount to empathy. One is *buren*, unable to bear, the suffering of another not necessary because one is feeling the suffering of another. Even Mencius's *ren*, translated as benevolence, while possibly involving the phenomenon of empathy, is not used as a concept of empathy in the *Mencius*. About King's claim regarding the role of empathy in moral approval and disapproval, Slote responds that King was mistaken to think that this is the first function of empathy for Slote. Slote regards the empathy playing this role as second-order empathy, which is modeled on first-order empathy, where one feels another's suffering and is motivated to help relieve the person of the pain.

In Chapter 9, Tao Jiang starts with a discussion of the Mencian model of moral persuasion, which he calls "moral therapy" in contrast to moral argument. While in moral argument, one aims to convince others the rightness of the paths he or she offers, in moral therapy, one as a moral doctor aims to cure a moral client (rather than a patient, who is incapable of "normal" moral sentiments and behaviors) of moral diseases. As Mencius's moral therapy involves empathy, Jiang relates it to Slote's moral sentimentalism, which also focuses on empathy, claiming that the type of empathy involved in moral therapy is what Slote calls second-order empathy. Given that empathy is partialistic, Jiang questions the ability of Slote's moral sentimentalism to deal with the issue of social justice, and he concludes that it cannot, appealing to Virginia Held's criticism of Slote.

In the spirit of his response to Richard King's chapter, Slote insists that Mencius may be aware of the phenomenon of empathy but lacks the concept of empathy. However, the bulk of his response is directed to Jiang's complaint that his moral sentimentalism centered on empathy cannot deal with the issue of social justice. An empathy-based ethics, for example, is against patriarchy, a type of social injustice, because parents in such social arrangement throw cold water on their daughters' hopes and desires and thus lack empathy with them. More generally, such an ethics can account for social/legal justice in terms of empathy operating at a social level.

In Chapter 10, On-cho Ng, to use his own word, attempts an intervention in Slote's moral sentimentalism by posing the multivalent Confucian notion of *qing*. At the same time as he acknowledges the inspirations that Slote's works afford the rethinking of *qing* as a philosophical conception, he sees the latter as an enriching conceptual and empirical resource for and even critical corrective of the former. In particular, unlike Slote's sentimentalism, which is thoroughly naturalistic, in Confucian Qing-ism, emotion's phenomenality and facticity are completely integrated into the ontology of *xing* (human nature), *xin* (mind-heart), and *qing* (emotion). Thus, while he applauds Slote's appropriation of *yin* and *ying* in expanding his sentimentalism, Ng points out that "in traditional Chinese *yin-yang* thinking, the question of *qi* (commonly translated as material force or psychophysical energy) is highly germane to emotions, such that it seems to be the metaphysical basis of Confucian *qing*-ism."

In his response to Ng, Slote takes the opportunity to explain how his naturalistic moral sentimentalism can deal with the normativity issue, as he believes that "empathy neatly bridges the supposedly unbridgeable gap between factual knowledge and motivation/reasons to act." Regarding Ng's complaint about the absence of *qi* in his attempt to use *yin* and *yang* to further develop his moral sentimentalism, Slote states that in his forthcoming book, *A Large Philosophy of Yin and Yang*, he does bring *qi* and even *taiji* into the picture. However, instead of going ontological or metaphysical, Slote claims that his use of *qi* and *taiji* "grows out of modern scientific thinking (in particular, what modern science says about the laws of motion)."

In Chapter 11, Aaron Stalnaker takes issue with Slote on the idea of impossibility of perfection. One of the main examples that Slote uses to show that is to seek the perfection of both virtues of frankness and tact, and Stalnaker argues that this is because frankness is not a virtue, especially in the Confucian tradition. In some cases, the reason that perfection seems impossible is that some social structures are unjust, one example of which is the seeming impossibility of seeking perfection of both career and family, especially for women. Thus, to believe that perfection is impossible in such cases is to abandon our fight for social justice before it even starts. Moreover, "perfect virtue is the right goal, even if that turns out to be impossible to achieve in one's lifetime, and even if that may jeopardize our individual happiness in important ways."

While Slote does not disagree on Stalnaker's last point summarized above regarding the worthiness of seeking the impossible perfection, he has difficulty with other issues. He disagrees with Stalnaker on frankness as not being a virtue simply because frankness is inappropriate or worse in many situations, as if so hardly anything will be counted a virtue: courage is often out of place and justice is often not the most appropriate way to treat people. Moreover, to acknowledge the impossibility of perfections in (for example) both career and family "might make women feel less bad about this if they realized that the inability is totally inevitable."

In Chapter 12, James Qingjie Wang focuses on Slote's idea of the self-other symmetry, a symmetry between a virtuous person's self-care and care for others, most clearly developed in *From Morality to Virtue*. While supporting Slote's argument against the idea of the self-other asymmetry, the view that a virtuous person ought to care for others more than for oneself, Wang also realizes some problem with Slote's view and ends up developing an alternative of his own. Wang analyzes the Confucian view of parent–child relationships, in which both parents' taking care of their young children and adult children's taking care of their elderly parents are not understood as one self's taking care of other but as parents'/children's self-realization and accomplishment. In light of this, Wang argues that the self-other symmetry/asymmetry issue should not bother us, since this very issue is based on a self-other dichotomy as a result of philosophical subjectivism and monistic individualism. Confucian virtue ethics emphasizes the self-other harmony, where the self-other relation is the relation of self with other, instead of self-other symmetry, where the self-other relation is the relation between self and other.

In his response, Slote states that, while he previously did argue for the symmetry between care of others and care for oneself, he now thinks that there are reasons to be less intolerant of the asymmetry between the two: to care for others more than oneself. The main reason, Slote states, has to do with empathy, which was not paid attention to in the book Wang engages with, as empathy also has the self-other asymmetry, and empathy is built into moral concepts like rightness, wrongness, and moral goodness. In this sense, ordinary moral judgments "have to be asymmetrical on purely conceptual grounds, assuming that we have empathy with others and not with our ongoing selves". Since he has given up his position on the self-other symmetry, Slote says that he hopes he may be excused from examining some interesting criticisms Wang makes of his position in that earlier book.

5 Conclusion

Before starting to respond to the critical and constructive engagements with his philosophy from Chinese philosophical perspectives by scholars of Chinese philosophy one by one, Slote mentions the op-ed piece in *The Stone* column of *New York Times* (May 11, 2016), "If Philosophy Won't Diversify, Let's Call It What It Really Is," by Jay Garfield and Bryan van Norden. Both authors of this piece, as well as Slote himself, blame contemporary Western philosophers for their negligence and even ignorance of Chinese philosophy as well as other non-Western philosophy. They certainly have a point. However, it is my conviction that scholars of Chinese philosophy must carry some of the blame too. If we continue to be contented with purely historical and textual analyses of classical Chinese philosophical texts, emphasizing how unique they are and largely ignorant of or, if not, setting aside the issues contemporary Western philosophers are tackling, then there are few reasons and motivations for contemporary Western philosophers to become interested in Chinese philosophy on their own initiative. Slote also claims that Western philosophy has been seriously misguided, and Chinese philosophy can help correct it. He may have a point on this as well. That said, I think the exchange is not one-directional. There are also misguided aspects in Chinese philosophy, which Western philosophy can help correct. It is my hope that bringing prominent contemporary Western philosophers and serious scholars of Chinese philosophy into critical and constructive dialogues can help change the current deplorable status of Chinese philosophy in the Anglo-European philosophical world on the one hand and facilitate the mutual learning of Western philosophy and Chinese philosophy on the other.

Notes

1 From Gary Watson's point of view, Slote's virtue ethics may have a different problem though. In his view, any virtue ethicist who claims that virtue is primary in his or her ethics faces a dilemma: "any ethics of virtue that lacks a theory of virtue will be non-explanatory but any ethics of virtue that has such a theory will collapse into an ethics of outcome" (Watson 1997: 62). What he means is that, if virtue is primary in an ethics, it is natural for people to ask what virtue is. If one tries to answer it by providing an account of virtue in terms of something else, then this something else becomes primary and virtue is at most secondary. This is the problem of Aristotle's ethics, as we have seen. However, if one tries to not provide an account of virtue in terms of something else in order to maintain the primacy of virtue, then virtue becomes non-explanatory. This seems to be the problem with Slote, as he is not willing to provide an account of virtue. When asked, he would respond that "you already know it" or "check this on yourself" (see, for example, Slote 2001: 12; 35). In order to avoid such questions altogether, instead of virtue and vice or good and evil, Slote prefers to use admirable and deplorable, as it is less likely that people will ask what you mean by admirable/deplorable. Elsewhere I presented a neo-Confucian philosopher Zhu Xi as a virtue ethicist who provides an account of virtue and yet in whose ethics virtue remains primary (see Huang 2011).

2 To what extent the third personal feeling can be regarded as second-order empathy, as Slote claims, is at least not immediately clear. An empathic person is supposed to be able to feel what a person in the negative conditions feels and motivated to help the person to get out of negative condition. In parallel, then, a second-order empathic person will not only (1) feel chilly toward a person displaying the cold-heartedness in his/her behavior but also (2) be motivated to help the person get rid of the cold-heartedness. Slote, however, doesn't include this aspect into his description of the second-order empathic person. For some more detailed discussion on this issue, see Huang 2015.

3 Michael Slote has also tried to expand his sentimentalism in other areas such as philosophy of education (see Slote 2013c), speech act theory (Slote 2017: 848–5 & Slote 2020b: Conclusion), and environmental philosophy (Slote 2013a: Chapter 8).

4 Michael Slote has published a few other pieces engaging Chinese philosophy elsewhere. For example, in 2016 he published a paper, "Moral Self-cultivation East and West: A Critique," in the *Journal of Moral Philosophy*, in which he argues against the very concept of self-cultivation in both Confucianism and Western philosophy, particularly in Aristotle and Kant (Slote 2016b). In addition, his *Between Psychology and Philosophy: East–West Themes and Beyond* (Slote 2020b) includes (revised/expanded versions of) three lectures he gave at Nankai University that sound major East–West themes: "Yin-yang, Mind, and Heart-Mind" (Chapter 2), "Moral Self-Cultivation East and West: A Critique" (Chapter 3), and "Philosophical Deficiencies East and West" (Chapter 4).

References

Huang, Yong (2011), "Two Dilemmas of Virtue Ethics and How Zhu Xi's Neo-Confucianism Avoids them," *Journal of Philosophical Research,* 36: 247–81.

Huang, Yong (2015), "Empathy with 'Devils': Wang Yangming's Contribution to Contemporary Moral Philosophy." in Michael Mi, Michael Slote, and Ernest Sosa (eds), *Moral and Intellectual Virtues in Western and Chinese Philosophy*, 214–34, New York: Routledge.

Hurka, Thomas (2001), *Virtue, Vice, and Value*. Oxford: Oxford University Press.

Santas, Gerasimos X. Santas (1997), "Does Aristotle Have a Virtue Ethics?" in Daniel Statman (ed.), *Virtue Ethics: A Critical Reader*, Washington, D.C. Georgetown University Press.

Slote, Michael (2001), *Morals from Motives,* Oxford: Oxford University Press.

Slote, Michael (2007), *Ethics of Care and Empathy,* London and New York: Routledge.

Slote, Michael (2009), "Comments on Bryan Van Norden's *Virtue Ethics and Consequentialism in Early Chinese Philosophy*," *Dao,* 8: 289–95.

Slote, Michael (2010a), *Moral Sentimentalism,* Oxford: Oxford University Press.

Slote, Michael (2010b), "The Mandate of Empathy," *Dao,* 9: 303–07.

Slote, Michael (2013a), *From Enlightenment to Receptivity: Rethinking Our Values,* Oxford: Oxford University Press.

Slote, Michael (2013b), "Updating Yin and Yang," *Dao,* 12: 271–82.

Slote, Michael. 2013c. *Education and Human Values: Reconciling Talent with an Ethics of Care*. New York: Routledge.

Slote, Michael (2014a), "Sentimentalist Epistemology," *Universitas: Monthly Review of Philosophy and Culture,* 41.3: 14–45.

Slote, Michael (2014b), *A Sentimentalist Theory of Mind*, Oxford: Oxford University Press.

Slote, Michael (2015a), "The Philosophical Reset Button: A Manifesto," *Dao,* 14: 1–11.

Slote, Michael (2015b), "Virtue's Turn and Return," *Dao,* 13: 319–24.

Slote, Michael (2016a), "From Virtue Ethics to Virtue Epistemology," in Chienkuo Mi, Michael Slote, and Ernest Sosa (eds), *Moral and Intellectual Virtues in Western and Chinese Philosophy: The Turn toward Virtue,* New York: Routledge.

Slote, Michael (2016b), "Moral Self-Cultivation East and West: A Critique," *Journal of Moral Education,* 45: 192–206.

Slote, Michael (2017), "Many Faces of Empathy," *Philosophia*, 45: 843–55.

Slote, Michael (2018), *A Philosophy of Yin and Yang*, Chinese-English bilingual edition, Beijing: Shangwu Yinshuguan.

Slote, Michael (2020a), "Natural Autonomy, Dual virtue, and *Yin-Yang*," *Dao,* 19: 1–12.

Slote, Michael (2020b), *Between Psychology and Philosophy: East-West Themes and Beyond,* Cham, Switzerland: Palgrave Macmillan.

Watson, Gary (1997), "On the Primacy of Character," in Daniel Statman (ed.), *Virtue Ethics: A Critical Reader,* Washington, D.C. Georgetown University Press.

2

Receptivity, Reason, and Responsiveness

From Feeling and Thinking to Action

Karyn Lai
*School of Humanities and Languages, University of New South Wales,
Sydney, Australia*
k.lai@unsw.edu.au

1 Introduction

Michael Slote places receptivity and reason, each enhanced by the other, in *yin-yang* complementarity, at the heart of sentimentalist morality. In *The Philosophy of Yin and Yang*, he highlights how emotion *and* reason[1] function together in moral life, artfully bringing together themes and elements from Western and Chinese philosophy. My discussion extends Slote's use of *yin-yang* in moral life by introducing the notion of responsiveness. I suggest that, by focusing on responsiveness, we may reinforce and invigorate Slote's account by (a) incorporating (more methodically) an action-oriented approach, and (b) using (more effectively and accurately) the Chinese tradition's resources on agency.

In Section 2, I briefly set out the key features of Slote's *yin-yang* morality pertinent to this discussion. This is followed by Section 3's focus on responsiveness in the *Zhuangzi*, where I draw out its implications for action. Finally, in Section 4, I articulate the importance of agency in responsiveness. I use this idea to support my proposal that Slote's account would be more sophisticated if it were to weave in responsiveness, especially as it is a distinctively Chinese theme, and will help turn our attention to action and agency.

2 Slote's *Yin-Yang* Morality

In *The Philosophy of Yin and Yang*, Slote develops earlier work to articulate an account of how our thinking about moral life could be enriched by engaging key themes from Western and Chinese philosophy. His account uses one component of *yin-yang* philosophy—their complementarity[2]—to engage Chinese and Western philosophy so as to develop a new methodological framework to incorporate emotion and reason, and to articulate a process for living a moral life. Slote's account marries directed active purpose (*yang*) and empathy (*yin*), highlighting how each augments the other in moral life. The *yang* aspect is underscored by reason: "directed active purpose" captures how a moral person's intentions, being intricately intertwined with empathy, are purposefully geared toward helping others (Slote 2018: 148–60). With the help of examples, Slote presents a persuasive account of how empathy and directed active purposiveness are involved in the interpersonal *communication* of *yin*. Compassion, the key characteristic of *yin*, (rightly, ethically) motivates a person to attempt to alleviate another person's distress. Complementarily, the capacity to control and direct one's motivations—*yang*—helps direct those empathic feelings toward effective action.

A forte of Slote's sentimentalist moral theory is its emphasis that reasons and emotions in our moral lives are not compartmentalized. Importantly, it also sees relationality as a basic fact of human life. Although relationality is not explicitly articulated in Slote's discussion, it is clear from his extended discussions about psychopaths, who do not care, that relationality figures in an important way in his view of morality. One of my tasks in this chapter is to create a more prominent place for relationality, a key feature of Chinese philosophy, through my focus on responsiveness (*ying* 應), drawing on a Daoist text, the *Zhuangzi*.

My discussion pushes Slote's interplay between empathy and purposiveness into the domain of responsive action. While I appreciate the intricate connection Slote draws between receptivity and purposiveness, I believe we need to give more consideration to their operational aspects. For instance, if a person is empathetically motivated to help a close friend in distress, and has worked out the best way she can achieve that purpose, how will these feelings and intentions be realized in appropriate action? How can she act in an appropriately responsive manner, in light of her friend's present circumstances? Although Slote's discussion provides a number of scenarios where a combination of empathy and directed purpose *may* ensue in right action, he does not discuss the dynamics of action. The discussion here addresses appropriate action in two ways. First, it reduces the gap between motivation and the production of appropriate *action*, a concern which receives some attention in Chinese philosophy. To be clear, Chinese philosophy does not propose a sure-fire account of how (right) motivation and intention result in appropriate action. However, some of its discussions—in both Confucian and Daoist traditions—address *practical ways* of cultivation that equip people with skills and abilities to follow-through with appropriate action.

Second, I appeal to the idea of *responsiveness*. The term *ying* (to answer; to be responsive), is evoked in in quite a few of the *Zhuangzi*'s passages. In the relevant sense, *ying* captures the nature of a person's response to the natural world, or to a situation, or to another person. I will demonstrate how responsiveness *completes* R&R (receptivity and reason),[3] building a theory of three R's working collaboratively—receptivity, reason, and responsiveness.

3 Responsiveness in the *Zhuangzi*

Responsiveness in the *Zhuangzi* is associated with perspicacity and depth of understanding of self and world. In this section, I attend to three aspects of responsiveness: what *not* to be responsive to; what to be responsive to, and why; and how responsiveness is a central feature of Zhuangzian agency. The idea of responsiveness sits at a critical juncture in our discussion because, for Slote, Daoist qualms about taking action—embodied in the notion *wuwei* (無為; non-action) and a cluster of associated ideas—are a stumbling block to a viable notion of agency. Slote writes,

> Daoism advocates wu wei, or natural, effortless action, and would be very critical of the whole idea of rational control, even as one side of an ideal ethical or life complementarity [sic]. Daoism rejects Confucianism utterly, rejects its ideas about virtue, about entrenched ethical habits, about the good life. But in so doing, Daoism also implicitly rejects the notion of an adult identity that I made so much of early on in this chapter. An adult identity involves habits and commitments, and since Daoism rejects such things, it would reject the very idea that we should have an adult identity. What I have described, therefore, as the choice about how much to emphasize relationships and how much to emphasize (career or personal) self-fulfillment is a choice that the Daoist will likely say should never be made.
> Slote 2018: 78[4]

I share Slote's concerns about how we interpret *wuwei*, although I would also emphasise that his hesitations are based on just one possible reading of *wuwei*. To allay these concerns, therefore, I draw out the point that responsiveness is an important element of Daoist philosophy. To begin with, we need to look at how the *Zhuangzi* pushes back on the matters we ought not to be responsive to. We begin, appropriately, by examining a passage from the *Zhuangzi* that discusses both *yin-yang*, and *ying*:

> In stillness, [the sage] and *yin* share the same virtue; in motion, he and *yang* share the same upsurge. He does not produce good fortune, nor does he generate calamity. Only when roused (by something else), does he respond (*ying*); only when pressed does he move; only when he has no choice, does he rise to act.
> *Zhuangzi* HY 40/15/10–11;[5] adapted from the translation by Watson 1968: 168[6]

How are we to understand the sage's responsiveness in light of the text's ambivalence about action? The passage suggests that the sage responds *only when* he needs to. Why does he not even seek to produce good fortune? Is good fortune not to be desired?

The *Zhuangzi*'s authors were sceptical of the proposals in its time that sought to deal with socio-political unrest. Many of the proponents, including the Confucians (the Ru scholar-officials 儒), assumed their methods were once-for-all remedies that could be devised independently of actual, concrete scenarios. These proposals lacked flexibility because they were fixated on prescriptive, norm-based approaches that applied to one and all.[7] Standards were communicated in codified forms, through word (*yan* 言) and practice. For the Confucians, the language that bound humans together included ritualized behavior, encapsulated in *li*-practices (禮).

Throughout the *Zhuangzi*, these concerns are expressed in different ways and in different conversations. In one of them, a favored follower of Confucius, Yan Yuan (顏淵), has a conversation with Jin (金), the music master, about Confucius' plans for quelling unrest. Jin admonishes:

> Nothing is as good as a boat for crossing water, nothing as good as a cart for crossing land. But though a boat will get you over water, if you try to push it across land, you may push till your dying day and it will hardly move. Are the past and present not like the water and the land, and the States of Zhou and Lu not like boat and cart? To attempt now to practice the ways of Zhou in the state of Lu is like trying to push a boat over land; much work without success, and certain danger to the person himself. The person who tries to do so has failed to understand the transmission (of teaching) that has no fixed direction, that responds [*ying*] to things and is never at a loss ... Rituals and regulations [must] change in response [*ying*] to the times. If you take a monkey and dress him in the robes of the Duke of Zhou, he will bite and tear at them, not satisfied until it has completely removed them. Look at the difference between past and present; the difference is as great as that between the monkey and the Duke of Zhou!
>
> *Zhuangzi* HY 38/14/35–42; adapted from the translation by Watson 1968: 160

With an analogy that offends Confucian sensibilities by making light of the revered Confucian Duke of Zhou, the *Zhuangzi* spells out the Confucian program's lack of sensitivity to changing times and circumstances. It is this kind of action (*wei* 為, as opposed to *wuwei*), the *active creation and imposition* of norms without regard for particular circumstances, that the *Zhuangzi* rejects. Referring to the previous passage about the sage not producing good fortune, the passage does not mean that Daoists should not strive to bring about positive outcomes. Rather, the statement should be understood in the following way: the sage does not produce "good fortune," nor does he generate "calamity," that is, the kinds of "fortune" and "calamity" specified in abstraction and imposed over one and all. Relating these observations to Slote's concerns articulated previously, I suggest that the *Zhuangzi* rejects *some, not all*, types of action. The term *wuwei* does not necessarily deny initiative; this discussion highlights Daoist reserve about approaches to life that impose a standardised solution for one and all, and for all time.⁸ This conception of *wuwei* is quite the opposite of one that denies "adult identity". At the very least, we need to be aware of the nuances of *wuwei* and its possible variant meanings.

Moving from the kinds of approaches that a person should not be responsive to, we consider next, the question of what we *ought* to be responsive to. In other words, what is the positive manifestation of *ying*? Chapter Two of the *Zhuangzi* ("Qiwulun"; "On seeing all things as equal"), which places significant emphasis on epistemological questions, highlights the importance of responsiveness by problematising epistemological inflexibility. Criticizing approaches to life that endorse only one correct view, one of its passages uses the indexical term "this" to pick out what is obvious to the self and valued by it, and "that" to denote what is of the other, and hence undetected or ignored by the self:

> Everything has its "that", everything has its "this". From one's own point of view, "that" cannot be seen, but it may be understood . . . the sage does not proceed in such a way, but illuminates all in the light of Heaven; this forms his view of what is right. The sage recognises a "this" which is also a "that", and a "that" which is also "this" . . . A state in which "this" and "that" no longer find their opposites is called the pivot of *dao*. When the pivot is fitted into the centre socket, it can respond limitlessly. Its "yea" is limitless and its "nay" too is limitless. So I say, the best thing to use is illumination.
>
> *Zhuangzi* HY 4/2/27–31; adapted from the translation by Watson 1968: 40

The antagonism between "this" and "that" arises from rigidity and defensiveness about what one holds to be true. In contrast, the sage's handling of matters is not bound by any one fixed prescription. Like a pivot rotating in its socket, his responses are unbounded, illuminated by his understanding of the limitlessness of the world. The language used in the text is particularly perspicacious; the idea of limitlessness is incorporated in the phrase *wuqiong* (無窮), which in this passage means to never be depleted (in responding).⁹

The point of highlighting this aspect of *ying* is to demonstrate that, contrary to a reading of *wuwei* as aligned with the lack of "adult identity" (Slote 2018: 78), or *yin* with "pliancy" (*ibid*., Chapter 1, note 6, p. 90), the sage's responsiveness is by no means marked by passivity. In fact, what we sense here is the sage's *liberation* from standardised and conventional norms that might constrain initiative, especially if the former are imposed insensitively to circumstantial cues. It seems apparent that a prerequisite of the *Zhuangzi*'s *ying* is agency, rather than the lack of it. Having examined *ying* in relation to what *not* to respond to, and what one ought to respond to, in the remainder of this section, I articulate what it means for agency. I begin with one of the text's stories on mastery—of the wheelmaker playfully called "Flat" (Bian 扁)—whose expertise is grounded in his responsiveness to the task at hand.

Bian seems reckless in his approach to matters of life and death. He insolently remarks to Duke Huan, reading in the hall above, that the Duke's book contains the "chaff and dregs of the men of old" (*Zhuangzi* HY 36/13/68–74; trans. Watson 1968: 152–3). Duke Huan calls the wheelmaker to account: If he cannot justify these remarks, he will lose his head! Bian provides an account of how his mastery is realised:

> Wheelwright Bian said, "I look at it from the point of view of my own affairs. When I chisel a wheel, if the blows of the mallet are too gentle, the chisel slides and won't take hold. But if they're too hard, it bites in and won't budge. Not too gentle, not too hard—you can feel it in your hand and respond [*ying*] to it in your heart-mind. You can't put it into words, and yet you know exactly how things stand in the midst (of the activity). I cannot teach it to my son, and he cannot receive it from me. So I've gone along for seventy years and at my age I'm still chiselling wheels. When the men of old died, they took with them the things that couldn't be handed down. So what you are reading there must be nothing but the chaff and dregs of the men of old."
>
> *Zhuangzi* HY 36/13/68–74. Adapted from the translation by Watson 1968: 152–3

Bian's mastery is based on responsiveness to the particular circumstances of each task. His actions are not bound by what he has learnt but rather by what he perceives, *there and then*, with his hands and his heart-mind (*xin*).[10] Yet, how could such a master *fail* to teach his skills to his son? Bian's mastery is based on his personal, in-the-moment responsiveness to the circumstances. Attempts to impart his carpentry skills are encoded in *his* words and *his* actions, and based on what *he* knows. His son could mimic his actions and perhaps handle the wood and tools as his father directs him to. But the son's *responsiveness* must be his own; his expert father cannot transmit responsiveness, a necessary condition for mastery, to him by either word or action. Therefore, Duke Huan's reading the words of the sages will yield limited returns; Duke Huan can never learn to *be* responsive in official life from simply reading books.

It is significant that wheelmaker Bian provides a coherent, discursive account of his skill—by articulating what might go wrong and what he needs to attend to—are these not constitutive of what Slote calls "purposiveness"? Another interesting feature of this story is that it uses *dialogue* as a means of communicating its point about the limitations of words. Here, we see the intelligent juxtaposition of what *can* be communicated in words—a fairly self-aware discursive presentation of the prerequisites of mastery—against the *ineffectiveness* of words in transmitting skill.

Moreover, this is not the only mastery story wherein the *Zhuangzi*'s figures demonstrate initiative and control, in a way relevant to Slote's discussion. The cicada-catcher presents a step-by-step account of what he needs to be attentive to at each stage in his training, an arduous program that perhaps renders him a hunchback (*Zhuangzi* HY 48/19/17–21).[11] Likewise, the boatman ferrying in deep gulfs (*Zhuangzi* HY 48/19/22–26) and the swimmer at the base of dangerous cascades

(*Zhuangzi* HY 50/19/49–54) are acutely aware of the conditions of their undertakings. None of these activities may be considered "passive" and all of them require the kind of control articulated in Slote's *yin-yang* morality. The masters are deeply aware that there are conditions in the environment that must be attended to and, *therefore*, reject the view that norms should primarily dictate how they should proceed.

Pertinent to our discussion here is an undercurrent in the mastery stories, that the proposals set out by other thinkers (including the Confucian program of self-cultivation)[12] are inadequate. In these proposals, individuals are required to familiarise themselves with prevailing norms and practices so as to belong, comfortably and familiarly, with others. From the point of view of the wheelmaker, norms and habits, perpetuated through the words of the "men of old," serve only to constrain responsiveness.

In contrast, the process of Daoist cultivation aims not to create habits associated with unthinking action but, indeed, to liberate the individual from such habits. In the *Zhuangzi*'s stories of mastery, cultivation *enables* responsiveness as it enlivens awareness of the situation's salient considerations. The cicada-catcher says, "I'm aware of nothing but cicada wings. Not wavering, not tipping, not letting any of the other ten thousand things take the place of those cicada wings—how can I help but succeed in taking them?" (*Zhuangzi* HY 48/19/17–21; adapted from the translation by Watson 1968: 199–200). The cicada-catcher succeeds because he is appropriately responsive to the task at hand. Likewise, the bellstand maker explains how he excels in producing marvellous bellstands. After having fasted for seven days:

> ... my dexterity is concentrated and distractions dissipate. Only then do I enter the mountain forest and observe the natural attributes (天性 *tian xing*) of the trees. Only when a tree with an exquisite form presents as a bellstand do I put my hand to it. Should I not encounter such, I will abandon the task. Thus I match what is *tian*'s (天; heaven) to *tian*. Is this why it seems the instrument was made by a daemonic person?
>
> *Zhuangzi* HY 50/19/57–9; trans. by Lai

In the *Zhuangzi*, responsiveness is a prerequisite of mastery. Responsivity must be cultivated *especially* because it hones the skills of an individual to be appropriately attentive to the conditions for a particular activity. Initiative—and agency—sit at the core of responsiveness. How does the *Zhuangzi*'s focus on responsiveness help us extend Slote's picture of morality? What is its impact on our understanding of agency? We explore these questions in the fourth and final section.

4 Agency in Responsiveness

Slote's examples in *The Philosophy of Yin and Yang* concerning how we treat others have an irreducible gravity. In contrast, the *Zhuangzi*'s mastery examples, about *ordinary* craftsmanship, seem relevantly *dissimilar*. But do we need to understand the mastery stories literally? In fact, the *Zhuangzi*'s objections to the traditionalism of its day—represented by figures such as Duke Huan—arise from a concern that traditionalism impoverishes the lives of the people. These objections are no less weighty than the question of how we morally respond to others.

The examples of ordinary activities can speak to us at different levels. At one level, they prompt us to consider the extraordinary power invested in officials, who take it upon themselves to design "ideal" ways of life for the common people. Is such power justified? At another level, these examples—which draw on the natural environment and the animal world—uphold the *superiority* of a life not encumbered by ritual and other courtly superfluities, so that a person can be appropriately responsive. Let me here demonstrate the significance of responsiveness with another mastery story from the *Zhuangzi*. Confucius, who figures in this story, witnesses a man swimming in treacherous waters at the foot of magnificent cascades. Confucius, thrown by the situation, fears for the swimmer's life. But a while later, the swimmer emerges from his swim and nonchalantly walks along the banks, oblivious to Confucius' anxiety:

> Confucius was seeing the sights at Lu-liang, where there were cascades of thirty fathoms with sprays of forty *li*, such that no fish, turtles or other water creatures could swim in it. He saw a man swimming in it and believed that the man was in some kind of trouble and intended to end his life. Confucius hastened his followers along by the cascades to pull the man out. But after the man had swum a couple of hundred paces, he came out of the water and began strolling along the base of the embankment, his hair streaming down, singing a song. Confucius ran after him and said, "I thought you were a ghost, but now, up close, I see you're a man. May I ask if you have a way (*dao*) of treading water?"...
>
> Zhuangzi HY 50/19/49–52, adapted from the
translation by Watson 1968: 204–05[13]

This experience has shaken Confucius because it has gone beyond the boundaries of the familiar. As a cultivated person, he *sees* what he has been taught to see, and not beyond. The threat from the cascades is obvious to him. *Therefore*, the swimmer's actions are interpreted as attempted suicide. By contrast, the swimmer seems unaware of these (perceived) dangers, relaxed and singing after his swim.

In the swimmer's response to Confucius, he says, "I have no way (*dao*). I began with what was originally there, developed what was natural (to me), and reached completion in keeping with fate. I go under with the swirls and come out with the eddies, following the way (*dao*) of the waters without thought of my (own) self. That's how I can tread water." (*Zhuangzi* HY 50/19/52-4, adapted from the translation by Watson 1968: 204–05). The swimmer has an openness—we could call this receptivity—to the ways of the waters. It would be foolish for him to assert his *dao* in light of the water's uncontrollable *dao*. Being receptive to the water's *dao*, he *responds* appropriately *by not asserting his own dao*. Here, using Slote's framework, and extending it, we have the rather elegant explanation: receptivity helps the swimmer understand the ways of the waters, reason alerts him to the fit between his *dao* and the water's *dao* (and, indeed, he should be aware that, in this situation, he should *not* have a directed purpose prior to his encounter with the cascades!), and responsiveness completes his swim, successfully, through deferring to the water's *dao* in his actions. How does this explanation add to Slote's account? To *be receptive* is to take in information in an open-minded way. To *have control* over one's motives in the relevant sense for Slote, is to consider, reasonably, what might or might not be feasible. To *be responsive* is to be in a frame of mind that considers oneself in a relation, and to be accountably so.

Slote argues that "it is only reasons, only emotions that make rational sense, that transmit rational force to those who empathically register the feelings of another" (2018: 216). In addition, I propose that responsiveness is necessary to bridge the gap between empathy and action: responsiveness, being *action-oriented*, brings receptivity and purposiveness to fruition. Earlier, I raised the question of how the *Zhuangzi*'s focus on action helps us gain a different perspective from Slote's picture of morality. I believe it does so in a critical way that challenges the tendency in Western philosophy to conceive of moral qualities or characteristics as relating to individuals, rather than to the *interaction* that arises from relating to others. This tendency remains in Slote's account of morality even though it garners the help of Chinese philosophical themes. How is this so? Are receptivity and (other-)directed purpose in Slote's account not *obviously* other-centred terms? They are, but I contend that they are other-centered only in a unidirectional way. Let me explain this by considering how we *measure* receptiveness. When we say a person is "receptive," we evaluate the moral capacity of an individual to be open to an "other." Although a favorable human capacity, receptivity is inward-directed, in that it primarily describes an individual who has, so to speak, made room in her moral life for others. The locus of evaluation is the *individual*. By contrast, the term *ying* derives its meaning from doing what is *fitting* (*dang* 當).[14] It draws our attention to the idea of reciprocity, focusing especially on the aptness of a person's actions *in light of her relationships*. In this way, *ying* is a bi-directional, relational term. Both receptivity and directed purpose, even if other-directed, do *not* necessarily result in action. The measure of purposiveness is whether a person *has* the objective (or an intention) to procure the well-being of another; what comes under scrutiny here are her *intentions* rather than actions.

In defense of Slote's account, it may be said that receptivity and directed active purpose, working together, will *ideally* produce right or appropriate action. However, the point I make here is that *ying*, responsiveness, centers on *fitting* action, based on relationality. Unlike either receptivity or directed purpose, it is bi-directional *and* therefore prompts us to cast our gaze on interaction. My proposal for responsiveness is not to have it replace receptivity and directed purpose, for they each have their place in how we understand an individual's moral capacities. However, we *also* need to focus on the *interactive space* in a relationship; relationality is what *ying* affords.

The importance of *ying* is even more pronounced when we consider that relationality is a key feature of Chinese philosophy. Further, the *Zhuangzi*'s stories on mastery and its cultivation can help us think through how we hone our capabilities and skills for acting and interacting. To reiterate, while the stories relate to mastery in ordinary craftsmanship, their accounts of observation, practice, familiarization, and attunement may be extended to our reflections on how we relate to others.

Slote is wary of cultivation as, in his view, the process may insidiously embed pressures to conform to dominant norms. It seems that cultivation of this kind is what the *Zhuangzi* seeks also to address. Although cultivation is important in the Daoist tradition, the *Zhuangzi*'s masters are not cultivating unthinking habits of simple agreement with others. Instead, they cultivate awareness of salient factors so as to be appropriately attentive to these salient factors in practice. The kinds of actions taken by the masters are far from habitual—to the extent that their actions seem to involve varying degrees of risk. In the case of the swimmer, life itself is at stake but in other stories, the masters are also putting themselves on the line to greater or lesser extents as they could fail to perform well, perhaps through a slip of the chisel, the hammer, or the butchering knife.

This is a *fascinating* aspect of agency embedded, and highlighted, in the *Zhuangzi*'s mastery stories. Strengths are involved, as are vulnerabilities. In relating to others, just as in undertaking skilled tasks, we need to cultivate ways of responding to others to ensure, insofar as we possibly can, that they are fitting. In the spirit of Slote's project, let me propose a *yin-yang* approach to cultivation. I suggest we need both Confucian and Daoist modes of cultivation. We need to cultivate familiarity with some prevailing norms and practices so that, in habitual actions—for example, returning a greeting with appropriate niceties—we are able to respond in a fitting way. But we must also cultivate sensitivity to situational variations. For example, if, upon greeting a close friend, we find out that she has suffered great distress, our empathic feelings for her situation should ideally be realized fittingly, in what we say to her and what we do to alleviate her sadness.

This brief example suggests a need for elements of both Confucian and Daoist cultivation, in *yin-yang* balance. Agency sits at the center of this model of cultivation and is, ideally, manifest in our responsiveness to others.

Let me complete my discussion about *yin-yang* cultivation with a simple example from contemporary life. As a driver, one would normally attempt to obey road rules. Driver training and testing seek to ascertain that new drivers are sufficiently familiar with these rules. We stop at red lights, though sometimes unwillingly, especially if we are running late. Even though we are aware that the safety of road users is paramount, often the lights are our primary cues: go when it's green, prepare to stop at amber, and stop at the red. These habitual practices, and their underlying culture, are often assumed and this is, on the whole, workable. When the lights break down, however, drivers typically begin to look, much more attentively than they usually do. They give way to other vehicles and pedestrians in a way not required if the lights were working. They *see* more, and they are more responsive to the needs of others. This is why Daoist-style responsiveness is important, as is Confucian-style compliance with road rules.

5 Conclusion

I have presented an account of responsiveness in the Daoist tradition, and its cultivation, that lend support to, and extend, Slote's *yin-yang* morality. Here, we have an account of the three R's—receptivity, reason (or directed purposiveness), and responsiveness. Not only does this account provide the link from feeling and thinking to action, it brings China's two significant traditions into interplay in relevant and important ways. It highlights the Chinese tradition's emphasis on cultivation and relationality, reinforcing Slote's conviction about the continuing relevance of Chinese philosophy. Most importantly, my proposal creates a place for Chinese philosophy, not simply to supplement ideas in the Western tradition but also to challenge Western philosophy's conceptual frameworks and attendant methodological assumptions about what it means to be moral.

Notes

1   Slote's account of the *yang* component of morality shifts in the text. He uses it first to refer to "reason" to highlight how it has overlaps with a prominent feature of ethics, that is, practical reason, in the Anglo-analytic tradition (Slote 2018: 12, 14; see also Chapter 3). In Chapter 3, *yang* is presented in a way that relates to a person's control of how his or her motivations are "directed" (see especially *ibid.*, Section 2.4: pp. 148–60). The reason for this shift is articulated in a footnote (note 7, Chapter 3: "…Once we recognize that practical reason and reasons are based in emotions that exemplify both *yin* and *yang*, it would be circular and would undercut the explanatory force of what we want to say, if we were to continue to characterize *yang* in terms of (practical) rationality," p. 242). This suggests that, to maintain the emotion/reason dichotomy, undermines the *yin-yang* approach Slote wishes to work with. In the book's conclusion, however, Slote uses the two terms, "reason" and "directed purpose", interchangeably (see *ibid.*, pp. 464–5).
2   The relation between *yin* and *yang* is dynamic and complex, especially as the referents of these terms have evolved across time in ancient Chinese texts, from referring to the sunny and shady sides of a hill to their more metaphorical meanings associated with darkness and light. Complementarity is only one aspect of the *yin-yang* relation, arising possibly in texts in the Warring States (戰國; 475–221 BCE), such as the *Laozi* (老子). For a nuanced account, refer to A. C. Graham's *Yin-Yang and the Nature of Correlative Thinking* (1986).

3   Note that when I refer to "reason," I mean "purposiveness," in the same way Slote does. The use of "R&R" is only for stylistic effect. Refer to my comments in note 1.
4   Slote continues, "However, by the same token, if we believe it is good for people to have or forge an adult identity, we will reject the Daoist rejection of this notion, and I am and have been implicitly assuming that that is what we should do," (2018: 78.).
5   References to the *Zhuangzi* (*Zhuangzi* HY) are from the Harvard-Yenching concordance, the *Zhuangzi Yinde*.
6   靜而與陰同德，動而與陽同波；不為福先，不為禍始；感而後應，迫而後動，不得已而後起。 It is interesting to note that this passage is from a chapter entitled "Ingrained Ideas" (*Keyi* 刻意; title translated by Legge 1891: 363).
7   The *Zhuangzi* speaks out strongly against those who deem themselves the measure of all things, imposing their standards on everyone (*Zhuangzi* HY 64/23/63–66).
8   In another story in the *Zhuangzi*, there is a conversation between Confucius and Yan Yuan in which Confucius speaks Daoist wisdoms. Yan Yuan had decided to take office in the court of the Prince of Wei, a notoriously difficult ruler. Confucius warns that Yan Yuan will be placing himself fin the way of danger, but Yan Yuan replies that he has thought through an effective strategy, to be "inwardly direct, outwardly compliant, and [to do his] work through the examples of antiquity' (*Zhuangzi* HY 8/4/1–9/4/24; trans. Watson 1968: 56). Instead of supporting Yan Yuan's aim to take on the (Confucian) responsibility to contribute to the reform of the Prince of Wei, Confucius, acting as spokesperson for the *Zhuangzi*'s views, says, "Goodness, how could that do? You have too many policies and plans and you haven't seen what is needed. You will probably get off without incurring any blame, yes. But that will be as far as it goes. How do you think you can actually convert him?" (trans. Watson 1968: 57). Confucius spurns Yan Yuan's *planning*, given that he has not even begun in the service of the Prince of Wei.
9   An extended discussion of my views on the responsiveness of the sage is presented in a co-authored paper (Lai and Chiu 2013).
10 Refer to a fascinating account of Bian by Lisa Raphals, in "Wheelwright Bian: a difficult *dao*" (2019).
11 Or, could it be that, being a hunchback makes him suited to this task? We do not know for sure, as the text does not say; this ambiguity is intriguing and fascinating.
12 Slote is rightly worried about self-cultivation programs. See his concerns in "Moral self-cultivation East and West" (2016).
13 Refer to my discussion in "Skill mastery, cultivation and spontaneity in the *Zhuangzi*: conversations with Confucius" (Lai forthcoming), which draws a distinction between cultivation in the Confucian and Daoist traditions.
14 This is the explanation of *ying* provided in the earliest Chinese lexicon, the *Shuowen Jiezi*, which states, "當也。从心…": (doing) what is fitting. The character *ying* incorporates the character for heart-mind (*xin*). *Shuowen Jiezi Zhu* (1981): 卷十一，心部, 6676.

References

Graham, Angus C. trans., (2001), *Chuang-Tzu: The Inner Chapters,* Indianapolis: Hackett Publishing Co.

Graham, Angus C. (1986), *Yin-Yang and the Nature of Correlative Thinking,* IEAP Occasional Paper and Monograph Series no. 6, Singapore: Institute of East Asian Philosophies.

Lai, Karyn, forthcoming. "Skill mastery, cultivation and spontaneity in the *Zhuangzi*: conversations with Confucius," in Justin Tiwald (ed.), *Oxford Handbook of Chinese Philosophy,* Oxford and New York: Oxford University Press.

Lai, Karyn and Wai Wai Chiu (2013), "*Ming* in the *Zhuangzi Neipian*: Enlightened engagement," *Journal of Chinese Philosophy,* 40 (3–4): 527–43.

Legge, James, trans. (1891), *Sacred Books of China: The Texts of Taoism, Part I: The Tao The King, The Writings of Kwang-Sze,* vol. 39, Oxford: Oxford University Press.

Raphals, Lisa (2019), "Wheelwright Bian: a Difficult *Dao,*" in Karyn Lai and Wai Wai Chiu (eds), *Skill and Mastery: Philosophical Stories from the* Zhuangzi, 129–42, London: Rowman and Littlefield International.

Shuowen Jiezi Zhu/Xu Shen zhuan; Duan Yucai zhu (*Shuowen Lexicon* by Duan, Yucai (1735–1815)), Shanghai: Shanghai gu ji chu ban she: Xin hua shu dian (1981); reprinted from the original (1815), China: Jing yun lou.

Slote, Michael (2018), *The Philosophy of Yin and Yang: A Contemporary Approach,* Beijing: Commercial Press.

Slote, Michael (2016), "Moral self-cultivation East and West," *Journal of Moral Education,* 45 (2): 192–206.

Watson, Burton, trans. (1968), *The Complete Works of Chuang Tzu,* New York: Columbia University Press.

Zhuangzi HY (Harvard-Yenching). *Zhuangzi Yinde* 《莊子引得》 (*A Concordance to Zhuangzi*). 1956. Hong, Ye (ed.) 洪業主編. Harvard-Yenching Institute Sinological Index Series, Supplement no. 20. Cambridge MA: Harvard University Press.

3

Michael Slote on *Yin/Yang* and Chinese Philosophy

Vincent Shen
University of Toronto, Canada

1 Introduction

I am very impressed by Michael Slote's works on sentimentalism, which resonate strongly with what was said in the recently unearthed text, *Human Nature Comes from Mandate* (Xin Zi Ming Chu 性自命出), that "*Dao* starts from human feeling. Human sentiments is born from human nature. He who starts from sentiments, will end up with meaningfulness" (*Guodian* 179; my translation). However, this will not be, though still related, the main subject of this chapter, which will discuss principally another topic, that is, Slote's philosophy of *yin* and *yang*.

2 Michael Slote's Philosophy of *Yin* and *Yang*

It is rare for an American philosopher, except when s/he is also a scholar in Chinese intellectual history or the like, to use a Chinese traditional philosophical term as title of his/her work. Now, here on my desk is a book by Michael Slote, in both Chinese and English, which is entitled *The Philosophy of Yin and Yang* 陰陽的哲學 (2018). Slote is most famous for his works on philosophy of emotions, sentimentalism, and ethics. It's amazing that this work assesses East/West philosophical traditions, focusing mostly on the Chinese concept of *yin/yang* and its philosophical potentials for both traditions. In this book, Slote argues that:

1. The relation between China and the West, in regard to their philosophies, can be balanced and viewed as a *yin-yang* relation.
2. Shortcomings in Western philosophy can be remedied by appealing to some ideas in Chinese philosophy.
3. Western philosophy, in particular in the areas of ethics, epistemology, philosophy of mind, and philosophy of science, too much emphasizes the *yang* side, and thus is one sided, unrealistic, and unbalanced.

4. Regarding ethics and morality, for example, Slote contends that *yin/yang* philosophy leads to a more balanced view of (felt) receptivity with (active) rational control.
5. Compassion, benevolence, and other moral sentiments have both a feeling aspect and a motivational aspect, seen by Slote as an instantiation of *yin* and *yang*.
6. *Yin* and *yang* involve a duality, but conceptually and metaphysically *inseparable*.
7. Not only *yin/yang*, but also other concepts such as *xin* (heart/mind), *Dao* (the Way), and Tian or Heaven, all these concepts' philosophical importance has been underestimated even by the Chinese. They should be reevaluated and promoted.

For me, *The Philosophy of Yin and Yang* is not only a comparative study in philosophy; it is also a reaching-out from Western philosophy to meet Chinese philosophy with an effort of self-reflection, even self-critique on the part of Western philosophy, using a Chinese comprehensive concept of *yin/yang*, with a view to promote both traditions into a higher synthesis. For me this is a very welcome work of linguistic strangification[1] on the part of Western philosophy done at the time of globalization.

As I see it, this work is in its line of thought similar to such works, though with different historical backgrounds and philosophical intentions, as *True Meaning of Lord of Heaven*, an overture from Scholasticism to Classical Confucianism by Matteo Ricci at the time of Renaissance; as, later at the time of Western modernity, Nicolas Malebranche's (1638–1715) *Entretien d'un philosophe chrétien et d'un philosophe chinois sur l'existence et la nature de Dieu*, which is more a critique of Neo-Confucianism, Zhu Xi in particular; and as Leibniz's *Novissima Sinica* and *Discourse on the Natural Theology of the Chinese*, which were more a defense of Confucianism, both classic and neo, and an appeal to a synthesis of European science with Confucian ethics. Now, at the time of globalization, we welcome to this work, *The Philosophy of Yin and Yang* that attempts an upgrading synthesis of both Western and Chinese philosophies through the Chinese concept of *yin/yang*.

I agree with Slote, who takes further steps to appropriate Chinese concepts of *yin* and *yang* to do self-examination and to promote both Western and Chinese philosophies. He says that *yin* and *yang* are duality yet "conceptually and metaphysically *inseparable*" (Slote 2008: 18). Thus, Slote emphasizes more the complementary aspect of *yin* and *yang*, not so much their difference. He stresses not only the general complementarity between East and West, but also the special complementarity in regard to ethics and morality, the complementarity between receptivity (passive) and (active) rational control, and the feeling aspect and the motivational aspect of human sentiments such as compassion, benevolence, and others.

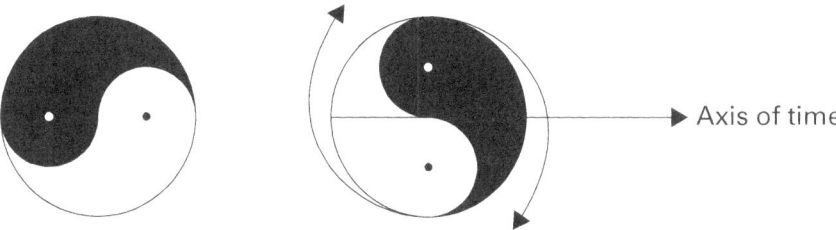

Figure 3.1   Figure 3.2

I should point out here that in Chinese philosophy, the relation between *yin* and *yang* not only demonstrates a complementary aspect, but also a differentiating aspect. *Yin* and *yang* are both different and complementary. The *Yijing* (*Classic of Changes*) expresses this structural difference/ complementarity relation between *yin* and *yang*. Moreover, since the *Yijing* belongs to a philosophy of change, its vision of *yin* and *yang* should be put into a higher dynamic vision so that *yin* and *yang*'s structural relation between difference/complementarity should be integrated into the dynamic process, and thereby becomes the relation between continuity and discontinuity in time. Yet, although elsewhere Slote appeals also to a historical reading of philosophy, like that of Enlightenment, David Hume, etc., he thereby implicitly refers to the historical, therefore temporal, dimension, and probably a dynamic vision of *yin* and *yang*, in the sense that he continues Hume's position, all in taking distance from what Hume said in regards to human emotions. However, this is not very clear in his treatise of *yin* and *yang*. There seems to be no explicit sense of dynamic reading of *yin* and *yang*, but only a structural one.

In the *Yijing*, it is said that "the successive *interaction* of *yin* and *yang* constitutes the Way (Dao)" (Chan 1963: 266, with modification and emphasis added). Similarly, Laozi in the *Daodejing* says something close to this: "The ten thousand things carry the *yin* and embraces the *yang*, and through the blending of the *vital* force they achieve harmony" (Chan 1963: 160, with modification). The traditional presentation of *Taiji* 太極 gives us a concrete image of the structural relationship between difference/complementarity (Figure 3.1) in its static situation. However, on the dynamic side of all that is, we have to put it into movement on the axis of time and thereby we have an image of the dynamic relation between continuity and discontinuity in time (Figure 2).

Since movement and change are the constant state of everything that is, the static situation should be integrated into the changing process. "Every thing changes except change itself" becomes the metaphysical motto of the *Classic of Changes*. As one of major origins of Chinese philosophy, it communicates to us the leading role of the dynamic aspect of *yin* and *yang*. In this perspective, Slote's explicit emphasis on the complementarity of *yin* and *yang*, therefore its structural perspective, with the implicit or even secondary role of the dynamic perspective, seems rather different from the Chinese tradition established since the *Yijing*.

3 Fang Yizhi, Chinese Predecessor of Michael Slote in Dealing with Philosophies of East and West

As to the relation between China and the West, we can move now to a Chinese predecessor of Michael Slote's view, Fang Yizhi 方以智 (1611–71). Fang Yizhi was the first Chinese philosopher, after Matteo Ricci's introduction of Western sciences into China, to have thought seriously and explicitly about the relation between East (China) and West in his *Humble Knowledge of Physics* (*wuli xiaoshi* 物理小識), *Equalizing East and West* (*Dongxi jun* 東西均) and other works.

There were several influences on Fang Yizhi's views on science and philosophy. He learned Western sciences from the Jesuits, and he sent his son, Fang Zhongtong 方中通, later a great Chinese mathematician, to study mathematics with the Western missionary J. N. Smogolenski (Mu Nige, 穆尼閣, 1611–56). Thus Fang has the prophetic vision of the feasibility and necessity of the cultural, scientific and philosophical interactions between East and West, which has become ever stronger over time. In comparison with him, the great Chinese philosopher Wang Fuzhi, a friend of Fang, focused squarely on Chinese philosophy and had no sense of the future interaction between East and West, which is now so extensive in the areas of science, philosophy, religion and culture in general.

One thing worth mentioning is Fang's understanding of Chinese and Western science and philosophy, in particular the fact that he classified sciences into three categories: the science of causes of concrete objects, named *zhice* 質測, like today's positive sciences; the science of governance and education, named *zaili* 宰理, like today's social and educational sciences; and the science of the ultimate and universal principles, named *tongji* 通幾, like philosophy. Fang said that he focused more on *zhice* 質測 and *tongji* 通幾 than on *zaili* 宰理. This classification is prophetic in the sense that it is much earlier in time than today's classification of natural sciences, social sciences and humanities (philosophy).

As to natural and physical sciences, Fang admired the Western versions of these, and corrected some of its data, like the distance between sun and earth and the nature of light etc. He combined both the Western science introduced by missionaries and Chinese traditional science, and improved them by his own findings, such as in the areas of astronomy, earth science, physics, optics, biomedical science etc. Even philosophers in the traditional Chinese sense like Wang Fuzhi agree with and admire Fang Yizi's approach in this regard, saying that:

> The learning of *zhice* that Master Mi (Fang Yizhi) and his son use is truly a practical approach for the attainment of both learning and thinking. For the investigation of things/*ge wu* 格物 was to exhaust principles through investigating objects or things. It was only *zhice* that could achieve this purpose.... Physics and chemistry recently transmitted from the Great West pertain to this level of principles.
>
> Wang 1992: 637

Unfortunately, Wang stays in the circle of his traditional Chinese, in particular Confucian, moral and political philosophy, and never tries to develop this tiny opening to Western science, thus having only an intuitive feeling rather than extensive knowledge of the West. Though himself a great philosopher in the sense of traditional Chinese philosophy, one might argue that he is too conservative and too short sighted regarding the issue of intercultural philosophy, in comparison with his friend, the prophetically open-minded Fang Yizhi.

As to metaphysics and purely philosophical study, Fang Yizhi regards the general principle in *the Yijing* as the highest principle/*tongji*, and as a result looks down upon Western metaphysics, as he makes clear in his preface to the *Wuli Xiaoshi* 物理小識 (*Humble Knowledge of Physics*): "Western science is proficient in *zhice* (investigation of concrete causes), but awkward in *tongji* (search of ultimate principle)" (Fang 1937: Preface). This is his critique of Western metaphysics, in particular its one-sided, stagnant view of leading in the end to a substantialist view of ultimate reality, instead of a dialectical and dynamic vision of change and of that ultimate reality manifesting in the *Yijing* 易經 (*The Book of Changes*).

Fang has developed an idea of dialectics that sees the universe as consisting of opposites, like *dao* 道 and *qi* 器, being and non-being, *yin* and *yang*, truth and false, day and night, water and fire, male and female, and the relation between East and West. These are all opposites yet mutually penetrating, leading towards mutual transformation. In this dialectical process between opposites, Fang presupposes a third term, an absolute, which is beyond the relative dialectics of oppositions but manifests or expresses itself through their dialectics. Thus we can say that, for Fan Yizhi, reality itself is in a dynamic process constantly changing due to opposites that are mutually penetrating, mutually including, and mutually transforming, that requests an ultimate reality, and absolute in itself, always expressing relative opposites.

Therefore, we can say that structural contrast is secondary to dynamic contrasts, including that between East and West. Fang Yizhi, in his *Yaodi Paozhunag* 藥地炮莊 (*Fang Yizhi's Processed Commentaries on the Zhuangzi*), expresses the idea that the distinction between East and West is relative: "Ordinary people put finger on the East as East, on the West as West; wise man knows that the East is not necessarily East and the West not necessarily West. Only the sage knows how to define East as East and West as West. It is through [Chan's dialectics of] three steps seeing Mountain and River that probably it is right to say so" (Fang 1975: 121–2).[2] For Fang, there are always ways everywhere in the East and West that elaborate the spiritual element, which is why they are all *dao* related to concrete things, changing, changeless and centrality, penetrating both extremes. He says: "Between Heaven and Earth there are a lot of methods for elaborating the spirit, in both East and West they are called the Way. *Dao* is things, and things are *Dao*, equalizing all things and not to be equalized with things, that's why *jun* is changing, changeless and centrality penetrating both extremes" (Fang 2001: 2).

Therefore, the so-called West and East have only a nominalist status, constructed by human beings and for human beings. In fact, there is no reference in reality, which is why Fang says:

> Thus it is called East and West; it is thus called outside and inside, or not inside nor outside; thus it is called South and North, thus it is called inside and outside, and we have the center because of inside and outside.
>
> Fang 2001: 293

and:

> Let me ask what is its center? Center is not at the outside, center is not at the inside, not inside nor outside; center is not at the center; how can center not at outside? inside? Center? South, North, East, West, where cannot be called center? Before and after South and North, before and after East and West, when can it not be at the center?
>
> Fang 2001: 295

This saying reminds me of what G. Aleni says about the *Global Maps* drawn by Matteo Ricci, that: "since the earth is round and round, nowhere on it is not the center. Thus the so-called distinctions among East/West/South/North are named after where one lives. There is no standard for them" (Wei 2011: *Juan* 75). One can reasonably derive from this that every point on the globe can be regarded as being at the center. Every nation is its own center. This is a pluralism of centralities. However, for Fang, all centralities point to a creative absolute.

Ultimately, Fang traces its concept of the Absolute to Zhou Dunyi's 周敦頤 (1017–73 AD) concept of the Great Ultimate, which itself is also based on the *Yijing*. Fang says: "It's Zhou Dunyi who starts to discuss an outline of Beginning and End, Void and Solid, Being and Non-being, Dao and Qi. There is void in the solid, solid in the void, before being here is non-being, before non-being there is being; the diagram of being is relative to the diagram of non-being. However, the real ultimate should be non-relative, and therefore there must be the absolute. Since being is relative to non-being, whereas the great ultimate should be the absolute, without any relativity" (Fang 2001: 49). Thus, in referring to the authority of Zhou Dunyi, Fang would say that, in all these opposites, before manifesting themselves into the status of opposites, there is already an absolute, the real ultimate, and therefore the absolute should not be taken as relative. Let us now turn to Zhou Dunyi.

4 *Yin* and *Yang* Unified by the Great Ultimate: Zhou Dunyi

Zhou Dunyi, the first pioneer of Neo-Confucianism, revitalized Confucianism after eight centuries of silence. With him, Confucianism began to revive during the

North Song Dynasty, taking up the challenges of Buddhism and Daoism, and was revitalized as Neo-Confucianism. He had a significant influence on its greatest synthesizer Zhu Xi (朱熹 (1130–1200) in the Southern Song and later on naturalist Neo-Confucians such as Fang Yizhi. Zhou Dunyi's *Explanation of the Diagram of the Great Ultimate* (*Taiji Tushuo* 太極圖說) is considered to be the pioneering philosophical work and has influenced Zhu Xi and Fang Yizhi. Here is its opening paragraph:

> *It's without limit (infinite), therefore named as the Great Ultimate* [my emphasis]. The Great Ultimate through movement generates *yang*. When its activity reaches its limit, it becomes tranquil. Through the tranquility the Great Ultimate generates *yin*. When tranquility reaches its limit, activity begins again. So movement and tranquility alternate and become the root of each other, giving rise to the distinction of *yin* and *yang*, and the two modes are thus established. By the transformation of *yang* and its union with *yin*, the Five Agents of Water, Fire, Wood, Metal and Earth arise. When these five vital forces (*qi*) are distributed in harmonious order, the four seasons run their course. The Five Agents are unified[3] by *yin* and *yang*; and *yin* and *yang* are unified by the Great Ultimate. The Five Agents arise, each with its specific nature.
>
> Chan 1963: 463

Here we adopt Zhu Xi's reading of the first sentence *wu ji er taiji* 無極而太極, that is, reading *wu* as "without" and *ji* as "limit;" therefore the whole sentence is saying that "it's without limit (infinite), therefore named as the Great Ultimate," and should not be read as Wing-tsit Chan did, as "Ultimate of Non-Being, then the Great Ultimate." In this essay, Zhou first develops a two-phase vision of the Ultimate Reality's manifestation into the cosmic process that starts with the birth of the universe as the phase of devolution, followed by human self-perfection as the phase of evolution. Thus, the creation of the universe has its origin in the infinite Great Ultimate, which moves from the infinite to more tangible and therefore finite manifestations.

First, in its act of creativity, the Great Ultimate launches a dynamic process of interaction between movement and tranquility, thus bringing forth the dialectics of *yin* and *yang*, in the process of which is produced five material forces, which upon further complications and combinations give rise to myriad other things. This process from the Infinite and formless to *yin* and *yang*, then five elements, then myriad things, with forms and finitude, seems therefore to be a process of devolution. The paragraph ends by summing up the whole process and reminding us of the unifying process and its origin in the Infinite Great Ultimate: "The Five Agents are unified by *yin* and *yang*, and *yin* and *yang* are unified by the Great Ultimate. The Five Agents arise, each with its specific nature."

One important thing to notice in regard to the Infinite is that the Infinite must be beyond its later differentiation or further division into *yin* and *yang*, which are finite, and whose interaction constitutes thereafter the law of nature. As textually evidenced here by Zhou Dunyi's *Explanation of the Diagram of the Great Ultimate*, and also by the *Laozi*,[4] the *Heng Xian*,[5] and many other Chinese philosophical texts, the Ultimate Reality, since it is infinite, is beyond the differentiation into being and nonbeing, *yin* and *yang*, movement and rest. Thus, the Infinite does not have, or goes beyond, differentiation or distinction between *yin* and *yang*. It is after the process of creating the universe or the giving birth of *qi*, which is the beginning of all finite beings, that there is *yin* and *yang*, the rhythmic interaction of which regulates the realms of finite beings. By contrast, Michael Slote seems to affirm *yin* and *yang* as pertaining to the ultimate category in Chinese philosophy, and does not notice the fact that they are finite, or with the finitude of their metaphysical status. It is worth mentioning that, after the process of devolution, then comes the evolutionary process according to Zhou Dunyi, in which human beings with intelligence and spiritual awareness emerged, and in their process of self-cultivation and self-perfection in achieving virtues extendable even to the whole universe, human beings could become sage. To establish a perfect model, as sage, for all human beings is therefore the ultimate goal of Zhou Dunyi's philosophy.

It follows that if the creation of the universe presented in the first part of the text is in a downward or devolutional process, the self-cultivation and self-perfection of human beings in the second part of the text creates an evolutional process in the universe. The basic concern is not only hominization but rather *humanization*; that is, the process in which human beings become genuinely human and in union with Heaven and Earth. Thus, both historically and philosophically, Chinese philosophy not only emphasizes the contrast between complementarity and difference, continuity and discontinuity between *yin* and *yang* and other pairs of opposites, but also their unification in the Infinite Great Ultimate as well as the manifestation of the Infinite into the dynamically and structurally contrasting opposites in a finite world.

5 A Philosophy of Contrast

Based upon previous discussions, I myself have proposed, since 1980, the concept of "contrast," not only as *yin* and *yang*, but also as opposites that are structurally different yet still complementary, dynamically discontinuous yet still continuous. This idea has its origin in Chinese philosophy. Laozi encourages us, for example, to think in terms of contrasts, more than as *yin* and *yang*, that Dao first manifests itself into *wu* 無 (non-being) as the realm of possibilities, and from this, some possibilities are realized as *you* 有 (beings); then, all beings are, structurally, constituted of opposites such as *you* (being) and *wu* (non-being), *yin* 陰 (feminine, negative, receptive) and *yang* 陽 (masculine, positive, creative), movement and rest, etc. More detailed opposites follow, such as "disaster and fortune," "correct and deviant," "good and evil" (*Laozi* 58); "beauty and ugliness," "good and not good," "being and non-being," "difficult and easy," "long and short," "high and low," "front and back" (*Laozi* 2); "the twisted and the upright," "hollow and full," "worn-out and renewed," "little and much" (*Laozi* 22); "heavy and light," "tranquility and agitation" (*Laozi* 26), etc. All these opposites are structurally different and yet complementary to each other, and they change dynamically in time into one another.

My proposal of a philosophy of contrast came earlier than Michael Slote's philosophy of *yin* and *yang*, but is similar to it. On the one hand, we both eschew structuralism in the sense that we emphasize both difference and complementarity, while structuralism sees only different elements in opposition, rather than in complementarity. Also Slote respects historicity, such as the history of Western philosophy, although he is not as familiar with the heritage of its Chinese equivalent. In contrast, structuralism over-emphasizes synchronicity to the negligence of diachronicity, and therefore human historicity is reduced to mere structural determinism.

On the other hand, it could be said that we are both similar to and yet different from Hegelianism. Historical movement is essential to Hegelian dialectics, which sees dialectics as both methodology and ontology, i.e., as the historical movement of Spirit seen as the True Reality. However, according to Hegel, Spirit moves by means of *Aufhebung*, understood in a negative way tending toward the ultimate triumph of negativity, and thus overlooking the positivity in its dialectical movement. However, my concept of contrast rediscovers the dynamic tension of both difference and complementarity, structurality and historicity, and it integrates both negative and positive forces in the movement of history as the process of reality's unfolding and manifestation. Probably we can say the same thing to Michael Slote when he, after criticizing Western and Chinese traditions, expects to arrive at an upgraded integration?

As I have said previously, the wisdom of contrast has its origin in the history of Chinese philosophy, such as the *Yijing*, the *Laozi,* and other Chinese philosophical texts. It epitomizes in the diagram of the Great Ultimate that gives us a concrete image of a philosophy of contrast, though apparently this represents explicitly only what I call "structural contrast." Still, based on the temporal nature of the Great Ultimate and its process of change, we can put its movement onto the axis of time and thereby we obtain an image of "dynamic contrast." By "structural contrast," I mean that in any moment of analysis, our perception, or any object under investigation, is constituted of interacting elements, different yet related, opposing yet complementing one another. It is synchronic in the sense that these opposing elements appear simultaneously to form a structured whole of phenomena. Being different, each element enjoys a certain degree of independence and difference. Being related, they are mutually interdependent and therefore complementary. This notion of structural contrast can be applied to all natural and human, both individual and social, phenomena.

In contrast, by "dynamic contrast" I mean that, on the dynamic axis of time, our individual life-story and collective history are in a process of becoming through the interplay between the precedent and the consequent moments, and among the past, the present, and the future. It is diachronic in the sense that one moment follows the other on the axis of time to form a history, not in a discontinuous succession but in a contrasting course of development. As discontinuous, the novel moment has its own originality which can never be reduced to any precedent moment. As continuous, it always keeps something from the precedent moment as residue or sedimentation of experience in time. Dynamic contrast therefore explains the interaction, scientifically between theory and empirical data, and historically between the traditional (past) and the modern (present and future).

Because of the fact that, in every structural or systematic whole, there is always a place for an actor or a group of actors to intervene, structural contrast and dynamic contrast are therefore also in a dialectical process, that, on the one hand, structural contrast determines in a certain sense the dynamic contrast; and, on the other, dynamic contrast integrates into itself structural contrast. Here we can situate the relations between theory and praxis, distancing and co-belongingness. Therefore, we should also take into account the element of subjectivity and intersubjectivity, and the existential dimension they bring with themselves. I have discussed these elsewhere, that, for limit of space, I will not discuss them here (Shen 1985: 7–8, 24–7).

Thus, I think it is more reasonable to extend the concept *yin/yang* into a philosophy of contrast, operated by oppositions not limited to *yin/yang* but rather open to groups of opposites like being and non-being, *yin* and *yang*, movement and rest, etc., both structurally complementary and differentiating, and dynamically continuous and discontinuous, to be ultimately unified or ideally referring to the infinite. In this sense, we may mention again our difference from structuralism, for which the structure is anonymous and it determines the constitution of meaning without being known consciously by the agent (see Shen 1985: 257–90). For us, on the contrary, a system or a structure is always the outcome of the act of "structuration" by a certain agent or group of actors in the process of time, which, can also be analyzed through our vision or intellectual gaze in order to uncover its structural intelligibility. An historical action can be analyzed in terms of systematic properties and be integrated into a structural totality. This is true, for example, in communication where system and agent are mutually dependent and promoting one another. The contrasting interaction between structure and dynamism leads finally to the evolutionary process of complexification. Structural contrast puts interacting elements into a kind of organized totality, but it is only through dynamic contrast that continuity and emergence of new possibilities can be properly understood.

The wisdom of contrast reminds us always to see the other side of the story and the tension between complementary elements essential to creativity in time. The wisdom of contrast reminds us too of the contrasting situation between concepts such as agent and system, difference and complementarity, continuity and discontinuity, reason and rationality, theory and praxis, understanding and translatability, process and reality, etc.

6 Conclusions

Now we are in a globalized world, in which every civilization goes beyond its physical frontiers to meet and interact with many others. Elsewhere I have defined "globalization" as "a historical process of deterritorialization or border-crossing, in which human desire, human interconnectedness and universalizability are to be realized on the planet as a whole, and to be concretized in the present as global free market, trans-national political order and cultural glocalism" (Shen 2004: 109–12). In this process, all people of the world are involved in the process of going beyond themselves to meet with and understand many others, either (ideally) for dialogue in view of mutual enrichment, or unfortunately for oppositional confrontation, even violent conflict.

In this context, philosophizing should not be self-enclosed in defining one's own vision of philosophy within the limit of one's own tradition, such as that of Western thought or Chinese thought. This is particularly necessary today when the type of rationality, so basic to Western civilization since the Enlightenment, is now challenged extensively. The world is open to other types of rationality, or rather to more comprehensive function of human reason and human sentiment, such as the Chinese vision of reasonableness and its emphasis on "Dao starts from human sentiment." This is the reason I admire Michaels Slote's philosophy of sentimentalism and his vision of *yin/yang* that goes out of Western philosophical tradition, in self-criticizing Western philosophy and in attempting to promote Chinese philosophy using an upgraded version of *yin/yang*. This approach has deep implications for intercultural philosophy.

I would say that, in the process of civilizational dialogue, intercultural philosophizing should not be limited to only doing comparative philosophy, just as comparative linguistics is often limited to the studies of resemblance and difference between two different languages. Although undertaking comparative philosophy in this manner could lead to a kind of relativism in philosophy, it will probably not really help the self/mutual understanding and the practice of philosophy itself. A maximal vision of comparative study should lead to interaction and dialogue among different cultural and philosophical traditions. For this, Michael Slote's *yin/yang* philosophy has resulted from such a communication, or more emphatically, is attempting a dialogue between Western and Chinese philosophies. Similarly, I have proposed a way of conducting intercultural philosophy: put into contrast rather than sheer comparison of different philosophical traditions. I understand "contrast" as the rhythmic and dialectical interplay between structural difference and complementarity, dynamic continuity and discontinuity, which leads eventually to the real mutual-enrichment of different agents, individual or collective, such as different traditions of philosophy.

At this time of globalization and high tech, when we can read all texts at the same time, from both East and West, from ancient to postmodern, the concept of incommensurability is less applicable than hitherto. It is questionable to emphasize the incommensurablity between China and the West. In fact, I would argue that incommensurability is already an out-of-date concept. If you can tell A and B are incommensurable, this presupposes that you understand both A and B; if not, you cannot say anything about their incommensurability. This means that A and B have something commonly understandable to you. This common understandability reveals their common intelligibility. So, the concept of incommensurability proposed by Thomas Kuhn, J. F. Lyotard etc., does not fit our reading experience today. How can one say that Western and Chinese philosophies are incommensurable if one does not understand them both, at least with a minimum degree of common intelligibility? They can be seen only as difference yet still commonly understandable.

What are the epistemological strategies we can adopt in view of a good comparative or intercultural philosophy? One would probably think of the strategy of appropriation of language, which means more concretely learning the language(s) of/understandable to other cultural/philosophical/ religious traditions. From a very young age, we learn a language through interacting with the generosity of those who take the initiative to speak to us, and thereby open to us a world of meaningfulness. Later, when grown up, we learn the languages of different disciplines, cultural practices, and different linguistic communities, which open us up to ever enlarging worlds. As Wittgenstein says, different language games correspond to different life-forms, therefore appropriation of another's language would give us access to the life-form implied in that specific language. By appropriating different languages within different cultural/philosophical/religious traditions, we could enter into different worlds and thereby enrich the construction of our own world.

We may also think of the strategy of strangification, or *waitui* 外推 in Chinese. By this I mean the act of going beyond oneself to go to many others, from familiar ground to unknown territory, from one's own cultural/religious world to those of many others. Three types of *waitui* (strangification) are in order: linguistic *waitui*; pragmatic *waitui*; and ontological *waitui*. I understand "dialogue" as mutual *waitui*. Thus, I speak the language understandable to you and to many strangers; I do things in ways that are acceptable to you and to many others; and I make the effort to enter into others' micro-worlds, scientific worlds, and even religious worlds, by meeting with reality itself, such as direct encounters with other individuals, social groups, civilizations, and nature, even with the Ultimate Reality, such as *dao* in Daoism, *tian* or sincerity or *li* or *xin* in Confucianism, or emptiness or One Mind in Buddhism, or God in Christianity, or Allah in Islam, etc.

From contrast to mutual strangification, hopefully this might suggest a way to bring optimistic mutual enrichment to dialogue among different traditions or civilizations. It is toward that end that it is significant to discuss the contribution of Michael Slote's *Philosophy of Yin and Yang* and his attempt to integrate both Western and Chinese philosophies into an upgraded synthesis.

Notes

1. Linguistic strangification requests that one translates the language of one's own philosophical/religious or cultural tradition into the language of (or understandable to) another tradition, to see whether it thereby becomes understandable or absurd. In the latter case, reflection on and self-critique should be made of one's own tradition instead of self-defense or other more radical forms of apologetics.
2. Chan's three steps: first, see the mountain as mountain, the river as river; second, see the mountain not as mountain and the river as not river; third, see the mountain as mountain and the river as river once more.
3. I have corrected Chan's translation of the first sentence, here in italic, "The Ultimate of the Non-Being and also the Great Ultimate" into "It's without limit (infinite), therefore named as the Great Ultimate," since I adopt Zhu Xi's reading, as explained in the main text.
4. Laozi says, "One gives birth to two, two gives birth to three, three gives birth to myriad of things. All things back up by *yin* and embrace *yang*, harmonized by breathing together" (*Laozi* 42).
5. The *Hengxian* says, "The Constant preceded non-being and being.... It was not satisfied with self-enclosure, therefore it rose to create Space. Since there was Space, there was *qi*. Since there was *qi*, there were beings. Since there were beings, there was beginning. Since there was beginning, there was passing away" (Ma 2003: 288).

References

Fang, Yizhi 方以智 (1937), *Humble Knowledge of Physics* 物理小識. Shanghai: Shangwu Yingshuguan.

Fang, Yizhi (1975), *Yaodi Paozhuang* 藥地炮莊 (*Fang Yizhi's Fusioned Commentaries of Zhuangzhi*), Taipei: Guangwen Book Store.

Fang, Yizhi, (2001), *Dongxi Jun* 東西均 (*Equalizing East and West*), in Pang Pu 龐樸 *Dong Xi Jun Zhushi* 東西均注釋 (*Annotations and Commentaries on Equalizing East and West*), Beijing: Zhonghua Bookstore.

Guodian Chu mu zhu jian 郭店楚墓竹簡 (1998) (*Guodian Chu Tomb Bamboo Slips*), ed. Jingmen Shi Museum, Beijing: Wenwu Chubanshe.

Laozia (1999), *Laozi Shizhong* 老子四種 (Four Versions of the *Laozi*). Taipei: Da'an Bookstore.

Ma, Chengyuan, ed. (2003), *Shanghai Bowuguan Chang Zhanguo Chuzhushu* (*Bamboo Scripts of Chu States During the Warring States Period Collected in Shanghai Mueseum*). Shanghai: Guji Chubanshe.

Shen, Vincent. 沈清松 (1985), *Essays in Contemporary Philosophy East and West*. Taipei: Lih-Ming Publishing Co.

Shen, Vincent (2004), "A Book Review of Michael Hardt & Antonio Negri's *Empire*," *Universitas: Monthly Review of Philosophy and Culture,* 361 (June 2004): 109–112.

Slote, Michael (2018), *The Philosophy of Yin and Yang* 陰陽的哲學 (A bilingual edition). Beijing: Shangwu Yingshuguan.

Wang, Fuzhi 王夫之 (1992), *Complete Works of Wang Fuzhi* 王夫之全集, vol. 12, Changsha: Yuelu Academy.
Wei, Yuan 魏源, ed. (2011), *Global Maps* 海國圖志. Changsha: Yuelu Shuyuan.
Wing-tsit, Chan (1963), *A Source Book in Chinese Philosophy,* Princeton: Princeton University Press.

4

Slote's Sentimentalist Theory of the Mind versus A Neo-Confucian Unified Theory of the Mind

JeeLoo Liu
California State University, Fullerton, United States
jeelooliu@gmail.com

1 Introduction

In *A Sentimentalist Theory of the Mind* (2014), Michael Slote argues for the importance of emotion in every aspect of our mental life.[1] In this book, he goes one step further from his previously advocated theory of moral sentimentalism, according to which morality fundamentally depends on emotion, and argues that the influence of emotion is pervasive even in our ordinary perception, thought, and action—emotion enters not just into moral deliberation and practical reason, but also into "intellectual/epistemic/cognitive rationality" (Slote 2014: xviii). In a nutshell, Slote's sentimentalist theory of the mind is the claim that emotion plays a crucial role in "unifying the mind" (*ibid.*). This chapter will critically examine Slote's sentimentalist theory of the mind and argue that it fails to proffer a genuinely unifying theory of the mind. In contrast, it will present a neo-Confucian view, which I call a "unified theory of the mind."

Using the word *xin* 心 (typically translated as *heart-mind*) as his case in point, Slote argues that intellect and emotion are inseparable in the tradition of Chinese language and thought. And because there was never a separation, there was also no effort of unification.[2] To refute his view, this chapter will present a neo-Confucian unified theory of the mind derived from an important neo-Confucian phrase: "the mind encompasses both nature and emotion (*xin tong xing qing* 心統性情)." This thesis was first proposed by Zhang Zai,[3] and further expanded by Zhu Xi. In this chapter, I shall argue that Zhang-Zhu's unified theory of the mind advocates both a form of "ontological unification" and a form of "regulative unification"—it is both a descriptive theory of the nature of the mind, and a normative theory of how the mind ought to function. In this respect, Zhang-Zhu's unified theory of the mind differs from Slote's *descriptive* theory. Another respect in which the two philosophies of the mind differ is that Slote declares himself to be an "empiricist" in the philosophy of mind, by which he means that our emotions are cultivated after birth and are the results of familial and social grooming alone. Slote frequently explains the existence of psychopaths or sociopaths in terms of the poor early family relationships such as neglect or abuse. In contrast, both Zhang Zai and Zhu Xi were committed to the Mencian view of the innateness of certain sentiments. Their unified philosophy of the mind can be called "innatist" in Slote's term. Neo-Confucians, on the basis of Mencius' theory of human nature, all advocate the innate goodness of the human mind, exemplified in the inborn moral sentiments of sympathy, shame and disgust, reverence and awe, and finally, the sense of right and wrong. The four groups of inborn sentiments in neo-Confucian moral psychology serve as the foundation of morality.

In this chapter I shall argue that in both respects, the Zhang-Zhu unified theory of the mind surpasses Slote's sentimentalist theory of the mind.

2 A Sentimentalist Theory of the Mind

Slote's main argument for his sentimentalist theory of the mind relies on his analysis of the nature of epistemic rationality: "Epistemic rationality turns out to require both empathy and certain emotions, and even sheer/mere belief turns out to involve, essentially involve, an emotional element" (Slote 2014: 12). According to him, one key emotional element is the role of empathy in our epistemic life: intellectual virtue such as "open-mindedness" consists in the agent's ability to "empathize with the other's point of view, sees things to some extent in the favorable light in which the other person sees them" (Slote 2014: 17). Furthermore, in Slote's analysis, believing in something (a proposition, a theory, or an argument) essentially involves a "favorable attitude, some positive feeling, affect, or emotion" (Slote 2014: 179); or, on a stronger point, belief simply "*is* a kind of emotion" (Slote 2014: 180). He thus concludes that "there is no such thing as a purely intellectual or purely cognitive belief or opinion" (Slote 2014: 179).

Slote construes his sentimentalist theory of the mind in contrast with "rationalism of the mind," which equates the unity of the mind with the mind's obeying principles of consistency and coherence of reason. To defeat rationalism of the mind, Slote aims to show that emotion is involved in all modes of thinking—conceptual, mathematical, scientific and empirical. He argues that to have a belief is "to have a favorable and positive attitude toward a certain way of seeing the world" (Slote 2014: 6). On the basis of this characterization of the nature of belief, Slote claims that "it follows that *there are and can be no purely intellectual or purely cognitive states of belief* because all belief necessarily involves some (perhaps mild) positive emotion" (Slote 2014: 6, emphasis added). His argument seems to rely on the role the sentiment of empathy plays in all epistemic rationality. According to Slote, the epistemic virtues such as open-mindedness or fair-mindedness require the agent to have "an ability and willingness to see things from other people's points of view" (Slote 2014: 15), and, to him, this attitude constitutes a form of intellectual empathy. Epistemic vices such as close-mindedness or intolerance are characterized as "epistemic anger" by Slote, again a highly emotive state of mind. These criteria of epistemic rationality assume an interpersonal relationship in the formation of belief. Even in the case of believing in theories and arguments, Slote argues, the agent must have a "favorable attitude, some positive feeling, emotion, or affect," and he concludes that "there is no such thing as a purely intellectual or purely cognitive belief or opinion" (Slote 2014: 18). Not only is belief such a cognitive state imbued with emotion, he thinks that positive or favorable attitudes are also "pervasively involved in cognition, learning, and knowledge" (Slote 2014: 22).

In contrast to those engaged in the reasons internalism/externalism debate on the belief-desire model for motivating human action, Slote is not suggesting, along with reasons externalists, that belief *needs* desire to motivate. On the contrary, he is arguing that emotion "plays a *constitutive* role in belief" (Slote 2014: 28), and belief is fundamentally a form of emotionally favorable attitude toward seeing the world in a certain way. Therefore, on his view, belief could by itself motivate action without the help of desire. In the chapter "Belief in Action," Slote presents a sentimentalist theory of human agency. He argues that under the standard belief-desire model, belief has merely a mind-to-world direction of fit in that the standard of justifiable belief is taken to rely on whether it fits reality. However, under such a view, belief is a passive, non-engaging, inert spectator attitude, and would of course lose its motivational efficacy. Slote proposes that we view belief with an additional *world-to-mind* fit, "because it involves emotion and motivation," and this can explain how belief can causally interact with the world and produce action (Slote 2014: 58). In other words, what Slote suggests is a revolutionary view of the mind, according to which the cognitive and the affective are no longer sharply divided but are unified as one sentimental mind, where emotion (which he characterizes as a positive attitude) is the dominant foundation penetrating every mental function. This is what he calls the "emotional unity of the self."

Slote's *emotional unity* thesis is that "emotions play a vital role in constituting the unity of our minds and ourselves as selves" (Slote 2014: 63). The thread of his argument seems to be based on the assertion that there is unity in belief, and since belief essentially involves emotion, emotion constitutes the unity of the mind. In other words, Slote takes unity of the mind as his starting point and traces the underlying factor of this unity to emotion. According to him, belief is a kind of unity of intellectual/conceptual and practical/emotional, and there is no purely intellectual state of belief. He also rejects the separation between theoretical reason and practical reason, taking the two to be "totally interfused" and mutually involved (Slote 2014: 65). In his view, believing that something is a means to an end "involves favoring a certain way of seeing the world and in acting practically on the basis of everyday desires and beliefs" (Slote 2014: 67).

I find Slote's sentimentalist theory of the mind, and especially his emotional unity thesis, muddled and confusing. In what follows, I will briefly lay out my criticisms before introducing the neo-Confucian unified theory of the mind.

3 A Critique of Slote's Sentimentalist Theory of the Mind

To begin with, what is unclear to me is whether Slote's thesis of a sentimentalist theory of the mind is meant to be *descriptive* or *normative*. I take it that the rationalists aim to provide a normative theory of human action. Kant's famous denouncement of the agent's good feelings, natural impulses, and even altruistic inclinations as having "no true moral worth" is not to deny that people *do* frequently act out of their emotions, however noble or praiseworthy those emotions may be. To Kant, a proper moral act *ought to be* one from the good will, the agent's autonomous self-regulation, or from the sense of duty. Kant acknowledges that reason is not always competent enough to guide the will, but he argues that the true role of reason is to produce a will that is "good in itself."[4] For this sole purpose, reason would have to suppress the heart's natural inclinations: "reason, which cognizes its highest practical vocation in the establishment of a good will, in attaining this purpose is capable only of its own kind of satisfaction, namely from fulfilling an end which in turn only reason determines, even if this should be combined with many infringements upon the ends of inclination" (Kant 1997: 9). According to Kant, our natural inclination for the desired effect of our action does not warrant our respect, even though we may approve it and even love it, "that is, regard it as favorable to my own advantage" (Kant 1997: 16). Kant declares: "Only what is connected with my will merely as ground and never as effect, that does not serve as inclination but outweighs it or at lease excludes it altogether from calculations in making a choice—hence the mere law for itself—can be an object of respect and so a command" (Kant 1997: 16). In other words, Kant's ethical rationalism is at the same time a normative theory, arguing for what reason *ought to* do, and an evaluative theory, assessing the moral worth of our action and its motive. Kant provides an argument that the more one allows one's reason to be governed by natural inclinations or the propensity of feeling (what Slote calls favorable attitudes) to pursue the enjoyment of life, the further one will "get away from true satisfaction," so much so that one ends up developing a certain "*misology*," hatred of reason (*ibid.*). Whether we accept this argument (and others) or not, Kant is at least providing some argumentation for his ethical rationalism. He does not deny that we often act out of our natural inclinations, but his main point is that reason ought to be master of inclinations. If Slote is offering normative sentimentalist theory of the mind, then he needs to present arguments to show why one ought to follow one's emotion in all cognition, learning, knowledge, practical reason, and morality. He has not done so to date.

On the other hand, if Slote is describing how emotion underlies *all* mental functions, then he will need far more empirical findings to back up this putative claim. His main argument is merely to point out that belief involves emotionally favorable attitudes. It may be true that in reality the mind cannot be sharply divided into different categories, where one uses *either* cognitive sagacity *or* emotive favoring in dealing with various affairs. However, this does not entail that such a distinction among our mental functions does not exist. Some fundamental differences between belief and emotion are that belief is *truth-apt* while emotion is not; the verification of the content of belief is generally world-directed while the verification of the content of emotion is not. People's self-ascription of a firm belief and their self-ascription of an emotion have different criteria: people claim to believe in *p* when they judge *p* to be true of the world, whereas people claim to have emotion *q* when they feel *q*-way. If asked for justification, people will cite evidence in support of *p*'s being true but will simply respond with their self-awareness in support of their feeling *q*-way. In the case of belief, rationality dictates that we defer to experts and be receptive to correction when our beliefs are refuted with strong evidence or discredited by those whom we trust to be experts. In the case of emotion, on the other hand, we believe ourselves to be the experts on what kind of emotion we have. Slote's conclusion that *there are and can be no purely intellectual or purely cognitive states of belief* is simply too strong. Even if people often do have emotionally driven beliefs, the pro-attitude that is characterized as *belief* is "take-it-as-true." Other pro-attitudes such as love and gratitude are not truth-apt and are not taken by the subjects as such either. If Slote claims that to have a firm belief is simply to have a favorable and positive attitude toward a certain way of seeing the world, then he needs to show how often one can be so emotionally driven to believe in something that one does not even attempt to provide justification when being asked, or that one would continue to hold such a belief even when confronted with compelling evidence against its credibility.[5]

As a descriptive thesis, Slote's emotional unity thesis also fails to explain away people's self-conflicted beliefs, emotions, desires, intention and action. The phenomena of *akrasia* (weakness of will, incontinence) are prevalent in the human mind. If one's belief is, as Slote claims, an emotional favoring of seeing the world in a certain way, then why would one also have another emotionally driven desire to act contrary to what one believes on the grounds of one's evidence and best reasoning? Emotions do not unify the mind, especially because emotions themselves are often acting against one another. One could love and hate the same person at the same time; one could simultaneously feel gratitude and resentful toward the same person. One could believe that one ought to do *x* as the means to one's desired end *y*, and yet one ends up not doing *x*. Davidson's *divided* or *partitioned mind* thesis was introduced to resolve some of the common paradoxes of irrationality. Davidson explains the paradox of irrationality this way: "What requires explaining is the action of an agent who, having weighed up the reasons on both sides, and having judged that the preponderance of reasons is on one side, then acts against this judgment" (Davidson 1982: 295). If the mind is indeed unified by emotion, then which emotion trumps all other conflicting emotions? If Slote's answer is "whichever that propels one to take the action," then his emotional unity thesis does not give us much insight into the struggles in the human mind.

In what follows, I will present a neo-Confucian theory of mind characterized by a key phrase: "The mind encompasses both nature and emotion (*xin tong xing qing* 心統性情)."

4 Neo-Confucian Unified Theory of the Mind

The thesis "The mind encompasses both nature and emotion (*xin tong xing qing* 心統性情)" was first proposed by Zhang Zai, and further expanded by Zhu Xi. In this brief quote, Zhang Zai introduces a unified theory of the mind: the mind unifies both the heavenly endowed nature (*xing* 性) and human emotion (*qing* 情). According to Wing-tsit Chan's assessment, this simple saying "makes the mind the master of a person's total being" (Chan 1963: 517). In a different quote, Zhang Zai takes the mind to be the unity of nature and perception/awareness (*zhijue* 知覺) (Zhang 1985: 9); in other words, he thinks that human mind is constituted both by *a priori* endowments and *a posteriori* experience and development. His unified theory of the mind first separates the metaphysical foundation of human existence from post-birth awareness and emotion, and then uses the mind to unify them both. However, the separate consideration of the mind's various sources—*a priori* and empirical—is not based on the dichotomy between the intellect and the affective, or reason and emotion, since Zhang Zai takes both perception and emotion to be part of our *a posteriori* mental functions, which cannot exist in humans without the endowed human nature.

On the empirical side, both perceptual awareness (the cognitive mind) and emotion (the affective mind) are derived from the mind's actual encounter with things. As Zhang Zai puts it, "From phenomena (*xiang* 象) the mind is discerned" (Zhang 1985: 24, cited in Tang 1956). According to Tang Chün-I's explanation, "'Phenomena' here means the appearances of things perceived by the mind and the impressions and ideas left on the mind due to its perceptions" (Tang 1956: 115). Tang thinks that Western Empiricists focus on the impressions and ideas in the mind, whereas Chinese thinkers emphasize the activity of the mind. The former takes the mind to be simply a collection (a storehouse) of numerous ideas and impressions, whereas the latter takes the mind to be the active production and transcendence of ideas. Tang argues that this is the "the basic conception in traditional Chinese thought toward an understanding of the mind" (*ibid.*, 116). This is a very insightful perspective. I think a further distinction between Empiricism and Zhang Zai's unified theory of the mind, as the standard Confucian view of nature and mind, is the latter does not take the mind to be any *tabula rasa*—the mind is predisposed to react to things in certain ways, and such predispositions are called "nature." Zhang Zai calls the intrinsic endowment what is "internal" and perceptual knowledge what is "external" (Zhang 1985: 25). To gain knowledge of the world, one must combine both the internal and the external, both the endowed and the empirical. He says: "Others think that our knowledge is derived from the passive reception (*shou* 受) of the eyes and ears. However, the reception of sense organs is actually the joint result of both the internal and the external. If one can see that the internal and the external jointly work beyond what mere sense organs such as eyes and ears receive, then one's understanding far surpasses those of others" (Zhang 1985: 25). In other words, in Zhang Zai's theory, there are two dimensions in human mind—the given and the acquired. He says: "Nature connotes what one can do by natural endowment. Ability (*neng* 能) connotes what one can do through one's own planning" (Zhang 1985: 21, modification of Chan's translation, Chan 1963: 508). Even though the mind, as part of our material existence, does not begin to function until after birth, it cannot accomplish all merely by what is perceived and cognized after birth. The mind is equipped with some innate abilities, and in Zhang Zai's view, such abilities enable us to surpass animalistic existence and be moral. They are what separate humans from other animals by nature.

Zhang Zai's division and unification of the two aspects of the mind—nature and emotion—is also a normative theory of the mind. In his view, our nature, that is, our "heavenly endowments," sets the norm for the mind's function. The aim of moral cultivation is to fully develop one's virtues to be in accord with the virtues of heaven. "If one's mind can fully develop one's nature, then one demonstrates that 'it is man who can make *Dao* great'" (Zhang 1985: 22, translated by Chan, Chan 1963: 510). To Zhang Zai, one's heavenly endowed nature is not simply one's biological makeup at birth: "To consider what is inborn as one's nature is to fail to understand the course of day and night" (*ibid.*). In other words, one's nature represents one's potential, and its full development awaits one's experience and one's accumulated practice (*xi* 習).

Zhang Zai endorses Mencius' view that human nature is good. According to Mencius, human nature contains four moral sentiments that are the beginnings of morality; hence, they are called "the four moral sprouts." Mencius argues that humans naturally have within themselves the heart that cannot bear the suffering of others, the sentiment of shame and disgust, the feeling of reverence and awe, and the sense of right and wrong. Mencius takes these four moral sprouts to be a universal trait in humans' psychological constitutions, which still need cultivation and maturation. Zhang Zai, however, treats human nature as exemplifying the highest good. He calls such endowments "the nature of heaven and earth." The manifestation of goodness in human conduct depends on one's effort to return to the heavenly endowed nature. Moral knowledge does not come from perceptual experience and the mind's interactions with things: "Knowledge coming from seeing and hearing is knowledge obtained through contact with things. It is not knowledge obtained through one's moral nature. Knowledge obtained through one's moral nature does not originate from seeing and hearing" (Supp. 2:21, Chan 1963: 515). Zhang Zai categorizes emotion and desire along with perceptual awareness; hence, on his view, neither emotion nor desire could have genuine moral worth. He regards those who follow human desires as people "who understand lower things" only (Chan 1963: 509). We ought to follow what heaven endows in us and try to overcome the inclinations that come from our *qi*-constitution, our experiential self, or simply our interactions with things. As he puts it, if one exhaustively investigates principles of things and fully manifests one's nature, then "nature becomes Heaven's virtue, and endowment (*ming* 命) becomes the principle of Heaven" (Zhang 1985: 23). In this respect, his normative position is closer to Kant's ethical rationalism.

Zhu Xi greatly admired Zhang Zai's unified thesis of the mind and developed it into a more structured theory of the mind as well as a normative moral theory based on this moral psychology. According to Zhu Xi, "The nature is simply the principle of the mind, while feelings and emotions are simply the manifestations of the nature.... Zhang Zai's doctrine of 'mind encompasses/commands (*tong* 統) both nature and emotion' is excellent" (Zhu 2002: 14.227). The reason why the word '*tong* 統' in this phrase is now rendered as both 'encompass' and 'command' is that Zhu Xi intentionally gave it two interpretations. Zhu Xi explains the meaning of '*tong*' in terms of "encompass or unify (*jian* 兼)" (cited in Zhang 1985: 338); at the same time, he also analyzes the role of the mind in this phrase as "command or rule (*zhuzai* 主宰)" (cited in Zhang 1985: 340).[6] On the basis of Zhu Xi's double connotations of '*tong*', I shall argue that Zhu Xi's unified theory of the mind advocates both a form of "ontological unification" and a form of "regulative unification"—it is both a descriptive theory of the nature of the mind, and a normative theory of how the mind *ought to* function. This analysis is based on Meng Peiyuan's exposition of Zhu Xi's doctrine of *xin tong xing qing*. Meng writes, "The word '*tong*' has two meanings: the first one is that *xin* encompasses nature and emotion; the second one is that *xin* commands nature and emotion. The former is an ontological claim, stating that the mind encompasses both the original state (*ti* 體) and its manifestation (*yong* 用), separating nature and emotion in terms of the original state and its manifestation.... The latter refers to the function (*gongneng* 功能) of the mind, meaning that the mind commands both nature and emotion in its function of awareness (*zhijue* 知覺)" (Meng 2011: 2, my translation). Both connotations of the word '*tong*' and both unification theses can be found in Zhu Xi's texts.

On the ontological dimension, Zhu Xi thinks that human nature, before empirical experience, already contains the principles of the four cardinal virtues—humaneness, righteousness, propriety, and wisdom. After one comes into contact with the outside world, one's mind is aroused into producing "thoughts, awareness, ideas, deliberation (*zhishi nianlv* 智識念慮)"—which are all categorized under the umbrella term 'emotion' by Zhu Xi (cited in Zhang 1985: 339). Zhu Xi takes the human mind to be ontologically grounded in the heavenly principle; in other words, he thinks that human existence is a moral existence. The reason why we can have morally praiseworthy emotions such as sympathy, for example, is that we are already creatures with the principle of humaneness in our nature. But to actually possess such moral sentiments, the mind needs to be actively engaged with things.

As he put it, "Humaneness is nature; commiseration is emotion. They both require the manifestation in the mind" (ibid.). That is to say, in Zhu Xi's view, the mind plays an active role in bringing the potential goodness into realization. "The mind contains both the inactive state (*jing* 靜), which is nature, and the active state (*dong* 動), which is emotion" (*ibid.*). Hence, the mind encompasses both nature and emotion. According to Meng Peiyuan, Zhu Xi's view that the mind is "simultaneously in an activated and inactivated state" not only "affirmed the position of the mind as an origin (a thing-in-itself), but also involved the issue of practices for the cultivation of mind and nature" (Meng 2010: 379). This is the path from the ontological unification in Zhu Xi's metaphysics to the regulative unification in Zhu Xi's normative theory.[7]

On the normative dimension, Zhu Xi's moral philosophy is close to that of Zhang Zai: the mind ought to use our moral grounding—our nature—as the standards of right and wrong. In Zhu Xi's moral psychology, human mind is fully responsible for our morality as well as our moral failure. In other words, the root of good and evil is in the human mind. He even says that the mind can sometimes be "not good (*bu shan* 不善)" (Zhu 2002: 14:228). However, if the mind encompasses both nature and emotion while nature is "purely good," then the part that could lead the mind to be deviating from good must be the mind's feeling and emotion.

Zhu Xi has a guarded view of human feeling and emotion. Even the four moral sprouts, the moral sentiments involving commiseration, righteousness, propriety and wisdom, which Mencius praised as the proof of the goodness of human nature, are not totally unproblematic, since they could also lead to wrongful acts. Zhu Xi says, "In human mind, if one has too much commiseration, then one could become indulgent and weak. If one has too much sense of shame and disgust, then one could end up feeling morally incensed towards the wrong things" (Zhu 2002: 14:193). In other words, our feeling and emotion, even when they are the so-called "moral sentiments" as the four moral sprouts, could deviate from the norm and lead us to commit moral ills. To Zhu Xi, "evil" results from the imbalance of feelings and emotions. As biological and moral beings, we have natural emotions and moral sentiments innate in us. "If our feelings and emotions are all expressed with due measure and degree (*zhongjie* 中節), then they are good; if they miss the appropriate measure and degree (*buzhongjie* 不中節), then they become evil. One's nature is complete and self-sufficient. How could there be anything bad in it? But men do not aim for good, and this is how they become evil" (Zhu 2002, 14:363). Zhu Xi links desire with emotion and gives the metaphor of water to explain their relations: "Desire is generated by feeling and emotion. Human mind is like water, and human nature is the water at rest, while feeling is the water in flow. Desire, on the other hand, is like the ripples and waves of water, which can be good and can be bad" (*ibid,* 14.229). From this metaphor, we can see that for Zhu Xi, emotion and desire are both activated mental states. Even though Zhu Xi did acknowledge that some desire is good, such as a moral agent's desire to achieve humaneness, in general he argues that human desire and heavenly principle are incompatible: "In one's mind, if heavenly principle is preserved, then human desire will disappear; if human desire wins over, then heavenly principle is extinguished. There has never been a mixture of heavenly principle and human desire in the same mind" (*ibid.*, 14.388). The reason why human desire is always bad is its intrinsically self-centered (*si* 私) nature. The precept of heavenly principle is to be impartial (*gong* 公), which stands in opposition to the self-centered desire. Zhu Xi says, "Everything can have the polarity of right and wrong: what is right is the impartiality of heavenly principle; what is wrong is the self-regarded human desire. One must carefully discern these two in every affair" (Zhu 2002: 14.390). For example, he says, eating and drinking is part of heavenly principle, but if one pursues delicious food and drink, then it becomes human desire (Zhu 2002: 14.389). This example shows that he rejects human desire primarily because desire belongs to the private realm and falls on the material level. One's desire should only be for the intellectual enrichment and spiritual gain.

According to Zhu Xi, there is a constant battle in one's mind between good and evil, between heavenly principle and human desire. "If one of them advances, then the other retreats; and vice versa. There is no way to stay neutral and not make any advancement or retreat" (Zhu 2002: 14.389). This is why one cannot do it alone; one needs to study and learn. "Before one learns, one's mind is filled with human desire. After one started learning, heavenly principle naturally becomes manifest and human desire gradually diminishes. This is of course good; however, there will be layer after layer of obstructions that need to be removed. Even after one has removed the major desires, one still needs to scrutinize one's deeper, subtler desires" (Zhu 2002: 14.390). Ultimately, the goal of learning is to "completely remove human desire so as to return to the precept of heavenly principle" (*ibid.*). According to his view, since heavenly principle is inherent in the human mind as human nature, the moral norm is internal to us. The more we learn about right and wrong, about truth and morality, the less desire we will have. Through the elimination of desire, we will eventually turn to the correct path if we had previously deviated from it through our emotion and desire. In other words, moral attainment must rely on moral education and ethical thinking. In this respect, Zhu Xi is clearly an ethical rationalist as well.

If evil derives from the mind's emotional manifestations and material desire, then human mind is not a sufficient grounding for human morality. We can see that even though Zhu Xi confirms the goodness of human nature, he is not optimistic about an individual's attainment of moral goodness. We have a purely good moral essence, but this a priori moral grounding is stuck in the physical constitutions which are manifested in our personality, temperament, emotion and desire. The latter obstructs the former from being completely realized in the individual's mind. To combat any moral impurity or moral failure resulting from our qi-constitutions, we need to resort to the mind for its effort in self-cultivation.

For Zhu Xi, our inborn nature is not what makes our moral accomplishment possible. In other words, our good nature is causally insufficient for our morality.

Even if we have an innate moral essence that defines what we are and what we ought to be, once born, our *qi*-dispositions immediately dominate our daily conduct. To retrieve the moral status granted us by our nature, we need to put in efforts to rectify our emotion and desire if they deviate from the heavenly principle inherent in our nature. Zhu Xi takes 'mind' to be where our agency resides. Without the human mind, human nature by itself is insufficient for our moral realization. He says, "If there were no mind, where do we place [human] nature? There must be a mind to administer the nature, to make it functional" (Zhu 2002: 14.192). Human nature without human mind is empty, while human mind without human nature would be without norms. Zhu Xi further explicates the unification thesis of the mind in terms of the mind's being the master-in-command: "Within the mind there is both active and passive aspects. The passive aspect is nature and the active aspect is feeling and emotion. 'The mind is *the master of* both nature and emotion.' Being the master is to be in command, like a general's commanding the troop of one million soldiers" (Zhu 1985: 7.2513, emphasis added). This quote clearly shows that in Zhu Xi's theory, nature is a passive given state, while the mind is the active agency. For our moral realization, human nature can be seen as the ontological grounding, but it is really the human mind that has the causal efficacy.[8]

However, we have seen that the mind encompasses both human nature and humans' affective states that include emotion and desire. If the former is causally ineffective and the latter is the root of evil, then there has to be some other function of the mind that is responsible for human morality. Zhu Xi identifies it with volition (*zhi*). Volition, as he sees it, is "the commander-in-chief of the mind" and it sets the direction of one's thinking (Zhu 2002: 14.358). Volition and desire are both intentional—they are about objects or events in the external world, but volition differs from desire in that desire is passively triggered by external objects while volition is the mind's taking the initiative to set out to do something.

Zhu Xi says, "To firm up one's volition to do good, one must be like the thirsty or hungry people's wanting to eat and drink. If one ever takes it idly, then one's volition cannot be set" (Zhu 2002: 14.282). In other words, there has to be an eagerness, an earnestness, and a directness in one's resolve to be good. This intent must always be preserved, and Zhu Xi calls it "not losing one's original mind (*bu shi benxin*)" or "retrieving one's lost mind (*qiu fangxin*)." The determination and direction come from the individual's effort, and they are not universally guaranteed in our given nature. Zhu Xi argues that the sages are simply "those who have done what human beings *ought to do*" (Zhu 2002: 14.280, emphasis added). In other words, the sages are the people who fulfill humans' moral status and realize their *nature*. Since to be a sage is simply to be a human being, every one of us should have the volition to learn from the sages, and further to have *possessing sagehood* as our responsibility. Moral accomplishment begins with this first step: to set the mind on the right direction toward sagehood.

To sum up, Zhu Xi's unified theory of the mind is both a metaphysical thesis and a moral theory. In Meng's analysis, the mind for Zhu Xi is both a peta-physical one and a moral one: "[In Zhu Xi's language] such a *xin* was obviously the mind of morality, and that had been a basic Confucian view about *xin* since Confucius and Mencius. But the mind of morality could not do without the mind of perception. Logically, the mind could be divided as the metaphysical one of morality and the peta-physical one of perception; but ontologically, mind was a whole composed of both the metaphysical and the peta-physical . . . . In particular, 'mind is composed of both its form and function" (Meng 2010: 384). We may conclude that Zhang-Zhu's unified theory of the mind, under Zhu Xi's elaboration, has become a rich theory that comprises of both metaphysics of the mind and a normative theory of the mind's role in morality.

5 Comparing the Two Unified Theories of the Mind[9]

From the above analysis, it is clear that Slote's unified theory of the mind and the neo-Confucian version thereof have different aims and scopes. Slote's theory advocates the unification of reason and emotion, using emotion as the unificatory basis of the empirical mind. In contrast, Zhang-Zhu's theory is the unification of the metaphysical foundation of the human mind and the various functions of the empirical mind. Slote's theory can at best serve as a descriptive theory of the mind and not as a normative theory of the mind. Slote might be right to point out that our mental functions do in fact contain an emotional element, but he could not be defending the normative position that all our mind's cognitive and rational operations *ought to* contain an emotional element. To defend such a normative view, he would be denying the value or even the existence of human rationality. I have argued that even as a descriptive theory of the mind, Slote's sentimentalist theory does not fully capture the nature of belief. Even if he is correct that belief is a form of "pro-attitude," it is not necessarily a form of empathic understanding of *someone else's* attitude, since belief is not merely an "interpersonal" attitude. One could entertain a belief even if no one else endorses this belief. Belief ultimately has a mind-to-world direction of fit; in other words, belief is an individual's assessment of the state of affairs in the world. Even if one's assessment of the verity of one's belief is not always purely based on available evidence and logical deduction, one nonetheless has an *epistemic responsibility* to achieve the truth-aptness of one's own belief.

In his most recent book, *The Philosophy of Yin and Yang*, Slote again underscores the emotional aspect of belief. He employs the Chinese philosophical division of *yin* and *yang* to depict the duo-aspect of belief: "the empathy or feeling side of compassion constitutes its *yin* aspect and the motivational side its *yang* aspect" (Slote 2018: 380). However, Slote is using the terms *yin* and *yang* in a very superficial way: to him, being receptive is the *yin* while being motivated to act or being active is the *yang*. Understanding *yin* and *yang* as metaphors for yielding and advancing without grasping the ontological roots of such notions, is similar to using a pair of contrastive adjectives such as soft and hard, weak and strong, etc. in delineating the various aspects of the mind. I cannot fathom what explanatory advantages Slote's *yin yang* theory could possibly give us in our understanding of the nature of emotion or the nature of belief.

The neo-Confucian unified theory of the mind that I have expounded in this paper, on the other hand, is primarily a metaphysical theory of human morality. This unified theory appeals to the human mind for the unification of our inborn nature (namely, our moral sentiments) and our affective mental states (i.e. our emotion and desire) to lay the *a priori* foundation for human morality. What the theory accomplishes is to affirm the moral attributes that humans have by nature—this view takes humans to be *homo moralis*. However, under Zhang Zai and Zhu Xi's view, even with the moral essence we have, it is nonetheless the human mind that actively unifies the *a priori* moral nature and the *a posterior* cognitive as well as affective functions. Our empirical mind has multiple functions. The cognitive functions of the empirical mind include what Zhang Zai refers to as "perceptual awareness" and what Zhu Xi refers to as "thoughts, awareness, ideas, deliberation." The affective functions of the mind, on the other hand, include emotion and desire. But the mind also has a volitional and a reflective function. Zhang Zai and Zhu Xi highlight the mind's volition (*zhi* 志) and reflection (*si* 思) in the human mind's deliberate unification of the various mental functions. Both downplay the significance of the cognitive aspects of the mind, taking them to be serving the insignificant part of human existence—our daily encounter with external affairs. Both of them also undervalue the affective aspects of the mind, especially with regard to unregulated human emotion and human desire. The regulative function of the mind, with volition and reflection, is to retrieve our innate moral sentiments, using them as the *norm* of our emotion, such that under the mind's regulative function, the release and expression of our emotion can be in accord with the norm. If everyone's mind can indeed achieve the unification of nature and emotion, then humans can indeed fulfill their moral essence and become moral beings.

In a nutshell, Zhang-Zhu's unified theory of the mind does not begin with the dichotomy of belief and desire, and thus does not aim to unify the two. However, their theory of the mind does not conflate the cognitive and the affective functions of the mind as Slote's theory seems to do. Their theory is also a distinctively normative theory of the mind, with moral fulfillment as the ultimate aim.

6 Conclusion

This chapter began with a critical examination of Michael Slote's sentimentalist theory of the mind and then introduces a neo-Confucian unified theory of the mind, which Slote thinks does not exist in Chinese philosophy of mind. Slote's understanding of the translation as "heart-mind" for the Chinese word '*xin*' has led him to claim that there is no unity of the intellectual and emotional since the two were never separated to begin with. However, it is not true that the polysemy of the word "*xin*" in Chinese language indicates a conflation of the intellectual and the emotional, or that "Chinese folk psychology lacked a contrast between cognitive and affective states."[10] Chinese words are typically polysemous, and this does not mean that the Chinese mind contains a confusing conceptual scheme. Instead, the polysemy of Chinese words reflects the economical usage of Chinese characters and the flexible combination of characters into terms or phrases in Chinese. We need to find appropriate translations of Chinese words depending on the context of use, and we should not jump to conclusion that because they can be translated differently, that they must reflect a conflation of concepts. The word "*xin*" can be translated as "the mind," which encompasses all mental functions, or "the affective mind" in particular, when it is used in the context of referring to our sentiments.[11] There is no conflation of the cognitive and the affective functions of the mind. As we have seen in Zhang-Zhu's unified theory of the mind, the mind encompasses not only the cognitive and the affective, but also the *a priori* and the *a posteriori* constitution of the mind.

The contemporary philosophy of mind in the West has been plagued with the mind-body dichotomy of the old, and the division between the physical and the mental in the standard forum of late. The multifarious debates between physicalism, emergentism, epiphenomenalism, reductionism, non-reductionism, and so on and so forth, have seriously undermined the causal efficacy of the mind as the seat of agency, and some philosophers have even pushed to eliminate the mind as a meaningful subject of discourse. The Chinese philosophy of mind is at the same time a metaphysical theory, placing the origin of human mind in the universe's production. Neo-Confucianism combines moral metaphysics with their philosophy of mind. As such, their philosophy of mind goes beyond the realm of science and cannot be reduced to the scientific language. It is perhaps partly because of this reason that Chinese philosophy of mind has not been able to enter into the discourse with analytic philosophy of mind. On the other hand, Chinese philosophy of mind is so far inadequately developed, also because philosophy of mind and moral philosophy are interwoven in the Chinese philosophical framework, and scholars have focused on moral philosophy based on their understanding of various theories of the mind. Chinese philosophy of mind is not a field independent of metaphysics and moral philosophy. This does not mean, however, that we cannot develop a distinctive Chinese philosophy of mind. We just need to recognize its distinctive features to make sense of it, rather than putting it in a mismatched philosophical framework to argue for its absence.

Notes

1 In Slote's reply to my paper, he lamented: "I wish Professor Liu hadn't relied exclusively on my book *A Sentimentalist Theory of the Mind* in formulating her view of my ideas about the mind or heart-mind and its unity. I now think that

yin/yang can be said to ground the unity of our functioning psychology, our so-called minds." However, I think Slote's *A Sentimentalist Theory of the Mind* is far better than his new *The Philosophy of Yin and Yang*. By focusing on the former, I am giving his philosophy more serious consideration. I will add a brief comment on the latter in the section where I compare the two theories.

2 Slote writes: "Chinese thinkers haven't set about showing the unity of the intellectual and emotional ... [because] their language doesn't sufficiently distinguish them to make it easy for someone to argue or assume that they are distinct and for someone else to then come along and argue that they are more unified than others have thought. I think one can be a sentimentalist about the mind only if one is able (and ready) at least on some level to distinguish intellect from emotion and then argue that the mind and/or its unity depends on a certain unity between intellect and emotion" (Slote 2014: 85).

3 This phrase appears several times in Zhang Zai's conversational records (*yulu*), see, for example, Zhang 1985: 339, 340, 374.

4 Kant writes, "Since reason is not sufficiently competent to guide the will surely with regard to its objects and the satisfaction of all our needs (which it to some extent even multiplies)—an end to which an implanted natural instinct would have led much more certainly; and since reason is nevertheless given to us as a practical faculty, that is, as one that is to influence the *will*; then, where nature has everywhere else gone to work purposively in distributing its capacities the true vocation of reason must be to produce a will that is good, not perhaps *as a means* to other purposes, but *good in itself*, for which reason was absolutely necessary" (Kant 1997: 9–10).

5 Granted, there are cases of such emotionally driven belief states. But they should be considered as exceptions rather than the norm of belief.

6 The double meaning of "tong" is not my own discovery. Many Chinese scholars, for example, Chen Lai (1986) and Meng Peiyuan (2011), have elaborated on the two meanings of '*tong*' in Zhu Xi's usage of *xin tong xing qing*.

7 In Meng's analysis, for Zhu Xi, the ontological unification of the mind consists not only in the unification of nature and perception, or "form and function of mind" in Meng's terms, but also in the unification of principle and *qi*—the former is manifested as *nature*, while the latter is realized in *perception* (Meng 2010: 383). Hence, this is clearly a metaphysical thesis.

8 As Zhu Xi empathically states, everything is the mind's doing: "In *the Doctrine of the Mean*, when it talks about 'Heaven's mandate is the so-called nature,' it means the mind. 'To follow our nature is the so-called *dao*' also means the mind. 'Cultivating dao is the so-called teaching' refers to the mind as well.... As for achieving knowledge (*zhizhi*), it is the mind's achieving knowledge; investigation of things (*gewu*) is also the mind's doing. To have self-discipline (*keji*), is the mind's having the disciplinary power." (Zhu 2002: 14.362)

9 This section is added in response to Slote's reply to my initial comment.

10 "Philosophy of Mind in China," http://philosophy.hku.hk/ch/mind.htm

11 I first came across this translation in reading Sky Liu's article, "A Moral Philosophy based on the Doctrine of Vital Energy (*Qi*) and Affective Mindset *(Xin)*: Wang Fuzhi's Study of Mencius and Its Contemporary Significance." He informed me that the translation of "*xin*" as "the affective mind" came from Chad Meyer. I wish

to acknowledge their contribution to this translation and hope that it will catch on and replace the cumbersome "heart-mind" translation so prevalent in the English discourse on Confucian and neo-Confucian moral psychology.

References

Chan, Wing-tsit (1963), *A Source Book in Chinese Philosophy,* Princeton University Press.

Chen, Lai (1986), "The Theory of *Mind Encompasses Nature and Emotion* in Zhu Xi's Philosophy (朱熹哲學的「心統性情」說)," *Zhejiang Academic Journal* (浙江學刊), 12–27: 76–78, 88.

Chen, Lai (2000), *Research on Zhu Xi's Philosophy* (朱子哲學研究), Shanghai, China: Eastern China Normal University Press.

Chen, Lai 陳來 (2011), *Song-ming Neo-Confucianism* (宋明理學), Beijing, China: SanLian Books.

Davidson, Donald (1982), "Paradoxes of Irrationality," in Wollheim and Hopkins (eds), *Philosophical Essays on Freud,* 289–305, Cambridge University Press.

Davidson, Donald (1985), "Incoherence and Irrationality," *Dialectica,* 39: 345–54.

Hume, David (1777), *An Inquiry Concerning the Principles of Morals,* London: A. Millar.

Hume, David (1896), *A Treatise Of Human Nature,* Oxford: Clarendon Press.

Kant, Immanuel (1997), *Groundwork of the Metaphysics of Morals,* Cambridge University Press.

Meng, Peiyuan (2010), "A Further Analysis of Zhu Xi's Theory of Mind," *Frontier of Philosophy in China,* 5 (3): 377–95.

Meng, Peiyuan 蒙培元 (2011), "On Zhu Xi's Thesis of *Mind Encompasses Nature and Emotion* (論朱熹的"心統性情"說)," *Journal of Tianshui Normal University* (天水師範學院學報), 31 (3): 1–8.

Slote, Michael (2010), *Moral Sentimentalism,* New York: Oxford University Press.

Slote, Michael (2014), *A Sentimentalist Theory of the Mind,* New York: Oxford University Press.

Slote, Michael (2018), *The Philosophy of Yin and Yang,* Beijing, China: The Commercial Press.

Tang, Chün-I (1956), "Chang Tsai's Theory of Mind and Its Metaphysical Basis," *Philosophy East and West,* 6: 113–36.

Zhang, Liwen 張立文. (2001), "The Contemporary Value of Zhu Xi's Thesis of *Mind Encompasses Nature and Emotion* (朱熹"心統性情"論的現代價值)," *Chinese Culture Research* (中國文化研究), 5 (28): 26–31.

Zhang, Zai (1985), *The Collected Works of Zhang Zai* 張載集. Beijing, China: Zhonghua shuju.

Zhu, Xi (2002), *The Complete Work of Zhu Xi (Zhuzi Quanshu).* Twenty-seven volumes. Shanghai: Guji Chubanshe.

Unknown author: "Philosophy of Mind in China," http://philosophy.hku.hk/ch/mind.htm

Two Paths to One Goal

The Unity of the Heart-Mind in Michael Slote and Wang Yangming

Xinzhong Yao and Yan Zhang[1]

Renmin University of China, Beijing and Ocean University of China, Qingdao

1 Introduction

Contrary to the traditionally and still popularly upheld notion of the mind in which reason and emotion are used to exclude each other within the overall structure of epistemology, Michael Slote tends to establish a specifically defined view of the mind that he on occasions prefers to call the "heart-mind" (*xin* 心). In his *A Sentimentalist Theory of Mind* (2014), he argues that the heart-mind involves not only reason but more importantly emotion, and insists that emotion has a central role in all mind-related states and activities. He further argues recently that the functioning heart-mind, expressed in belief, desire, will etc., has *yin* and *yang* as its nature, and that both intellect and sentiment have intrinsic *yin* and *yang* attributes.[2] In his *Moral Sentimentalism* (2010), Slote takes the cognition of moral situation and moral judgment as empathic responses, and argues that belief (traditionally regarded as a result of reason and as a cognitive state) not only contains emotion but is itself emotion. In this way, he tends to reduce all functions of the heart-mind to the functions of emotion, and to pave the way for his ambitious project on unifying the mind. While admirable in revoking the stronghold of rationalism, it is apparent to us that this path risks dissolving intellect in emotion. In arguing against the rationalist overemphasis on reason most likely at the expense of emotion, Slote's unifying drive seems to have gone too far. It may be useful for us, therefore, to examine the strength and weakness of his project in light of the Chinese understanding of the heart-mind. To do so, we will come to examine Slote's path to the unity of the heart-mind from the perspective of a similar project launched more than 500 years ago by a Ming Dynasty Confucian philosopher, Wang Yangming (1472–1529). Wang takes the notion of *xin* (the heart-mind) as a whole, composed of nature (*xing*性), cognition (*zhi*知), emotion (qing情), reason/principle (li 理), will/intention (yi意) and action (xing行), and idealistically unifies all these components in the so-called "innate entity" (liang zhi 良知) of knowledge-sentiment-will. In comparing the two paths respectively advanced by Michael Slote and Wang Yangming we intend to highlight the different characteristics of their versions of "sentimentalism," and to generate a critique of Slote's path to the unity of the heart-mind, in particular by referring to Wang's understanding of a priori unity between cognition and emotion, and between knowledge and action.

2 Slote's Sentimentalist Unity of the Mind

In the tripartite theory of the soul or psyche discussed in the *Republic*, Plato divides the human soul into three parts and seeks to unify them by placing the thinking part in the dominant position to rule and control the other two parts, the temperamental and the appetitive. Plato takes this kind of unity as the manifestation of justice either in individuals or in the state (Bremmer 1983). Since then, seeking unity between different parts of the mind has been taken as a priority in Christian theology and later in European philosophy, with the former insisting that all must be unified in faith (belief) in Christ while mainstream of the latter persisting that all mind's elements must be unified by reason which is hence known as "rationalism." There are exceptions to rationalism in modern philosophy where empiricism or non-rationalism-oriented philosophers, such as Francis Hutcheson (1694–1746), David Hume (1711–76), Adam Smith (1723–90) and Friedrich Nietzsche (1844–1900), to name but a few, place an emphasis not on reason or rational activity, but rather on a non-rational element as the underlying line, and argue for the unity of the mind respectively based on moral sense, sentiment or will. Michael Slote takes traditional sentimentalism one step further, claiming that the mind and its functions are constituted, and can be reasonably explained, by and only by emotional activities such as empathy, sympathy, favor, and aversion.

Apart from following traditional threads of epistemic and ethical sentimentalism, Slote revitalizes it by taking into account the Chinese concept of *xin* (the heart-mind), drawing on the fact that in *xin* there is no distinction between the mind and the heart. To him, the Chinese notion of *xin* differs from the narrowly defined mind in Western philosophy according to which, to assure the proper functioning of the mind—such as knowing, believing, and reasoning—we must exclude sentimental elements. Insisting that sentimental elements exist in all activities of the mind and that emotion must not and cannot be reduced to reason, Slote argues for the central position of emotion in all intellectual activities such as knowing, believing, judging, approving, or disapproving, claiming that moral approval is preconditioned by empathizing with an agent's motives. He believes that "real open-mindedness requires (one to be able to acquire) a certain degree or amount of sympathy for what others think, and such sympathy clearly means having an at least somewhat favorable opinion of what others think" (Slote 2014: 16). Different from his predecessors in the long tradition of sentimentalism, however, Slote has gone one step further by claiming that not only moral approval or disapproval but also almost all that are traditionally regarded as rational activities, such as believing and judging, are none other than emotional processes, initiated by emotion, driven by emotion, and ended in emotion. This way he comes to the conclusion that "belief not only involves emotion but is a kind of emotion" (Slote 2014: 180). For him, the mind is perfectly unified in emotion which we may be justified to term as a "thorough sentimentalist theory of the mind."

Unlike "almost all previous Western philosophy," Slote claims that his sentimentalism is characterized by "not assuming or saying that mind and emotion can be separated," and is founded on "the interpenetration of mind and emotion." To him, only the Chinese mode of thinking anticipates his theory, because "in a Chinese language and mode of thinking," it is "almost impossible to think about mind and emotion separately" (Slote 2014: 86). What he values in the Chinese philosophy of *xin* is its tendency towards the unity of the mind. In this sense he sees his sentimentalist theory of mind as a kind of "vindication of the way the Chinese thought has proceeded" (Slote 2014: 86). Despite his sentimental appreciation of the Chinese concept of *xin* based on the presumption "that intellect and emotion cannot be separated," Slote draw our attention to the fact that Chinese philosophy merely "presumes" or "presupposes" this and should be therefore regarded only as a primitive mode of the unity of the mind. In his own words, "Chinese thinkers have not set about showing the unity of the intellectual and emotional in anything like the manner attempted" in his theory, because "their language does not sufficiently distinguish them to make it easy for someone else to then come along and argue that they are more unified than others have thought" (Slote 2014: 85). One advantage his sentimentalism has over any type of traditional Chinese philosophy, as he argues, is that he is able not only to clearly distinguish "intellect from emotion" but also to philosophically justify "that the mind and/or its unity depends on a certain unity between intellect and emotion" (Slote 2014: 85).

Slote's theory goes beyond traditional sentimentalism as an ethical theory, and is extended to many other fields including epistemology and politics. He seems to be determined to construct an epistemic sentimentalism or sentimentalist epistemology by claiming that all knowing processes are in essence none other than an emotional process. To the question of "whether there really is such a thing as a purely intellectual viewpoint, belief, assumption, or doubt", he is "to some extent inclined to think not" (Slote 2010: 147), because "the fact that we say that those who accept certain viewpoints or assumptions favor them indicates that there is no such thing as purely intellectual science or purely intellectual work in other disciplines either" (Slote 2010: 148). In social and political fields it is the same, and "a sentimentalist ethics of empathic caring can say that institutions and laws, as well as social customs and practices, are just if they reflect empathically caring motivation on the part of (enough of) those responsible for originating and maintaining them" (Slote 2010: 125).

For Slote, similar to all other virtues, epistemic virtue must also start with, and complete by, empathy and sympathy: "if we can empathize with cognitive states independently of other people's emotional/hedonic/orectic states or processes, then it should be possible to empathize with another person's intellectual point of view" (Slote 2010: 146). He believes that "real open-mindedness requires…a certain degree or amount of sympathy for what others think, and such sympathy clearly means having an at least somewhat favorable opinion of what others think" (Slote 2014: 177).

While we admire the thoroughness and comprehensiveness of Slote's sentimentalism, it might be worth being cautious about its treatment of epistemic processes concerning, in particular, belief. Emotion does of course play an important role in any believing, and a committing attitude or passionate favoring may have been present in a strong belief. However, as far as epistemology is concerned, we must not deny that belief is both a reasoning process and a rational commitment, and we must not put aside simply Plato's insistence that belief must satisfy the criteria of being justified and being true before it can be called "knowledge," and when Socrates claims that an unexamined life is not worth living, what he has in mind surely is rational examination rather than emotionally favoring. Even in a common sense, we can see that while involving emotion this or that way, epistemic belief can be eventually justified (proved or disproved) only in terms of rational reasoning and examination.

Discarding rationalistic epistemology of the mind, Slote intends to set up a sentimentalist epistemology by emphasizing the central role that sentiment plays in all epistemic states. It seems that he is aware of the difficulty in so doing, and states that "The idea that there is an emotional element in belief that we have been ignoring does not get us all the way to a sentimentalist epistemology"; he admits it needs much more effort to convince people of his conclusion, which has taken him further down the road into an extreme version of sentimentalism: "The further step involves realizing, first, that belief not only involves emotion but is a kind of emotion, and, second, that this means there is a sentimentalist aspect not only to the epistemic standard or virtue of open-mindedness but also to not committing the Monte Carlo Fallacy and to such ordinary epistemic/cognitive tasks as gathering evidence intelligently and carefully" (Slote 2014: 180). To this sentimental project, it suffices here for us to caution him that it is one thing to confirm that "all the elements of a functioning mind or psyche necessarily involve emotion" (Slote 2018: 11), but it is quite another to assert that all the elements are a kind of emotion.[3] By attributing all mind's activities to emotion, Slote inevitably risks overemphasizing sentiment at the expense of intellect.

3 Yin-yang and the Unity of the Heart-mind

In criticizing traditional philosophies about the rational mind, Slote has rightly pointed out that Western rationalism places too much emphasis on rational projection and ignores receptivity. In opposition to this tradition, Slote's sentimentalism reads the mind in terms of emotion, and asserts that it is emotion rather than reason that is universal to all mind-related states and determines all the mind's activities. It is therefore natural for Slote to come to the Chinese uses of *yin* and *yang*, and claims that "emotion by its very nature involves and is constituted by a yin-yang structure" (Slote 2018: 11).

To ensure the unity of the mind, Slote takes the mutual supplementation of *yin-yang* as the fundamentals of the mind, and by the *yin-yang* analogy he justifies again that reason and emotion must not be taken as exclusive of each other. Slote takes "receptivity" as *yin* and "directed active purpose" as *yang*, and believes that both *yin* and *yang* are exemplified in "the situation where someone has, among other things, the emotion of compassion" (Slote 2018: 9). The way he goes by is to be consistent with his "thorough sentimentalism", interpreting *yin* in terms of "receptive empathy" towards others, open-mindedness about different views, and accepting the world as it is unless having sufficient reasons to doubt or reject it. He regards *yin-yang* as the foundation of his philosophy of the heart-mind, and uses it to illustrate all mental activities such as sympathy, approval, disbelief, etc. Taking empathy and sympathy as an example of the mind's unity, as Slote is attempted to do, *yin* enables one to feel and perceive the suffering of others while *yang* enables one to take active action to reduce their suffering and to help them. The mutuality of *yin-yang* means that none of the two can exist and function alone; if there is *yin*, there must be *yang*, which is proved in the process from empathy leading to sympathy, namely from emotion to the motive to act. In the same way, empirical senses lead to belief, and belief leads to a directed active purpose, which in turn leads to action. Hence there is the perfect unity of the beginning and the end, of knowledge and action, and of sentiment and intellect. While drawing on *yin-yang* mutuality to explain his sentimental unity of the mind, to his disappointment, however, he finds that such a clear connection "between heart-mind and *yin-yang* has never even been hinted at by Chinese thinkers" (Slote 2018: 11).[4] Therefore he seems to take it as his mission not only to convince Western philosophers of the connection, but also to remind East Asian philosophers of this rich resource in their own tradition and of their unfulfilled task to philosophize the bridge between the mind and *yin-yang*. His agenda is of course more than convincing and reminding. In fact, he works very hard to magnify the power of *yin-yang* to illustrate the sweeping function of emotion in the whole structure of the heart-mind.

Consistent with that his attempt to revoke the dominant position of rationalist philosophy of the mind leads to the dissolving of reason in emotion, and Slote's sentimental appreciation of the *yin-yang* structure seems also to bear a kind of risk that the obvious mutuality is being rendered as an inequality between *yin* and *yang*. Placing more emphasis on the emotional and receptive, it seems logical for him to elevate *yin* above *yang*, and to reduce *yang* to a secondary position. In a similar way as dissolving belief in sentiment, he may have, willingly or unwillingly, dissolved *yang* in *yin*. Although *yin* and *yang* need each other to exist, in accordance with Slote's theory, *yin* turns out to be more fundamental than *yang* in his interpretation where *yang* must rely on *yin* to function. This way, *yang* seems to have been rendered as a merely additional attribute of *yin*. In his own example, the belief that there is no food in the room has the *yin* attributes, namely accepting what the senses has revealed; its *yang* attribute, "the directed active purpose", is also related to desire which in the final analysis is a *yin* attribute, because even it directs one to action, it is nevertheless a pure desire, not a rationally and logically guided action, if we accept the traditional differentiation of yang as rational and yin as emotional. Further, in Slote's philosophy of *yin* and *yang*, both *yin* attributes and *yang* attributes are rendered as human feelings and emotions. In his "Epistemology of Yin and Yang" (Slote 2015 [6]: 29–37), Slote sees receptivity and decisiveness as two epistemic virtues, the former as the *yin* virtue and the latter as the *yang* virtue. It is true that he has confirmed that either receptivity or decisiveness contains both *yin* attributes and *yang* attributes, and that receptivity justifies our perception, while a certain epistemic decisiveness characterizes the making of rational inferences, and this applies as much to abduction as to induction.[5] However, in the end, both receptivity and decisiveness are in the category of emotion: receptivity is an emotional trust of what we have perceived, while decisiveness is an emotional tendency to satisfying our desire. Either in receptivity or in activity, the mind has become simply a sentimental structure, and all properties of the mind such as belief, desire, and will not only depend on *yin* to function, but they themselves are *yin* functions. Furthermore, *yin* and *yang* are both considered emotional states, and the qualities traditionally attributed to *yang* such as decisiveness, muscularity, activeness, rigor, rigidity etc. all seem to have been dissolved in receptivity, in order to pave the way for his sentimentalist use of *yin-yang* mutuality. Seeing his overemphasis on receptivity and undermining the role of activity, we cannot help but say that *yin-yang* are used by Slote simply as yet another conceptual tool to prove that emotion rather than reason unifies our heart-mind.

There is no doubt that Slote intends to go beyond the dispute between rationalism that our concepts and knowledge are gained independently of sense experience, and empiricism that sense experience is the ultimate source of all our concepts and knowledge. As a philosopher going for the unity of the mind, Slote replaces reason and sense experience with emotion as the single source for all concepts and knowledge. Using the *yin-yang* metaphor, he reaches the singularity of sentimentalist epistemology. For Slote, "Belief needs to have a mind-to-world direction of fit that it seems apt to characterize as exemplifying yin; but it also needs to have a world-to-mind direction of fit that motivates or helps motivate specific, directed, instrumental or other actions, and that, of course, represents the yang that I am saying characterizes all states of belief"; however, from this balanced way of *yin* and *yang*, Slote goes one more step to confirm that this has enabled us to "see more clearly now how and why belief can be characterized as an emotional state, an emotional state whose yin and yang aspects are no more separable than are the yin and yang of compassion for someone or of (a strong) concern to escape fire through a given door" (Slote 2018: 396).

4 Unity of *Xin* in Chinese Philosophy

For Slote, Chinese philosophy can be seen as a mode of his sentimentalism, but a merely primitive mode given that Chinese philosophers are unable to distinguish intellect from sentiment in their uses of the important concept of *xin*. He believes that this has obstructed them not only from consciously unifying the heart and the mind but also from taking emotion as the central line running through all activities and components of *xin*. He may be justified in saying that *xin* in Chinese philosophy contains multi-dimensional elements including reason and emotion, and the Chinese concept may be employed as a potentially useful tool for the unity of the heart-mind operated in other philosophical systems. However, his conviction that few Chinese philosophers have consciously made good use of the tool to highlight the difference between parts and then to unify them is somehow misleading. Despite a clear disagreement between Western and Chinese philosophies concerning how to define the heart-mind, the majority of Chinese philosophers, like those in the Western tradition, also attempt to seek the unity of *xin*'s components and in so doing they explore different senses of *xin* in accordance with particular contexts.

Xin is fundamental to almost all Chinese philosophies where it refers to both the organ of senses/feelings and the reasoning faculty. In the *Analects of Confucius*, *xin* is comparatively unimportant (only six times of appearance) and is nevertheless used as the unity of virtue, intellect, and sentiment, as demonstrated in the saying attributed to Confucius that only when he was seventy years old could he do whatever his *xin* desired without going over [moral] boundaries.[6] The significance of this concept dramatically increases in the *Book of Mencius*, where *xin* appears 124 times. It seems probable that *xin* in this text can justify Slote's claim that sentiment rather than reason is the foundation of goodness and virtue. For example, the "sensitive heart to the suffering of others" (*bu ren ren zhi xin* 不忍人之心) is taken as the foundation of the compassionate or humane government (*ren zheng* 仁政). The "four hearts" (*si xin* 四心), the heart of commiseration, the heart of shame and dislike, the heart of deference and compliance, and the heart of right and wrong, central to Mencius' understanding of the heart-mind, are also translated in English as "four feelings" or "four senses" which indicates that they are primarily perceptive rather than cognitive. It is these perceptive senses that are said to be the beginnings of the four virtues, humanity, righteousness, propriety and wisdom (*Mencius* 2A6, in Chan 1963: 65). However, in Mencius *xin* is not a simple locus of feelings. It has multidimensional meanings and multilayered functions, which is illustrated at least on two occasions. First, he uses *si* 思 (thinking) to define *xin*, asserting that "The function of the mind [*xin*] is to think

[*si*]. If we think, we will get them. This is what Heaven has given to us" (*Mencius* 6A15, in Chan 1963: 59). When he says this, it is more likely that Mencius refers it to the rational faculty rather than an emotional entity, as thinking is more on the side of reasoning than favoring. Second, he uses "*qiu*" (seeking or desiring) to qualify *xin*'s function when urging people to seek their lost heart-mind: "if one seeks, then one will find it." For this we have reasons to say that thinking in Mencius is not only an intellectual activity but also an emotional pursuit, or the "embodied knowing".

It seems clear for Mencius that both the emotional heart and the rational mind are the properties of *xin* that is endowed by Heaven. Without resorting to any single element to unify the heart and mind, Mencius simply sees *xin* as an undivided unity. *Xin* is taken not only as the organ for thinking and feeling but also as the *a priori* location of all our intellectual and emotional faculties. For him, to exert *xin* to the utmost is the necessary step for knowing one's own nature, knowing the nature of all other people, knowing and serving the Confucian ultimate power, Heaven (*Tian*) (*Mencius* 7A1).

Although Neo-Confucianism is responsible for promoting Mencius to the orthodox line of Confucian tradition, not all of them have continued Mencius's project on unifying *xin*. In particular in the Cheng-Zhu School (Cheng Yi 程頤 1033–1107 and Zhu Xi 朱熹 1130–1200), *xin* is divided into two kinds, *ren xin* (the human heart 人心), and *dao xin* (roughly and conveniently the moral heart道心). Zhu Xi asserts that the human heart and the moral heart correspond respectively to self-centered desire (*ren yu* 人欲) and universal principle (*tian li*天理). The equivalent of the former refer to human consciousness, perception, physical desire, feeling and emotion, while the equivalent of the latter refer to (human) nature (*xing*性), reason (*li*理) and virtue (*de*). However we must point out that even Zhu Xi is not a dualist in its real sense. In the Preface to his *Collected Commentaries on the Doctrine of the Mean*, Zhu Xi does not intend to separate *xin* into two unrelated entities; rather, he insists that both physical desire and universal principle exist in the heart (*fang cun*方寸 the "square inch"). However, one thing is clear, that in general Neo-Confucians do not claim that the emotional is the defining quality of humans. For them, human heart (*ren xin*) is confined to the body, desire and private behavior, and occasionally to the intellect as Zhu Xi says so in his commentary on the *Great Learning*.[7] It is *dao xin* (道心) that defines humanity, the original state of humans and what humans should be, and therefore becomes the unifying force for emotion and intellect. Zhu Xi also makes use of *yin* and *yang* to prescribe *xin*, saying that "the activity and tranquility of the mind are the yin and yang" (Chan 1963: 628), but he is more concerned with the unity of principle (*li*) and material force (*qi*气) than about the two aspects of *xin*, intellect and emotion. For him the mind and the nature, or the consciousness and the principle are originally one and already pervade each other.

Although Zhu Xi struggles for the unity between human heart and the moral mind, he underpins the contradictory nature of these two kinds of *xin*, which leads him to an uncertain position about the relationship between the absolute, rational and virtuous mind and the relative, emotional and physical heart, the latter of which is limited, finite and desirous and must be judged, restrained and guided by the former. For him, life is a process of human grasping of heavenly principle, in which emotional desires, must be washed away day by day through investigating the principle of things and learning sagely teachings. For this reason, Zhu Xi is often classified as a "rationalist" and his position is often interpreted, probably not precisely, as "dualism" (between the heart-mind and the nature, between things and the principle).

Regardless of interpretations, Zhu Xi's difficulty in accommodating human heart and the moral mind causes great problems for the people who seek to unify the intellect and emotion of *xin*. Of these people Wang Yangming stands out as most successful in terms of integration between human heart and the principle, between the mind and the things, and between knowledge and action. In this sense, Wang can be said to have been the predecessor of Slote as an early monist philosopher of the mind. Wang starts his unifying project from the epistemological problem that has been presumably caused by Zhu Xi's dualist theory that takes things as the objects of the consciousness and claims that "the physical world and the mind are separate and their unity is inconceivable" (Chang 1962: 29). Contrary to this doctrine, Wang follows the same line of *xin* monism as Lu Jiuyuan (陆九渊 1139–93), who heavily criticized Zhu Xi's tendency towards dualism and made such famous assertions as that "Perfect truth is reduced to a unity; the essential principle is never a duality. The mind and principle can never be separated into two," that "The universe is my mind, and my mind is the universe," and that "All people have this mind and all minds contain this principle in full" (Chan 1963: 574, 579, 580). Wang proceeds to establish his unity doctrine by targeting the following contradictions implied in Zhu Xi's theory: "(a) the individual versus the universe, (b) mind versus the physical world, (c) mind versus body, (d) desire versus reason, and (e) knowing versus doing" (Chan 1963: 33). Although Wang is primarily focused on the unity between *xin* and *li* 理 (the universal principle), in the process of overcoming the seemingly dualist doctrine of the heart-mind and the things, he comes to the unity of all elements within the heart-mind.

In a similar way as Slote's project, Wang places an emphasis on "sentiment" as the focal point of the heart-mind, which in a sense he may be qualified as a Confucian sentimentalist. While we cannot see a direct use of "empathy" as the unifying force in the teachings of Wang, it is apparent that Wang follows the suit of Mencius in regarding the "commiserate heart" as the foundation of human virtues and of the unified world. Seeing a child about to fall into a well, one would naturally arouse a feeling of commiseration (alarm and alert), which proves that all humans have the commiserate heart within. This human-heartedness, Wang argues, has enabled one to the unity (*yi ti* 一體) with the child. When we observe the pitiful cries and frightened appearance of birds and animals about to be slaughtered, we could not help but feel an "inability to bear" their suffering. This fact, he again argues, demonstrates that our human-heartedness leads us to the unity with the birds and animals. When we see plants broken and destroyed, we could not help but feel pitiful and even when we see tiles and stones shattered and crushed, we would not help but feel regretful, these have proved that our human-heartedness forms the unity with the plants, tiles and stones (Chan 1963: 659–60). Through human-heartedness, we become unified with the whole universe of humans and things, and this has laid the foundation for Wang's theory of the heart-mind.

5 Convergence and Divergence

Despite a gap of more than 500 years between Wang Yangming and Michael Slote, it is still worthwhile for us to bring them together and examine their similarities and differences. Similarities would make it possible for a better understanding of their respective theories while differences may well shed new light on the strong and weak points of the sentimentalist unity of the mind proposed by Slote.

Slote's sentimentalism is unique in the sense that it is both thorough and comprehensive. Main points of this theory can be summarized as follows. First, he takes empathetic caring as the foundation of morality, arguing that it is natural feelings rather than rationalist intellect that should be taken as the source of the value for any action. Second, he bases his sentimentalist concept of the mind on receptivity, insisting that we should be open both epistemically and ethically to sentiment, to relationship and to different ways of living. Third, he makes use of *yin-yang* to characterize the heart-mind, taking the mutuality and interdependence between *yin* and *yang* as the essence and structure of the heart-mind, and arguing that only in receptivity (*yin*) can we justify all our beliefs, motives, and actions. Fourth, he argues not only that belief contains emotion but also that any belief is a kind of emotion (curiosity, desire, favoring), taking the unionist standpoint to call that we must see the connection between belief and desire, and between compassionate motive and moral action. In one word, Slote reduces not only all heart-mind states such as tranquility, emotion, and intellect but also all heart-mind related activities, such as knowing, believing, perceiving, reasoning, motivating, and acting into what he calls the sentiment to complete his monist sentimentalism of the mind.

From a historical perspective, Slote's unity of the mind and the heart, dissolving all things into the heart-mind and then reducing all internal elements to sentiment are already attempted in Wang Yangming's unity of knowledge and action. Wang does not think of knowing as a kind of purely rational process involving reasoning only, because for him knowledge is nothing more than sense experience and moral preference. Wang takes it for example what is said in the *Great Learning* about "loving beautiful colors and hating bad odors"; for him, seeing "beautiful colors appertains to knowledge, while loving beautiful colors appertains to action"; however, knowledge and action are not separate as they seem to be, nor is one ahead of the other, because "as soon as one sees that beautiful color, he has already loved it. It is not that he sees it first and then makes up his mind to love it"; similarly, "smelling a bad odor appertains to knowledge, while hating a bad odor appertains to action. However, as soon as one smells a bad odor, he has already hated it. It is not that he smells it first and then makes up his mind to hate it" (Wang 1963: 10).

As we can see, knowledge in Wang Yangming is a kind of sense knowledge, while action is primarily not the actual behavior, but an internal intention, the will or desire. In this kind of theory, knowing and emotional desiring are in fact the same, and knowing the beautiful color and loving it take place simultaneously. As far as the unity between outward knowing and internal appreciating is concerned, it seems not to be much different between Wang and Slote, as the latter also insists in his aesthetic analysis that knowing the beautiful and appreciating it are not separate, despite the fact that Wang and Slote base their unity projects on different theoretical presumptions.

Slote elaborates on the emotional nature of belief by which he establishes the connection between belief and sentiment. The same has also been achieved by Wang who insists that knowing and acting are not separate, because knowing is acting, and if it does not pertain to acting, then it would not be a true knowing: "when a thought is aroused it is already action" (Wang 1963: 201). What Wang intends to explain here is that the heart-mind can naturally discern the good from evil, and that moral judgment contains not only the emotion of preferring the good to evil, but also the motivation and will to do the good and to remove evil, in the same way as one's desire for food: "A man must have the desire for food before he knows the food. This desire to eat is the will; it is already the beginning of action" (Wang 1963: 92).

Both Slote and Wang may be said to be "mind monists."[8] Wang insists that the heart-mind (*xin*) is the master of human beings, and all meaningful manifestations of *xin* are none other than different conditions of the sentimental. It seems apparent that as an idealist, Wang is more thorough than Slote as Wang applies the unity not only to the intellect-emotion, but also to the mind-body and the human-the world. For Wang, all senses and indeed the whole body are determined by *xin*. His *xin* monism is clearly seen in the following statement: "The master of the body is the mind [*xin*]. What emanates from the mind is the will. The original substance of the will is knowledge, and wherever the will is directed is a thing" (Wang 1963: 14). He further explains why there are no principles nor things outside *xin* as follows: "when the will is directed toward serving one's parents, then serving one's parents is a 'thing'. When the will is directed toward serving one's ruler, then serving one's ruler is a 'thing'. When the will is directed toward being humane to all people and feeling love toward things, then being humane to all people and feeling love toward things are 'things', and when the will is directed toward seeing, hearing, speaking, and acting, then each of these is a 'thing'" (Wang 1963: 14). Therefore, *xin* does not passively accept what we have perceived, in the similar way as Slote repeatedly emphasizes, it actively "creates" the entire world we live in. *Xin* is further identified with the innate knowledge, which permeates all beings and is intrinsic to all things: "The innate knowledge of man is the same as that of plants and trees, tiles and stones. Without the innate knowledge inherent in man, there cannot be plants and trees, tiles and stones. This is not true of them only. Even Heaven and Earth cannot exist without the innate knowledge that is inherent in man" (Wang 1963: 221).

Xin is able to unify one and the world because of the innate knowledge, and innate knowledge is both the nature and the function of *xin*. This explains Wang's conviction that all the principles [of things] are in *xin* and are the same as *xin*: "the mind [*xin*] and principle are identical. When the mind is free from the obscuration of selfish desires, it is the embodiment of the Principle of Nature.... The main thing is for the mind to make effort to get rid of selfish human desires and preserve the Principle of Nature" (Chan 1963: 667). From this we can see that all Wang's theories about *xin* are utilized to pave the way for his understanding of how to enable the virtuous individual and the moral world. There is no need to differentiate the human heart and the moral heart as Cheng-Zhu school was supposed to have advocated; Wang differentiates the *xin* that is obscured by private desires and the *xin* that is not. The former is the selfish mind while the latter is the innately good heart. Therefore not the heart in general but the heart of innate knowledge that underlies Wang's unity of *xin*. The heart of innate knowledge does not exclude emotions and feelings, as Wang confirms that "Pleasure, anger, sorrow, fear, love, hate, and desire are the seven feelings. These seven are also natural to the mind" (Wang 1963: 229). While natural to *xin*, empirical emotions are not necessarily good because it is always possible for emotions to be obscured or not to be emanated by following their natural courses. "When the seven feelings follow their natural courses of operation, they are all functions of innate knowledge, and cannot be distinguished as good or evil. However, we should not have any selfish attachment to them. When there is such an attachment, they become selfish desires and obscurations to innate knowledge. Nevertheless, as soon as there is any attachment, innate knowledge is naturally aware of it. As it is aware of it, the obscuration will be gone and its substance will be restored. It is only when one can penetrate this point that his task becomes simple, easy, and thorough" (Wang 1963: 229).

It has become clear that although Wang stresses the importance of sentiment, he does not intend to make empirical emotions the substance of *xin*, but merely as *xin*'s attributes to be guided and directed by *a priori* sentiment (innate knowledge). It is innate knowledge that is taken as the substance of the mind. This has revealed another difference between Wang and Slote. For Slote, human intellect and emotion are explained in epistemology and ethics, but going beyond epistemology and ethics, Wang draws on metaphysical presumptions to interpret what underlies the unity of *xin*, and how human feelings, originally of a neither good nor evil nature, could lead to moral emotion, moral knowledge and right action. For Wang, "Our nature is the substance of the mind and Heaven is the source of our nature" (Chan 1963: 672). With this metaphysical presupposition, Wang idealistically carries his unity to completion. The universe is the whole but is not outside of human beings. At the center of the universe is *xin*, which is universal to all things, all beings, all emotions and all principles. *Xin* does not rely on things to exist and function; on the contrary, the meaning, existence and function of all things depend on *xin*. Wang is clearly aware that not everybody is able to realize this, and only the morally great man or the sage can regard "Heaven and Earth and the myriad things as one body" and regard "the world as one family and the country as one person" (Chan 1963: 659). The sage or great man is the full embodiment of innate knowledge. Because of innate knowledge *xin* in Wang is not only fully moralized but also underlies the unity of the three dimensions of the mind: intellect, will and emotion. This has been famously explained in his "Doctrine of the Four Axioms" (*si ju jiao* 四句教): "In the original substance of the mind [*xin*] there is no distinction of good and evil. When the will becomes active, however, such distinction exists. The faculty of innate knowledge is to know good and evil. The investigation of things is to do good and remove evil" (Wang 1963: 244).

Despite the fact that Wang and Slote both see the heart-mind as one entity, and both insist that intellect and emotion must be united, there is no doubt a huge difference between Wang's *xin* and Slote's mind. Unlike Slote who asserts the independence of sentiment which underlies the unity of the mind, Wang reduces intellect, sentiment, and will to the functions of the innate entity. Wang regards feelings and senses as something that may go wrong and should be carefully guarded against. By identifying *xin* and principle, Wang tries to unveil the universal nature of the individual *xin*, to justify his ethical and metaphysical unity of knowledge and action.

As an idealist, Wang's unity of *xin* has an advantage over Slote's. While Slote's unity of intellect and emotion requires him to prove both theoretically and empirically how the mind of the people is motivated by emotion and how their emotion is directed to action, Wang does not have to undertake such a difficult task. Instead he differentiates the properly functioning *xin* and the not properly functioning *xin*. For both ordinary people and the great man (sage) alike, principle and *xin* are originally the same. But ordinary people are simply not aware of this; instead they see *xin* and principle from selfish desires, and their *xin* is therefore obscured. As a moral teacher, Wang makes his students aware that they cannot realize the original *xin*, unless they have rectified wrong motives and overcome selfish desires. As soon as they have realized that we innately "know" and intuitively appreciate good and evil, then *xin* would be fully unified, where knowing, feeling, willing, and acting would be perfectly directed to moral virtue and universal principle.

6 Conclusion

As a sentimentalist, Michael Slote is surely more thorough and comprehensive than most of his predecessors and contemporaries, at least partly due to his skillfully making use of the Chinese concepts of *xin* and *yin-yang* to strengthen his argument for the unity of the heart-mind and to justify the dominant position of emotion in the heart-mind. While Wang Yangming shares the sentimental commitment to the role of emotion in the discussion of *xin*'s nature and function, he should not be considered a sentimentalist in the same sense as Slote. Although both Slote and Wang consciously aim for the unity of the heart-mind, and both place an emphasis on the importance of sentiment in the unifying process, they follow two different paths. The differences of their paths are determined by their philosophical perspectives on the heart-mind and by their conceptual constructions of the heart-mind, intellect and emotion as a whole.

Both Slote and Wang argue enthusiastically for the unity of the heart-mind, but their notions of *xin* differ. For Slote, the heart-mind is primarily an epistemic entity, which, as he claims, is dominated by sentiment. From his perspective, motivated by emotional activities such as empathy and sympathy, the heart-mind proceeds from receptivity to directed purpose, then to understanding, embracing, and acting. For Wang, *xin* is the trinity of the locus, agent and activity of the innate knowledge, and is identical with the universal principle (*li*). *Xin* is where the innate knowledge is located and demonstrates how it functions. As the moral agent, *xin* is responsible for motivating people to have morally approved motive for action, while riding us of all immoral desires. Knowledge and action are therefore unified in *xin*, not in nor by the outside world.

Both Wang and Slote employ a kind of sentiment in order to realize the unity of the heart-mind, but they have taken different views concerning what the sentiment is and how it works. For Wang it is primarily human-heartedness (*ren* 仁), *a priori* and pure "sentiment," which underlies not only the unity of the heart and the mind but also manifests one's unity with the world. The world is already one, and what humans must do is simply to realize this within. Sentiment for Slote is empirical and *a posterior*, and its function is to unify cognitive and non-cognitive states, knowing and doing, and to manifest the interconnection among human beings, and between human beings and external things.

To a great extent, their difference in paths is caused by the conceptual instruments available to them. For Wang, *xin* is not only the thinking and feeling faculty, but is particularly also the entity of innate knowledge that is endowed by Heaven. Therefore apart from *a priori* "sentiments", Wang adds a significantly transcendental dimension to mind-sentimentalism to explain where the sentiments come from. The three constituent factors, empirical, *a priori*, and transcendental, are thus molded together as the innate knowledge to safeguard *xin*'s unifying process. The three-in-one innate knowledge has made it easier for Wang to ensure that intellect and emotion or knowing and acting are intrinsically and functionally unified. This kind of metaphysical idealism is, however, impossible for Slote to take for granted, or better to say, for him to willingly accept. The world in which Slote comes to unify the heart-mind is psychologically approvable, and the instrument he employs is empirically observed empathy. The starting point of his path cannot be anything but dualist in which things and the body exist outside of the heart-mind, and human cognition is inevitably a process from the internal to the external, *via* the interaction between the two elements, cognitive and non-cognitive, of the heart-mind. This explains why Slote comes to unify intellect and emotion but claim strongly to dissolve cognition in emotion. It seems that he has no other choice but to internalize outside things as human desire or feeling in order to reach the unity of the heart-mind. But for Wang, the whole world is in *xin*, or there is no world outside of *xin*; therefore knowing is essentially the self-cognition of innate knowledge, because in Wang's doctrine there is no external thing as the object, nor opposition between the subject and the object. The cognitive unity of intellect and sentiment is part of, or essence of, the ontological unity of the universe.

Slote's sentimentalist views on cognition and emotion break away from the modern or scientific way of thinking, by attacking the opposition between the knowing agent and the known object, and by recognizing the interdependence between the human and the world. Despite Slote making good use of Chinese concepts of *xin* and *yin-yang*, his project is significantly different from the Chinese monism as demonstrated in Wang's doctrine of the unity between knowledge and action. For Wang there is no need to internalize the world and to prove that cognition involves emotion, because the human and the world, whether it is called Heaven (*Tian* 天) or myriad things (*wan wu* 万物), is intrinsically one body, and cognitive elements and non-cognitive elements, whether they are called knowledge (*zhi* 知) or emotion (*qing* 情), are already unified in *xin*, underlain by *a priori* human-heartedness innate to *xin*.

It has been made sufficiently clear above that Slote and Wang aim at the same goal of the unity but the same goal is spelled out in different contexts. Cognition and sentiment, are mostly a tool used by Slote and Wang to understand how people interact and interdepend in the world. Slote endeavors to prove in his sentimentalism that all parts or elements of the world are interrelated and interconnected. He therefore calls us to recognize the emotional connections between the people, magnifying the significance of caring and empathy as the mechanism to interconnect people. But as an empirical and psychological mechanism, empathy has to rely on the similarity and common feelings between persons. Caring is possible only when people share similar empirical emotions and its strength depends on the degree of intimacy between them. It seems apparent, however, that Wang has already disregarded this as problematic.[9] Instead of empirically proving this, Wang opts for a mystical and yet straightforward way to demonstrate the interconnectedness between people, between *xin* and principle, and between humans and the world. His way cannot be undertaken as an empirical scheme. Wang indeed claims that innate knowledge is already in our heart-mind, and oneness of the world and the principle would be manifested itself as soon as we are aware of our heart-mind. In this transcendental realm, Wang has completed his project by reaching the perfect oneness between the heart and the mind, intellect and emotion, knowledge and action, that Slote's project may not be ever able to achieve nor would it be intended to. For these reasons, we would have to conclude that, despite their sharing the same enthusiasm in stressing [innate or psychological] the importance of sentiment over reason and in aiming at the unity of intellect and sentiment or between the human and the world, Slote and Wang have launched two different projects and advanced in two different paths, and we have reason to doubt whether these paths would lead them to the same goal.

Notes

1. A previous version of this chapter was presented at the international conference entitled "Slote Encountering Chinese Philosophy", March 16–17, 2018, organized by the Chinese University of Hong Kong. The authors wish to thank Michael Slote and all participants of the conference for their insightful comments and suggestions, some of which have been incorporated into this revised version.
2. Michael Slote, "Yin-Yang and the Heart-Mind," *Dao: A Journal of Comparative Philosophy* (2018) 17: 1–11.
3. Slote confirms that one must be open-minded towards a different view which requires empathy. At the same time, he also insists that the belief or preference in believing is also a matter of emotion which is a positive emotional attitude. He suggests that we must take into account such non-cognitive factors such as desire and attitude. This reminds us of what Charles Stevenson presents in his *Ethics and Language*, that the meaning of ethical terms and statements can be nothing but an emotional expression (Stevenson 1944).
4. We will come to test this claim later when we examine Wang Yangming's doctrine of the unity between knowledge and action.
5. "The first thing to note about the decisiveness that characterizes a willingness to make inferences in an unhesitating or non-vacillating way is that inference itself involves what, making use of William James's celebrated phrase, we can call mental flights and perchings" (Slote 2015 [6]: 32).
6. "At fifteen my mind was set on learning. At thirty my character had been formed. At forty I had no more perplexities. At fifty I knew the Mandate of Heaven (T'ien-ming). At sixty I was at ease with whatever I heard. At seventy I could follow my heart's desire without transgressing moral principles" (Chan 1963: 22).
7. "If we wish to extend our knowledge to the utmost, we must investigate the principles of all things we come into contact with, for the intelligent mind of man is certainly formed to know [*ren xin zhi ling, mo bu you* zhi 人心之灵，莫不有知]" (Chan 1963: 89).
8. For a discussion of Wang's monism, see Chang 1962: 33–43.
9. Wang considers this an impossible task as he tried to investigate the principle of bamboo when he was young, and after failing this, he became a fierce critique of Zhu Xi's way to the unity between the mind and the principle (see Yao 2013).

References

Bremmer, J. (1983), *The Early Greek Concept of the Soul*, Princeton: Princeton University Press.

Chan, Wing-tsit. trans. and ed. (1963), *A Source Book in Chinese Philosophy,* Princeton: Princeton University Press.

Chang, Carsun (1962), *Wang Yang-ming: Idealist Philosopher of Sixteenth-Century China*. Jamaica, NY: St. John's University Press.

Slote, Michael (2010), *Moral Sentimentalism,* New York: Oxford University Press.

Slote, Michael (2014), *A Sentimentalist Theory of the Mind,* New York: Oxford University Press.

Slote, Michael (2015), "Study on Yin and Yang Features of Moral Epistemology 认识论的阴与阳," *Hubei University Journal* (Philosophy and Social Sciences Editions), 6: 29–37.

Slote, Michael (2018a), "Yin-Yang and the Heart-Mind." *Dao: A Journal of Comparative Philosophy,* 17: 1–11.

Slote, Michael. (2018b), *The Philosophy of Yin and Yang: A Contemporary Approach,* The Chinese-English bilingual edition, Beijing: The Commercial Press.

Stevenson, Charles (1944), *Ethics and Language*. New Haven, CT: Yale University Press.

Wang, Yangming (1963), *Instructions for Practical Living and Other Neo-Confucian Writings by Wang Yang-ming,* translated, with Notes, by Wing-tsit Chan, New York and London: Columbia University Press.

Yao, Xinzhong (2013), "Philosophy of Learning in Wang Yangming and Francis Bacon," *Journal of Chinese Philosophy,* 40: 417–35.

6

Belief, Desire, and Besire

Slote and Wang Yangming on Moral Motivation

Yong Huang
The Chinese University of Hong Kong

1 Introduction

The Humean belief-desire model is still the mainstream theory of moral motivation, according to which an agent is motivated to act if the person has a desire, which is coupled with a means-end belief of the agent that this desire can be served by a particular action (section 2). In the contemporary philosophical scene, there are some anti-Humeans, mostly rationalists, who claim that belief alone is sufficient to motivate a person; there are also some anti-Humeans, mostly emotivists, who claim that there is no such a thing as moral belief: if it is moral, it is not a belief but merely an emotion, and if it is a belief, then it has nothing to do with moral motivation. However, this chapter is interested in a third group of anti-Humeans, who agree with Humeans that both belief and desire are needed to motivate a person to act, but belief and desire here are not two separate mental states but, instead, form a single, unitary one, the so-called "besire." This chapter will focus on Michael Slote as a representative of this third group of anti-Humeans (section 3). Recognizing the significant contributions that Slote's idea of besire makes to the issue of moral motivation (although his main concern is philosophy of mind), this chapter will also reveal some of its limitations, which it argues can be overcome by Wang Yangming's conception of *liangzhi*, literally "good knowledge," a kind of besire (section 4). It concludes with a brief summary of the main arguments.

2 The Humean Belief-Desire Model

Donald Davidson presents a belief-desire account of action which is characteristically Humean: "Whenever someone does something for a reason... he can be characterized as (a) having some sort of pro attitude toward actions of a certain kind, and (b) believing (or knowing, perceiving, noticing, remembering) that his action is of that kind" (Davidson 2001: 3–4). Here (b) is simply belief, while (a) is largely desire and desire-like mental states, such as "wantings, urges, promptings, and a great variety of moral views, aesthetic principles, economic prejudices, social conventions, and public and private goals and values in so far as these can be interpreted as attitudes of an agent directed toward actions of a certain kind" (Davidson 2001: 4).

Along the same lines, Bernard Williams presents what he calls the internal interpretation of reason for action: "A has a reason to ø iff A has some desire the satisfaction of which will be served by his ø-ing. Alternatively, we might say ... some desire, the satisfaction of which A believes will be served by his ø-ing" (Williams 1982: 101). Here, Williams uses desire, which is representative of members of what he calls the subjective motivational set, S, including virtually same things as Davidson's list of pro-attitudes: "dispositions of evaluation, patterns of emotional reaction, personal loyalties, and various projects ... embodying commitments of the agent" (Williams 1982: 105). Williams contrasts this internal interpretation of reasons for action with what he calls the externalist interpretation, according to which, "there are some cases of an agent's ø-ing because he believes that there is a reason for him to ø," even if his ø-ing does not serve any member in his subjective motivational set (Williams 1982: 107).

The example that Davidson uses is one's action of flipping a switch, which is rationalized by (a) one's desire or pro-attitude to turn on the light and (b) one's belief that flipping the switch can satisfy this desire to turn on the light. Here, without the desire to turn on the light, one would not flip the switch, even if (or precisely because) one believes that flipping the switch can turn on the light; similarly, one would not flip the switch if one does not believe that doing so would turn on the light even if (or precisely because) one has the desire to turn on the light. We can construct a similar example based on Williams' discussion. A person's action of mixing the stuff in front of him with tonic and drinking it is rationalized by his desire to drink gin mixed with tonic and his belief that the stuff in front of him is gin. Without the belief that the stuff in front of him is gin, he would not mix it with tonic and drink it even if (or precisely because) he has the desire to drink gin mixed with tonic; similarly, without the desire to drink gin mixed with tonic, he would not mix the stuff in front of him with tonic and drink it, even though (or precisely because) he believes that the stuff in front of him is gin. All these show that a rational action is impossible unless one has both the relevant desire and relevant means-end beliefs.

Of course, there are more complicated cases, where an action is not rationalized even though one has relevant desires and beliefs. Williams gives an example. Suppose a person has a desire to mix gin and tonic and drink it, and he also has a (false) belief that the stuff in front of him is gin. The two, desire and belief, combined, cause his action to mix it with tonic and drink it. While the belief and desire the person has can explain his action perfectly, i.e. why he is motivated to act, "it is just very odd to say that he has a reason to drink this stuff, and natural to say that he has no reason to drink it, although he thinks that he has" (Williams 1982: 102). In other words, his action is not rationalized in this case, as it is based on his false belief. Williams also mentions another scenario in which an action, or the lack thereof, is not rationalized, where "*A* may be ignorant of some element in *S*" (Williams 1982: 103).[1] While in the previous case, an action is not rationalized because of the false belief, in this current case, the lack of an action is not rationalized due to the agent, *A*, being not aware of a desire, *D*, in his subjective motivation set, *S*, which would be served by his ø-ing.

Belief and desires are here considered to be of two different mental states. Anscombe illustrates their difference with the following metaphor: "Let us consider a man going round a town with a shopping list in his hand. Now it is clear that the relation of this list to the things he actually buys is one and the same whether his wife gave him the list or it is his own list; and that there is a different relation when a list is made by a detective following him about. . . . If the list and the things that the man actually buys do not agree, and if this and this alone constitutes a mistake, then the mistake is not in the list but in the man's performance. . . . whereas if the detective's record and what the man actually buys do not agree, then the mistake is in the record" (Anscombe 2000: § 32).

In this metaphor, the man's list is equivalent to desire, while the detective's record is equivalent to belief. What Anscombe's metaphor aims to illustrate is the so-called the opposite directions of fit between belief and the world and that of desire to the world. Just as the man has to do something with the things he buys instead of the list when the two don't agree, so one has to do something with the world instead of the desire when the two disagree; and just as the detective needs to do something with his record instead of the things the man buys when the two disagree, so one needs to do something with his belief instead of the world when the two don't agree. In other words, the desire and the world have a world-to-mind direction of fit, while the belief and the world have a mind-to-world direction of fit. Mark Platts summarizes this Anscombean distinction most clearly: "Beliefs aim at the true, and their being true is their fitting the world; falsity is a decisive failing in a belief, and false beliefs should be discarded; beliefs should be changed to fit with the world, not vice versa. Desires aim at realisation, and their realisation is the world fitting with them; the fact that the indicative content of a desire is not realised in the world is not yet a failing in the desire, and not yet any reason to discard the desire; the world, crudely, should be changed to fit with our desires, not vice versa" (Platts 1979: 256–7).

3 Slote's Besire

Michael Slote poses two questions to this Humean model: "[1] How can things [beliefs and desires] with opposite directions of fit interact to successfully cause something [action], and [2] how can they and why should they in particular cause something [action] that has the direction of fit of one of them [desire] but not the other [belief]?" (Slote 2014: 56). It seems that the second question is relatively easy to answer. Presumably, Slote here means that the action that is produced by belief and desire has a world-to-mind direction of fit, which is the same as the direction of fit of belief, one part of the cause of the action, and not that of desire, another part of the cause of the action. However, direction of fit is supposed to be between a mental state and a state of affairs in the world, and action, while being caused by mental state(s) and thus intentional, is itself not a mental state, and so it does not seem that the issue of its fit with the world will arise in the first place, to say nothing about the direction of the fit.

Slote acknowledges that the first question does not arise in common sense but occurs only to philosophers, but I wonder whether it should be a question even for us philosophers. To say that belief and desire have the opposite directions of fit is not to say that belief and desires are two contrary forces that would mutually cancel each other so that they cannot cause anything when brought together (and thus there will be a question about how they can work together to cause action). It says only that when an action caused by belief and desire fails to reach its intended goal, we realize that there is a conflict between our belief and the world and/or one between our desire and the world; and we should now change our belief to fit with the world or demand the world to be changed to fit with our desire, and our changed belief may help us redirect our action so that our desire may be satisfied, that is, the world is changed to fit with our desire.

In any case, the main point Slote aims to make is that, in order to answer the two questions he raises to Humeans, we have to argue that, contrary to what Humeans assume, no beliefs are inert; rather, they are inherently motivating. In this sense, he is sympathetic with such rationalist philosophers as Thomas Nagel and Thomas Scanlon, who also argue that belief can motivate the believer to act without appealing to anything independent in Williams' subjective motivational set or Davidson's list of pro-attitudes. For example, Thomas Scanlon claims that "[a] rational person who judges there to be compelling reason to do A normally forms the intention to do A, and this judgment is sufficient explanation of that intention and of the agent's acting on it (since this action is part of what such an intention involves). There is no need to invoke an additional form of motivation" (Scanlon 1998: 33–4). It is in this sense that Slote defends the rationalist philosophy against the emotivist philosophers such as J. L. Mackie, who considers the rationalist view to be queer because it entails the possibility of objective prescriptivity. Slote claims that "there are cases where this combination or interfusion of elements seems plausibly in fact to exist" (Slote 2014 33).[2]

However, under this agreement lies a more fundamental difference between Slote and rationalist philosophers. Rationalists share with Humeans the view that belief is purely rational and intellectual. Their disagreement with Humeans is that the belief of a purely rationalistic and intellectual nature is itself motivating. While agreeing with rationalists that belief is motivating, Slote argues that belief is motivating precisely because it is not a purely intellectual or cognitive mental state: "first ... because any belief involves a certain favorable or positive emotion toward a certain way of seeing the world (or reality); and second.... because any belief has to involve a favorable attitude not only to certain intellectual assumptions and enterprises, but also to using and relying on that belief in non-intellectual practical contexts" (Slote 2014: 36–7).

So Slote argues that all beliefs have aspects of desires intrinsic in them, with opposite directions of fit with the world (Slote 2014: 72). Slote argues that belief, which, in contrast to desire, has commonly been considered to be purely rational, particularly on the Humean belief-desire model, itself contains emotional elements. To have a belief at least in part means to have a favorable attitude toward it and to have a desire to defend it whenever it is challenged. However, Slote does not stop here. Inspired by his colleague Elijah Chudnoff's view that, to believe the validity of a certain form of inference, one must have some motivation to reason in accordance with it, Slote argues that to hold a belief as true is to be motivated to act according to this belief. For Slote, any account of human action, even by belief alone, has to contain both rational and irrational elements. Beliefs, while rational, always contain irrational desires in them, and thus all beliefs are really *besires*.

The word "besire" is coined by J. E. J. Altham when he talks about the awareness of a moral property that "is a unitary mental state which has properties both of belief and desire.... It would not be two mental states, one a belief and the other a desire.... It would be rather what I call a 'besire'" (Altham 1986: 284). Michael Smith claims that Altham's is an excellent term to refer to the mental state "having both directions of fit with respect to the same content"; it is "'besire' because, though this state is belief-like, it is also desire-like"; instead of "the contingent co-existence of beliefs and desires", it is a third single, unitary mental state in addition to belief and desire (Smith 1994: 118–19).

As we can see, for both Altham and Smith, as well as almost all others who have discussed on this topic, besire is only an additional mental state along with belief and desire. In other words, they still leave room for the purely cognitive state of belief and purely affective state of desire. This, however, does not seem to be radical enough for Slote. He complains that the existing discussion of besire "doesn't ... suggest that ordinary beliefs (or even besires) have an emotional/affective component or aspect. In effect, the idea that all beliefs have the emotional aspect we have spoken of here translates into the idea that not just some beliefs but *all* beliefs are besires, a view that has never been advocated in the literature on besires but somehow also extends or develops what is said in that literature"; and instead of pointing, as Nagel, McDowell, and Scanlon do, "to particular kinds of cases where belief is intrinsically motivating ... I have been saying here that *all* beliefs have motivating properties/aspects" (Slote 2014: chapter 2, note 2).

However, Slote does not notice, nor does he thus address, the derogatory tone of "besire" as it is used in most of the existing literature. Immediately after the statement quoted above, "It would be rather what I call a 'besire'," Altham add a parenthetical sentence: "If that reminds one 'bizarre', I have no objection" (Altham 1986: 284). Similarly, for Smith, while they Humeans need not deny the contingent co-existence of beliefs and desires, they do deny the existence of besire, the "*single, unitary kind of state*" (Smith 1994: 119). The problem they identify with besire is the so-called conflict of directions of fit. To say that a mental state has a mind-to-world direction of fit is to say that when the two are in conflict, the mental state has to be modified to fit the world; and to say that a mental state has a world-to-mind direction of fit is to say that when the two are in conflict, the world has to be modified to fit the mind. In the Humean tradition, belief has a mind-to-world direction of fit, while the desire has a world-to-mind direction of fit. So they have the opposite directions of fit. This is not a problem, however, since belief and desire are two separate mental states.

Now if a single, unitary mental state called besire is both cognitive and affective, and thus has two opposite directions of fit to the world involved in this single mental state, then when a conflict arises between this mental state and the world, should we change the world to fit the mind (as we should since it is a desire) or change the mind to fit the world (as we should since it is also a belief), since apparently we cannot do both at the same time? About this "bizarre" nature of besire, Michael Smith explains most clearly. He first explains the distinction between belief and desire through "a difference in the counterfactual dependence of belief that p and a desire that p on a perception with the content that not p": in face of this perception with the content of not p, the belief p will go out of existence, while the desire p tends to endure (Smith 1994: 115). Now, the problem is that "[a] state with both directions of fit [besire] would therefore have to be such that, both, in the presence of such a perception it tends to go out of existence, and, in the presence of such a perception, it tends to endure, leading the subject who has it to bring it about that p. Taken quite literally, then, the idea that there may be a state having both directions of fit is just plain incoherent" (Smith 1994: 118)

As we have just said, Slote does not address or even notice this apparently bizarre nature of besire, but is Slote's besire also bizarre in the sense of being incoherent as Smith indicates? It does not seem to be so. Slote emphasizes the two aspects of desire entailed in belief. The first is that when we have a belief, we will have a favorable attitude toward it and a desire to defend it when it is challenged. While I'm not entirely sure whether this counts as a besire in the strict sense,[3] if it is a besire, then it is not bizarre because when there is a conflict between our belief p and the perception not p, we will not only change our belief to fit the world but will also change our desire, that is, we will no longer have the favorable attitude toward it or desire to defend it.

The second is that when we have a belief, we will have a desire to use it: "I am saying that one (metaphysically and/or logically) can't have a belief unless one is motivated to make use of it" (Slote 2014: 41). The example Slote uses to illustrate his point is the following. If a person believes that something is the largest rock in the vicinity, he has the desire to have more money, and he is told that he will be given a lot of money if he brings the largest rock in the vicinity to a particular woman, then the person will have a desire to use the belief to satisfy his desire for more money, which motivates him to bring her that rock. However, let us suppose that he is not given any money after he brings that rock to the woman because it turns out that the rock is not the biggest in the vicinity, that is, his belief is false. Then he has to change his belief to fit the world. Will he still maintain the desire to use that (false) belief? Of course not. There are two options here. On the one hand, the desire to use the belief is intrinsic to the belief (which I doubt is the case, since it is not common that a person somehow stumbles upon a belief first and only then form a desire to use it), so that when the belief is abandoned, the desire will be abandoned as well. On the other, the desire to use the belief is merely derivative from his independent desire for money (which I suspect is the case, as normally a desire first arises in a person and only then does the person start to look for beliefs to satisfy it; if the person already has such a belief, he will have the desire to use it; if he does not have it yet, he will have a desire to form a new belief), so that when he maintains his desire for more money, he has to abandon the desire to use that (false) belief, since the latter desire does not serve to satisfy the former desire.

So in both senses, Slote's besire is not bizarre. However, there are two conditions that have to be met. The first is that, in both cases, the belief element and the desire element of the besire have the same mind-to-world direction of fit: when one's belief (p) comes into conflict with the perception with the content of not p, one not only gives up the belief but also gives up the desire to defend it (in the first sense) or the desire to make use of it (in the second case). While this is not necessarily a problem in itself, as we can see later, this is a problem for Slote since he clearly states that his concept of desire-entailing belief, besire, has both directions of fit: "Belief has a mind-to-world direction of fit, therefore, in virtue of the fact that its propositional content is true if and only if it fits the real world; and it has a world-to-mind direction of fit because its motivation to rely on that content for practical/theoretical purposes will be fulfilled when and only when the belief actually is used for such purposes" (Slote 2014: 72). If Slote really wants to insist that his desire-entailing belief has both directions of fit, he would need to respond to what Altham regards as its bizarre nature or what Smith regards as its incoherence.

The second condition is that Slote's concept of besire is not radical enough (although in due course I'll also show that it is too radical in a different sense). The reason I say that it is not radical enough is that his desire-entailing belief, as besire, still needs to work together with an independent desire. This is particularly clear in the example he uses to illustrate the second sense of besire discussed above: the person who has the beliefs that the rock is the biggest in the vicinity and that he will be given a large sum of money if he brings it to a woman who needs it and the desire to make use such beliefs will not be motivated to bring the rock to the woman unless he has an independent desire for money.[4] This reminds us of the very motive

Slote has in emphasizing the emotive aspect of belief. As we have seen, Slote complains that Humeans who recognize nothing but the intellectual, rational, and cognitive element in belief and who claim that belief has only the mind-to-world direction of fit cannot explain how such a belief can interact with desire that has the opposite direction of fit. While we have argued above that it is not necessary for two mental states to share the same direction of fit in order for them to interact with each other to produce action, Slote does think it is necessary, and so he argues that:

> [i]f belief is partially world-to-mind, because it involves emotion and motivation, then it is easier to see how it can causally interact or combine with something else that is world-to-mind in fit to produce something with that same fit.... [T]he problem ... about how the afferent and efferent, or items with opposite directions of fit, can work together efficaciously is at least partially answered by arguing and claiming that belief ... has a previously unsuspected efferent or world-to-mind aspect that allows it to combine with desires efficaciously to produce actions.
>
> Slote 2014: 58

In this sense, Slote's besire is still very much consistent with and acceptable on the Humean model of belief and desire: belief, even if it contains the two aspects of desire that Slote discusses, cannot motivate a person to act without an independent desire the belief in question is supposed to serve to satisfy.[5] This is essentially a Humean account of reason for action, which is in contrast to the rationalist account that claims that belief alone can motivate a person to act without any desire, whether the desire is contained in the belief or is an independent desire. In the sense of and to the extent that Slote aims to provide an alternative account of reason for action to both Humeanism and rationalism, he thus fails in his project.

To have a more radical (although also less radical in another sense) concept of besire, the besire that can motivate one to act without the assistance of an independent desire (and, for that matter, without the assistance of an independent belief), we need to turn to Wang Yangming, the most influential neo-Confucian in the Ming Dynasty of China.

4 Wang Yangming's Besire

One of Wang's trademark notions is *liangzhi* 良知, literally "good knowledge." What he means is not simply knowledge about the good or the moral, such as the merely intellectual knowledge that one ought to love one's parents; rather he means the knowledge that itself is good or moral, the affective knowledge—that (for example) one ought to love one's parents—which inclines one to act accordingly, that is, to love one's parents. In other words, it is the moral knowledge that has motivation built into it. Elsewhere I characterize such knowledge as knowing-to, as a type of knowing that is different from and in addition to Gilbert Ryle's knowing-that and knowing-how (Huang 2017). While knowing-that is intellectual knowing and knowing-how is capacity knowing, knowing-to is motivating knowing. Here, I want to argue that it can also be adequately characterized as a kind of besire: a mental state that includes both belief and desire, although Wang prefers to use the term "knowledge and action," where knowledge is equivalent to belief, while action is better understood as desire, and his trade mark theory is the unity of knowing and acting.

To illustrate this feature of his *liangzhi*, Wang uses the analogy from the Confucian classic, *The Great Learning*:

> *The Great Learning* shows us what genuine knowledge and genuine action are. It asks us "to love the good as we love the beautiful color and to hate the evil as we hate the bad odor." Here seeing the beautiful color belongs to knowing, while loving it belongs to acting. However, at the very moment one sees the beautiful color one has already loved it; it is not the case that one decides to love it only after seeing it. Similarly, smelling the bad odor belongs to knowing, while hating it belongs to acting. However, at the very moment one smells the bad odor, one has already hated it; it is not the case that one decides to hate it only after smelling it.
>
> Wang 1992: [1] 4

What Wang emphasizes here is that, at the same time one believes that a flower is beautiful, one must also love it (or at the same time one loves a flower, one must also believe that it is beautiful); and at the same time one recognizes a bad odor, one must also hate it (or at the same time one hates an odor, one must also believe that it is a bad odor). It is impossible that one believes that a flower is beautiful without the emotion, feeling, or desire of loving it (or that one believes that an odor is smelly without the emotion, feeling, or desire of hating it), just as it is impossible that one loves the flower without believing that it is beautiful (or that one hates the odor without believing that it is smelly). It is not the case that one first believes that the flower is beautiful and then starts to love it (or first believes that the odor is bad and then starts to hate it), just as it is not the case that one first loves the flower and then realizes that it is beautiful (or that one first hates the odor and only then realizes that it is bad). Here the belief that flower is beautiful and desire to love it (or the belief that the odor is bad and the desire to hate it) constitute one single, unitary mental state, a besire.

As mentioned earlier, Wang prefers to talk about knowing and acting, which can be made better sense of, however, only in terms of belief and desire, especially in light of his notion of knowledge and action as one (*zhi xing he yi*). To illustrate their oneness, Wang borrows and modifies an analogy of water with the natural tendency to flow downward used by Mencius for a different purpose. While Mencius uses it to show that human nature (water) is naturally good (naturally flows down), Wang uses it to show that knowledge (water) naturally inclines one to act (naturally flows down) (see Wang 1992: [8] 277). It is in this sense that Wang claims that "The effort to know and the effort to act are originally inseparable. Only because learners later separate them into two separate efforts and the original state of knowledge and action is lost, is there a need for a theory about their unity and simultaneous progress" (Wang 1992: [2] 42). It is also in this sense that he complains that people tend to regard knowing and acting as two separate endeavors, thinking that one has to know before one can act; one shall first make an effort to know today, and only after one really knows does one start to make an effort to act. As a result, one does not act the whole life, nor does one know the whole life. This is a serious disease, and the "doctrine of oneness of knowledge and action that I am advocating today is precisely to cure this disease" (Wang 1992: [1] 4–5).

To paraphrase what Wang says above using the Humean terminology (though not the Humean perspective), we can see that Wang is against the view that one first acquires a belief and only later acquires a desire to act according to this belief. Instead one acquires the belief and desire to act accordingly simultaneously. It is important to notice that when Wang talks about knowledge and (desire for) action, he is talking about knowledge and (desire for) action with the same content. For example, corresponding to one's knowledge (belief) that one ought to love one's parent is one's (desire) to love one's parent, and only in this sense that knowledge and (desire for) action are one. It is in this sense that it is different from the belief and desire in the Humean belief-desire model, where belief and desire do not have the same content. For example, according the Humean model, what motivates me to drink the stuff in front of me is my belief that this stuff is water and my desire to drink it. Here the content of my belief (this stuff is water) and that of my desire (to drink water) are not the same.

Thus, Gu Dongqiao, one of his students, misunderstood Wang when he (the student) argues that knowledge and (desire for) action cannot be the same, as the former must precede the latter, saying that "only after I know that this is food do I eat it, and only after I know that this is soup do I drink it"[6] (in Wang 1992: [2] 41). Precedence of knowledge (belief) to (desire for) action in this sense is of course something that Wang also accepts. Indeed, in this sense, Wang also allows the opposite temporal sequence: action precedes knowledge. Thus, in his response to Gu Dongqiao, Wang says that one can know that the soup is delicious only after one drinks it (Wang 1992: [2] 42). For Wang, the reason that knowledge can precede action in some cases and action can precede knowledge in some other cases, either of which shows that knowledge and action are not one, is that knowledge and action in each pair do not have the same content, while his oneness of knowledge and action is meant to refer to knowledge and action with the same content. Thus, when he claims that "there has never been one who knows and yet does not act. To know and yet not to act is not genuine knowing" (Wang 1992: [1] 4). Here, the desire to act that is inseparable from knowledge (belief) is the desire to act according to the knowledge. For example, one's knowledge that one ought to be filial to one's parent is inseparable from one's desire to be filial to one's parents, one's knowledge that one ought to love one's siblings is inseparable from one's desire to love one's siblings, and one's knowledge that one ought to commiserate with people is inseparable from one's desire to commiserate with people. In the sense that Wang's knowledge and (desire for) action have the same content, Wang's *liangzhi* is a genuine sense of besire.

If Wang's *liangzhi* is a genuine sense of besire, then is it also something bizarre or incoherent in the sense that it contains two conflicting directions of fit with the world? Before we try to answer this question, we need to realize that it is not always the case that belief has a mind-to-world direction of fit, nor is it always the case that desire has a world-to-mind direction of fit. Indeed, even when she uses the metaphor of a man's shopping list and a detective's record to illustrate the opposite directions of fit for belief and desire, Anscombe has already introduced the qualification for desire's world-to-mind direction of fit:

> If this and this alone constitutes a mistake. For the discrepancy might arise because some of the things were not to be had and if one might have known they were not to be had, we might speak of a mistake (an error of judgment) in constructing the list. If I go out in Oxford with a shopping list including "tackle for catching sharks", no one will think of it as a mistake in performance that I fail to come back with it. And then again there may be a discrepancy between the list and what the man bought because he changed his mind and decided to buy something else instead.
>
> Anscombe 2000: § 32

Here, Anscombe is telling us that desire sometimes also has the mind-to-world direction of fit, but we can also make a case that belief sometimes also has the world-to-mind direction of fit. Indeed, I shall argue that certain type of belief, the type that Wang Yangming talks about, typically has the world-to-mind direction of fit. As we have seen, the type of belief/knowledge that Wang says is in one with desire for action is *liangzhi*, literally good knowledge: it is the knowledge about what we ought to do. In other words, it is normative knowledge.

Here we can see that, while in one sense Wang's besire is more radical than Slote's (as it can motivate a person to act without the need for an independent desire), in another sense it is less so than Slote's. As we have seen, Slote claims that all beliefs are besire (although he does not claim that all desires are also besires, which should be equally plausible as a number of philosophers have pointed out the cognitive nature of desires or emotions; in other words, just as beliefs are not merely intellectual, desire are not purely non-intellectual). In contrast, for Wang, only moral (or more generally normative) knowledge/beliefs are besires.

This difference establishes two advantages of Wang's conception of besire over Slote's. On the one hand, only normative beliefs can be besires in the genuine sense. As we have shown, a mental state can be regarded as a besire not simply because it is both belief-like and desire-like but the content of the belief and the content of desire should be the same. So a besire p is both belief p and desire p, which, however, is only applicable to normative belief. For example, my belief that I ought to love my parents and my desire to love my parents have the same content (love my parents): the desire in question is the desire to act according to the belief. Now if we look at a non-normative belief, for example, my belief that it will be a sunny day tomorrow, without an independent desire, there is no way for me to act according to this belief, since this belief is neutral with respect to what I'm going to do. If I have an independent desire to be sun-tanned, this belief may lead me to go to the beach; but if I have an independent desire to keep cool, this same belief may lead me to stay home. Without any independent desire, this belief cannot tell me what to act, and this independent desire does not have the same content as the belief.

On the other hand, and more importantly, if we focus on normative belief, we will realize that the direction of fit between normative belief and the world is not the mind-to-world one but the world-to-mind one. For example, if I believe that everyone ought to love his or her parents, and if the content of our perception is that not everyone or even no one loves his or her parents, this does not necessitate our modification of our belief to fit the world. In the contrary, I would think that the world is not what it ought to be and it ought to be modified (I ought to modify it) so that everyone in the world will love his or her parents, and as a result the world fits with my belief. This forms a stark contrast with non-normative belief. Suppose my belief is that everyone in the world loves his or her parents. Then if my perception of the world has the content that not everyone in the world loves his or her parents, then I will have to modify my belief to fit with the world. So, while the non-normative belief has the mind-to-world direction of fit, normative belief typically has a world-to-mind direction of it. This means that normative belief has the same direction of fit as desire, which also has a world-to-mind direction of fit. Since besire is both belief-like and desire-like, and since belief in besire is only normative belief, and since normative belief has the same direction of fit as desire, then besire, despite its being both belief-like and desire-like, doesn't have conflicting directions of fit and thus is not bizarre.

All claims that a single, unitary mental state of besire is bizarre or incoherent are based on the assumption that besire has both (as a belief) mind-to-world direction of it and (as a desire) the world-to-mind direction fit, something Slote also accepts and, indeed, emphasizes, and these two directions are in conflict, making the very idea of besire that is based on this conflict unintelligible; and this very assumption of besire consisting of two conflicting directions of fit is, in turn, based on the dogma that belief always has a mind-to-world direction of it, and the desire always has a world-to-mind direction of fit. I have been arguing here that this dogma has to be jettisoned. This is primarily not because desire sometimes also has the mind-to-world direction, as cautioned by Anscombe herself. After all, desire's mind-to-world direction of fit is exception, and desire typically has the world-to-mind direction of fit. The main reason for us to reject this dogma is that there is one type of belief, moral or normative belief, which typically has the world-to-mind direction of fit.

So, crucial to our argument is the distinction between non-normative beliefs and normative beliefs. The kind of distinction we want to make between the two, however, is not new at all. Kant essentially makes the same distinction when he distinguishes between reality in theoretical reason (corresponding to non-normative belief) and reality in practical reason (corresponding to normative belief). In the former, the reality of something is the cause of our belief about it and our belief has to fit with the reality; in the latter, however, the reality of something is inseparable from our belief in it and our willingness and ability to act accordingly. To discern the reality in the latter sense, according to Kant, is "only to discern the possibility or impossibility of willing the action by which a certain object would be made Real, provided we had the ability to bring it about" (Kant 1956: 59). This Kantian distinction is stated in a more easily understandable way by John Rawls, also a Kantian: "practical reason is concerned with the production of objects according to a conception of these objects ... while theoretical reason is concerned with the knowledge of given objects" (Rawls 1993: 93). In the former, then, there is a world-to-mind direction of fit, while in the latter there is a mind-to-world direction of fit.

However, it seems that our emphasis on the normative nature of moral belief and thus the besire's lack of conflicting directions of fit in explaining the belief-like element of besire also carries a risk. If the belief-like element or besire has the same world-to-mind direction of fit as the desire-like element of besire, then is normative belief, as Ayer claims, really not a belief but merely emotion or desire, and thus we are really not talking about a mental state of besire, which is simultaneously belief-like and desire-like; instead do we just have the mental state of desire? The question here comes down to the issue of objectivity of moral belief. If it does not have any objectivity, then it is hardly distinguishable from desire. One initial way to respond to this question is to take notice of the proviso that Kant makes in the quote above: "provided we had the ability to bring it about." This proviso is necessary. When we say that we ought to change the world to fit our normative belief, in contrast to changing our descriptive belief to fit the world, we are not saying that we can hold whatever normative belief, however absurd it is, and demand the world to fit with it. For example, we cannot hold a normative belief that human beings ought to be immortal and then try to change the world so that it can fit with our normative belief. The reason is that it is impossible for humans to be immortal, or it is not within our ability to change the world so that it can fit with our beliefs. This is really what the slogan "ought implies can" means: what we think people ought to do must be something that they can do (although it is not necessarily what people actually do, as people may not do what they can do), so that when people do not do what we believe that they ought to do, we can blame them in order to make them do it (i.e. change the world to fit our belief). For example, according to Owen Flanagan's principle of minimal psychological realism, we need to "make sure when constructing a moral theory or projecting a moral ideal, that the character, decision processing, and behaviour prescribed are possible, or are perceived to be possible for creatures like us" (Flanagan 1991: 34).

This, however, is not unique to moral beliefs, which require that the world be changed to fit with them; desires are the same. When we say that we change the world to fit our desires, it also means that our desires must be realistic. If we desire to be immortal, then perhaps we can never change the world in such a way that it will fit with our desire. This is indeed what Anscombe meant to stress with her qualification discussed above. So the Kantian proviso is far short of delivering us the needed objectivity of moral belief, especially because it fails to enable us to make the distinction between normative belief and desire, and without this distinction, we cannot be sure that we have a genuine case of besire instead of a simple case of desire. What the Kantain proviso establishes about our normative belief is only that what we believe we humans ought to be (do) must be things that we human beings can do. However, what we human beings can do is not necessarily what we human beings ought to do, which is the concern of morality or normativity. We human beings can do a lot of things, some of which we ought to do and some not. So is there any objective reality of our moral belief? Or is there a world to which our belief must fit with? In other words, while moral beliefs, being *moral*, have the world-to-mind direction of fit, do these same moral beliefs, as *beliefs*, also have a mind-to-world direction of fit? Wang Yangming has a positive answer to this question. However, this involves the complicated issue of Wang Yangming's unique version of moral realism, the topic of a different essay of mine, and so here let me just point out one of its central features.

Unlike other types of moral realism that focuses on the action and/or its environment, from which moral rightness and wrongness can be perceived or upon which they supervene, Wang's moral realism, which takes a virtue ethics approach, focuses on the human agent, the characteristics a healthy and non-defective human being ought to have. Wang takes the mainstream Confucian view of human nature as being moral, although he develops his own unique arguments for this view, details of which I will not be able to go into. It suffices to say, for the purpose of this essay, that, while familiar versions of moral realism stress that moral quality or property exist out there in the world (this also applies to the so-called response dependent theory, represented by John McDowell, who uses John Locke's secondary quality as an analogy of moral quality), Wang's moral realism emphasizes that moral qualities or properties reside right within us and yet are nevertheless not subjective but objective, since the question about what is a healthy, non-deficient, and characteristic human being must be based on an objective and even scientific study of human beings, just like the question about what is a healthy, non-deficient, and characteristic wolf or poison ivy must be based on scientific study of such beings. So a moral belief about what human beings ought to be or do must reflect this reality of human nature, and a belief that does not reflect this reality has to be changed to fit this reality. It is in this sense that moral belief also has the mind-to-world direction of fit.

5 Conclusion

In this chapter, I have been developing a third anti-Humean position regarding moral motivation, as a contrast to the rationalist anti-Humean view represented by Thomas Nagel and Thomas Scanlon and the emotivist anti-Humean view represented by Ayer and Altham. This third anti-Humean position is unique in its embracing the idea of besire, a single, unitary mental state that is both belief-like and desire-like, which motivates a person to act. In the analytic tradition, Michael Slote is one of the representatives of such a view. However, I have argued that his notion of besire is both unnecessarily too radical (as he claims that all beliefs are desires) and not sufficiently radical (as he needs an independent desire to explain the motivation of human action). I have then argued that both limitations of Slote's besire can be overcome in the neo-Confucian philosopher Wang Yangming's notion of *liangzhi*, which, as a besire, only applies to the realm of morality or normativity and can motivate a person to act without the need for an independent desire. More importantly, I have argued that Wang's *liangzhi* as a besire can adequately respond to the Humean view of it as bizarre or incoherent due to their perceived opposite directions of fit of belief-like element and desire-like element of besire. In Wang, the belief-like element of besire is of a normative nature and thus has the world-to-mind direction of fit, which is the same as the direction of fit as the desire-like element of the same besire, and thus there is no conflict between these two elements' respective directions of fit with the world.

Before concluding, I would like to make brief responses to two questions a careful reader up to this point would raise. First, emphasizing the objectivity of moral belief as the *belief-like* element of besire, I have pointed out that it (the belief-like-element of besire) has the mind-to-world direction of fit. Then what about the desire-like element of besire? Does it still have, as it typically does, the world-to-mind direction of fit? If so, the problem of conflicting directions of fit remains. A simple answer to this question is that here we are not encountering a typical case of desire; instead this is an exceptional case to which Anscombe's qualification should apply: the desire to act according to a false belief is not a desire that a rational person should have!

Second, I have said that moral belief, the belief-like element of besire, as *moral*, has a world-to-mind direction of fit, but as a *belief*, it has a mind-to-world direction of fit. Then, it seems that the conflicting directions of fit have simply shifted: from the conflict between the belief-like element and desire-like element within the besire to the conflict between the *moral* element and the *belief* element within the belief-like element of besire; if so, instead of having a bizarre and incoherent besire, we have a bizarre and incoherent *belief-like* element of besire. One way to respond to such a criticism is to start with an analogy. The idea of a healthy dog also has two directions of fit. First, in order to know what constitutes a healthy dog, we need to study dogs. In this sense, the idea of a healthy dog has a mind-to-world direction of fit. So if our idea of a healthy dog comes into conflict with the result of most up-to-date and reliable scientific studies of dogs, we have to modify our idea to fit with the world. Second, however, after a view of what constitutes a healthy dog is adopted, veterinarians can use the idea to determine whether a given dog is healthy or not and thus needs treatment or not; the idea of a healthy dog becomes a normative one and thus has a world-to-mind direction of fit. Here the issue of conflicting directions of fit does not arise because the two directions of fit don't function at the same time but sequentially: when we need to determine what constitutes a healthy dog, the idea of a healthy dog has the mind-to-world direction of fit; only after this idea is accepted does it start to have the world-to-mind direction of fit. Our conception of a healthy, non-defective, and characteristic human being is precisely the same: when we form the conception, it is descriptive and has the mind-to-world direction of fit; after we form the conception, it becomes normative and has the world-to-mind direction of fit. These two opposite directions of fit don't occur simultaneously but only sequentially and thus do not constitute any conflict.

Notes

1 Although Williams immediately adds: "But we should notice that an unknown element in S, D, will provide a reason for A to ø only if ø-ing is rationally related to D" (Williams 1982: 103).
2 So here we can see that there are different groups of anti-Humeans on the issue of motivation. As we have seen, Humeans claim that a person is motivated to act by the fusion of two separate mental states: desire and the means-end belief. As we have also seen, rationalist philosophers claim that belief alone can be motivating without an independent desire. In contrast, emotivists argue that desire alone is motivating. For example, Ayer claims that if "moral judgment" is indeed a *judgment* (belief), it cannot be about morality and therefore cannot result in action; if it is indeed about *morality*, then it cannot be a judgment. *Moral statements are really not statements but "are simply expressions of emotion which can be neither true nor false"* (Ayer 1946: 103); Moreover, "it is worth mentioning that ethical terms do not serve only to express feeling. They are calculated also to arouse feeling, and so to stimulate action" (Ayer 1946: 108). Although Ayer is talking about moral motivation, what he says certainly also applies to non-moral motivations. Slote belongs to a third group of anti-Humeans, who agree that both belief and desire are needed to motivating one to act, but they are not two separate mental states; instead, they form one single, unitary mental state. For Slote, the very fact that belief can be motivating, as rationalists have observed, shows that belief is not merely intellectual but also emotional, as rationalists are unwilling to acknowledge.
3 Besire is a mental state in which belief and desire have the same content, a belief p and a desire p. So If I have a belief p and have a desire to defend p, then the content of the belief is p, while the content of desire is defending p. Thus they don't have the same content and thus don't constitute a besire. Of course we may think

that the desire to defend p can be abbreviated as desire p, just as the belief that p is true can be abbreviated as belief p, and thus we have an instance of besire.
4 Slote is not entirely consistent on this issue. While here he says that the desire entailing belief still needs to work with an independent desire to motivate the agent to act, in some other places, he seems to think that the desire entailing belief alone can have such a motivation. He states that since "belief entails emotion, the emotion of favoring a certain way of seeing things, and … emotion is something we find it easy to connect with motivation," we can understand how "belief can, on its own, sometimes motivate us and reinforces whatever else we can say in favor of objective prescriptivity" (Slote 2014: 34).
5 Indeed, Slote somewhat acknowledges that when he says that "Davidson's desire-belief model for explaining human actions is fundamentally more plausible than the Kantian picture, but that it also depends on the idea that belief isn't purely intellectual in ways that Davidson and those who have followed him haven't explicitly recognized" (2014: 37), and that what he is doing "constitutes a way of philosophically buttressing Davidson's model of action in a way or ways that, unbeknownst to Davidson, it seems to need buttressing" (Slote 2014: 55).
6 In Chinese, it is customary to say to "drink soup," and not "eat soup" as in English.

References

Altham, J. E. L. (1986), "The Legacy of Emotivism," in Graham Macdonald and Crispin Wright (eds), *Fact, Science, and Morality: Essays on A.J. Ayer's* Language, Truth, and Logic, Malden, MA and Oxford: Basil Blackwell.

Ayer, A. J. (1946), *Language, Truth, and Logic*, New York: Dover Publications.

Anscombe, G. E. M. (2000), *Intention*, Cambridge, MA: Harvard University Press.

Davidson, Donald (2001), *Essays on Actions and Events*. Oxford: Oxford University Press.

Flanagan, Owen (1991), *Varieties of Moral Personality: Ethics and Psychological Realism*, Cambridge, MA: Harvard University Press.

Huang, Yong (2017), "Knowing-that, Knowing-how, or Knowing-to: Wang Yangming's Conception of Moral Knowledge," *Journal of Philosophical Research*, 42: 65–94.

Kant, Immanuel (1956), *Critique of Practical Reason*, New York: Macmillan Publishing Company.

Platts, Mark de Bretton (1979), *Ways of Meaning: An Introduction to a Philosophy of Language*, Cambridge, MA: MIT Press.

Rawls, John (1993), *Political Liberalism*, New York: Columbia University Press.

Scanlon, Thomas (1998), *What We Owe to Each Other*, Cambridge, MA: Harvard University Press.

Slote, Michael (2014), *A Sentimentalist Theory of the Mind*, Oxford: Oxford University Press.

Smith, Michael (1994), *The Moral Problem*, Malden, MA and Oxford: Basil Blackwell.

Wang, Yangming 王陽明. (1992), *The Complete Works of Wang Yangming* 王陽明全集. Shanghai 上海: Shanghai Guji Chubanshe 上海古籍出版社.

Williams, Bernard (1982), *Moral Luck*, Oxford: Oxford University Press.

The Value of Receptivity and *Yin/Yang* Clusters for Philosophy

Robin R. Wang

Professor of Philosophy, Loyola Marymount University, Los Angeles, United States

1 Introduction

We are very much grateful for Michael Slote's recent work. His critique of Western philosophy has led him to dig into the ancient Chinese conceptual treasure box and locate *yinyang* as an underappreciated philosophical notion and suggest that we make good use of it. He has shown us how this centuries-old concept can make a valuable and unique contribution to contemporary philosophy.

> I came to recognize that the *yin/yang* complementarity can be understood or interpreted as emphasizing (and balancing) both receptivity and rational control in a way one doesn't typically find in the West. Then, even later, I came to realize that we can use *yin/yang* thus understood to deal plausibly with major current and historical philosophical issues in (Western) epistemology, ethics, and philosophy of mind.
>
> Slote 2018: 98

I fully support Slote's claim that philosophers both today and historically (East and West) have neither taken *yin* and *yang* seriously, nor employed it systematically or foundationally. *Yinyang* can "pervade the philosophical areas/topics that epistemology, ethics, and the philosophy of mind deal with, but also serve as a justif*ying* basis, perhaps the ultimate justif*ying* basis, for what it makes most sense for philosophers to say about these matters" (Slote 2018: 38). However, I would like to complicate his *yin/yang* complementarity by introducing the *yinyang clusters*, which more accurately clarify the deeper meaning of *yin/yang* theory and more effectively employ *yin/yang* philosophical practice in our time. The main argument of this effort is to illuminate that *yinyang* is a multilevel structure that cannot be reduced to a single string of complementarity or balance. *Yinyang* is constituted of a broad web of various meanings and logics, and it cannot be subject to a simple definition or understanding. Such *yinyang* clusters resist a univocal definition degree and reserve a proper range of semantic diversity. The *yinyang clusters* show a more faithful and responsible way to the classical Chinese theory and practice of *yinyang* and bring out a new perspective on a wide range of philosophical problems and justifications. Roger Ames explains the way of knowing in Chinese philosophy. According to him, Chinese texts are rooted in a process cosmology so that their epistemic vocabulary seeks a "mapping" of the context that allows for a productive "forging ahead" within it, and thus promises only practical rather than apodictic knowledge: that is, "finding one's way" (*zhidao* 知道), "unraveling the patterns within the context" (*lijie* 理解), "seeing with full clarity" (*liaojie* 瞭解), "getting through with facility" (*tongda* 通達), "being well acquainted with everything" (*baishitong* 百事通) and so on (Ames 2018: xxx).

2 From the Genealogy of *Yinyang* to the Value of Receptivity: The Conceptual and Practical Origin

Slote rightly claims that: "Western philosophical thought has on the whole overemphasized rational control at the expense of the countervailing and important virtue/value of receptivity" (Slote 2018: 16). He calls for a perspective on moral sentimentalism by turning to the *yin/yang* notion in Chinese philosophy. For him, *yin/yang* assumes a greater philosophical importance at the same time that it adds strength to the case for moral sentimentalism.

In order to fully grasp this *yinyang* usage, let us trace back the origin and foundation of the *yinyang* notion. Joseph Needham (1990–95) states that *yinyang* concepts "were the most ultimate principles of which the ancient Chinese could conceive" (Needham 1954: 224). At its conception, *yinyang* was an attempt to reconcile human life with the sun. *Yin* and *yang* in their earliest usage in Chinese history were separate terms that were connected through an effect of the sun reflecting on a hill. The first written record of using the two characters together is found in the *Shijing*: "Viewing the scenery at hill, looking for *yinyang*" (Zhou 2002: xxx).[1] The shady side of the hill is *yin* and the sunny side is *yang*. This original meaning of *yinyang* demonstrates that *yinyang* is not a particular object, being, or substance, but rather a phenomenon—a concrete reference and an observable fact. In this sense, *yinyang* is quite different from the sun itself, *ri* 日. The sun is an entity, a being, a particular object; however, *yin/yang* is the effect of this entity and not the entity itself. It is a way of thinking—that is, *yinyang* thinking. This *yinyang* thinking has at least two characteristics: a) thinking takes place within the intersection of a complex context, not simply an isolated consciousness activity; b) focusing on a primacy of the interplay between interrelated elements, such as the sun, the hill, and the light. In the earliest meaning, *yin* and *yang* are described as functions of something, and they are inevitably attached to relationships or contexts. Any fixed definition of *yin/yang* will, thus, lead to a problematic understanding of the terms.

The period of the Zhou Dynasty (eleventh century BCE to 221 BCE) and its decline is commonly taken as a time in which Chinese thought gradually moved toward more and more humanistic and rationalistic understandings of the world and the place of human beings in it. Around the third century BCE, China experienced a particular shift from a mystical–religious view of the operations of the world toward naturalistic analyses of specific causes. The rise of the *yinyang* thinking paradigm at that time is intimately connected with this shift, as *yinyang* became an important conceptual tool that facilitated this transition. The shift has analogies with the step from mythos to logos in the ancient Mediterranean world, and *yinyang* thinking functions in ways similar to the recognition of natural laws and the reduction of phenomena to elements. It advocates a rational effort to furnish an intellectual and coherent account of the natural world and the human condition. This period was directed toward increasing "existential autonomy," allowing human beings to take ever more control over their own lives (Unschuld 2010). *Yinyang* became the most effective and multifarious concrete conceptual tool for explaining our associations and relationships with each other, the world and cosmos.

Huangdi Neijing, the classical text of the Han dynasty, can be taken as an example of treatise on *yinyang* theory and practice, illustrating a distinctive union between pre-qin philosophical thought and various practical techniques. This thinking paradigm assumes that all natural occurrences can be incorporated into a single system of correspondence. This system of correspondence also encodes again the fact that *yinyang* is not a substance, thing, or fixed essence, but rather a way of unfolding and coordinating multidimensional relationships that are both complex and changing. More specifically, the naturalistic account rests on the following assumptions: the human body shares the same categorical structure (*xianglei* 相類) with heaven, earth, and myriad things; the pattern of pathology is the same pattern as the changes of heaven and earth; human biological rhythm should change according to the rhythms of heaven, earth, and the four seasons. However, we could also say that the understanding of the natural world is modeled on the structure of the body, insofar as the cosmos itself is conceived on a biological model. These presuppositions also display a central tenet in Chinese thought and culture: the unity of heaven, earth, and human being. This hypothesis relies heavily on *yinyang* for its rational explanation and coherence. The development of *yinyang* through many social practices including medicine, the cultivation of the human body, the arts and so on, secured a permanent and powerful place for *yinyang* in Chinese thought and culture at the same time that it broadened and systematized the meaning of *yinyang*.

Slote is not simply interested in the *yin/yang* notion, but more specifically in seeing the value of *yin*. Although he points out that Chinese does not have a term for receptivity, he maintains that, for modern purposes, *yin* is equated with receptivity, can apply to epistemology, and can construct something such as a *yinyang* epistemology. How, then, should we understand *yin* as receptivity?

To understand *yin* as a valuable and philosophical relevance to the Western concept of receptivity, we must return to the *Daodejing* to consider *yin*'s hidden meaning and the construction of the epistemic virtue of *yin*. (Though it could be argued that Slote has a biased view about Daoism.)² According to the modern Chinese intellectual Liang Qichao 梁啓超 (1873-1929), the terms *yin* and *yang* in the Shang and early Zhou dynasties were primarily descriptions of natural phenomena and did not form a philosophical system until the *Daodejing* (see Liang 1982: 347). Although there is only one usage of the term *yinyang* in the *Daodejing*, the text has a persistent orientation toward the paradoxical interdependence of opposites in the world. We read from the *Daodejing* (chapter 42): "All the myriad things *fuyin baoyang* (負陰抱陽) [carrying (embodying) *yin* and embracing *yang*]" (Moeller 2007: 103). In this, *yin* and *yang* are woven into the condition of the myriad things.

The word *fu* (負), translated here as "embod*ying*," has more than twenty meanings in the classical Chinese dictionary *Shuowen Jiezi*. One of the main meanings of *fu* is to carry or bear something on your back, not in front of you but behind you or in the background. Thus, this word *fu* in the *Daodejing* can be taken as *bei* 背 (on your back). *Fuyin* (負陰) then refers to things that are not confronted, or not seen, but still carried along—i.e. *yin*. It is carr*ying* something unseen or non-present. Later it develops and expends to the term of *ti* 體(structure). The *fuyin* always predicates a set of situations, a unique way of being with the world.

This understanding is rooted in natural phenomena. According to classical Chinese thought, everything emerges from the dark ground and hidden places. A plant comes from a seed that has been hidden in the depths of the earth. The power of growing and nourishment below the surface allows it to spring up and be displayed. In the same way that the soil provides nourishment for the seed, the mother provides a nourishing physical context that allows the child to grow and flourish, just as the female body supplies all nutrients for a fetus to survive and develop. When the male's sperm meets the female's egg, the former's function in the process of creating new life is complete. The female, however, works slowly, nourishing the fetus for nine months. *Yin* is *jing* (stillness) because it exemplifies the potency of nourishing. This *yin* ability wins *Daodejing*'s philosophical recognition and admiration. It is called "dark efficacy" (Mysterious Virtue).

Bao (抱) means to embrace, and literally refers to putting your arms around something, often in a sense of holding something valuable, as in "to *bao* your child." The myriad things embrace or wrap their arms around that which is in front of them, i.e. apparent *yang*. Like the development of *yin*, it becomes the paired term of *yong* 用 (function). The idea of *baoyang* is derived from the sun: one faces south and embraces direct sunlight. Another extension is confronting what is in front and seeing what is present (*you* 有).

The *fuyin* and *baoyang* or *tiyong* reveal awareness of two aspects of reality: the *yin* as the hidden underl*ying* structure, and the *yang* as the explicit presence in front of us. This is what Slote describes: "adult human lives need to exemplify, ideally do exemplify, a kind of balance or fusion between receptivity and rational control" (Slote 2018: 46). Although *baoyang* and *fuyin* are inseparable, the *Daodejing* argues that our natural tendency is to look more at what stands before us, which is *yang*, and to ignore *yin*. The *Daodejing* counteracts this tendency with a focus on *yin*. The *yin* should be guarded (*shou* 守) and protected (*bao* 保). One should remember to "stay at the front by keeping to the rear" (Moeller 2007: 158).

Take the case of the silent transformation, which is the very basis of our life but has not been entered into our epistemic mindset. Francois Jullien claims: "We view change but we do not perceive it. We do not perceive it because our intelligence separates, isolates and stabilizes" (Jullien 2011: 41). For example, we notice that children or plants have grown, but we do not see the actual growing; we remark that we are getting old, but do not see actual aging. These experiences illustrate that "Transformations are silent not simply due to their mode of emergence but also because they are infinitely gradual and not local but global, unlike action and thus do not differentiate themselves nor are they notice in consequences (just as everything ages within us and in the duration, we do not see ourselves becoming old" (Jullien 2011: 98).

In its broader sense, *yin* can be seen as receptivity because it concerns utilizing resources, evaluating situations, and accepting conditions. Its focal point is "stimulus and response" or "sympathetic resonance" (*ganying* 感應) among things, events, and people. Take Slote's example of a man in a burning house. The man's state of caring, or strongly felt desire, has both a *yang* and a *yin* aspect. It involves motivation to get through the door (*yang* force) but also reflects (his take on) the situation he is in (*yin* strength). He sees that he is in grave danger and that escape is only possible through the given door, and that involves his being epistemically receptive to what is going on around him; but he also is motivated to escape through that door, and the motivation is in fact inseparable from his recognition of his danger and of the circumstances that limit his ways of escaping that danger. Slote applies the *yin/yang* structure exemplified by the man in the burning house as constituting not only his situational caring/desire, but also his reason to act as he is acting, the reason that justifies him in tr*ying* to do what he is attempting to do in his circumstances.

Slote also extends *yin*/receptivity to other aspects of human moral psychology. According to him, there are both a receptive aspect and a controlling/purposeful aspect to compassion and other altruistic emotions that instantiate the *yin/yang* duality, but something similar occurs in cases of prudential rationality, in cases where someone seeks to promote or preserve their own well-being, like the case of the man in the burning house. Such *yinyang* can help us to solve some contemporary philosophical problems.

At a simplistic interpretational level or at its first encounter of *yinyang*, this *yinyang* handling might be somewhat acceptable. However at its basic core, *yin* and *yang* continuously support and consume each other, forming a changing pattern or continuum called "mutual restraint." It is neither the case that *yin* and *yang* are separate, nor that they become one; rather, *yin* and *yang* multiply each other to form a dynamic but sustainable system. Consequently, any *yin* and *yang* interaction serves as the vastly context-dependence aspect of any relationship and thinking. Thus, *yinyang* thinking cannot be truthfully described, analyzed, and evaluated independent of its contextualizing situations, including first and foremost the conditions in which they have been. We must be cautious about using *yinyang* to set apart of receptivity with rational control or suggest "a kind of serial epistemological order: with perception and memory in *yin* fashion providing the beliefs on the basis of which we in *yang* fashion generalize or theorize" (Slote 2018: 94).

3 The *Yinyang* Clusters and *Yinyang* Epistemology

With a textual and historical background knowledge of the origin of *yinyang*, we can now return to Slote. According to him: "Epistemic rationality has a *yin/yang* basis by defending the idea that the epistemic rationality of ordinary beliefs involves natural epistemic virtues like receptivity and decisiveness that together realize a *yin/yang* structure, this too then favors the idea that belief is an emotional state with a *yin/yang* structure or character" (Slote 2018: 80).

We can learn a great deal from Slote's application of the *yinyang* usage, especially his unfolding and analytic methodology. Yet there is a precautious concern or worry about whether he has reduced the *yinyang* structure to simply complementarity while defining *yang* as rationality and *yin* as receptivity. This dualistic orientation in application of *yinyang* is truly problematic. He states: "One's life will go better if it demonstrates a certain *amount or degree* of active rational control and a comparable *amount or degree* of receptivity" (Slote 2018: 66). One may ask, what is this *amount or degree* of rational control and receptivity? Further, is there a relationship between epistemic rationality and the epistemic virtue of receptivity? If we want to construct the *yinyang* epistemology, we need to go a little deeper into this *yinyang* thinking structure.

As we discussed above, the terms *yin* and *yang* gradually developed from ways of naming the sun into a complex way of thinking. *Yinyang* is not merely a term, but it also represents an underl*ying* order in an enduring thinking. At its root, this order is built on relationships and dynamic tendencies rather than on a discrete property. Another extension is confronting what is in front and seeing what is present (*you* 有). It is something that can be described using Brook Ziporyn's terms: "internal coherence, or hidden coherence, as opposed to explicitly manifest intelligibility" (Ziproyn 2011: 326). A range of classical texts demonstrates that the *yinyang* thinking is a pervasive spectrum of differences within relatedness, connection, and mutual influence. From the *yinyang* epistemic perspective, this spectrum is situated in the rhythm of interactions and mutual integration. There are six aspects of any given *yinyang* relation which we can see as *yinyang* clusters.

1. *Maodun* 矛盾: Contradiction and opposition. Although *yinyang* thinking may prompt us to think of harmony, interconnection, and wholeness, the basis of any *yinyang* distinction is difference, opposition, and contradiction. Any two given sides are connected and related, but they are also opposed in some way, like light and dark, male and female, forceful and yielding. It is the tension and difference between the two sides that allows for the dynamic energy that comes through their interactions. This aspect of *yinyang* is often described in terms of *maodun* 矛盾, which literally means "shield-spear" and originates from a story in the *Hanfeizi* 韓非子 (280–233 BCE). A person who sells shields and spears promotes his shields by sa*ying* they are so strong that nothing can penetrate them, whereas he promotes his spears by *saying* they are so sharp they can penetrate anything. Then someone then asks him what happens if one tries to use your spear to penetrate your shield? (Gu 1996: 204)

The *Hanfeizi* story raises opposites as logical contradictions. In this sense, something cannot be *yang* and *yin* (light and dark, masculine and feminine) in precisely the same way, at the same time, and in the same context. This approach to distinctions can be seen as the one of most fundamental in European philosophy. Such an approach, however, works only in the abstract. In reality, we not only find that opposites exist through interaction with and in dependence on each other, but also that the same thing can be considered to have opposite qualities depending on the context, as it is not a logical contradiction to say that one thing is small (in comparison to a mountain) but large (in comparison to an ant). In thinking about opposition and difference, Chinese thinkers concentrate much more on these latter aspects. This can apply to the dynamic connection between rational control and receptivity. It might be very difficult to separate rational control with receptivity at a real-life decision-making process.

2. *Xiangyi* 相依: Interdependence. One side of the opposition of *yinyang* cannot exist without the other. This interdependence can be seen on several different levels. On one level, it points out the interdependence of opposites as relative concepts. In labeling something as "high," one must implicitly label something else as "low." One cannot have a concept of "good" without existing a concept of "bad" (*Daodejing*, Chapter 2). According to *yinyang* thinking, however, the interdependence of opposites does not simply refer to the relativity of our concepts, but also to how things themselves exist, grow, and function. One way that this interdependence appears most clearly is through the alternation of *yin* and *yang*. The sun is the best example of *yang*—bright, warming, stimulating growth, and lending rhythm—but when the power of that *yang* is developed to its logical conclusion, it is necessary for it to be anchored, regenerated, and sustained by the force of *yin*. The sun must set. Although *yang* is the obvious, it cannot thrive without attention to *yin*. This interdependence appears in traditional Chinese medical texts, where the surge of *yangqi* 陽氣 depends on the regeneration of *yinqi* 陰氣, of the five internal organs. Without that basis, the *yinqi* of the organs, there will be no surge of *yangqi* or its extension outward.

The *Gui Guzi* 鬼谷子 (*The Master of Spirit Valley*), a classic text of the school of Zongheng縱橫 (School of Strategy) in the Warring States Period (451–221 BCE), illustrates this interdependence, using an opening and closing door as a metaphor. To be a door, it must be able to open and close as two interrelated modes; otherwise, it will be simply a wall (that does not move) or an open space (that does not close). The *Gui Guzi* gives this a cosmic significance: "Opening and closing are the way of heaven and earth. Opening and closing change and move *yinyang*, just as the four seasons open and close to transform the myriad things" (Xu 2008: 13). In this sense, rational control and receptivity should be interdependent and inter-reliant in a given situation.

3. *Huhan* 互含: Mutual inclusion. Interdependence is linked closely to mutual inclusion. If *yin* depends on *yang*, then *yang* is always implicated in *yin*; in other words, *yin* cannot be adequately characterized without also taking account of *yang*. The same is true of *yang*: it necessarily involves *yin*. Regarding things themselves, even something that is strongly *yang* can be considered *yin* in some relations, as we have seen. The constant alternation between *yin* and *yang* also entails that *yang* always holds some *yin* and *yin* holds some *yang*. In the cycle of four seasons, summer is the most *yang* of the seasons, yet it contains a *yin* force, which will begin to emerge in the summer, extend through the fall, and reach its culmination in the winter. Winter is the highest stage of *yin*, yet it unfolds a *yang* force that will attain its full momentum through spring to summer. This mutual inclusion is best captured in the famous *yinyang* symbol, which includes a small circle of *yang* within the fullest *yin* and a small circle of *yin* within the fullest *yang*.

Similarly, in the *Yijing* 易經 (*The Book of Changes*), all *yin* hexagrams have a dominant *yang* line and all *yang* hexagrams have a dominant *yin* line. This mutual inclusion has important consequences in terms of strategy because it indicates that, when one thing appears to you as present, that thing also entails opposite forces that are hidden and in motion but that have not yet appeared. In the context of rational control and receptivity one may argue that rational control must contain a degree of receptivity and any receptivity should be inclusive of rational control.

4. *Jiaogan* 交感: Interaction or resonance. Each element influences and shapes the other. If *yin* and *yang* are interdependent and mutually inclusive, then a change in one will necessarily produce a change in the other. Thus, as *yang* ebbs in the autumn, *yin* strengthens, and as *yin* declines in the spring, *yang* grows. For example, in Chinese traditional medical diagnoses, too much *yin* in the body is a sickness of *yang*, and too much *yang* in the body is a sickness of *yin*. Changes in *yin* will affect *yang*, and vice versa. This mutual resonance is crucial to *yinyang* as a strategy because it entails that one can influence any element by addressing its opposite, which in practice most often takes the form of responding to *yang* through *yin*.

The text from the Eastern Han dynasty (25–220 CE) *Taipingjing* 太平經 (*Classic of Great Peace* 31–7 BCE), also known as a valuable resource for early Daoist beliefs and practices, applies this *yinyang* resonance to oppose female infanticide. In medical treatment, *yin* and *yang* should be fostered at the same time. It is said, for example, that *yin* will not respond to the drug or acupuncture without a certain amount of *yang*. The *Lüshi Chunqiu* 呂氏春秋 (*The Annals of Lü Buwei c.* 240 BCE)[3] takes this resonance as a general principle, approached through the relationship between action and nonaction: "Not to venture out is the means by which one does venture out; not to act is the means by which one acts. This is called 'using the *Yang* to summon the *Yin* and using the *Yin* to summon the *yang*'" (Knoblock and Riegel 2000: 410). Slote's discussion of emotions exhibits an interesting resonance between rational control and receptivity.

5. *Hubu* 互補: Complementary or mutual support. Each side of *yinyang* supplies what the other lacks. Given that *yin* and *yang* are different but interdependent, properly dealing with a situation often requires supplementing one with the other, which is a way of achieving the appropriate balance between the two. For example, the *Zhouli* 周禮 (*The Rites of Zhou*, 5–221 BCE) describes the craft of making a wheel:

> The way of making the hub of wheel must be measured according to *yinyang*. *Yang* is densely grained and thus is strong; *yin* is loosely grained and thus is soft. Therefore, one uses fire to nourish its *yin*, making it even with its *yang*. Thus, even if the wheel is worn, it will not lose its round form.
>
> Wang 1972: 424

This passage addresses the difficulty of creating a wheel that is firm but made of materials that are soft enough to bend into a circle. Here, softness and hardness complement and support each other. This complementarity is different from the submission of one to the other, because both sides stand on equal ground in performing different roles. Such rational control and receptivity should be in a pair of mutual support.

6. *Zhuanhua* 轉化: Change and transformation. One side of *yinyang* becomes the other in an endless cycle. *Yinyang* thinking is fundamentally dynamic and centers on change. In nature, there is decline, deficiency, decrease, and demise, as well as flourishing, surplus, increase, and reproduction. In the human world, life is filled with trouble, failure, exhaustion, and insufficiency, as well as fullness, fruition, mastery, and success. Considering these various states of being, one can derive that change is perpetual, never-ending. Reversal (*fan* 反) is a constant theme in Chinese thought, especially in the *Daodejing*. It invokes the image of a circle, or more precisely, a spiral movement that forever continues in a ring formation.

The *He Guanzi* 鶡冠子 (*Pheasant Cape Master*), a text most likely from the Warring States Period (475–221 BCE), gives an influential characterization of this movement: "Beautiful and ugly adorn each other: this is called returning to the full cycle. Things develop to their extremes and then reverse. This is called circular flowing" (X. Wang 1936: 9).[4] The character translated as flowing, *liu* 流, refers most literally to the flowing of water, and the character itself contains the image of water on the left. The term for circular or ring is *huan*環. We might thus also translate the phrase as "flowing circulation."

The *Huangdi Neijing* often identifies *yinyang* interplay as a cycle (*huan*) without beginning or end: "*Yinyang* are mutually connected, like a cycle without beginning. Thus, one knows that attack and defense always follow each other." Another passage says: "*Yinyang* are interlocking like a cycle without limit, *yinyang* follow each other and internal and external interlock each other like a cycle without limit" (Niu 1993: 59).

The discussions above help us see now the ambiguity and complexity in sa*ying* that two things "are like *yin* and *yang*." Everything is bound up in a plurality of relationships at the same time, related both to multiple things and to the same thing in multiple ways (Wang 2012).

When we apply this *yinyang* thinking to Slote's work, we might ask whether rational control and receptivity can change or transform toward each other? In other words, will rational control and receptivity change a place in time?

The *yinyang* thinking is a highly interpretive process. It presupposes knowledge of the *yinyang* scheme or a pattern. If we see a *yang*, we cannot be ignorant all those *yin*-like things, since they have been always there, both in time and space. For example, if we discuss the *yang*-rationality then we must pay the same attention to *yin*-receptivity. *Yinyang* claims must be taken as a point of reference that is defined by location (*wei* 位) and time (*shi* 時). This *yinyang* structure accentuates these complex, multidimensional frameworks to explore the wide array of practices that constitute *yinyang* understanding. The defense of this pluralistic picture of *yinyang* thought illuminates the diversity and variety within the paradigm itself, a diversity that has enabled *yinyang* to serve so many different functions throughout various aspects of Chinese thought and culture.

These relations are not distinct but reflect the actual complexity of life and nature. This is how fortune-tellers can manufacture your life in the image or patterns of this gestalt. By means of a combination or a manipulation of your information, one can build one's life into a pattern of perceptual cognitive activity. The *yinyang*-knower locates himself or herself within this perceptual world. It is not so much that we build knowledge based on what we objectively perceive, but that we perceive according to what we know.

Slote has made a bold claim that *yin/yang* offers a single form of justification within ethics, epistemology, and the philosophy of mind.

> *Yin/yang* epistemologist can account for all the basic forms of epistemological justification and can extend his or her same categories to justify claims in ethics as well. So *yin/yang* philosophy valuably balances values we intuitively accept and applies them in unif*ying* way across (traditionally) different fields of philosophy—something that other philosophical approaches don't even attempt to do.
>
> Slote 2018: 188

However, we do want to question whether *yin*-receptivity and *yang*-rational control be discernable through the *yinyang clusters*, and more specifically in the six *yinyang* relationships. Can the *yinyang* justification be verified through these *yinyang* clusters due to the complexity of *yinyang* itself? For example, Slote maintains: "Belief and desire are the *yin* and *yang* of the mind. The mind as functional contains and has to contain *yin* belief and *yang* desire in necessary relation to one another and to that extent constitutes or is constituted by a *yin/yang* complementarity of belief and desire" (Slote 2018: 189). It seems to be a reasonable expectation from above *yinyang* clusters discussion that the relationship between *yin*-belief and *yang*-desire should go beyond the single dimension of complementarity to a cluster of mutual dependence, mutual containment, and mutual transformation. In other words, "the philosopher's stone" using Slote's expression, should entail a more complicated element. The more interesting inquiry might be whether the philosophical and epistemological justification can be multidimensional? Otherwise we will be facing the question of whose *yinyang* we are talking about: Slote's version, or that practiced in Chinese thought and culture? Should we eschew the use of *yinyang* as an afterthought or merely as "decoration" for one's own purpose?

4 Conclusion

There is no doubt that the notion of *yinyang* has played a significant role and central function in Chinese thought and culture for thousands of years. This well-established theory also traveled around world long before Western thinkers picked up on it. Hegel (1770–1831) "took advantage of non-European culture to establish a Eurocentric system of philosophy. The non-European components, especially those from Chinese *yin-yang* philosophy, were used not only in his lectures on the history of philosophy, the philosophy of world history, aesthetics and religious philosophy but also in his philosophical masterpieces like the great Logic and the Less Logic" (Ma 2016:10). It is a known fact that Hegel learned *Dao* from Jean-Pierre Abel-Remusat (1788–1832), a French sinologist.[5] This historical fact shows that human life is composed of encounters, and the events caused by them constitute the part of understanding and knowing. The question of how the cross-fertilization of ideas and concepts are influenced and shaped by each other remains a contested ground. There are many inescapable cultural, social and historical differences. Metaphysical and value commitments, somatic and conceptual habits, and culturally distinctive notions of social roles and persons are active in a fundamental way, creating frameworks through which we reason and live.

Let's take a case in comparison of *yinyang* theory with the Hegelian thesis–antithesis–synthesis method. At first glance, they seem to share some interesting aspects of dialectic movement. However, *yinyang* focused mainly on unraveling world's connectivity problem while the Hegelian dialectic method excelled at solving the problem of human consciousness. *Yinyang* is built on the structures of relationships and dynamic tendencies rather than on the individual characteristics of things or beings. For Hegel, the thesis and anti-thesis are not necessarily as intrinsically connected as the *yin* and *yang* connection. They can be independent; one can exist without other. The third moment of the dialectic, the "determinate negation," does not stand only in reference to the first two moments. The third moment has a wholeness that frees it from the overly simplistic polarity of the lower two moments. Once the determinate negation is reached, the lower two levels vanish beneath it.

Hegel's dialectic is progressive; the movement does not imply a return to its previous oppositions. This is unlike *yinyang* clusters, which see the movement going in both directions at the same time. From a *yinyang* perspective, the dialectical terms make sense only in relation to one another (e.g., *yin* is nonsense without *yang*), whereas for Hegel, dialectical terms seek lined forwarding. There is no move back and forth between opposed terms. It is only moving upwards and toward a one-way unity.

In Slote's usage of *yinyang* notion, we have indicated that he rips away the multiple meanings of *yinyang* clusters and reduces them into a single element. Charles Taylor has articulated a concept of "the holism of meaning." According to him: "A word only has meaning within a lexicon and a context of language practices, which are ultimately embedded in a form of life" (Taylor 2016: 17). The holism of meaning amounts to that individual words can only be words within the context of an articulated language. Language is not something which could be built up one word at a time. Mature linguistic capacity is not built up in this way, and never could be: each word supposes a whole of language to it its full force as a word (Taylor 2015: 18). This "holism of meaning" has even more relevance to the Chinese language itself. Like other Chinese characters, *yinyang* in Chinese is a symbolic image which contains meaning (*yi* 义), figure (*xiang* 象), and implications (*yi* 意). It has deeply rooted linguistic background and dimension yet is different than an atomism of meaning. Its relationships cannot be grasped through conceptual terms, instead it requires a participations, something more like poetry or music.

The coherence of the notion of *yinyang*, along with other philosophical terms that have their beginnings in classical China, can be understood in terms of the conceptual framework of focus and field. Understood within this framework, the notion of *yinyang* is a wide variety of context-dependent meanings. This field of meanings is constituted of a plurality of clusters of meanings that focus the field of meaning from a particular and finite perspective. Furthermore, these clusters of meanings are constantly transacting and mutually transforming one anothe; as a result, the field itself is constantly transforming. In light of this, the notion of *yinyang* must be understood in terms of process, plurality, and relations in contrast to permanence, singularity, and essence. In Taylor's view: "Language can be compared to immense web, in which every parts stands in a more or less clearly recognizable connection with others and all with the whole" (Taylor 2015: 20). If language is seen as a web, then any term gets its meaning only in the field of its contrast and connections.

It is worthy of notice that the purpose of the above inquiry is to highlight the fact that *yinyang* is a semantically pluralistic notion that transforms its meaning and logic according to the context in which it operates. Thus, it is most properly understood by investigating it within the diverse contexts in which it is used and developed. The discussions of *yinyang* clusters have also performed a useful heuristic function, that its characteristics cannot exhaust the vast and rich meanings and logics of the notion. Furthermore, what is valuable about investigating the notion of *yinyang* clusters is that we are inevitably led to learn about the various contexts in which it is embedded due to the intrinsic contextual nature of the notion. Thus, an investigation of *yinyang* clusters requires us to expand our horizons and to broaden our perspective, rather than spiral down into a narrow tunnel of isolated inquiry.

Let's take the examples of parent–children, teacher–student, or employer–employee relationships to illustrate the *yinyang* intrinsic interaction. There is structure or movement within each of these relationships; nonetheless, parents should use their power to empower their children, teachers should empower their students, and employers should empower their employees. These are complex dynamic processes in constant flux. Sometimes the more dominant side of these relationships must give up some of their power-as-dominance in order to empower the other: parents must let children create their own identity, teachers must let students ask questions, and employers must give employees freedom. The transformative relationship is also seen as "shifting" or "revisable": children will become stronger than their ageing parents, and students may well surpass their accomplished teachers. Consequently, any interaction is a vastly context-dependent aspect of human relationships.

I would like to end this essay by stating an intellectual's mission as articulated by Sima Qian (145–87 BCE), a great historian in Chinese history, "researching changes of heaven and human being; penetrating the history of past and present; establishing your own school of thought." According to him, in order to establish one's own teaching or theory, we must learn a broader context (in a religious and earthly realm) and be well versed in the past and present history of ideas. Only under these conditions can we attempt to forge our own ideas and perspectives.

Notes

1 James Legge translated the word *yinyang* as "the light and the shade" (Legge 1994: 488).
2 Slote 2018: 102: "I think Daoism gives us an inadequate picture of successful adult living."
3 The *Lüshi Chunqiu*, compiled around 240 BCE, is the one of the great monuments of Chinese thinking. As Knoblock and Riegel put it, it is: "a philosophical manual

for the universal rule of the coming dynasty.... It belongs in the first rank of classical Chinese philosophy" (Knoblock and Riegel 2000: vii–viii).
4 The statement of *wuji zhefa* 物極則反, "a thing will reverse after developing to its extremes," has become a popular idiom in contemporary China. There is a term in contemporary Western science called "self-organized criticality," which refers to the tendency of large dissipative systems to drive themselves to a critical state, with a wide range of length and time scales. The idea provides a unifying concept for large-scale behavior in systems with many degrees of freedom. It has been looked for in such diverse areas as earthquake structure, economics, and biological evolution. It is also seen as "regression toward means."
5 Alexander Statman has done substantial research on this topic.

References

Ames, Roger (2018), *Theorizing Persons for Confucian Role Ethics: A Good Place to Start*.
Jullien, François (2011), *Silent Transformation*. Seagull Books.
Gu, Guangqi 顧廣圻 (1996), *Commentary on Hanfeizi* 韓非子, Shanghai: Shanghai Guji Press.
Knoblock, J. and J. Riegel (2000), *The Annals of Lü Buwei: A Complete Translation and Study*, Stanford: Stanford University Press.
Legge, James, trans. (1994), *The Chinese Classics*, vol. 4. Taipei: SMC Publishing Inc.
Liang, Qichao 梁啓超 (1982), "The Origin of *Yinyang* and Wuxing 陰陽五行說之來歷," in Gu Jiegang, ed., *The Debate on Ancient History* 古史辨, vol. 5. Shanghai: Shanghai Guji Press.
Ma, John Z. G. (2016), "Comparison between Hegel's Being-Nothing-Becoming and I-Ching's Yin-Yang-I (Change)," *Asian Research Journal of Arts & Social Sciences* 1 (6): 1–15.
Moeller, Hans-Georg (2007), *Daodejing*, translated with illuminating explanation. Open Court.
Needham, Joseph (1954), *Science and Civilisation in China*, vol. 2. Cambridge: Cambridge University Press.
Niu, Bingzhan 牛兵占, ed. (1993), *Huangdi Neijing* 黃帝內經. Shijiazhuang: Hebei Science and Technology Press.
Slote, Michael (2018), *The Philosophy of Yin and Yang* 阴阳的哲学, Beijing: The Commercial Press.
Taylor, Charles (2016), *The Language Animal: The Full Shape of the Human Linguistic Capacity*, Cambridge: Harvard University Press.
Unschuld, Paul (2010), *Medicine in China: A History of Ideas*, 25th edition, Berkeley: University of California Press.
Wang, Robin (2012), *Yinyang: The Way of Heaven and Earth in Chinese Thought and Culture*, Cambridge: Cambridge University Press.
Wang, Yunwu 王雲五, ed. (1972), *New Commentary and Translation of The Ritual of Zhou* 周禮今注今譯, Taipei: Taiwan Commercial Press.
Wang, Xinzhan 王心湛, ed. (1936), *Collection and Interpretation of He Guanzi*, 鶡冠子集解, Shanghai: Guangyi Press.

Xu, Fuhong 許富宏, (2008), *Collected Commentaries on Master of Spirit Valley* 鬼谷子集釋, Beijing: Chinese Press.

Ziporyan, Brook (2011), *Ironies of Oneness and Difference: Coherence in Early Chinese Thought: A Prolegomena to the Study of Li*, Albany: SUNY Press.

Zhou, Zhenfu 周振甫 (2002), *Commentary on The Book of Odes* 詩經, Beijing: Chinese Press.

8

Empathy, Meaning, and Approval in the *Mencius* and Michael Slote

R. A. H. King
Institute of Philosophy, University of Berne

1 Introduction

A philosopher's reading of early Chinese texts is a perilous enterprise which assumes some kind of answer to many questions; for example, what business is it of the philosopher in particular to read these texts? After all, philosophers read many kinds of texts that need not be philosophical, and Michael Slote's work is grounded in psychology, sociology, linguistics, and of course the history of what is now called philosophy. Of course, the history of philosophy is not always philosophy. Furthermore, we are confronted with many interpretative decisions, choices, and quicksands when turning back to early China. Much difficulty is caused simply by translation; this may seem a triviality, but it must be borne in mind even by those used to turning these texts into modern languages; perhaps, especially by those who do this as a matter of course. And there is always also the question of the relation of the language used to the conceptual apparatus at work behinds the scenes. A case in point for the present enquiry is "empathy". This is a term of art, and terms of art are, like anything artificial, useful even if they tend to reflect the preoccupations of the maker.[1] It is remarkable that "empathy" is a term of art, supposing it to be central to our deepest concerns relating to others. Insofar as it only relates to others, and insofar as ethics is a matter of leading lives, *tout court*, empathy cannot be the basis for all ethics. As a term of art, it has one part of its history in Hume's notion of sympathy, which is a passion in his marvelously simple taxonomy of the contents of our minds, and hence stands in contrast to reason. And what he means by "reason" is constrained by Newtonian science, mathematics, and logic. Thus passion, and so sympathy, are contrastive concepts to reason; indeed, if one takes his talk of vivacity at face value, in part distinguished merely by being more or less vivid, as well as by being a representation or not. And whatever one may think of expressions for empathy in early Chinese, to which we will turn shortly, there are only rough analogues of science, maths and logic, at best. This leaves one wondering whether any traction is to be had for a comparison between pre-Qin and Enlightenment ethics.

Philosophers turn to the past for many reasons, for authority, for a treasury of arguments and concepts which may now enjoy a revival, to name some of the more reputable reasons. In each case, one may well wonder how essential the reference to past masters may be. My own interests, however, make it unavoidable to turn to the early texts in detail, to pursue the mapping of their concepts onto ours; which is why I welcome this opportunity to ponder Michael Slote's rich philosophical theory and its relations to the *Mencius*. The first point one must make is that the speaker in the *Mencius*, the statesman and counselor Meng Ke from the end of the fourth century BCE, thinks that his debating is necessary, to get the Mohist and Yangist teaching out of the way, that is: to prevent this being the form of leadership that takes hold in the court (3b14: references of this form are to the *Mencius*, translations are James Legge's). The reason against these ways of thinking is that they lead to famine, on the one hand, and on the other that they lead to neglect of roles and their correct fulfilment, "preventing 仁 *ren* benevolence and 義 *yi* righteousness (i.e. justice)."

In the competitive situation in which the 士 *shi*, the lowest rank eligible for administrative and magisterial duties, worked, talk has a practical purpose relative to the powerful monarchs officials, and their competitors, but also their own followers, who are the addressees. Meng Ke, as a *shi*, is of course someone with an official career. This background is fundamentally different from that of contemporary academic philosophers; the status of theory, and its relation to practice are very different. The point of this remark is that when Mencius pushes empathy, whatever the relation between his terms and ours, he is doing something other than we are when we construct a theory of action, and even virtue, which in some way depends on empathy. Above all, he is confronted with incompetent, thoughtless and cruel rulers, and he is constrained to work against the inveterate tendency of things to go very wrong.

The *Mencius* is concerned with kinds of humans, specifically, kinds of administrators and rulers. If they are to fulfil their roles well, they have to be good at it, in other words they have to have virtue in some sense. Virtue requires both action and feeling. Empathy is an element in virtue which, perhaps, fulfils several functions: as a) a motive of action; b) providing understanding of others; c) and the understanding of practical concepts. Finally, in virtue there has to be stability. The long term is what counts, in the long term; and pre-Qin thinkers have a long view of human life, and this requires a certain stability in agents. This is something that many early Chinese texts agonize about, also with reference to the speaker's own life. Yet there is an oddity about empathy and myself: I cannot have empathy with myself, and practical thought also has to do with me leading my life, in view of the good within the many roles I fulfil. The topic of self-cultivation, as it is called in the literature, 修身 *xiushen*, is an important one, and one that Michael Slote has also addressed, but it is something I shall leave aside here. We are not dealing with the whole of ethics here, only where one agent faces another. Questions thus arise as to how our concern for others is built into a good life; there is here an assumption that the good of others cannot be my good, *pace* Joseph Butler.

2 Baptism, Definition, and Examples

We use general terms, and are able to subsume instances under them. Now, this is a chapter in practical philosophy, not the philosophy of language. Knowing how to act and understanding the language of action are two different skills but ones that are closely intertwined. After all, we would like to understand the kinds of action we should perform, the kinds of people around us. In this section, I wish to consider briefly different approaches to terms, within practical philosophy, following Michael Slote's method in *Moral Sentimentalism*, then move onto the term "empathy."

Introducing his term "empathy," Michael Slote uses an example (whether fictitious or not) of a prominent leader saying "I feel your pain." This attitude towards others' feelings, rather than the act of putting oneself in someone's shoes, is what is to be understood by "empathy". On the one hand, there are elements of stipulation here, for we are asked to go along with a decision. On the other, there are elements of referring to a situation we are presumed to be familiar with. Thus, we have at least some notion of what empathy is. Whatever the history of empathy, it appears to have gained currency in ethical contexts. Michael Slote emphasized this everyday language aspect of the term; and my son Kilian tells me that it is empathy when his contemporaries say one to another "I feel you." Great as the respect is that I have for the way we speak, and its importance in making sure we do not talk nonsense, as philosophers very often do, it is perhaps nonetheless worthwhile to note that current use of a term hardly earns it a permanent place in ethical vocabulary. For example, the work that has been done on non-human animals and empathy would tend to show that there is something there, assuming for the moment that "empathy" there means what Slote means by the term.

When it comes to action in everyday life, we do understand terms connected with acting, and with people's abilities to act, for example, bravely or cruelly. We might distinguish three ways in which the meaning of these terms is determined, namely, baptism, definition, and examples. These three methods then lay the basis for our knowledge of the meaning of these terms, in other words for our understanding of them. In turn, these methods will decide how assertions about practical matters, and hence knowledge of practical matters relates to the terms. Among these terms are those which *we* might class as emotional, and among these, some relate to our knowledge of the emotional states of others; roughly, states that fit the question: how do you feel about that? These terms have some obvious peculiarities; they relate to, may be used of, others and myself. They are contrasted in some way with knowledge terms. They do not refer to actions, but may be intimately related to them. Clearly, here, I am homing in on "empathy".

Let us begin with baptism, as a way of approaching the meaning of general terms. Michael Slote suggests that "moral" terms may be treated on a par with natural kind terms, in some ways as suggested by Saul Kripke in his *Naming and Necessity*. We baptize something as, for example, water, and from this baptism then follow necessary features, ones that belong to water in all possible conditions. This procedure appears to operate in abstraction from all actual (past) use, under the pretence that such terms do not exist, just as a child before christening answers to no name. But there are two other ways for reflective use of terms, whether natural kind terms or not, to be made manageable; a rather different project from that of *Naming and Necessity*. One is that we define the terms. This is a method sometimes associated with a Socratic approach to enquiries. Another approach is that one takes an example of the thing in question. Thus Aristotle writes when tackling *phronêsis*, practical wisdom: "We should look at those called *phronimoi*, practically wise, in order to determine what *phronêsis* is" (Nic.Eth. VI 5). I wish to suggest that in the *Mencius*, terms are fixed on the basis of examples. In this way, they are brought to the attention of interlocutors. This procedure is deeply embedded in the procedure of the *Mencius*. For one important claim is that we have in us the beginnings of stable forms of behavior, and that part of the persuasion undertaken by Meng Ke in the stories about him is to confront his interlocutors with these beginnings.

3 A Term for Empathy in the *Mencius*, Buren 不忍?

"*Ren* 仁" is often translated as "benevolence" and is typically seen as a virtue, perhaps even the founding or grounding virtue in the *Mencius* (e.g. Bryan Van Norden 2007). This may be the principal reason for thinking the *Mencius* as scooping Hutcheson, Hume, and Smith on the moral sense, or on the claim that goodness makes itself felt rather than known to us. In other words, translating *ren* as "benevolence" suggests that the *Mencius* is concerned with empathy. Because we feel for others, and naturally act in accordance with this feeling, we are well disposed to the good of others. However, I will concentrate here on another term, "not bearing the suffering of others," not in itself a virtue, but a prelude, and also a criterion for good forms of behavior. The term "不忍" *buren*,[2] not being able to bear something, has a variety of meanings, which we will now look at very briefly. First off, it has the simple meaning of being highly adverse to something, for example different kinds of food: "Mencius said, 'Zeng Xi was fond of sheep-dates, and his son, the philosopher Zeng, could not bear (*buren*) to eat sheep-dates.' Gong Sun Chou asked, saying, 'Which is best, minced meat and broiled meat, or sheep-dates?'" (*Mencius* 7b82)

"*Ren* 忍," the positive term on its own, can also have a causative meaning, "make something or something able to endure," or "harden," as Legge has it:

> Thus, when Heaven is about to confer a great office on any man, it first exercises his mind with suffering, and his sinews and bones with toil. It exposes his body to hunger, and subjects him to extreme poverty. It confounds his undertakings. By all these methods it stimulates his mind, hardens (*ren*) his nature, and supplies his incompetencies.
>
> *Mencius* 6b35

But the phrase may also have the meaning, if not in the *Mencius*, "bear to do something improper": "Confucius said of the head of the Ji family, who had eight rows of pantomimes in his area, 'If he can bear to do this, what may he not bear to do?'" (*Lunyu* 3.1)

The point in citing this material is to dispel the impression that there is a specific vocabulary for "moral feelings." Some aversions are important, some less so, from food to matters of ritual propriety. However, the term also plays a very special role in the *Mencius* in diagnosing the way in which humans may come at good government: "things you cannot endure" are to be found in all humans, and these things, especially, the suffering of others, that is, may be "extended" into *ren* 仁 benevolence. Here, *buren* 不忍 "what you cannot endure," is interpreted as not wanting to hurt others:

> Mencius said, 'All men have some things which they cannot bear; extend that feeling to what they can bear, and benevolence will be the result. All men have some things which they will not do; extend that feeling to the things which they do, and righteousness will be the result. If a man can give full development to the feeling which makes him shrink from injuring others, his benevolence will be more than can be called into practice. If he can give full development to the feeling which refuses to break through, or jump over, a wall, his righteousness will be more than can be called into practice …
>
> *Mencius* 7b77

That "government that does not bear the suffering of others" serves as a measure, to wit for good government:

> When they (the sages) had used their power of hearing to the utmost, they called in the pitch-tubes to their aid to determine the five notes – the use of those tubes is inexhaustible. When they had exerted to the utmost the thoughts of their hearts, they called in to their aid a government that could not endure to witness the sufferings of men – and their benevolence overspread the kingdom.
>
> *Mencius* 4a1

One famous story in the *Mencius* concerns the way in which a powerful king is persuaded to admit to having pity with an ox about to be slaughtered. He hears the oxen's cries "like an innocent human being led to the place of execution":

Mencius said "I heard the following incident from Hu He: 'The king,' said he, 'was sitting aloft in the hall, when a man appeared, leading an ox past the lower part of it. The king saw him, and asked, Where is the ox going? The man replied, We are going to consecrate a bell with its blood. The king said, Let it go. I cannot bear its frightened appearance, as if it were an innocent person going to the place of death. The man answered, Shall we then omit the consecration of the bell? The king said, How can that be omitted? Change it for a sheep.' I do not know whether this incident really occurred."

Mencius 1a7

The question at issue is whether or not the king has the capacity to protect the people (*baomin* 保民), and so act as a proper king (*wang* 王). The point of the story, on one reading, is that the king is forced to admit having compassion for the ox, and hence to his having the stuff in him to protect the people: all that is needed is the compassion for the ox. The king says: "I cannot bear its shivering and trembling with fear." How are we to see this "inability to bear the suffering of others"? First, there is no sign that it is an active process. It just happens to the king; to such an extent that he seems unaware of some aspects of the event, for example, its relevance to ruling. There is a cognitive element in this reaction: he reacts to what he hears; the lowing of the ox, its affective state, and what is about to happen to it. The way he *understands* the lowing is interesting, namely "like an innocent man being led to the place of execution," for this suggests the possibility that strictly he is not being compassionate toward the ox—he is compassionate only because it puts him in mind of undeserved human suffering. I will not pursue this line of thought here, and assume that the king's reaction really is to the ox as a sentient being. And there is a motivational aspect to this reaction: hearing the ox moves him to action. The reason this reaction is important is the king's role: he is a king and much depends on the way he fills his role. In turn, Meng Ke is fulfilling a role towards the king—a potential advisor, indeed, minister. The commoners say that the king is just being mean, begrudging the expense of an ox, only using a sheep. But Meng Ke turns the story positively, putting pressure on the king to admit to having pity on the beast:

> "There is no harm in their saying so," said Mencius. "Your conduct was an artifice of benevolence. You saw the ox, and had not seen the sheep. So is the superior man affected towards animals, that, having seen them alive, he cannot bear to see them die; having heard their dying cries, he cannot bear to eat their flesh. Therefore, he keeps away from his slaughter-house and cook-room."
>
> *Mencius* 1a7

Here we have a major problem with pity: surely the sheep deserves just as much our pity as does the ox. It may be true that we are moved more by the ox, seeing it. But this feeling does not track the deserts of the case. A proper response to suffering is not to ensure we do not notice it. Here, emotion and obligation come apart. The feeling is stuck in the here and now, whereas obligation is not. This problem becomes even more acute when Meng Ke turns the king's pity toward the business of ruling. First of all, he sees it in terms of a comparison with the capacity to lift things and see things: someone who says he can lift a heavy load should not deny he can lift a feather, someone who can see a hair cannot deny seeing a load of logs. The king admits this. There are knotty problems here with the concept of capacity, and how this applies to compassion and virtue. For virtue is not a mere capacity. Let us return to the story. Mencius said:

> Now here is kindness sufficient to reach to animals, and no benefits are extended from it to the people. How is this? Is an exception to be made here? The truth is, the feather is not lifted , because strength is not used; the waggon-load of firewood is not seen, because the eyesight is not used; and the people are not loved and protected, because kindness is not employed. Therefore your Majesty's not exercising the royal sway, is because you do not do it, not because you are not able to do it.
>
> <div align="right"><i>Mencius</i> 1a7</div>

So the king's kindness (*en* 恩) touches animals, but not the people, simply because he does not do it, not because he cannot do it. His capacity to do it has been proven by his reaction to the ox; presumably this is a greater sign of kindness, a greater sensitivity to suffering than being sensitive to humans' suffering. And yet this sensitivity has not been active in the case of the humans, has not motivated the king to "protect the people".

What the king is then concerned with is the difference between being able to do something and doing it; a point again illustrated by obvious inabilities of humans, jumping over the sea with a mountain under the arm, and obvious abilities, breaking a twig when ordered to do so. Once again, there are questions here about the kinds of capacities involved in action. On the one hand, being able to do something, and wanting to do it are clearly different things; on the other, the crucial thing about a virtue is the reliable presence of motivation, not the bare capacity to do something ("able to break a twig on command"). Is the king's sensitivity a virtue? Surely it is only the first step towards a virtue, a capacity we all have, perhaps, and which only needs to be developed to be applied to all. Meng Ke describes the extension of the treatment of others on the basis of this pity:

> Treat with the reverence due to age the elders in your own family, so that the elders in the families of others shall be similarly treated; treat with the kindness due to youth the young in your own family, so that the young in the families of others shall be similarly treated – do this, and the kingdom may be made to go round in your palm.
>
> <div align="right"><i>Mencius</i> 1a7</div>

Order in the "world," "what is under the sky" (Legge: "kingdom"), depends on roles being fulfilled, firstly within one's clan or family, and then extending this to all.

In sum, "what one cannot bear" would appear to be closely related to aspects of the concept of empathy. It refers to a capacity relative to others capable of suffering, but also to the actualisation of this capacity; it may finally develop into a fixed disposition, *ren* benevolence. Admittedly, the *Mencius* is more interested in the scope of *ren* and the inability to bear suffering, not their relative fixity.

4 Establishing the Meaning of "a Heart that Does not Bear the Suffering of Others"

The topic of basic feelings, as we might say, and their development into settled forms of behavior is the subject of another well-known text in the *Mencius*. This text also serves as a foil to examine the idea that the meanings of practical terms, "moral" ones, if you will, point to, or even are grounded in empathy:

> All men have a mind which cannot bear to see the sufferings of others. The ancient kings had this commiserating mind, and they, as a matter of course, had likewise a commiserating government. When with a commiserating mind was practised a commiserating government, to rule the kingdom was as easy a matter as to make anything go round in the palm. When I say that all men have a mind which cannot bear to see the sufferings of others, my meaning may be illustrated thus: even now-a-days, if men suddenly see a child about to fall into a well, they will without exception experience a feeling of alarm and distress.
>
> *Mencius* 2a6

Can one be moved by an imaginary example? Literature suggests that we can be; but there are distinctions in the ways we may be moved. The logical point that is important here is that we are not dependent on actual cases for having compassion on someone. Just imagine it and you will see what you are made of. Thus this example contrasts with that of the sheep and the ox in 1a7 above; for there, absent sufferers arouse no pity. But what the story shows is the *meaning* of not being able to bear the suffering of others: what it means not to be cruel.[3] But the way this meaning is fixed is not a baptism. Mencius does not say: let us call this empathy with suffering! He says: But think of this case, which is what we call pity.

Mencius considers this possession to be like that of our limbs. This comparison raises the question, perhaps, of the naturalism of our practical tendencies: we naturally tend to have compassion with a child about to fall into the well. We should be wary, however, of assuming an oversimplified naturalistic reading of the passage. For there is also a traditional line of interpretation of this passage which has it that the child is the world, and those affected by it are *ren* 人 (translated by Legge as "men"), in the sense of nobles: it then fits with a role based ethic, where anyone without this heart fails to meet the criteria for being a *ren* 人 in this sense.

Buren, the inability to bear is (a) a capacity that people have to react to the suffering of others; (b) on this basis, i.e. embedding the activation of this disposition in more complicated behavior, we are motivated to very wide ranging social activity; (c) *buren* takes in the situation of the other human; however, it is not clear if the agent is affected *exactly* as the sufferer is. Thus it may not count as empathy in Slote's sense. The important point is that *buren* is a form of awareness. Thus, a cognitive element is involved, whether presupposed by the emotion or presupposing the emotion.

5 What Is Empathy?

If empathy is to be developed into a reliable disposition, there has to be recognition of like cases, by responding to them emotionally, and seeing the like cases requires a form of understanding, perhaps even reasoning in difficult cases. This understanding may of course be embedded in, and made reliable by, emotion (not cognitively reliable, but motivationally).[4]

My suggestion is that the Mencian use of *buren* has interesting similarities with empathy in this sense.[5] But we have seen that it is cognitively loaded: it has content.

Following on from empathy, we have approval and disapproval—a positive attitude to something, in serious cases, the well-being of someone or something else: "empathy helps to create or constitute (something like) moral approval and disapproval" (Slote 2010: 27). This is the first function of empathy. Does this imply that empathy itself is moral or not? If empathy is not moral, how can it make something else moral? And if it is already moral, then why? Perhaps, the position is quite simply: this is what "moral" means: "So a recognition or awareness of (what can be described as) empathy is also part and parcel of, or a priori to, our understanding of morality" (Slote 2010: 61).

But there is a difference here: does empathy constitute our understanding of morality, or is it prior to it? (I take it that a priority here is that priority relating to knowledge, and not the order of coming to be.) For if empathy constitutes understanding, then one might want to argue that it is necessarily a form of cognition. If it is merely a priori to our understanding, then it might be a non-cognitive foundation for morality, in a much more Humean spirit. Approval is, apparently, a quasi-physiological change, almost Aristotelian in its simplicity: "Approval is empathic warming, an agent's warming empathically to others approval: we empathically warm to empathic agential warmth toward others and that approval consists in our having such a reaction" (Slote 2010: 35). However, I would wish to argue that approval requires a proposition to be positive about: you can only say "yes" to a proposition. For Slote, approval or disapproval are prior to moral judgment. And in the *Mencius*, the sense of approval and disapproval (saying "yes" and "no") is the beginning of knowledge. While this may be knowledge how, it still has some propositional content, how an agent does something.

As to the second function of empathy: empathy moves, it provides a motive. This would appear to be a push-me pull-you motive, a cause of action, rather than grounds for action: "empathy is a motivating psychological mechanism that constitutes a key element both in ordinary moral motivation and in the making and understanding of moral claims" (Slote 2010: 5) The two further functions of empathy are to enable us to make and understand moral claims. I take it that both of these in fact are forms of approval and disapproval.

Finally, empathy serves as a criterion of moral evaluation: "empathy and the notion of empathic caring for or about others in fact offer us a plausible criterion of moral evaluation" (Slote 2010: 21).

These functions are of course related: our awareness of the well-being, or ill-being, of someone is the touchstone for saying yes or no to a course of action, like sending the ox to slaughter. Saying "yes" to an action may motivate. And this action is then evaluable. Action is then moral, i.e. good, (or right?) when empathy is a motive in that action.

What about obligation here? Are we obligated by empathy to do something? This might be one reading of the *Mencius* 2a6: we feel an obligation to help the child. But to begin with, the mere presence of the motive is at issue. If the persuader is to catch all humans in his net, then the bar has to be set very low, the merest twitch of commiseration is all that is needed. But this twitch is far from complete virtue.

> In other words, the same empathy that leads us to certain preferences or choices as agents also governs our empathic reactions of chill and warmth as spectators or contemplators of what (other) agents do. And this is not so surprising when one considers that for an attitude to be experienced as warm, it has to resemble ordinary physical warmth at least to the extent of affecting what is (metaphorically) near more strongly than what is (metaphorically) distant.
>
> Slote 2010: 62

Empathy produces obligations. The degree of suffering we have empathy with produces a corresponding degree of obligation, and the degree of suffering we have empathy with produces a degree of obligation: the greater the empathy, the greater the obligation. In fact, the *Mencius* stresses the need to extend what one cannot bear to others. Rather than resting with partiality, the *Mencius* utilizes partisan feelings, viz. those to our nearest and dearest. The king is to extend them either to all, or to all within the four seas. We have already seen this in 7b77, above. This has an analogue in the obligation to care for others on the basis of empathy:

And:

> The Ethics of Care and Empathy: moral goodness consists or is embodied in certain sorts (or a certain pattern) of empathic concern for or about (the wellbeing of) those who may be affected by given actions or traits ...
>
> Slote 2010: 34

A further question is if there is a link to rationalism in this sentimentalism. Consider this:

> Almost everyone knows that empathy can (often) help us identify those who need our help more immediately or quickly than other modes of cognition, and this clearly makes empathy epistemically relevant to the moral life. But empathy also can help us recognize the virtue or vice of those we come into contact with (or read about). In fact, I think it is our primary mode of access to (the) moral attributes (of individuals or groups).
>
> Slote 2017: 845

Empathy is thus a form of cognition, but it is unclear to me if there is a further story to be told about empathy, explaining how this works and how this cognition works with other forms; perhaps we are meant to rely on contemporary science to supply this story. There are ways in which empathy itself may be a passion, and so non-representational, in a good Humean manner, whilst the awareness of empathy is actually the cognition. But it remains unclear what enables empathy to tell us about others, if it is merely a passion itself. If it is a cognition, informative about the world, other humans, then its relationship with heavy duty knowledge (aka reason) becomes very interesting. Sentiment, yes, but sentiment with content, unlike Humean passions. This allows empathy to be justified by its objects, and also explained by them. Unlike the senses, there is no organ of empathy (contrast Slote 2017, and think of the heart, e.g. in *Mencius* 2a6).

Practical terms, such as character traits, come in varying degrees of generality, but they all have meaning on the basis of empathy, on the Slotean view; thus, empathy is the pivotal capacity that gives rise to moral qualities:

> The account just given is a reference fixing account of "right" or "morally good" and, by extension, of other moral terms. But what fixes or helps to fix the reference is not some thin, subjective notion of experience but, rather, certain experiences as directed toward others and as reflecting what others feel. These latter notions are both causal and both contained within the idea of empathy, and we can, therefore, say that on the present account a certain phenomenon of empathy understood as a causal mechanism serves (or helps) to fix moral reference in an a priori way.
>
> Slote 2010: 63

Leaving aside for the moment the problem that the good and the right are distinct notions,[6] the question of how empathy feeds into other terms is very interesting. For one might be concerned that "right" and "good" are evaluative terms which have no descriptive content. So their application to things in the world, as Hume might say, is not a matter of fact, merely of feeling. With "thicker" terms, such as "cruel" or "brave", or "father" or "son," we are on safer ground. Such terms are plausibly held both to be evaluative and descriptive, such that evaluation and description are logically related to one another. In this way, such thick terms (cruel, brave) are attributed to or withheld from things on the basis of the way these things are. And at the same time, they carry necessary evaluation with them. Cruelty must be bad.

In Slote's picture, the evaluation is grounded not in the way things are, but in our empathy with those affected the actions, people or circumstances so described: Slote says that, in *Ethics of Care and Empathy* (Slote 2007), he "argued in argued, in particular, that we can use facts about the differing empathic responsiveness of agents to justify (or as criterial for) normative moral claims and distinctions, but that argument, that discussion, can be deepened or solidified in the light of the fuller metaethics offered here. If empathy derived approval and disapproval fix the reference (and help constitute the meaning) of moral terms, that gives us more reason than ECE (Ethics of Care and Empathy) ever offered to think that we can justify normative moral claims by reference to how we as agents empathically respond to different situations" (Slote 2010: 68)

The crucial thing about empathy, as about *buren* in the Mencius, is that it tells us the way things are—it is a way of knowing:

> The kind of empathy that takes in the feelings, attitudes, etc., of others (what is sometimes called associative or receptive empathy) clearly allows us to pick up on, to recognize, what others are feeling, and to do so without any belabored form of inductive or abductive inference. Empathy is a direct way of knowing about other minds, and the literature on empathy frequently emphasizes that.
> Slote 2017: 844

Empathy here gives us knowledge of obligations and their rankings. Yet measuring these degrees of obligations seems to be very difficult. If the obligations are to be binding (enforceable), one needs rules, even if the rules have exceptions. Clearly, the *Mencius* is deeply concerned with rules and regulations, quite apart from the standing dispositions of people. We can see this in the case of Mencius's sister in law. According to the rites, males are not allowed to touch their sisters-in-law, but *in extremis*, if she were drowning, of course Meng Ke may fish her out, and so touch her:

> He who would not so rescue the drowning woman is a wolf. For males and females not to allow their hands to touch in giving and receiving is the general rule; when a sister-in-law is drowning, to rescue her with the hand is a peculiar exigency.
>
> *Mencius* 4a17

The problem of ethics versus laws runs thus: if the strictures of ritual are to be enforced, on pain of punishment, then we need rules; and these are mentioned often enough in the *Mencius*. Their relation to the "government that does not bear the suffering of others" deserves more study.

6 Sympatheia—Cosmic Sympathy?

In fact, I suspect that the *Mencius* might be read profitably not on the basis of isolated individuals, who have to be cemented together again using sentiment,[7] but rather in terms of the Hippocratic *sumpnoia mia*, "one breathing-together" or Stoic-Neoplatonic *sumpatheia*:[8] which holds the cosmos together, prior to any individuals, and on the basis of which the abilities of individuals are explained. (It is also worth thinking of Humean sympathy in this tradition.) Consider these pieces of the *Mencius*:

> Chou pursued, "I venture to ask what you mean by your vast, flowing passion-nature!" The reply was, "It is difficult to describe it. This is the passion-nature: It is exceedingly great, and exceedingly strong. Being nourished by rectitude, and sustaining no injury, it fills up all between heaven and earth. This is the passion-nature: It is the mate and assistant of righteousness and reason. Without it, man is in a state of starvation. It is produced by the accumulation of righteous deeds; it is not to be obtained by incidental acts of righteousness. If the mind does not feel complacency in the conduct, the nature becomes starved."
>
> *Mencius* 2a2

And Mencius said,

> All things are already complete in us. There is no greater delight than to be conscious of sincerity on self-examination. If one acts with a vigorous effort at the law of reciprocity, when he seeks for the realization of perfect virtue, nothing can be closer than his approximation to it.
>
> *Mencius* 7a4

In 2a2, *qi*, Legge's "passion nature," is clearly something in Mencius with cosmic repercussions. So too is "the presence of the ten thousands things" in Meng Ke himself. Admittedly, many readers of the *Mencius* find especially the last passage an alien intrusion into the more sedate political discussions of the earlier part of the work. But it is a warning not to assume atomic individuals in need of cementing together, as the baseline from which practical thought must start.

7 Finally, to Virtue

For Slote, "Moral virtue, in other words, is that property of other individuals or their attitudes or actions that is empathically registered in us as a feeling of being warmed" (Slote 2017: 846–7). There is no general standpoint here, where we abstract from our interests. Where Hume takes trouble to distinguish the pleasure we take in virtue from other sources of pleasure in our fellow humans, here we only have a warming. The radical aspect of this standpoint would seem to be that there is no further explanation to be had: the end of the story is being warmed by virtue. In Mencian terms, extending empathy produces *ren* 仁. Episodes of empathy can be developed into a habit of empathizing. Then the question is why this is any better, as an explanation or prescription for our sociality, than entirely general rules, applying both to oneself and to others, in other words, adopting an impartial standpoint.

The problem of one's own virtue: it is perhaps plausible that one cannot attribute virtue to oneself, as this view of virtue implies. In the *Mencius* itself, there is no term for virtue in Slote's sense; and none either in the sense of goodness in the species *human*, in a more Aristotelian and Platonic vein. What we have are fairly fixed forms of behavior, related above all to human relationships (*renlun*), but also to governmental, administrative, and judicial roles (*wei* e.g. Mencius 2a5, 2b15, 4b8). The fact that these virtues relate to roles makes their attribution to individuals problematic: everyone fulfils many roles, and these roles change—from son to father, from advisor to minister, from duke to prince and co. Roles change, and then so must the corresponding virtues.

> To walk slowly, keeping behind his elders, is to perform the part of a younger brother. To walk quickly and precede his elders, is to violate the duty of a younger brother. Now, is it what a man cannot do – to walk slowly? It is what he does not do. The course of Yao and Shun was simply that of filial piety and fraternal duty.
>
> *Mencius* 6b22; trans. Legge

There is no word here of motivation, or of understanding what you are doing: apparently, only actual behavior is relevant. Legge translates *ti* as "the duty of a younger brother." This is perhaps an unhappy rendering, but it does point to a feature of the Mencius' thought: relationships place you under obligations. Here, difficult questions for anyone interested in virtue arise: Why do relationships place you under obligations? And are there obligations above and beyond those imposed by particular relationships? Are there obligations to other rational beings or humans, as such? And also: how do obligations relate to virtues? This last is a complicated question. A first, no doubt overly simple thought, might be that possession of a virtue consists in fulfilling obligations. Thus virtuous activity consists in performing your duty. This leaves open what the source of these obligations are—what imposes the obligations? Why do these obligations hold? In this text, all that implied about this is that humans should act like Yao and Shun—these are the models, one might think. And the way in which following these models provides obligations relates to parents and elders generally. In the context of empathy, the point is that fellow feeling is obviously, even in societies without hard and fast roles, at home within close relationships. This does not mean that empathy needs to remain confined to relationships, but that this is a good starting point for persuading others of their capacity to be affected, as we have seen in the story of the king and the ox in *Mencius* 1a7.

The final point that I wish to make about this last text cited (6b22) concerns filial piety and respect for elders (*xiaoti* 孝悌) as the whole of the way of Yao and Shun: "The way of Yao and Shun is filial piety and fraternal piety and that is all." On the surface this may seem to leave no room for the other virtues; at best, it leaves unclear how all the others relate to *xiaoti*. Various relations are conceivable—*xiaoti* may be derived from ren or ren may be the kind that *xiaoti* belongs to or it may represent the exercise of this. If we were to accept this last suggestion, the question would then arise how we are to think of other exercises of *ren*. For example feeling pity towards a child, as in *Mencius* 2a6, or the developed pattern of behavior based on this, may be an exercise of *ren*, but can hardly be conceived of as *xiaoti*, filial and fraternal duty.

One of the puzzles with *Mencius* 2a6 is what is the relationship between the four forms of behavior noted there: *ren*, *yi*, *li* and *zhi*. Four beginnings, "tips" (*duan* "principles" in Legge's translation) are identified for these four forms of behavior:

> The feeling of commiseration is the principle of benevolence. The feeling of shame and dislike is the principle of righteousness. The feeling of modesty and complaisance is the principle of propriety. The feeling of approving and disapproving is the principle of knowledge. Men have these four principles just as they have their four limbs. When men, having these four principles, yet say of themselves that they cannot develop them, they play the thief with themselves, and he who says of his prince that he cannot develop them plays the thief with his prince.
>
> *Mencius* 2a6

In some way, *ren* would appear fundamental to the other three. The situation of the child about to fall into the well, cited above, relates to commiseration and fear (*chuti zhi xin*), and this in turn is the beginning of *ren*, benevolence. There is no parallel "thought experiment" to establish that the interlocutor also has these other beginnings. This beginning needs development, in order to produce *ren* behavior; it is a principle in the sense of a starting point, not in the sense of a premise from which other things develop. Thus, the tip of good behavior, present in all of us like our limbs, is merely the starting point for further development towards good behavior.

Is this the kind of involvement of empathy with good behavior that Slote has in mind? First, there is no suggestion that not bearing the suffering of others is left behind, when developed into a standing form of behavior. Second, we must take note of the fact that the "thought experiment" does not involve any behavior at all, only a minimal reaction. And finally, pity is not explicitly the motive for any behavior that may or should result. What is said is that the commiseration has no ulterior motive,[9] which is a rather different point. In sum, there are many similarities with Slote's empathy, but both the function, and the content of *buren* are distinct.

Approval and disapproval (to follow Legge's translation of *shifei* for the moment) are here said to be the principles of knowledge. There are many ambiguities here which deserve to be discussed. But one point may be made briefly. Approval and disapproval are separate from *ren*. But one might tell a story of the way in which compassion (*buren zhi xin*: the heart that cannot bear the suffering of others), develops into approval and disapproval. Or else it may feed into approval and disapproval, as a criterion. This would allow one to tell a story about the way empathy feeds into knowledge, or may be cantilevered up, to use a phrase of David Wiggins', to cover our needs and desires. Clearly, we are not dealing with deduction.

A final word about sentimentalism. This project, showing morals to be properly a matter of feeling, and not of thought, depends on a contrastive use of passion. It is far from clear that the *Mencius* distinguishes between passion and reason is a way that can be responsibly or profitably compared with some of the ways these were contrasted in early modern philosophy. It deserves to be noted however, how important knowledge for Mencius is—witness his use of measures and weights as analogues for practical judgment (4a2). If empathy, like *buren*, tells us about the way things are, then it is amenable to supporting argument and persuasion, very much in the vein of the *Mencius*.

Acknowledgments

My thanks to Huang Yong for organizing a very stimulating meeting, and to Michael Slote for his engagement, as well as for his written comments on an earlier version. I am also very grateful to Anders Sydskjør for his probing suggestions.

Notes

1   Apparently introduced as a translation of *Einfühlung*, which is an aesthetic, not an ethical term, see Curtis and Koch 2009. As an aesthetic term, it is used prominently by von Vischer 1843, and it means that aesthetic qualities such as beauty are rather projections of the perceiving subject than qualities of the object itself (and is thus more akin to Malebranche's and Hume's view that the mind tends to spread itself on external objects). Vischer is considered as the founder of the German tradition of "*Einfühlungsästhetik*" which became prominent in the late nineteenth century; cf. Müller-Tamm 2005. (The word occurs neither in Grimm nor Adelung.) My thanks to Martina King for putting me onto this history.

    OED s.v. empathy "1. In the psychological theory of K. Lasswitz: a physical property of the nervous system analogous to electrical capacitance, believed to be correlated with feeling. Obs. Rare. 2 a. Psychol. and Aesthetics. The quality or power of projecting one's personality into or mentally identifying oneself with an object of contemplation, and so fully understanding or appreciating it. Now rare. 2. b. orig. Psychol. The ability to understand and appreciate another person's feelings, experience, etc."

2   For a rather different take on this term, *see* Sung, Winnie. (2019). *Bu Ren in the Mencius: I Cannot Let You be Harmed. Philosophy East and West* 69 (4):1098–119.

3   Contrast e.g. D. C. Lau's translation, which makes the story *the reason* for making the assertion that we have a heart that cannot bear the suffering of others.

4   See Michael Brady 2013 on the emotions.

5   Empathy is meant to be both negative and positive, unlike sympathy: you have empathy with both bad and good feelings. *Buren* is restricted to negative empathy, but see Mencius' dancing feet, a scenario described without *buren*: M4a27 Mencius said, "The richest fruit of benevolence is this: the service of one's parents. The richest fruit of righteousness is this: the obeying one's elder brothers. The richest fruit of wisdom is this: the knowing those two things, and not departing from them. The richest fruit of propriety is this: the ordering and adorning those two things. The richest fruit of music is this: the rejoicing in those two things. When they are rejoiced in, they grow. Growing, how can they be repressed? When they come to this state that they cannot be repressed, then unconsciously the feet begin to dance and the hands to move." I take it this refers not to solitary performances, but acting out roles with others: the pleasure in the performance on all sides makes the performance extend itself.

6   Notably, Kant insists that goodness is determined by the law, i.e. right (AA V 63), a point reiterated by the great Aristotelian and Kantian, Sir David Ross (1930).

7   Cf. Slote 2010: 305: "So in recent years I have been attempting to show that empathy is central to the moral life—that it is, to borrow from Hume in a different context, the cement of the moral universe." Reading ancient texts from a post-Enlightenment perspective can be distorting. Cf. Slote 2010: 304, fn. 1 "After speaking of the "ten thousand things" that are within us, Mengzi goes on to say that we should treat others as we would wish to be treated. The latter idea could be derived from a Kantian Categorical Imperative, but in Mengzi's case, it is derived from the sense of things' being within or part of us, i.e., from an empathic identification with others. So in the Mencius, altruism is clearly based in or on empathy." That "i.e." is a bold bound over a deep gulf.

8   *Stoicorum Veterum Fragmenta* 2.145, 170, 172, Plotinus 4.5.1.35, 2.3.7.14–20.

9   "They will feel so, not as a ground on which they may gain the favour of the child's parents, nor as a ground on which they may seek the praise of their neighbours and friends, nor from a dislike to the reputation of having been unmoved by such a thing."

References

Brady, Michael S. (2013), *Emotional Insight: The Epistemic Role of Emotional Experience*, Oxford: Oxford University Press.

Curtis, Robin and Gertrud Koch (2009), *Einfühlung: zu Geschichte und Gegenwart eines ästhetischen Konzepts* Munich: Wilhelm Fink Verlag.

Mencius, 1893. Vol. 2 The Chinese Classics with a translation, critical and exegetical notes, prolegomena, and copious indices. Oxford: Oxford University Press (with James Legge's translation: (http://ctext.org/mengzi).

Müller-Tamm, Jutta (2005), *Abstraktion als Einfühlung*. Rombach Wissenschaften. Litterae; Bd. 124, Freiburg/Brsg.: Rombach.

Oxford English Dictionary. http://www.oed.com.

Philosophy East and West 69 (4): 1098–1119.

Ross, W. D. (1930), *The Right and the Good*, Oxford: Oxford University Press

Slote, Michael (2007), *The Ethics of Care and Empathy*, London: Routledge.

Slote, Michael (2010a), *Moral Sentimentalism*, Oxford: Oxford University Press.

Slote, Michael (2010b), "The Mandate of Empathy," *Dao*, 9: 303–07.

Slote, Michael (2017), "The Many Faces of Empathy," *Philosophia*, 45: 843–55.

Sung, Winnie. (2019). *Bu Ren in the Mencius: I Cannot Let You be Harmed*. Philosophy East and West 69 (4):1098–119.

Van Norden, Bryan (2007), *Virtue Ethics and Consequentialism in Early Chinese Philosophy*, New York: Cambridge University Press.

von Vischer, Friedrich Theodor (1843), *Plan zu einer Neugliederung der Ästhetik*. Reutlingen und Leipzig: Mäcken,

9

Moral Therapy and the Imperative of Empathy

Mencius Encountering Slote

Tao Jiang
Rutgers University, United States

1 Introduction

Contemporary discourse on classical Confucian moral cultivation characterizes it, at least implicitly, as primarily a self-oriented project, its avowed communitarianism notwithstanding. More specifically, although scholarly discussions on classical Confucian moral psychology have presented a complex and nuanced picture of moral sentiments and their transformation, such discussions are largely confined to a moral agent herself. However, classical Confucian moral discourse also has a significant component that is primarily other-oriented, especially in the form of moral persuasion. This is most clearly demonstrated in the *Mencius*, much of which offers detailed accounts of Mencius trying to persuade a ruler to adopt the Confucian/Mencian moral-political-economic program. What is involved in moral persuasion is drastically different from self-cultivation and merits a separate discussion, especially given the fact that moral persuasion requires a deep understanding of the moral client, the particular context of the dialogue, and the moral agent herself. In other words, moral persuasion highlights three aspects of moral cultivation that are more salient than the self-oriented effort, namely a deep understanding of the heartmind[1] of another moral agent, an acute sensitivity toward the context of a particular dialogue, as well as a high degree of conscientiousness of one's own motivations when engaging in moral persuasions.

On the other hand, moral persuasion is usually interpreted by contemporary scholars to be conducted through moral argument. That is, early Chinese moral thinkers are understood to engage in moral argument, trying to convince their contemporaries the rightness of the paths they offer. However, such an approach to moral persuasion is more appropriate when the target of their effort is their intellectual peers, whereas if the target of this effort is rulers and those in power, as is often the case in many of the early texts such as the *Mencius*, this approach does not necessarily offer the most fitting interpretative framework. I will argue in this essay that, when dealing with rulers, Mencius resorts to a mode of moral persuasion that can be better characterized as moral therapy.

In this connection, it is interesting to note that contemporary discourse on classical Confucianism sometimes also characterizes it as a form of moral therapy.[2] However, if moral therapy means the curing of moral diseases, it requires a moral doctor and a moral client ("moral patient" in contemporary ethics means something completely different, referring to someone who is incapable of "normal" moral sentiments and behaviors). But the contemporary interpretation of Confucianism is largely confined to the self-cultivation of a moral agent who is at the same time the moral doctor and the moral client without distinguishing the two, likely due to the self-oriented interpretation of classical Confucianism, whereas a therapeutic model implies such a distinction, at least in the modern sense of the term "therapy." As we will see in the following, the distinction between a moral doctor and a moral client is central to the moral therapy described in several famous passages of the *Mencius* wherein fascinating dynamics between the two parties unfolds in front of our eyes.

In this essay, I take seriously the characterization of Confucian moral philosophy as therapeutic and develop a framework of moral therapy to explore the therapeutic aspect of the Mencian moral project. I argue that Mencius, the moral doctor, attempts to change the interpretative script of cost/benefit in his moral clients' (often rulers') self-understanding to a moral script he discerns to be actually operative in the client's actions. The goal is to push a ruler to repair his relationship with the people in his political maneuvers.

In the latter part of the essay, I will engage Mencian moral therapy with Michael Slote's moral sentimentalism, especially with respect to their shared emphasis on the central role empathy plays in our moral life, in order to provide a broader context for the Mencian moral therapy. I will argue that Mencian moral therapy operates within moral sentimentalism that sees empathy at a moral imperative in our life, especially when dealing with people who are morally challenging.

2 Moral Therapy and Human Relations

It is important to observe, at the outset, that interpreting the Mencian mode of moral persuasion through the lens of moral therapy is different from doing it through that of moral argument. Clearly both methods are present in the text, but moral persuasion through argument has dominated the modern discourse on Mencian thought given the way philosophy is practiced in the modern academy. In this connection, it is important to point out that as methods of moral persuasion, moral argument and moral therapy actually have rather different objectives. Conducting a therapy is about clarifying and transforming a moral client's self-understanding and *winning over* the client as a result whereas engaging in an argument is often more about *winning* an argument with the pretense that winning an argument itself *should* win over the opponent without taking into considerations of the psychological dynamics of those who lose an argument as well as the relationship between the two sides engaging in the argument. One can win an argument without winning over the person who has lost the argument, just as one can win over an opponent even when the former loses an argument to the latter. Clearly, moral persuasion is more than winning a moral argument. It requires that the moral doctor takes the totality of the moral client's heartmind into consideration and effects changes in the moral client's self-understanding in a way that resonates with the client.

Furthermore, what is also salient about moral argument is that any two persons can engage in an argument, without presupposing any relationship between the two; on the other hand, in order for moral therapy to be effective such that the client is won over and the goal of changing his/her heartmind and/or behavior is achieved, there needs to be a relationship of trust such that the client can trust the doctor. This relationship of trust can potentially open the client's heartmind to being persuaded. Without such a relationship, any argument, however sharp and powerful, is often futile, if not outright counterproductive, when the goal is to persuade the other side to change their heartmind. Another way to put it is that moral argument is about moral truth (whatever conception of truth it might be) irrespective of the relationship status of the parties involved whereas moral therapy is about understanding another person's heartmind in its totality within the context of a therapist/client relationship in order to bring about a better self-understanding of the clients themselves and effect changes in their behaviors and their troubled relationships with others. In the case of Mencius, helping a ruler to repair his frayed relations with his people is the primary objective of Mencius' therapeutic effort.

In a famous passage where Mencius is asked what he is good at, he replies, "I have an insight into words. I am good at cultivating my flood-like *qi*" (*Mencius* 2A2; trans. Lau 1970, with modifications). Most commentators focus on Mencius' rumination about the flood-like moral energy and do not pay as much attention to the first aspect of Mencius' strength, namely his claim to have insights into a person's state of heartmind by the way that person uses words. Clearly, Mencius sees himself as being good at both self-oriented moral cultivation and other-oriented moral persuasion. This essay will highlight the significance of the latter aspect, especially through the lens of moral therapy.

Mencius elaborates his insight into words this way: "From biased words I can see wherein the speaker is blind; from immoderate words, wherein he is ensnared; from heretical words, wherein he has strayed from the right path; from evasive words, wherein he is at his wits' end" (*Mencius* 2A2; trans. Lau 1970). This is a succinct summary of Mencius' thinking on how to get through to another person, given their particular state of heartmind. Mencius does it by paying close attention to the way words are used which offer invaluable clues to what the clients think and feel about a particular issue. Indeed, much of the text portrays a Mencius who is adept at discerning the state of heartmind of his interlocutors. This is critically important in a therapeutic context that the doctor understands the client well.

Let us take a closer look at how Mencius offers a distinctly therapeutic approach to the moral ills of his time, especially when dealing with powerful rulers, in his effort to help rulers repair their problematic relationships with their people. As we will see, the Mencian moral therapy is to help a ruler to reset his strained relationship with his people such that both sides can enjoy a more mutually satisfying relationship, therefore helping to fulfill the ruler's political ambitions. Aided by his extraordinary discernment of his clients' heartmind, Mencius creatively crafts an alternative moral script that explains the state of heartmind shown through the clients' words/behaviors far more effectively than even the speakers themselves realize, in order to reorient their moral compass to the Confucian path.

3 Mencius' Therapeutic Approach to Problematic Desires

There is a cluster of remarkable passages in the *Mencius* 1B we will call "passages of problematic desires" (PPDs). These PPDs have a uniform theme: a king, in a conversation with Mencius on the grand topics of good governance and political ambitions, admits one or two weaknesses he has, believing they are a hindrance to fulfilling his dream of a virtuous leader. More specifically, in 1B1, a king tells Mencius that he is fond of music but embarrassed that the kind of music he enjoys is not that of former kings but rather popular music. In 1B3, King Xuan of Qi confesses to Mencius that he has a weakness, namely he is fond of valor, in the context of a discussion about the king's political ambitions. In 1B5, the king confides in Mencius that he has two weak spots, namely fondness of money and women, when Mencius is discussing how to practice kingly governance with the king.

What is fascinating about these PPDs is that the king is well aware of the problematic nature of his particular desires, be they his fondness for pop music, valor, sex, or money, and that the king is ashamed to admit those desires to Mencius. Such a sense of shame seems natural to the king. Indeed, much of the Mencian discussion of human nature dwells on the inborn nature of our moral inclinations, including the sense of shame which is the root of the virtue of righteousness. However, what is surprising is that Mencius, in his dialogues with the king, celebrates the fact that the king has those desires, instead of chastising or condemning him for harboring them, as might be expected from a well-known moralist:

> If you have a great fondness for music, then there is perhaps hope for the state of Qi. Whether it is the music of today or the music of antiquity makes no difference.
>
> *Mencius* 1B1; trans. Lau 1970, with slight modifications

In other words, Mencius is saying that there is some close relationship between having fondness for music and hope for the state of Qi. This is rather surprising as the relevance of the king's fondness for pop music to the ideal of good governance is not immediately obvious. The king is understandably intrigued, asking to hear about it more. Mencius goes on to prod the king to sharing his fondness of music with his people, instead of monopolizing the joy. We find Mencius making a similar point in 1B5 with regard to the king's fondness for money and sex.

1B3 makes a somewhat different point. Here the king considers his fondness for valor a weakness when the king asks Mencius for advice about how to promote good relations with neighboring states. Mencius makes the point that fondness for valor is not itself problematic and that such a fondness, if properly channeled toward the worthy case of bringing peace over the world, would actually be a great virtue and asset.

1B1 and 1B3 suggest that Mencius lays down two routes in dealing with problematic desires, namely, the sharing route and the rechanneling route. The common interpretative trope in the contemporary discourse on the Mencian thought focuses on Mencius' message of sharing and rechanneling the king's personal desires as a matter of moral cultivation or application. Few contemporary commentators have dwelled on Mencius' puzzling response to the king's admissions of problematic desires. But the reasons for Mencius' response is not as obvious as many interpreters might have assumed.

There are several ways to interpret Mencius' response in 1B1. An obvious one is to see it as a savvy Mencian tactic to gain the king's ear. Given how readily Mencius is willing to confront a king in uncomfortable situations registered throughout the text, this interpretation, while plausible, certainly does not preclude other possibilities. Another way to unpack this is to highlight the critical importance of music in the Confucian teaching. As is well known, music occupies a special place within traditional Chinese political discourse in representing the ideal of harmony.[3] However, Mencius' focus in this passage is not really on music *per se* since it is not important to him whether the king likes the kind of music that is more about political harmony or he prefers the popular kind that is for entertainment only. Rather, Mencius' emphasis is on the king's fondness, regardless of the particular object of such a fondness. That is, Mencius' celebration of the king's fondness for music is not really about king's music taste—the right kind can have a more apparent connection to political governance—but rather about the king's ability to be fond of things.

The third way to approach Mencius' surprising response is to see it as Mencius' genuine expression of relief of a certain kind. That is, Mencius is relieved that the king is capable of fondness for music, regardless of kind of music involved. It is possible to imagine that among the many rulers Mencius has encountered there are some who are not even capable of enjoying music. It clearly implies that if a king is not even capable of such a fondness, there would have been no hope for the kingdom under his rule. This begs the question: why does Mencius elevate the king's mere fondness for music to such a height that his kingdom's political future is dependent on it? The third interpretation is more philosophically interesting as it demonstrates Mencius' keen sense of what fondness for music can reveal about the moral potentials of the king. We will focus on the third interpretation in the following discussion.

In this connection, Christopher Small, in an influential book on music or what he calls "musicking" (i.e., participating in any activities of music performance that includes performing, listening, practicing, or dancing), observes:

> The act of musicking establishes in the place where it is happening a set of *relationships*, and it is in those relationships that the meaning of the act lies. They are to be found not only between those organized sounds which are conventionally thought of as being the stuff of musical meaning but also between the people who are taking part, in whatever capacity, in the performance; and they model, or stand as metaphor for, ideal relationships as the participants in the performance imagine them to be: relationships between person and person, be- tween individual and society, between humanity and the natural world and even perhaps the supernatural world.
>
> Small 1998: 13, my italics

He further points out that when we are musicking, we "explore, affirm and celebrate" those relationships (Small 1998: 215). There is quite a bit of contemporary scholarly literature on the connection between music and empathy. What emerges from these discussions, for the purpose of this essay, is a strong connection between music and empathy. In light of this, we can interpret Mencius' response to the king's fondness for music as well as the king's apparent sense of shame in his admission that he prefers pop music to ritual music as important indicators that the king is not lacking in terms of "normal" human sensitivities and emotional range. The king is not morally sick. No wonder Mencius is relieved.

Furthermore, Small's observation on the music's implications on human relationships is also relevant to what Mencius points out to the king. The king's fondness for music gives Mencius a glimpse into the king's heartmind pertaining to his relationship to those around him. Indeed, helping the king to repair his relationships with his people lies at the heart of the Mencian moral therapy. To accomplish this, Mencius offers an alternative moral script that affirms the king's problematic desires by bringing out in the open their implications in morality and relationships. This means that Mencius discerns a moral script operative in many of his conversations with the rulers. His moral therapy hinges on such a discernment as well as an effective way to articulate the script.

4 Moral Script

A moral script, according to Martin Hoffman (2000: 10–12), is a habitual association between transgression and guilt (actual and/or virtual), developed early in childhood, that forms the basis of the moral behaviors and motivations of a moral agent. Because of its early formation, the impact of moral script in our lives is powerful, if at times hidden. Due to the king's expression of shame or self-doubt in his admissions to Mencius his harboring of problematic desires listed above, it is clear that there is such a moral script operative in the king. More specifically, what is operative in the kings Mencius talks to in the text is a moral script of an ideal ruler that pits morals against desires, pleasure, and ambition. Put differently, there is an implicit script in a king which says that to be good ruler he must guard against his problematic desires like the desires for money, sex, valor, and even his political ambition. We will see that Mencius discerns such a moral script in the king's heartmind, taps into it, and reformulates it in his therapeutic approach. In so doing, Mencius takes advantage of precious and often fleeting moments in order to persuade a ruler to be more humane and benevolent to his own people.

In the PPDs we examined previously, Mencius advises the king to let his people have a chance to enjoy what he himself enjoys, such as sex, wealth, and music on the one hand and to channel his fondness for valor and political ambition toward the worthy cause of bringing peace to the world on the other. The first advice is more universally applicable whereas the second advice is more relevant to a ruler. Let us put aside the second advice for now (we will come back to it later in the essay) and focus on the first.

What Mencius is doing in the first case is to recast the operative moral script that pits virtues against problematic desires by affirming the legitimacy of those desires, considered problematic even by the king himself, while encouraging the king to let his people have a chance to enjoy them. Such a move problematizes the *monopoly* of desired objects, rather than the desire itself or any particular desired object. This effort is evident in all of the PPDs we have examined above.

However, the most striking passage that details Mencius' effort to reshape a client's moral script can be found in *Mencius* 1A7, the famous ox-sparing passage, wherein Mencius asks the king whether the following incident happened:

> The King was sitting in the hall. He saw someone passing below, leading an ox. The King noticed this and said, 'Where is the ox going?' 'The blood of the ox is to be used for consecrating a new bell.' 'Spare it. I cannot bear to see it shrinking with fear, like an innocent man going to the place of execution.' 'In that case, should the ceremony be abandoned?' 'That is out of the question. Use a lamb instead.'
>
> trans. Lau 1970

Once the king admits that it indeed happened, Mencius asks the king to explain why he spares the ox but substitutes a lamb for it. Apparently, many people regard the king's action as being stingy since an obvious explanation for what motivates the king's action is the difference in value between the two. But as a king he is unlikely concerned about the cost of an ox versus a lamb. If that difference in cost between an ox and a lamb cannot be the reason for the king's action, the only explanation seems to be that the king is just silly and that he does not really know what he is doing. The king readily concedes this point since no sensible alternative has presented itself. This is precisely where Mencius demonstrates his extraordinary discernment of a precious teaching moment.

Mencius latches onto the king's own perplexity and sees some flicker of humanity, however fleeting, in such an incident as it provides Mencius a way into the king's heartmind. He manages to identify an unconventional perspective from which the king's action makes better sense than king's begrudging about the cost of an ox and, more importantly, sheds light on the moral sensitivity the king exhibits. Furthermore, Mencius views the incident from the perspective of *relationship* instead of cost. That is, Mencius sees the difference between the ox and the lamb not in terms of their cost but in terms of the king's relationships with them:

> It is the way of a benevolent man. You saw the ox but not the lamb. The attitude of a gentleman towards animals is this: once having seen them alive, he cannot bear to see them die, and once having heard their cry, he cannot bear to eat their flesh.
>
> 1A7; trans. Lau 1970

In other words, the king saw the ox, but not the lamb. This means that the relationship between the king and the ox is more immediate and concrete than his relationship with some poor lamb which is more distant and abstract, as captured in the common expression "out of sight, out of mind." Reorienting the episode in the direction of the king's relationship brings forth the moral implications of the king's actions.

What Mencius is doing here is to bring out in the open the moral script operative in the king's heartmind and dismiss the script of profit. In the script of profit, there is a cost–benefit analysis that involves calculation and evaluation of the cost versus benefit. This is clearly the script people resort to when commenting on the king's motive in substituting an ox with a lamb to perform a sacrificial ritual. According to the script of profit, the king is miserly. However, the problem with this analysis is that it does not make sense since as a king he is unlikely to be concerned with the minor difference in the cost of an ox versus a lamb. An alternative analysis is that the king does not know what he is doing. Mencius is perceptive enough to see that the script of profit is an inappropriate one to interpret the king's actions and motivations, but Mencius does not think the king is just silly, either.

As a skilled moral doctor, Mencius sees a different script at work, namely the moral script, that is reflected in the sympathetic reaction at the sight of the suffering of another sentient being, activated by the king's sighting of a trembling ox. In

Mencius' eyes, the king's action is motivated by pity toward the ox in fear. In so doing, Mencius points out to the king his own benevolence toward the ox of which he is unaware:

> The heart behind your action is sufficient to enable you to become a true King. The people all thought that you grudged the expense, but, for my part, I have no doubt that you were moved by pity for the animal.
>
> Mencius 1A7; trans. Lau 1970

The king is impressed by Mencius' ability to see something in him that eludes even the king himself:

> For though the deed was mine, when I looked into myself I failed to understand my own heart: You described it for me and your words struck a chord in me. What made you think that my heart accorded with the way of a true King?
>
> ibid.

Here the king expresses his awe of Mencius' extraordinary discernment. Of course, it does not hurt that Mencius tells the king that he has what it takes to be a true king. When the king says that Mencius' words have struck a chord in him, it is a good indication that a relationship of trust is established between the king and Mencius which is required of any effective therapy.

It is interesting to observe in this connection that at the very beginning of the *Mencius*, a king asks Mencius how he can profit (*li* 利) his kingdom. Mencius brushes aside the concern for profit and insists on a discussion of righteousness (*yi* 義). In light of what we have discussed here, it is clear that the script of profit is the dominant one that guides a king's thinking and behavior. What Mencius is doing there is to shift the profit script to the moral script. That is, from the very beginning of the text, the *Mencius* embarks on changing the dominant script of the time from profit/benefit/cost to that of morality/benevolence/righteousness. The script of profit clearly does not apply in the case of the king sparing an ox and replacing it with a lamb whereas the moral script provides a more sensible explanation about the king's motivation in that anecdote. Such a theme persists throughout the *Mencius*, both as a central topic of discussion and as the method by which moral persuasion is conducted and this is sometimes referred to as the debate between profit and righteousness in the text (*yi li zhi bian* 義利之辯).

5 From the Personal to the Political

In order to create a therapeutically effective environment, Mencius has to be able to discern an opportune moment when conversing with the king, taking into considerations the king's reactions and other sentiments expressed in the course of their interactions on that occasion. The breakthrough comes precisely when the king realizes that he does have the potential to be a benevolent ruler, similar to the extolled figures of sage kings. This demonstrates Mencius' perceptive discernment in trying to persuade the king that the latter already has what it takes to become a benevolent ruler. According to Mencius, all that the king has to do "is take this very heart here and apply it to what is over there" (*ibid.*). Mencius is making the point that if the king is capable of showing benevolence toward an animal he certainly can be benevolent toward his people. Indeed, the primary motivation in Mencius' moral therapy is to push a ruler to repair his relationship with his people. One way to repair the king's relationship with his people is shown in the many passages wherein Mencius advises the king to let his people have a chance to enjoy the things the king himself takes pleasure in that include music, garden, money, and sensuous pleasure. This is the sharing route of the Mencian moral psychology as noted above.

However, there is another aspect of Mencian thought that specifically targets rulers. We have encountered this earlier when discussing PPDs. In *Mencius* 1B3, the king is well aware of his fondness for valor as a hurdle to becoming a benevolent king. Mencius' response is again fascinating:

> I beg you not to be fond of small valor. Putting your hand on your sword and snapping with anger, "How dare you oppose me!" is to show the defiance of a common fellow which can only be pitched against a single adversary. You should make it something greater . . . .
>
> If there was one bully in the Empire, King Wu felt this to be a personal affront. This was the valor of King Wu. Thus he, too, brought peace to the people of the Empire in one outburst of rage. Now if you, too, will bring peace to the people of the Empire in one outburst of rage, then the people's only fear will be that you are not fond of valor.
>
> *Mencius* 1B3; trans. Lau 1970, with slight modifications

Mencius is making the point that fondness for valor is not itself problematic. What *is* problematic is the pettiness of its expressions. If the king could model himself after ancient sage kings, who are motivated by moral outrage on behalf of people suffering under tyrannical rules, and channel that moral outrage toward the worthy case of bringing peace to the world, fondness for valor would actually be a great virtue and asset for a political leader.

In 1A7, Mencius deals with a similar issue concerning the king's political ambition. Here Mencius confronts the king for the latter's warmongering endeavors. He asks the king to explain why he launches wars: "Perhaps you find satisfaction only in starting a war, imperiling your subjects and incurring the enmity of other feudal lords?" The king rejects this and mentions his ambition as the motivation to starting a war. When Mencius prods the king to tell him what his ambition is, the king is reluctant to answer. Mencius goes through a list of regular objects of desire and the king says no. Mencius ventures a guess about the king's ambition:

> In that case one can guess what your supreme ambition is: You wish to extend your territory, to enjoy the homage of Qin and Chu, to rule over the Central Kingdoms and to bring peace to the barbarian tribes on the four borders. Seeking the fulfilment of such an ambition by such means as you employ is like looking for fish by climbing a tree.
>
> 1A7; trans. Lau 1970, modifications

There are at least two points worth noting. First, here Mencius is no longer dealing with the king's basic desires for money, sex, and other pleasures as we have seen previously. As a ruler, those desires can be easily met. Here Mencius is addressing the king's political ambition. Second, Mencius does not belittle the king's ambition or doubt his abilities to realize such an ambition. Many places in the text show that Mencius actually lauds such an ambition. In other words, just like Mencius' affirmation of the king's desires for pleasure and wealth discussed above, Mencius also affirms the legitimacy and appropriateness of the king's political ambition. Mencius points out to the king that the problem is not with his ambition per se, but with his way of accomplishing it. He reminds the king that if the king continues to do what he is doing in order to realize his ambition, it will not end well. The king is clearly interested in what Mencius has to say:

> "I am dull-witted," said the King, "and cannot see my way beyond this point. I hope you will help me towards my goal and instruct me plainly. Though I am slow, I shall make an attempt to follow your advice."
>
> 1A7; trans. Lau 1970

This gives Mencius an ideal opening to pitch to the king a comprehensive Confucian program which includes economic policies, family policy, and others. Clearly, Mencius' effort, when conversing with a ruler, focuses on persuading the king: first, that the Confucian program is conducive to the king's realization of his political ambitions; second, that it is laudable and not shameful to harbor grand political ambitions; and third, that the king has what it takes to be a sage king.

To sum up, I have tried to make the case that the Mencian moral therapy is an effective way to reveal the presence of a moral script operative in "normal"[4] human beings, even in rulers. Such a moral script points to universalist human moral inclinations that are often hidden but can be manifested in our everyday behaviors and desires. To accomplish this, Mencius takes on (conventionally considered) problematic desires and effectively uses the moral script to demonstrate subtle ways desires express themselves that disclose a hidden well of moral sentiments that can be harnessed for personal wellbeing as well as political ambition. At the center of the Mencian moral therapy is to tap into the operative moral scripts and reformulate them such that they can be used towards more worthy goals of repairing the frayed, often abusive, relationships between a ruler and his people.

6 Mencius Meets Slote: Empathy in Moral Therapy

According to Michael Slote, one of the few prominent contemporary Western thinkers who have taken an interest in Chinese philosophy in recent years, Mencius' approach to ethics resonates strongly with Hume, whose sentimentalism places a great deal of "emphasis on compassion, sympathy, and benevolence as the basis for moral thought and action" (Slote 2009: 290) and sees a great deal of possibilities in the joining of hands between the contemporary efforts to revive interest in empathy and traditional Chinese philosophy (Slote 2010b: 306). The sentimentalist approach to ethics is in sharp contrast with Aristotle's rationalist approach with which many contemporary Confucian scholars have drawn much of their comparison, despite the fact that the Aristotelian ethics leaves little room for those moral sentiments. Slote's own works represent contemporary revival of sentimentalism that can be traced back to eighteenth-century British thinkers like David Hume, Francis Hutcheson, and Adam Smith, etc., and can provide a helpful framework to articulate some of the underlying assumptions of the Mencian ethics, especially the role of empathy in Mencius' moral therapy.

As we have discussed in this essay, moral therapy can be a more effective method of moral persuasion than moral argument, if the goal is indeed to win over another moral agent instead of winning an argument, because moral therapy attempts to understand moral agents in a way moral argument does not take into much consideration. At the heart of the Mencian moral therapy is the moral doctor's attempt to understand the moral client's underlying motivations or "moral script," often opaque to the client him/herself. Slote's methodic articulation of empathy offers unique insights into the central role played by empathy in a Mencian doctor's attempt to understand his moral clients.

Empathy is often distinguished from sympathy, although their distinction is not always clear-cut. As Slote puts it,

> Empathy occurs when ... you feel another person's pain or joy. But sympathy for the person who, say, feels pain doesn't require us to feel their pain and is a matter, rather, of wanting their condition to improve (and hoping or wanting to do something oneself to bring that about).
>
> Slote 2014: 12

In other words, empathy is feeling what another person is feeling whereas sympathy is more specifically the feeling of sorrow for another person's misfortune. Our earlier discussion of Mencius' moral therapy clearly indicates that both empathy and sympathy are at work. Indeed, there is quite a bit of evidence showing that sympathetic concern for others is dependent on our empathic capacity (*ibid.*), which resonates with what is operative in Mencius' thought. As Bryan Van Norden observes,

> Regarding the distinction between "empathy" and "sympathy," I suspect that Mengzi would regard *sympathy* as merely the "extension" or "filling out" of

empathy, rather than marking a categorical distinction between the two reactions. I think Mengzi would worry that any fundamental distinction between empathy and sympathy would come close to the sort of "two sources" view of ethics that he criticizes the Moist YI Zhi for holding (*Mencius* 3a5)."

Van Norden 2009: 305

Therefore, for the purpose of the following discussion, especially when it comes to Mencius' thought, we will not strictly differentiate between empathy and sympathy.

One of the most interesting theoretical developments on empathy by Slote is the distinction he draws between empathy with others' joy/suffering and empathy with those agents' empathic concerns for other people or objects. The former is directed at the state of affairs of another being including human, animal, or even inanimate objects—let us call it first-order empathy—and the latter refers to empathy with agential empathy—let us call it second-order empathy (Slote does not use first-order/second-order to describe empathy). As we will see in the following, Mencian ethics operating on both orders of empathy, differentiating a moral doctor's empathy with the clients in the therapeutic context from moral clients' empathy/sympathy with their objects. I will argue that the Mencian moral doctor often operates on the level of second-order empathy, appealing to a ruler's first-order empathy in order to help the king extend his empathy/sympathy to his people so as to become a benevolent ruler. Let us delve into the two orders of empathy in some detail.

First-Order Empathy

In the sentimentalist discourse, discussions around first-order empathy tend to focus on its partialist character, often in contrast with the utilitarian rationalist approach to ethics with its universalist aspirations. That is, "we empathically react to nearby and visible suffering or need more than to suffering or need we merely hear or know about" (Slote 2010a: 21) and "we are empathically partial not only to what we perceive (and what is therefore, given the way things are in the actual world, in our vicinity) but also to what is contemporaneous with our concern" (Slote 2010a: 22). Indeed, much of the attraction as well as the problem with sentimentalism is its partialism. Slote offers the examples of trapped miners and a drowning child in need of immediate help to illustrate the attraction of sentimentalist partiality:

> When miners are trapped in a mine, we feel more empathy for them than for the greater number of future miners we might save by installing safety devices, and we also think it morally better to save those miners than to invest in safety devices. (The suggestion that we should invest in safety equipment *rather than* saving the miners would actually *horrify* most of us.) Similarly, it goes more against the grain of empathy to ignore a child drowning right in front of one than to not give money to Oxfam that one believes will save a single child in a

distant country, and we tend to think that it is morally worse to ignore the drowning child than to not give to Oxfam.

Slote 2010a: 22, original italics

The *prima facie* similarities between Slote's examples and some of Mencius' cases are striking. The moral deliberation that privileges those who are spatiotemporally close (and/or perceptually immediate) to the moral agent over those who are more distant and only heard about (and/or conceptually known) is in sharp contrast with the utilitarian critique of partialism that carries problematic implications on the central moral issue of justice. On the other hand, sentimentalism appreciates human beings as embodied beings and intrinsically partialist, implying that universalist and rationalist approach does not appreciate human beings in their complicated embodied existence. Therefore, if the challenge for rationalism is how to reach the particular, given rationalism's commitment to the universal,[5] the challenge for sentimentalism is the opposite, namely, how to reach the universal given sentimentalism's partialist orientation. So the question for Slote is whether or not he can account for justice in his sentimentalism. One of Slote's theoretical ambitions is precisely to provide such an account.

Slote believes that "social justice could be conceived entirely in sentimentalist care ethical terms" (Slote 2010a, 124) and that "empathy is the key to care ethics' greatest potential development and plausibility, both in general and in the sphere of justice" (*ibid.*). According to Slote,

> it is possible to understand the justice of (a given society's) laws, institutions, and social customs *on analogy with* the ethics of individual acts and attitudes of caring.... So a sentimentalist ethics of empathic caring can say that institutions and laws, as well as social customs and practices, are just if they reflect empathically caring motivation on the part of (enough of) those responsible for originating and maintaining them.
>
> Slote 2010a: 125, original italics

Slote essentially treats the problem of justice as a case of more consistently extending our empathy to others. He uses women's equality as an example to illustrate how empathy-based justice should work: "patriarchal social attitudes can embody a lack of empathic concern and respect for the aspirations of girls and women (e.g., to become doctors), and we can certainly say that all laws, customs, and institutions that reflect such attitudes are as unjust as the attitudes themselves (and the situation or society in which they flourish)" (Slote 2010a: 126–7).

However, as Virginia Held points out in her critique of Slote, empathy alone is not adequate in raising women's and girls' own expectation of their rights:

> The problem here, as I see it, is that Slote presupposes what he tries to provide. If women and girls already believe they have rights to equality and have a

sense of entitlement to be treated as equals, then not respecting them in this way will be a failure of empathic concern. But girls may have been well-cared for and yet have grown up without developing aspirations for equal political power or equal careers. Centuries of caring parents failed to apply ideas of justice to girls, and it was not until girls understood their rights to equality that they developed aspirations to equal careers and political power. If women believe it is appropriate and right for men to support their wives and daughters and for women to be subordinate to their male "providers," then suddenly expecting them to be economically self-sufficient might show inadequate empathic concern.

Held 2011: 316–17

In other words, empathy alone is insufficient in generating the ideal of gender equality, as evidenced by centuries of parental care in human history much of which did not produce—or has not produced—the ideal of gender equality. Due to the difficulty, if not impossibility, in generating the ideal of gender equality from within empathy itself, Held proposes that "the meanings, goals, and practices of justice can be different from those of care, and to arrange that different values are given priority in different domains of society" (Held 2011: 317).

Interestingly, Held's worry about the inadequacy of empathy in accounting for justice can be seen in Mencius' thought, which does not have a robust notion of justice to begin with. In some ways Mencius faces a similar challenge, namely how the concern for the near and dear be extended to the far and distant. Indeed, the objective of the Mencian moral therapy is to help a ruler channel his partialist moral sentiments toward the universalist aspiration of becoming a benevolent king. However, it is clear that the Mencian (and Confucian more broadly) extensionist strategy is not meant to completely transform the graded nature of empathy but rather to render it more open (instead of being completely blocked by selfishness and self-centeredness[6]). Slote echoes such a sentiment:

> [P]eople are likely to develop more empathy for (groups of) people they know than for those they don't. Still … we do have the capacity to develop *some* substantial empathy and concern for distant people we don't know, and in that case, it is perhaps not too much to expect people to develop a *greater degree* of empathic concern *for their compatriots*.
>
> Slote 2010a: 215, original italics

But such an empathic care does not necessarily translate into concern for equality and justice specifically. It could well have been empathic concern for the well-being of others, however well-being is understood in different cultures and societies, many of which do not entertain the idea of equality.

Since there is no separate notion of justice in Mencius' thought, notions of empathy and benevolence are allowed to do all the conceptual work. One of the consequences of the Mencian moral partialism is that the problem of justice remains unresolved. Mencius, and the Confucians more generally, is known to be rather unapologetic about one's special treatment accorded to one's family members, parents in particular.[7] If Mencius is indeed a sentimentalist (and there are good reasons to categorize him as one), the problem he faces in regard to the partialist nature of empathy/sympathy provides an interesting test case, at least in historical terms, about the viability of a robust notion of justice that is grounded in empathy. Without the challenge posed by a robust notion of justice separate from his empathy-based sentimentalism, Mencius does not really struggle with the imperative of justice that is expected of a moral philosopher. Mencius' willingness to bite the bullet and pay the price of justice in order to retain benevolence as the defining quality of being human points to the task facing contemporary Western ethicists who work in the intellectual environment wherein the ideal of justice reigns supreme.

Second-Order Empathy

Having dealt with first-order empathy, let us move to its second-order version. Second-order empathy, namely empathy with agential empathy, takes on the issue of moral evaluations within the empathy-based moral sentimentalism. Slote offers an astute description of its dynamics in the following passage:

> When we empathize with agential empathy, what we are doing is very different from what the agent is doing. The empathically concerned agent wants and seeks to do what is helpful to some person or persons (leaving aside animals for simplicity's sake). Empathic agents feel empathy, for example, *with* (the point of view of) certain people their actions may affect and are concerned *for* or *about* (the welfare or wishes of) those people. But when we feel empathy with empathically concerned agents (as agents), we empathize with them, not with the people they are empathizing with or focused on. We empathize, in other words, *with what they as (potential) agents are feeling and/or desiring*, and such empathy is, I believe, the core or basis of moral approval and disapproval.
>
> Slote 2010a: 34, original italics

Slote finds in second-order empathy a sentimentalist basis for moral evaluation. More specifically, in developing a sentimentalist, empathy-based framework of moral evaluation, Slote connects moral approval/disapproval with agential warmth/coldness. Accordingly, when one shows empathy toward others, one experiences what others are experiencing vicariously. When we empathize with that very empathic agent, we experience warmth toward that person. And this empathic agential warmth constitutes moral approval of the agent's empathy toward others (Slote 2010a: 35). As Slote elaborates,

People whose capacity for empathy is fully developed will ... have a different empathic reaction to (the characteristic actions of) agents whose empathy is also fully developed from that which they will have to (the characteristic actions of) agents who have less developed empathy. In particular, if agents' actions reflect empathic concern for (the well being or wishes of) others, empathic beings will feel warmly or tenderly toward them, and such warmth and tenderness empathically reflect the empathic warmth or tenderness of the agents. I want to say that such (in one sense) reflective feeling, such *empathy with empathy*, also constitutes moral approval, and possibly admiration as well, for agents and/or their actions.

Slote 2010a: 34–5, original italics

On the other hand, unempathetic actions exhibit coldness towards others which registers the agent's disapproval of others' actions. Slote believes that moral judgment is grounded in such second-order empathic warmth or coldness in a sentimentalist account which "correspond[s] pretty well to differences in the (normative) moral evaluations we tend to make about those situations" (Slote 2010a: 21). Slote gives the example of its correspondence with the deontological distinction we make with regard to the degree of seriousness of moral wrong between doing harm and letting it happen to support his empathy-based account of moral judgment.

One of Slote's challenges is to make the case that empathy is relevant to moral thinking and moral justification. In that regard, he hopes to demonstrate that "empathy has something important to do with our *understanding* of moral claims and moral distinctions" (Slote 2010a: 25, original italics). This reflects the philosophical landscape of Western ethical discourse which tends to privilege the rational (Aristotle famously touts it as the defining quality of being human) over the emotive such that an appeal to the emotive needs to be justified in a way the appeal to the rational does not. Slote hopes to provide a more philosophically sensible explanation for many of our common moral reactions and judgments that match traditional deontological evaluations but questioned by the utilitarian approach whose moral calculation problematizes much of our commonsense moral intuitions and judgments.[8]

In this respect, it is interesting to observe that Mencius and the Mencian moral tradition does not seem to have any problem with empathy, compassion, and benevolence. Rather, such sentiments are regarded as self-evident points of departure that need no further justification, other than their constitution of human nature endowed by Heaven, within much of the Mencian moral discourse.

The Imperative of Empathy

It should be clear from our discussion that both orders of empathy are at play in the Mencian moral universe. Mencius' empathic response to the king when the king expresses embarrassment about his various problematic desires, e.g., his desires for wealth, sex, pop music, and even power, are examples of first-order empathy. Mencius' counsel of a ruler about the latter's reaction to an ox being led to its own sacrifice is a case of second-order empathy, namely Mencius' empathy with the king's sympathy for a helpless animal. Slote's observation of second-order empathy/sympathy is especially relevant to the king's sympathy toward a sacrificial ox as Mencius is clearly concerned not so much with the wellbeing of the ox, which is the object of the king's sympathy, as with the king's sympathy itself. This is evidenced in Mencius' warning that a gentleman should not be close to the kitchen where he would be exposed to the killing of animals, which would presumably make it hard to eat meat.[9] Furthermore, Mencius' effort to see flickers of compassion and benevolence toward an animal shown by a usually ruthless monarch means that Mencius resorts to empathy as a response to the king's sympathetic reactions to the ox, in contrast with others who see the king's action as a sign of his stinginess or simple idiocy.

It is worth pointing out that empathizing with a cruel ruler is not an easy task, especially for a well-known moralist who is willing to confront a ruler directly. Mencius' empathic response to the king's sympathetic concerns or even problematic desires should be understood as a conscious decision he makes in order to find hope in a hopeless situation. Mencius clearly believes empathy is more effective in changing the heartmind of another person, especially a ruler, than condemnation under certain circumstances. It is conceivable that in order to be empathic with a cruel ruler Mencius has to dip deep into his own heartmind and finds that fountain of empathy, the flood-like moral energy (*haoran zhi qi* 浩然之氣), consciously directs it toward the moral client, usually a king, in front of him in order to help the king preserve his humanity in the way he governs. He sees it as his mission to persuade the rulers of his time to adopt a more humane and benevolent policy toward their suffering people during an extremely violent period in Chinese history. This is the imperative of empathy in Mencian moral therapy.

7 Conclusion

To conclude, in this essay we have tried to develop a framework of moral therapy in order to better appreciate certain distinct features in Mencius' approach to moral persuasion, especially pertaining to his unique way of dealing with problematic human desires and connecting them to the cultivation of moral virtues. We have shown that critical to the Mencian moral therapy is his ability to discern an implicit moral script operative in everyday actions of another moral agent, often a ruler in the *Mencius*. Mencius' objective is to bring such a script out in the open and help the ruler repurpose it for the moral-political cause of benevolent governance.

Our brief examination of Michael Slote's moral sentimentalism has shown that an empathy-based, rather than rationalist, virtue ethics offers a potent interpretative framework to rearticulate certain unique features of the Mencian moral discourse, especially the ubiquitous role played by empathy. We have seen that Mencius sees empathy as both a critical aspect of our moral nature and an effective way to engage with another moral agent who might not be receptive to moral persuasion under normal circumstances. As Slote observes,[10] knowing the motivation of another moral agent is critical in the Mencian moral philosophy, especially when compared with Aristotle for whom such a knowledge does not even come into consideration.

Clearly, Mencius has a lot to contribute to contemporary moral discourse, being among the earliest moral sentimentalists if we accept Slote's categorization of him. Edward Slingerland goes as far as claiming that "Mencius is arguably a much better resource as moral psychologist than Aristotle, the premodern thinker to whom contemporary virtue ethics typically turns" (Slingerland 2007: 380). Slote's systematic and nuanced deliberations on empathy, care and their moral and political potentials can be especially useful for contemporary moral philosophers sympathetic to the Mencian (and the Confucian more broadly) paradigm to explore core Mencian moral insights for a more robust Confucian moral and political project in the contemporary world.[11]

Notes

1 In this essay I translate the Chinese word *xin* 心 in the classical texts as "heartmind," instead of heart, mind, heart-and-mind or heart-mind as adopted by other translators. Heartmind is obviously not an English word, but a neologism trying to capture the widely shared scholarly consensus that ancient Chinese did not differentiate between heart and mind the way they are used in contemporary English. Since we are dealing with classical Chinese texts that are translated into contemporary English for contemporary Western readership in this context, it makes sense to highlight this point in the way the word *xin* is translated. For me, the attraction of heartmind as a single term is precisely its ambiguity, much like *xin* in different texts and contexts. It runs the gamut of the emotive, cognitive, evaluative, calculative, voluntary and whatever other functions *xin* performs, with different texts leaning toward different aspects. In other words, the fact that pre-modern Chinese thinkers allow *xin* to perform such a wide range of roles (without feeling the need to clarify which one) suggests the underlying assumption of the singularity of heartmind. Heartmind has the advantage of being both familiar and strange, not unlike *xin* in all its complexity and ambiguity in various Chinese texts through the ages.
2 For example, Philip J. Ivanhoe portrays Confucius's *dao* as "a kind of therapy for his disordered age" (Ivanhoe 1991: 57). Edward Slingerland calls Mencius a moral psychoanalyst (Slingerland 2011a: 98)
3 Readers can refer to Erica Brindley 2012 for a detailed study of the role of music in early Chinese politics and philosophy.

4 "Normal" here is a statistical concept.
5 This is not uncontested, but we will leave it to another occasion as the focus in this essay is sentimentalism rather than rationalism.
6 Ivanhoe usefully differentiates selfishness from self-centeredness: "Being self-centered overlaps with but is different from our normal conception of being selfish. Being selfish means to give excessive or exclusive weight to one's own narrow interests over and against the interests of others; being self-centered means to take the self as the center of one's thoughts about the world" (Ivanhoe 2015: 243).
7 One of the problematic implications of this partialism is nepotism of which the Confucians are sometimes accused of (Graham 1989: 302). While Mencius is certainly susceptible to such a charge, there are resources in his thought that can help to mitigate it.
8 What Slote has in mind here is Peter Singer's famous critique of commonsense moral judgment with its implicit partialism in Singer's essay "Famine, Affluence, and Morality."
9 As Slingerland observes (2011b: 407), despite the lament of hypocrisy by some contemporary commentators, Mencius' advice makes sense in the environment wherein even the notional possibility of vegetarianism does not exist. Of course, this does not mean that the Mencian empathy-based moral sentiment should not be developed to its logical conclusion in the contemporary world wherein the wellbeing of animal world and the broader ecological concern are of utmost urgency.
10 This is from Slote's comment on my presentation during an international conference, "Slote Encountering Chinese Philosophy," held on March 16–17, 2018, at the Chinese University of Hong Kong.
11 I would like to express my appreciation to Yong Huang for organizing the wonderful conference, "Slote Encountering Chinese Philosophy," on March 16–17, 2018, at the Chinese University of Hong Kong, and for inviting me to be part of this conversation. I would also like to thank Michael Slote for his comments on an earlier version of this essay as well as all the conference participants for their helpful critiques. Of course, all errors and inadequacies remain mine alone.

Bibliography

Brindley, Erica (2012), *Music, Cosmology, and the Politics of Harmony in Early China*, Albany: SUNY Press.
Graham, A. C. (1989), *Disputers of the Tao: Philosophical Argument in Ancient China*, La Salle, IL: Open Court.
Held, Virginia (2011), "Care, Empathy, and Justice: Comments on Michael Slote's Moral Sentimentalism," *Analytic Philosophy*, 52 (4): 312–18.
Hoffman, Martin (2000), *Empathy and Moral Development: Implications for Caring and Justice*, New York: Cambridge University Press.
Ivanhoe, Philip J. (1991), "Character Consequentialism and Early Confucianism," *Journal of Religious Ethics*, 19 (1): 55–70.

Ivanhoe, Philip J. (2015), "Senses and Values of Oneness," in Brian Bruya (ed.), *The Philosophical Challenge from China*," Boston, MA: MIT Press.
Lau, D. C., trans. (1970), *Mencius, Translated with an Introduction and Notes*. London & New York: Penguin.
Slingerland, Edward (2007), "Chinese Thought from an Evolutionary Perspective," *Philosophy East & West*, 57 (3): 375–88.
Slingerland, Edward (2011a), "'Of what use are the *Odes*?' Cognitive Science, Virtue Ethics, and Early Confucian Ethics," *Philosophy East & West*, 61 (1): 80–109.
Slingerland, Edward (2011b), "The Situationist Critique and Early Confucian Virtue Ethics," *Ethics*, 121: 390–419.
Slote, Michael (2007), *The Ethics of Care and Empathy*, London: Routledge.
Slote, Michael (2009), "Comments on Bryan Van Norden's Virtue Ethics and Consequentialism in Early Chinese Philosophy," *Dao: A Journal of Comparative Philosophy*, 8: 289–95.
Slote, Michael (2010a), *Moral Sentimentalism*. New York: Oxford University Press.
Slote, Michael (2010b), "The Mandate of Empathy," *Dao: A Journal of Comparative Philosophy*, 9: 303–07.
Slote, Michael (2014), *A Sentimentalist Theory of the Mind*, New York: Oxford University Press.
Small, Christopher (1998), *Musicking: The Meanings of Performing and Listening*, Middletown, CT: Wesleyan University Press.
Van Norden, Bryan (2009), "Response to Angle and Slote," *Dao A Journal of Comparative Philosophy*, 8: 305–09.

10

Slote's Moral Sentimentalism and Confucian *Qing*-ism

On-cho Ng
Penn State University, United States

1 Introduction

There is much to appreciate in Slote's endeavor to tap into the resources afforded by Chinese traditions with regard to the role of emotions in moral thinking, aptly showing that the *soi-disant* East–West divide is, in fact, imminently bridgeable. Even without appealing to the faintly quaint notion of a human condition, cross-cultural comparative studies of all sorts have shown that the possibilities for intellectual convergence, if not consensus, abound, notwithstanding vastly different historico-cultural circumstances. Insofar as the goal of our present conversations is to further tease out such intercultural resonance by using Slote's reference to Chinese thought as a point of departure, it behooves us to attempt an intervention in his "moral sentimentalism" by posing the multivalent Confucian notion of *qing* (emotions, sentiments, feelings) as a counterpoint in the guise of a confected philosophical "ism," thereby throwing into relief the seemingly universal resonances and apparently particular discords, as we traverse, intercultural and hermeneutically, the verbal and semantic terrain of mind/*xin*, nature/*xing*, emotions/*qing*, desires/*yu*, and so on, in an effort to make sense of the nature and role of emotions and desires in the morphology of morality, in terms of both their objectivity and normativity. Thus, at the same time that I acknowledge the inspirations that Slote's works offer in my endeavor to rethink *qing* as a philosophical concept in the Chinese context, I see the latter as an enriching conceptual and empirical resource for, if not critical corrective of, the former.

2 Slote's Sentimentalism

Let us first set the scene by limning at least the gist of the sort of philosophy that Slote has been doing in the past two decades or so, which offers affinities as grounds for companionable juxtaposition and dialogue with aspects of Chinese thought. One might suppose that the ideational and intellectual rapport begins with his rejection of the priority accorded to cold and pure reason in ethical construal in the Western philosophical traditions. Arguing on behalf of an agent-driven virtue ethics that militates against the conventional Aristotelian approach of justifying the good and the right in terms of virtues, he seeks to delimit and circumscribe the prevailing role of rationalism in much of ethico-moral thinking in the West, from ancient Greece to the present day. In his *Morals and Motives* (Slote 2001), Slote began to propound a virtue ethics premised on the intent and impulse of caring. He does so by drawing from the alternative stream of sentimentalism, *à la* Hume and Hutcheson, in which the test and criterion of right action is its leaning toward enhancing the welfare, and its propensity to enable the care of fellow human beings. Several subsequent works served to flesh out his agent-based ethical theory, most notably *The Ethics of Care and Empathy* (Slote 2007), *Moral Sentimentalism* (Slote 2010a), *Essays on the History of Ethics* (Slote 2010a, and *The Impossibility of Perfection: Aristotle, Feminism, and the Complexities of Ethics* (Slote 2011). In the first book of this tetralogy, Slote posits that a well-developed ethics of care, as a "total or systematic *human* morality" (Slote 2007) featuring empathy (the capacity to feel others' pain) and not mere sympathy (feeling bad for others in pain) as a self-sufficient criterion of moral discriminations, can be a self-contained system of thinking that, in contradistinction to long-established ethical formulations, affords us better insights into a vast array of moral issues, including respect, autonomy, practical reason, and justice, such that it is actually preferable to liberalism, according to which the moral agent is incapable of the "*fullest sort* of love" (Slote 2007: 76).

To flesh out this ethics of care so that it becomes a metaethics, in *Moral Sentimentalism*, which replicates verbatim sections of the earlier book and reiterates many of its main arguments, Slote conceives of empathy as the basic premise of moral actions as well as the point of reference for moral terms (good-and-bad/right-and-wrong), adjudicated by psychological, affective, and conative attitudes, especially those of approval and disapproval, the former being "empathetic warmth," the latter "empathetic chill." Once again, insofar as Slote is concerned that the good and the right may have been unjustifiably downplayed or elided in modern moral philosophical theories, such as the liberal rights-driven one, his sentimentalist metaethical exposition seeks precisely to restore their central places in relation to empathy: "[I]t is *a priori* that goodness (or rightness) is whatever causes us to be warmed by the warmth displayed by agents, and since it is trivial and obvious that it is agential warmth itself that causes this warming, it follows that agential warmth, as displayed in actions, is just what the goodness (or rightness) of actions consists in" (Slote 2010a: 61). Hence the natural intrication of fact and value in the moral sentimentalism, in the sense that *that which is* may cohere with *that which ought to be*—compassionate actions are morally good and right. As such, it may play fruitful roles in matters of justice (social, and global), extending its utility to intellectual and scientific pursuits.

Slote's *Essays on the History of Ethics* reviews and rethinks the history of ethics from the vantage point of his sentimentalism. In particular, he upholds the sort of elevationism espoused by Plato, Aristotle, and the Stoics to be the most warrantable of the ethical theories that define the interrelations between virtues and well-being (or self-interest), to the extent that it reduces well-being to virtue, whereas Kantian dualism dichotomizes them and utilitarian reductionism subordinates virtue to well-being. Building on Hume's sentimentalist explanation of approval and disapproval, Slote seeks to integrate normative sentimentalism with a sentimentalist metaethics. One essay engages with Bryan Van Norden's construal of virtue ethics in the Chinese context, arguing for the expansion of its comparative reach so that Hume may be a meaningful correlative exemplification.

The Impossibility of Perfection brings Slote's care ethics of empathy to bear on the philosophical feminist critique of patriarchal view of values and virtues, arguing for the revision of and resistance against gendered assertions of values, and thus, virtues. The way to do so is "to introduce a new category of values, a new way of thinking about our parsing goods and virtues—we need the notion of a *partial* value, of a *partial* virtue or human good" (Slote 2011: 28). A partial good perforce entails a contending good, such as the antagonistic nexus of frankness and tact, in which the realization of one means the diminution of the other, and therefore absolute unanimity of the virtues is not possible. For Slote, "patriarchy sees gender-relative dependent or non-dependent values, while feminism ethical thought sees or can see paired partial values that are equally relevant to men and women" (Slote 2011: 36). Therefore, a good life nevertheless must mean one in which there is compromise between goods and virtues. Countervailing the Greek and Enlightenment attestations that all ethical values may be harmonized under the auspices of reason, Slote posits disunity in human good and virtue.[1]

In other words, for Slote, conventional Western ethics premised on rationality, from Kantian deontology, through utilitarianism, to the ethics of rights, leaves much to be desired. I am in sympathy with his discontent. In much of this dominant strand of ethics, the realization of the good has indeed come to mean not restraining and limiting others' ability and opportunity to realize their own interests, underpinned by the concepts of individual freedom and autonomy, and buttressed by the application of law as the guarantor of procedures whereby individuals may pursue, mediate, and work out their various self-interests. Thus, anything is acceptable and admissible as long as there is no violation of the law, such that ethics, to the extent that it exists, is minimalist, as enacted legal imperatives trump unwritten moral mandates. Slote's sentimentalist moral philosophy is a purposeful corrective. At the same time that it makes sense of the practical aspects of morality, it situates morality in a naturalistic worldview. In his *A Sentimentalist Theory of Mind* (Slote 2014), through engaging with the philosophy of mind, Slote seeks to further explicate and justify the apparent objectivity and normativity of an ethico-morality based on emotions (especially love and gratitude), anchored on the idea that belief is in fact an emotion—emotion is a propositional attitude, such that evaluation is a critical important component of any analysis of emotion. In other words, he defines and shapes the questions of why and how emotion may be a subject of philosophical inquiry.[2]

3 Confucian *Qing*-ism

While Slote is a philosopher, his work has a historical subtext, showing that views of emotions do change and evolve.[3] His engagement with empathy reflects a moment of socio-political change, as our increasingly globalized world redresses and rethinks values and priorities. In particular, Slote's appeal to empathy and receptivity as the basis and predicate of a care ethics strikes chords of harmony with Chinese ruminations on conditions of moral action with regard to *qing* qua emotion. In the Chinese construal of *qing*, which I conveniently but inelegantly call *qing*-ism, emotions do indeed take center stage in the morphology of morality, so that moral thoughts can be said to be sentimental, and if moral facts correspond with sentimental responses, then emotions are the principal source of moral knowledge.

If we take this *qing*-ism seriously, we may say that emotions involve not only "active entanglements with the world" but they are also constitutive of the moral dimensions of the human self (Solomon 2004: 68). Emotions frame a "philosophical hub" that in essence involves questions of ontology, epistemology, and ethics (de Sousa 1987: 18–20). Significantly, these questions in terms of emotion are often couched in the form of antinomies. Epistemologically speaking, is emotion merely *subjective* effusions of our will that shed little light on the *objective* nature of the world? Is it *arational-irrational* spontaneous projections that offend the better senses of our deliberate *rational* self? Is it after all ontologically *posterior* to our *prior* nature, although humanity cannot be without emotion? Can it ever be the *foundation of ethics* or is it doomed to be the *source of antinomian chaos*? Precisely because of emotion's evocation of such philosophical ambivalence that invites opposite conclusions, it is often treated as a second-order entity and activity—a mere personal outward expression that is peripheral to the primary integrity of an essential being anchored on sound objective rationality.[4] Nevertheless, in contemporary Western thought, emotions have increasingly been interpreted and dissected not as nonintentional feelings but as intentional and object-directed phenomena. They represent a sort of cognitive state that involves belief, judgment, and thought. Desires themselves, or the conative related to the body, can be the legitimate wellspring of actions and behaviors. If one subscribes to a philosophy of the mind that sees it as socially mediated and constructed, then indeed "emotions are not feelings that well up in some natural and untutored way from our natural selves.... They are in fact not personal and natural at all [but] are, instead, contrivances, social constructs" (Nussbaum 1988: 226). In short, whether in terms of a socialized philosophy of emotion or a more general philosophy of the mind, the inexorable interpenetration of the conative (subjective) and cognitive (objective) seems to be at the heart of the argument.⁵

This short reference to the Western conceptions of emotion, apart from the earlier one on Slote's, has a two-fold goal. First, I seek to establish, and then loosen and expand, the conceptual parameters around which an analysis of *qing* qua emotion in the Chinese philosophical context may be built. Second, I want to hint at the fact that the discourse on emotion in Confucianism evokes certain resonance with our current rethinking of emotion. A crucial caveat here is in order. At the same time that I appeal to comparison, I am aware that the deontological demands and prescriptions discernible in Platonism and Kantianism, or for that matter, Judeo-Christianity, were never as systematically, rigidly, and unyieldingly articulated in classical and Neo-Confucianism. Moreover, the anti-ontological tendencies integral to the contemporary Western views on emotion as highly personal, registering of the fleeting conative-epistemological dimensions of ephemeral realities, are quite antithetical to the Confucian ontological conception of emotion, which asserts the ontogenetic oneness of the affective and nature.

Constructing *qing*-ism is an exercise in historical semantics that lays bare the accrued meanings and connotations of the conceptual term of *qing* (emotion). It is a sort of taxonomy of the Confucian models of the person in terms of *qing* qua emotion. A comprehensive historical semantics on *qing* is obviously impossible here, and so I will be highly selective and perhaps even unhistorical by simply selecting what I deem to be representative cases. In talking about classical Chinese conception of *qing*, one should be reminded of the late A. C. Graham's contention that despite its ubiquity in Pre-Han texts, it does not mean "passions." Rather, as "a noun it means 'the facts,'" and "as an adjective 'genuine.'" Thus, *qing* refers to the naming of reality: "[T]he *ch'ing* of X is what X cannot lack if it is to be *called* 'X'" (Grahm 1989: 59–66). On the other hand, as Chad Hansen points out, although it is valid to define *qing* in terms of the reality—and the naming of it—of a thing, such definition ignores the affective states that inhere in such naming. Hansen refines Graham's theory by seeing *qing* more specifically as "reality responses" or "reality inputs." *Qing* "are all reality-induced discrimination or distinction-making reactions.... They guide the application of terms ... in real time in real (and inevitably unique) situations. Thus, the fundamental sensory distinctions ... are *qing*. But so also is the reality feedback we get from executing a *dao* (guiding discourse) ... —pleasure, anger, sadness, fear, love, hate, desire" (Hansen 1994: 194–7). When Hansen describes *qing* as "reality inputs," he is asking us to see that emotion, in an ontogenetic way, correlates with human nature and nature. Nature, as it is, can be felt as emotion through the mediation of the human heart-mind. This ontogenetic structural chain of action and reaction is most elegantly explained in the "Records of Music" (*Yueji*) in the *Records of Rites* (*Liji*). The *Yueji* does state that the seven emotions of *xi* (delight), *nu* (anger), *ai* (sorrow), *le* (joy), *ai* (affection), *hen* (hate), *yu* (desire) are "not nature" (*feixing*) (*Shisanjing* 1: 885–6). But it is also unequivocal in affirming that innate responses are aroused from the very core (*zhong*) of the mind-heart (*xin*) and are therefore inextricably tied to things-as-they-are (*wu*), that is, nature (ibid., 885–6). In other words, emotion, issued from the depth of our tranquil (*jing*) nature, responds in the most accurate and appropriate manner to reality. Emotion is the changing existential inputs into the reality of a constant nature. Thus, in the *Yueji*, there is the unmistakable conflation of emotion with nature, and this nature-with-emotion (*xingqing*) is the basis on which the sage-rulers instituted rites and music (ibid., 886, 889). Graham was therefore right to suggest that *qing* is the naming of reality, but he was wrong to deny that emotions, or the "passions" in his word, play both ontological and epistemological roles in such naming. The structural holism of emotion-in-nature may also be seen in the following examples.

Confucius does not explicitly and directly explore *qing*, but for him, a full and fulfilled emotional life is deemed to be an integral part of everyday living. For instance, on the impact of sadness, it is said that "when the Master was eating by the side of a mourner, he never ate to the full. He did not sing on the same day in which he had been weeping" (*Analects* 7.9). On the pathos evoked by the aesthetic power of music, the *Analects* tells of Confucius forgetting the taste of meat for three months after he had heard the powerful Shao music in Qi (*Analects* 7.13). He also gave free rein to his emotion of grief when this favorite disciple Yan Yuan passed away: "When Yan Yuan died, the Master bewailed him exceedingly, and the disciples who were with him said, 'Master, your grief is excessive?' 'Is it excessive?' he said. 'If I am not to mourn bitterly for this man, for whom should I mourn?'" (*Analects* 11.9). Emotion is in fact an expression of supreme virtue since, according to him, "[o]nly those who are endowed with *ren* (humaneness, humanity, humanheartedness) can love or hate others" (*Analects* 4.3). It is therefore discriminating and preferential. What Confucius seeks is a life-long joy through the attainment of knowledge: "He is simply a man, who in his eager pursuit [of knowledge] forgets his food, who in the joy of its attainment forgets his sorrows, and who does not perceive that old age is coming on" (*Analects* 7.18). The securing of joy necessarily means the dissipation of anxiety and fear. A *junzi* (a morally sovereign person) is burdened with neither anxiety nor fear, for "when introspective examination discovers nothing dysfunctional, what is there to be anxious about, what is there to fear?" (*Analects* 12.4). The person with superior noble character is "satisfied and composed," whereas a "mean person" (*xiaoren*, that is, a morally defective and deficient person) is always "full of distress" (*Analects* 7.36).

Thus, to Confucius, emotion is the natural manifestation of our moral-ethical constitution, an instance of the holism of inner virtues and outer joy, or vice versa, inner evil and outer anxiety. It cannot therefore be simply an intrapersonal, subjective psychological state. Emotion has everything to do with the unbreakable relation between the exertion of moral virtues, which is cognitively judicious, and its conative affects and effects in emotional terms. As such, it cannot be a mere subjective emotive paroxysm devoid of the objective grounding of moral right and wrong. Supreme emotional contentment is part and parcel of superior moral attainment. If this interpretation of Confucius's conception of *qing* is correct, it shows that Graham's translation of *qing* as that which is genuine and essential in humanity is very sensible but nonetheless incomplete. *Xing* (human nature) and *qing* are indeed, as Graham noted, "overlapping concepts, and the combination of *hsing ch'ing* is common" (Graham 1989: 65). But he dissolved the affective elements as *qing* becomes totally submerged in the ontological state of *xing*, thereby failing to appreciate the fundamental fact that the very entity of *xin* given both the faculty (mind) and organ (heart) effectively blur the line between the cognitive and affective.

Mencius, like Confucius, does not directly engage *qing*, but his famous thesis that the cardinal virtues of *ren* (humanity), *yi* (rightness), *li* (propriety), and *zhi* (moral wisdom) are fulfillment of the four innate "sprouts" (*duan*) of the senses of sympathy, shame, humility, and judgment suggests the affective root of moral action. However, in his conversation with Gaozi, Mencius does use the word "*qing*" in his assertion of the goodness of nature (*xing*): "As far as his essential emotion (*qing*) is concerned, a person is capable of becoming good" (*Mencius* 6a6). To the extent that Mencius actually uses the word *qing* to illustrate his central anthropological message of our inborn capability to do good, *qing*, as the "essential emotion," can reasonably be understood as the fundamental and original emotion-in-nature, the moral but also affective sprouts (*duan*), that is, the authentic unadulterated state of humanity. Moreover, Mencius clearly elucidates the sprout of sympathy-humanity, as is well known, by referring to the feeling of alarm and horror that one would have if one saw a child about to fall into a well. According to David Nivison, acting morally in the Mencian scheme is a process that begins by "extending" (*tui*) our embryonic emotions prescribed by our nature. Our innate moral "deep structure," as it were, is developed, in the absence of force, in the right direction. To do good is to involve our whole and full sensibility in that which is right (Nivison 1996: 109–13). Mencius's "sprouts" are at once instinctual emotional responses and their moral reasoning basis. As such, they need to be properly channeled so that they play customary and quotidian roles in our practical deliberations (Wong 1991: 31–44). To put it another way, in Mencius's words, one must "retain the mind-heart" (*cunxin*) by means of *jen* and *li*, and thereby become a *junzi* free from vexations, a state of emotional tranquility:

> The benevolent person loves others, and the decorous person respects others. He who loves others is always loved by them; he who respects others is always respected by them. . . . Hence while a superior person has perennial worries, he has no unexpected vexations. His worries are of this kind: Shun was a man; I am also a man. Shun set an example for the empire worthy of being handed down to posterity, yet here I am, just an ordinary man. That is something worth worrying about. If one worries about it, what should one do? On should become like Shun. That is all. On the other hand, the superior person is free from vexations. He never does anything that is not benevolent; he does not act

except in accordance with propriety. Even when unexpected vexations come his way, the superior person refuses to be perturbed by them.

Mencius 4b28

Thus, in extending our emotion and feeling in connection with our nature and mind-heart, one ultimately arrives in an unperturbed state of tranquility. Mencius describes this as "not stirring the mind-heart" (*budongxin*), which is a sort of moral courage that comes only with moral rectitude: "If, on looking within, one finds oneself to be in the wrong, then even though one's adversary be only a common fellow coarsely clad, one is bound to tremble with fear. But if one finds oneself in the right, one goes forward even against men in the thousands." Mencius goes on to explain that this supra-emotional state of non-perturbation is also a result of one's ability and success in nourishing the "flood-like *qi* (breath)" that "fills the space between Heaven and Earth," and "unites rightness and the Way." In short, by pursuing rightness (*yi*) and acting in accordance with "the standard set in one's mind-heart," that is, by "taking hold of one's will and not abuse one's *qi*," one is finally in tune with incipient emotion and returns to our nature, wholly immersed in the profound cosmic breath (*Mencius* 2a1). Not stirring the mind-heart does not mean achieving a state of emotionlessness, but rather forestalling the mind-heart from being overtaken by circumstances, resulting in ingrained and unresolved emotions, and selfish desires.

It is in the *Xunzi* that we find a clear reference to and definition of *qing*: "The feelings of liking and disliking, of delight and anger, and of sorrow and joy that are inborn in our nature are called 'emotions'" (Knoblock 1988: 3.127). The emotions are crucial as the "inner content" that renders meaningful the pursuits of rites (*li*) (Knoblock 1988: 3.62). Like Confucius and Mencius, Xunzi certainly sees a clear linkage between emotion and moral judgment and action. In exploring the question of "self-cultivation" (*xiushen*), he tells us that delight will be felt when one sees good, yielding the urge to preserve the good. The witnessing of evil, on the other hand, induces "sorrowful apprehension," coupled with "loathing" and "hate," prompting the effort of internal self-examination (Knoblock 1988: 1.151). Yet, in the same context, Xunzi emphasizes the need to curtail excessive expression of emotion. A superior person has the capacity to rise above and go beyond his immediate emotional responses and therefore to maintain a state of spiritual equilibrium: "He does not commit the excess of snatching things back out of anger or that of giving things away out of joy. The superior person can broaden his sense of purpose even in times of hardship and poverty because he exalts the virtue of humanity.... [T]he superior person's ability consists in his use of a sense of common good to prevail over personal desires" (Knobloch 1988: 1.158). Thus, it is the fruitful interpenetration of emotion and moral virtue rather than their separation that defines the self. Moreover, a trans-emotional state of presence forged by the tempering of emotion by virtue is considered to be the ultimate psycho-spiritual constitution. In other words, emotion cannot be reduced to the manifold impacts or impressions recorded on the passivity of the mental apparatus, that is, our mere sensory faculties.

That emotion is at once the primordial background (being an integral part of nature) and the actualized foreground (being the manifestation of that nature) is elucidated in the *Doctrine of the Mean* (*Zhongyong*):

> Before issuance of the feelings of pleasure, anger, sorrow and joy, it is called equilibrium (*zhong*, or centrality, the mean). With the issuance of these feelings and their attaining due measure and degree, it is called harmony (*he*). Equilibrium is the great foundation of the world, and harmony its universal path. When equilibrium and harmony are realized to the utmost, heaven and earth will attain their proper order and all things will flourish.
>
> Chan 1963: 98; translation slightly modified

The very givenness of emotion, before any axiological predicates, is the primordial foundation of all-under-heaven with intrinsic openness and intentionality, teleologically proceeding toward its actualization. The *zhong* of emotion forms a background of plenitude that dissolves antinomies. Emotion is not pitted as subjective effusions of our will against the objective nature of the world; it is ontologically coeval with nature. Far from tending toward antinomian chaos, its harmonious issuance (*he*) lays down the universal path. This harmony is reminiscent of Mencius's idea of the unperturbability of the mind-heart (*budongxin*).

How does this morphology of *qing*-emotion in classical Confucianism compare with that in the reformulated Song Confucianism, that is, the tradition of Learning of the Way (*daoxue*)? It appears that as ontology in the latter becomes increasingly couched in terms of the dualistic anthropology of the axiologically distinct *li* (principle) and *qi* (material force, psychophysical energy) and their correlates, despite constant philosophical reiterations of their oneness, emotion's ontological role undergoes changes. Let us chart these changes by looking at the treatment of *qing* by the Cheng brothers and Zhu Xi.

To Cheng Yi, it is an ontological given that emotion is integrally a part of nature (*xing*). He subscribes to the *Mean*'s conception of the pristine emotion as nature in the original state, that is, before its issuance as emotion. He sees the oneness of nature, destiny, heaven, mind-heart and emotion: "The origin of nature is called destiny. The very natural being of nature is heaven. Nature, after assuming form, is called the mind-heart. Nature, with its arousal, is called emotion. These various entities are all one" (*Er Cheng yishu* 25//11b). When asked if pleasure and anger came from nature, he affirmed that "once there is life and the awareness of it, there is nature. Once there is nature, there is emotion. How can there be emotion in the absence of nature?" When asked further why pleasure and anger, being from nature, nevertheless expressed themselves outwardly, Cheng Yi answered, "It is not that [emotion] is manifested outwardly. It is that [emotion] responds to the outer but issues from the very core in the center" (*Er Cheng yishu* 18/17b). There is thus no question that he sees emotion as rooted in nature. To the extent that emotion is part of nature, nature does not stifle emotion, as he and Cheng Hao told us: "A person's possessing pleasure, anger, sorrow and joy is nature as it naturally is. If now we recklessly claim that they should be extirpated in order to apprehend heaven's truth, it can be said that heaven's truth is destroyed" (*Er Cheng yishu* 2A/8b–9a). Cheng Yi therefore rejects characterizing "nature as good and emotion as not good." The description (*ming*) of "not good" should not be applied to emotion since it is "the arousal of nature" (*qing zhi dong*) (*Henan* 2/25a).

However, Cheng Yi also says that at times emotion "has to be returned to that which is correct," thereby implying emotion's tendency toward the bad (*ibid.*). Moreover, emotion is clearly a second-order entity or activity in that it cannot be equated with nature. He explains by using the analogy of water: "Nature's possessing pleasure and anger is like water's making waves." Water's nature is its placidity, flat, clear and still as a mirror. But with sands and rocks on the unleveled underlying ground, or if there is wind brushing the water's surface, there will be ground swells and waves. Just as these turbulences are not the nature of water, neither are pleasure and anger human nature. What human nature consists in are the "four sprouts" (*siduan*), that is, the innate feelings and emotions embedded in the primordial nature before arousal. Both water itself and nature itself are prior. Without them, there would not be waves and emotion (*Er Cheng yishu* 18/17b). Cheng Yi also views emotion as the "issuance" (*fa*) of the mind-heart (*xin*) which is really one with nature: "The mind-heart is originally good, but when it is issued in thoughts and deliberations, there is what is good and what is not good. Once it has been issued, it can no longer be called the mind-heart; it should be called emotion." He uses the comparison with water again: "Take the similar case of water. It is called water, but when it flows in different streams, some moving east, some moving west, it produces what are called tributaries" (*Er Cheng yishu* 18/17a). Cheng Hao, in conceptualizing emotion as the arousal of nature, also points to the fact that only the latter is the "root" (*ben*), which is in a state of "favorable prosperity" (*shunli*), whereas the former can periodically lapse into evil, requiring "rectification" (*zheng*) (*Er Cheng yihsu* 2a/15b).

As the latency and stillness of nature (pristinely good) becomes separate and distinct from the movement and actualization of emotion (potentially bad), emotion also becomes the source of antinomy. This severance is a result of the Cheng brothers' identifying the truly authentic self, nature, with the ontological ultimate of heaven (*tian*) or principle (*li*): "What humanity receives from heaven is destiny. What is inherent in things is principle. What is endowed in humanity is nature. As the master of the body, it is the mind-heart" (*Er Cheng yishu* 18/17a). As emotion is now consigned to a posterior metaphysical space, a gap appears between it and nature. To bridge the gap, there is a veined determinate route, that is, the processes of arousal (*dong*) and issuance (*fa*), along which emotion emerges from the background into the foreground. In contradistinction to the classical conception of *qing* which is axiologically neutral, the Cheng brothers' emotion, in its passage from the ontological to the ontic and back, assumes different valuation. Emotion is now the function (*yong*). Love (*ai*), for instance, is emotion, while humanity (*ren*) is nature. The former alone cannot represent the latter as a whole. "How can love alone be taken as humanity?" Cheng Yi asks (*Er Cheng yishu* 18/1a). "Love is the function of humanity" (*Er Cheng yishu* 15/8b). Such assignation of value splinters emotion into two. On the one hand, emotion is good as a part of nature. On the other, emotion with its affective essence and expressive function, in tuning into and submitting to the corporeal world, is the source of the bad. Hence the necessity to control it:

> Heaven and earth, in preserving and nurturing the essential, obtain the best of the Five Agents. It is endowed in humanity as the root. In its authentic stillness before issuance, all the five natures are complete, namely, humanity, rightness, propriety, wisdom and trustworthiness. When forms come into being, external things touch the forms which are then aroused from within. As the inside is aroused, the seven emotions come forth to the outside, namely, pleasure, anger, sorrow, joy, liking, disliking and desire. As emotion burns and becomes recklessly heedless, nature then becomes vulnerably open. Therefore, the sagacious restrains emotion so that it corresponds with that which is the core, rectifies the mind-heart, and nurtures nature. This is thus called developing emotion in accordance with nature (*xing qi qing*). The foolish knows not how to control it, indulging in emotion to the point of being crooked, and killing nature by fettering it. This is called stifling nature by emotion (*qing qi xing*).
>
> *Yichuan* 4/1a

This passage by Cheng Yi not only clearly shows nature and emotion as axiologically unequally, but also reveals the potential and imminent adverse moral and ethical consequences of giving rein to emotion.

Cheng Hao is similarly wary of the caprice and restlessness of emotion. Our pleasure and anger are often merely the selfish functioning of our limited thinking. In a letter he wrote to Zhang Zai (1020–77) on the difficulty of maintaining the quiescence of nature as a result of the intervention of emotion, he expounded on the role of emotion and its proper management. Anger is "easily aroused but difficult to control," Cheng Hao asserts. His solution to recalcitrant emotion is to abandon intrapersonal subjective affective expressiveness in favor of an object-oriented conative channeling, which is the sages' way of coming to grips with pleasure and anger. He continues in this letter: "The pleasure of the sages comes when a thing deserves pleasure. The anger of the sages comes when a thing deserves anger. Therefore the sages' pleasure and anger do not hinge on the mind-heart but on things." Cheng Hao appeals to the objective right and wrong prescribed by principle (*li*) as the measure and control of our emotion: "We should be able to forget our anger when we feel angry, and instead look at the right and the wrong in terms of principle, and we will see that external temptations will not amount to evil" (*Yichuan* 3/1a–b). In other words, emotion after all is subjective projection that demands the intervention of objective criteria laid down by principle.

Such anthropology of emotion generates antinomy both in ontological and epistemological terms. Ontologically speaking, emotions must exist as a part of nature. The sages do express them. As such, they make up the true self; they define the integrity of being. But emotions are also pathological, affronts on our nature. Epistemologically speaking, emotions do inform us of the world. They are nature's arousal and issuance when responding to things. They are a set of reasonable, hence, rational, qualities instantiated by a person in his or her confrontation with the world. Our anger and pleasure tell us about the objects. On the other hand, emotions tell us nothing but the subject himself or herself, especially his or her selfish feelings. The epistemological question is the *Euthyphro* question: Do the gods love piety because it is piety, or do they simply describe as pious whatever they love? (Cf. De souse: 9). Cheng Hao asks us to answer the former in the affirmative—we are angry because that which makes us angry calls for this one emotion and no other. Nonetheless antinomy remains, and in an effort to resolve it, Cheng Hao proposes the universalization of emotion into a sort of supra-temporal and supra-spatial "non-emotion" (*wuqing*): "The constant principle of heaven and earth is that their mind is in all things, and yet they have no mind of their own. The constant principle of the sage is that his emotion is in accord with all creations, and yet he has no emotion of his own" (*Mingdao* 3/1a).

As is well known, Zhu Xi's ontology is premised on his notions of principle (*li*) and psycho-physical force (*qi*). It is also well known that despite their ultimate oneness and mutual identification, Zhu is "obliged to say that principle is prior" (Chan 1963: 634). This fundamental ontological principle, in humanity, is nature (*xing*): "Nature is principle. The mind-heart is its embracement and reservoir, and issues it forth into operation" (Chan 1963: 631; translation slightly modified). Emotion/*qing* is an integral part of humanity's constitution, and it distinguishes between the good and bad:

> But if humanity possesses a nature, it also possesses a certain form, and if it possesses a form, it must be that it also possesses a certain min-heart. This mind-heart cannot but be stirred by things, and being stirred by things, it is set into motion, and the desires of the nature emerge from it. From this there emerges the distinction between good and bad. The desires of this nature are what are called emotions.
>
> Virag 2007: 57

Zhu explains the interrelation between nature, mind-heart, and emotion in this way: "The mind-heart embraces both nature and emotion. Nature is substance (*ti*) and emotion is function (*yong*)" (*ibid*). Another way of describing the substance-function dichotomy is to view nature as the "root" (*gen*) and emotion as the "sprouts" (*ya*) (Qian 1986: 377). As with the Cheng brothers, Zhu also provides a teleological pattern of the interrelated movement of these entities:

"Humanity is nature; love is emotion. While emotion is issued in function, nature refers to that which is not yet issued" (Virag 1986: 378). Nature as the primordial principle in humanity "is the state before activity begins. Emotion is the state when activity has begun, and the mind-heart includes both of these states. For nature is the mind-heart before it is issued, while emotion is the mind-heart after it is issued.... Desire emanates from emotion." Zhu continues by using the familiar analogy of water to illustrate the sequential pattern of movement: "The mind-heart is comparable to water, nature is comparable to the calmness of still water, emotion is comparable to the flow of water, and desire is comparable to its waves." He further develops the analogy to demonstrate that there are good and bad desires:

> Just as there are good and bad waves, so there are good desires, such as when "I want humanity," and bad desires which rush out like wild and violent waves. When bad desires are substantial, they will destroy heaven's principle, as water bursts a dam and damages everything. When Mencius said that "emotion enables people to do good," he meant that the correct emotion flowing from our nature is originally all good.
>
> Chan 1963: 631; translation slightly modified

Indeed, Zhu endorses the show of emotion under the proper circumstance. "What affair in the world does not involve delight and anger, joy and grief?" he waxes rhetorical (Qian 1986: 379). When asked if the sages ever displayed anger, he replied that "when they ought to be angry, they will show it in their countenance. But if one has to punish someone for his crime and purposely smile, that would be wrong.... When one becomes angry at the right time, he will be acting in the proper degree. When the matter is over, anger disappears, and none of it will be retained" (Chan 1963: 632). Grief similarly can be expressed (Chan 1967: 39ff, 53), not to mention the basic instincts to satisfy hunger and thirst (Chan 1967: 155, 163).

But insofar as nature, a state antecedent to activity, is the substance of humanity, Zhu Xi privileges the phase of equilibrium prior to the issuance of emotion: "Unless one's mind-heart is tranquil by being absolutely quiet and without desire, how can one handle changing events and become one with the activities of the world?" (Chan 1967: 7). For with issuance comes the problem of evil: "There is nothing that is not good in nature. What the mind-heart issues is emotion, which may be no good. To speak of evil is not to say that the mind-heart does not apprehend [truth]. However, even though the original substance of the mind-heart is nothing but good, its flow results in evil because emotion moves with things" (Qian 1986: 378). Emotion begs proper control and restraint. It is an existential and experiential fact that in living, one cannot avoid being moved by things. It is "nature's desire." But it nevertheless requires the "control of the mind-heart" (*xinzai*). With the control of the mind-heart, "emotion can obtain its rectification and follow the constancy of nature, so that it can no longer be spoken of as desire. If it is not ruled, the flow of emotion submerges nature, which becomes only human desires" (Qian 1986: 380). The rule of the mind-heart which checks desires consists in the application of thought: "If we think through the right and wrong, and thought and ought-not of a thing, in accordance with its principle, then our thought will surely be correct" (Qian 1986: 378). With the application of principle as the reasonable yardstick, emotion finds proper manifestation: "We then take delight in things that call for delight without exceeding the bounds of delight, and are angry at things that call for anger without misdirecting our anger, so much so that sorrow, joy, liking and disliking can all be expressed in due degree and measure without exaggeration" (Qian 1986: 379).

Zhu Xi, in aligning human nature with the ontological ultimate of principle, does seem to at times create a metaphysical distance in the commerce between nature and emotion. Nature-qua-principle is the true substance that has infinite aspects and attributes, emotion being one. Although Zhu always reiterates the oneness of principle and material force, and the mutual reinforcement of nature and emotion, axiological ordering nonetheless forms the bedrock of his anthropology. The ordering brings forth all the attendant antinomies that we discussed above: First, emotion, albeit a part of the absolutely good nature, is the reality of contingent feelings that may lead to the bad. Second, emotion responds to and is moved by things, as nature dictates, and yet it is epistemologically unreliable, until the intervention of principle, which provides the needed objective and indeed universal insight. Third, emotion is an indispensable part of the integrity of the self and personhood, but it is not the firm ground on which ethics and morals can be built, unless it is properly issued with the mediation of the mind-heart. Fourth, emotion straddles the objective (nature-cum-emotion) and the subjective (individual instantiation of affective qualities), but only the objective mode of emotion transcends particular feelings and coheres with the universally right and wrong. Nevertheless, in the final analysis, emotion is ultimately conceived as a transcendent expressive quality of humanity in its ideal state. The fundamental assertion and assumption of *qing*-ism is that emotion is innately and integrally a part of the moral agent's quest of ethical self-realization, as Zhu Xi reminds us:

> Humaneness, rightness, ritual propriety and wisdom are all in the realm of nature. The nature has no form or image that one uses to discern it: all it has are these principles. Only if there are feelings is it possible to see it, and these are the sense of sympathy, shame, modesty and judgment. Therefore, Mencius spoke of the nature, saying, "Only on the basis of the feelings can one speak of goodness." The nature has no form or image/reflection, and only the feelings can be seen. Observing how its expression is good, we can know that the nature is originally good.
>
> Quoted in Virag 2007: 82

4 Juxtaposing Slote's Sentimentalism and Confucian *Qing*-ism

Qing-ism, as a philosophical hub embodying a host of philosophical questions, does seem to resonate with many of the concerns and contentions of Slote's moral sentimentalism. Both accept the sheer phenomenality and facticity of emotion, which necessitates the collapse of the subjective (emotion)-objective (reason) dichotomy. But in Confucianism, emotion's phenomenality and facticity are completely integrated into the ontology of *xing* (mind-heart), *xin* (mind-heart), and *qing* (emotion). In Slote's sentimentalism, there does not seem to be the Confucian metaphysical sense of organic and holistic oneness in which emotion is accommodated. Let's look at Zhu Xi's explication of Zhang Zai's claim that "the mind-heart unites the nature and emotions:"

> Afterwards, when I read Heng Qu (Zhang Zai)'s statement, "The mind-heart unites the nature and emotions," I realized that it was a great theoretical achievement, and only then did I find the character *qing* being mentioned— one that was consistent with the ideas of Mencius. Mencius said, "The feeling of sympathy is the beginning of humaneness." Humaneness is the nature, and pity and commiseration are feelings. This is the mind-heart as regarded from the emotions. He also said, "Humaneness, rightness, ritual propriety and wisdom are rooted in the mind-heart," and this is the mind-heart as regarded from the nature. The mind-heart encompasses the nature and emotions; the nature is the substance and the emotions are the function. The character, "*xin* (mind-heart)," is simply the etymological root, therefore both the terms "nature (*xing*)" and "emotions (*qing*)" share the same radical, the mind-heart.
>
> Quoted in Virag 2007: 75–6

Zhu elsewhere says:

> The nature has no form or image that one uses to discern it: all it has are these principles. Only if there are emotions is it possible to see it, and these are the senses of sympathy, shame, modesty and judgment. Therefore, Mencius spoke of the nature, saying, "Only on the basis of the emotions can one speak of goodness."
>
> Quoted in Virag 2007: 81–2

Accordingly, just as Hegel refers to the cunning of Reason, so Zhu appeals to the cunning of emotions, in which case emotions are constitutive interpretations of the world, in that they are perceptual judgments and, therefore, intentional. As with any other judgments, emotional judgments involve presumptions and accompanying relations with a host of beliefs, which may not be a part of the emotion itself. They are, however, distinguished by their inextricable ties with our self-esteem and self-worth; in fact, they stem from our very being.

If we juxtapose the Confucian cardinal virtue of *ren* (which is the fully realized emotion of sympathy and compassion, according to Mencius) with Slote's empathy, then we can see how both *ren* and empathy demand their fulfillment in the wider world. Slote sees a care ethics based on empathy to be superior to liberalism based on reason and justice as the philosophical underpinning of a body-politic. I agree. In a liberal community of citizens, justice is defined in terms of and safeguarded by rights. A citizen, as a free and independent person, is first and foremost a rights-holder, who is invariably a beneficiary of the rights he or she is entitled to. Another person's welfare, which is already defined and protected by rights, is theoretically not a moral agent's concern. The consequence of this lack of concern may very well be the sentiment expressed in this statement by Charles Taylor, who is disgruntled with the rights-based discourse: "Instead of saying that it is wrong to kill me, we begin to say that I have a right to life" (Taylor 1999: 127). In that sense, as Slote argues, a liberal moral agent is incapable of extending the fullest sort of love to others. Hence the need for care ethics as a replacement of conventional moral thinking, a shift from attending to the symmetrical relations of the public domain of the *polis* to nurturing the asymmetrical ones in the private realm of the *oikos* (household), where love (not rights) reigns supreme (see Dallmayr 2003).

As Zhu Xi makes clear, *ren* is the Way, both human and cosmic:

> Now, as for humaneness constituting the Way, it is the mind-heart of Heaven and Earth to produce things, which is present in all things. Before the emotions have issued forth, this substance is already complete; after the emotions have issued forth, its operations is inexhaustible. If we are sincerely able to embody and preserve it, then there is no place where the origin of all goodness and the root of all action does not reside.
>
> Virag 2007: 84–5

The empathy of *ren* connects all. Confucius has told us that empathetic persons "establish others in seeking to establish themselves and promote others in seeking to get there themselves" (*Analects* 6.30), and hence this golden rule: "Do not impose on others what you yourself do not want" (*Analects* 12.2). Such are the basic lineaments of a Confucian care ethics. The empathetic moral agent, unlike the right-holding one, is first and foremost a benefactor. He brings both empathy and sympathy into play. He imagines being X who is the object-figure, thus feeling X's terror, and being sympathetic, that is, having "the recognition-response tie" (Goldie 2000: 178–80), in Peter Goldie's words, cares about X's terror and wants to assuage it. Wang Yangming (1472–1529) offers us a grand vision of a universe as a moral community animated by *ren*/empathy:

> The profound person regards Heaven, Earth, and the myriad things as one body. He sees the world as one family and the country as one person.... Forming one body with Heave, Earth, and the myriad things is true not only of

the great person. Even the mind-heart of the small person is no different. Only he makes it small. Therefore, when he sees a child about to fall into a well, he cannot help a feeling of alarm and commiseration. This shows that his humanity (*ren*) forms one body with the child. Again, when he observes the pitiful cries and frightened appearance of the birds and animals about to be slaughtered, he cannot help feeling an inability to bear their suffering. This shows that his humane empathy forms one body with birds and animals.... Everything from ruler, minister, husband, wife, and friends to mountains, rivers, spiritual beings, birds, animals, plants should be truly loved in order to realize my humanity that forms one body with them, and then my clear character will be completed manifested, and I will really form one body with Heaven, Earth, and the myriad things.

Wang 1963: 272–3

This ideal of the universe as a moral community affords the moral agent a unifying perspective for his or her engagement with the world. *Ren* is thus a diffusive system of affection with intentions, desires, and hopes of ethical commitment. I wonder if this is not also the ideal polity of care ethics.

What is particularly interesting and striking to me as a student of Chinese thought is that Slote's work, in the Western scholarly quarters, develops, and is evaluated, within the oppositional framework of reason-versus-emotion. Much of the polemic and dialogue revolves around the epistemological questions of the nature of moral belief, judgment, decision, and justification, and the extent to which they are mediated by reason or emotion. What we have in Confucian *qing*-ism is a moral psychology that does not feature such a stark tension, although as pointed out, there is no dearth of antinomy of one sort or another when it comes to the adjudication of the relative roles of the components of this psychology. The central question is not whether it is emotion or reason that determines and defines moral behavior and understanding; it is how we, through incessant self-cultivation as guided by tradition, fully realize our natural, original endowment of *ren*—the moral emotions of love and empathy—by extending our mind-heart with its broad range of abilities and dispositions: the awareness, cognizance, and perception of, and the sensitivity and responsiveness to, the myriad things and their englobing circumstances. *Ren* is not an abstract principle or rational concept to be discursively studied, ratiocinated, and comprehended; it is a deeply moving emotion that is felt and acted out. On the other hand, an empathetic person is an achieved state of being, the result of the painstaking process of character cultivation and formation, even though everyone is endowed with *ren*.

It is to Slote's credit that he gives due attention to the importance of moral emotions in our moral growth and existence, making a powerful case that they are by no means as brittle and dubious as the deontologists make them out to be.[6] To ignore them is to perhaps engage in what Collingwood calls "the corruption of consciousness," an unfaithful act of elision in the process of converting psychic emotions into other manifested forms of emotions. The disowning of moral emotions corrupts consciousness in such a way that it cannot draw an accurate picture of what our rational mind wants to articulate: "A truthful consciousness gives intellect a firm foundation upon which to build; a corrupt consciousness forces intellect to build on a quicksand" (quoted in Boucher 1989: 224–5). Both Slote and the Confucian thinkers, in their different ways, affirm the psychological nubs and beginnings of our moral senses and sensibilities.

Most recently, Slote has sought to develop his understanding of emotions as moral sentimentalism via the architectonics of the *yin-yang* philosophy, as evidenced by the publication of *The Philosophy of Yin and Yang* (Slote 2018). Unlike his previous works, his current effort to expound sentimentalism within the overarching yin-yang framework moves his thinking much closer to the Confucian metaphysics of emotions as an expression of organismic and holistic oneness. Although the present essay does not aim to address this latest work by Slote on *yin-yang*, there are some questions arising from it that do intrigue me. As Slote points out, for our contemporary purposes, *yin* is equated with receptivity as an epistemic virtue while *yang* is decisiveness. And to the extent that all rational/ justified belief is or involves emotion, belief is an emotional state with a *yin-yang* structure or character. In fact, our own psychology is characterized by the *yin-yang* complementarity. Therefore, *yin-yang* should figure prominently as a unifying framework and justifying basis in the philosophy of mind, epistemology, and ethics. Agreed. I am persuaded that Slote's appropriation of the *yin-yang* scheme is not merely an after-the-fact syndication of *yin* and *yang* as instantiations of one thing or another in our life-world.

Nevertheless, in traditional Chinese *yin-yang* thinking, the question of *qi* (commonly translated as material force or psychophysical energy) is highly germane to emotions, such that it seems to be the metaphysical basis of Confucian *qing*-ism (Harbsmeier 2004). I alluded to this in my earlier references to Zhu Xi. Indeed, especially in Neo-Confucianism, *yin/yang*-qua-*qi* appears often in discourse and debates on human nature (*xing*) and innate constitution. The nature is dichotomized into "the nature of heaven-and-earth" (*tiandi zhi xing*)—the original and pure moral nature—and "psychophysical nature" (*qizhi zhi xing*)—the secondary nature which is the energy of which human beings are unevenly and differently constituted, allowing for the expressions of emotions and feelings, that is, *qing*. To use the words of Zhang Zai: "A person's firmness, docility, slowness, quickness, and talent or lack of talent are due to the one-sidedness of psychophysical energy. Heaven (nature) is originally harmonious and not one-sided. If one cultivates this psychophysical energy and returns to one's original nature without being one-sided, one can then fully develop one's nature and [be in harmony with] heaven" (Chan 1963: 512). Cheng Hao has this to say:

> "What is inborn is called nature:" nature is the same as psychophysical energy, and psychophysical energy is the same as nature, as they are both inborn.

Psychophysical energy with which humanity is endowed at birth, according to principle, can be good and evil. However, a person is not born with these two opposing elements in the one's nature to start with. Some people become good from childhood and others become evil, owing to the psychophysical energy with which they are endowed. Human nature is of course good, but it cannot be said that evil is not human nature. It is called nature for what is inborn. "By nature humanity is tranquil at birth." The state before birth cannot be discussed. As soon as we talk of human nature, in fact it is no more the pure nature [as it cannot be distinguished from the endowed psychophysical energy to which principle is attached from the birth.

de Bary and Bloom 1999: 691–2; translation modifed

Lü Kun (1536–1618) elaborates on this dual nature (moral and physical) vis-à-vis the workings of *yin-yang*:

There are two kinds of heaven: the moral and metaphysical heaven (*lidao zhi tian*), and the natural heaven (*qishu zhi tian*). Therefore, humanity is endowed with a moral nature and a concrete psychophysical nature. Both heavens come from the Great Ultimate (*taiji*). The moral and metaphysical is the prior one, the pure good principle before the original separates into yin and yang, and the five agents.... The natural heaven is the posterior one, after the original energy has split up onto the two poles and the five agents, with the distinction between good and evil.

Quoted in Santangelo 2010: 138

Wang Fuzhi (1619–92), the well-known Qing polymath, averred:

Heaven creates humanity through the five phases of the *yin-yang* energy. Principle is thus located in humanity, and when it is concentrated, it is [human] nature. There are sounds, images, smells, and tastes that enrich their [human beings'] lives, and there are humaneness, rightness, propriety, and wisdom to rectify their virtues. If the sounds, images, smells, and tastes follow their natural way, then they do not run counter to humaneness, rightness, propriety, and wisdom. The integration of the two forms the dual substance (*ti*).

ibid.: 145

All of these examples illustrate the fact that the philosophy of *yin* and *yang* is part and parcel of a philosophical anthropology that features the tension and harmony between a moral nature and a physical nature. This anthropology in turn serves as the basis for the Neo-Confucian philosophy of cultivation and education devoted to the retrieval of the original moral nature, of which *qing*-ism is an expression. I suppose for Slote's purposes, his appropriation of the *yin-yang* philosophy does not quite need to address directly this metaphysical aspect. But insofar as he claims that yin-yang is absolutely fundamental to understanding the human psyche and mental functioning, I do wonder if it is not a fruitful exercise to rethink the dual-nature in light of Slote's construal of the mind-heart, *xin*, as a *yin-yang* entity. Just as he contends that Chinese philosophers have never made claims about the mind-heart in such terms, so we may say they have not thought about the two natures with reference to the relation between belief and desire, and Slote could be one to break new interpretive grounds through his, so to say, *yin-yang qing*-ism.

5 Conclusion

It bears repeating that Slote's current intellectual project is an ambitious enterprise of altering the terms of intercultural philosophical dialogue. His business is to "reset" certain predominant predilections in Western philosophy. Just look at the bold proclamation he makes in "The Philosophical Reset Button: A Manifesto" (Slote 2015), where he bemoans the overly intellectualistic and rationalistic tendencies in Western philosophy and sees hopes for their rectification and amelioration in plumbing the resources proffered by the Chinese counterpart. The fact that we bothered to hold a conference and produce a volume attests to our very assent to the rhetoric and value of his daring, even though there are varying and divergent degrees of concord with the substance of his argument. To the extent that Slote's preoccupation involves critical interrogation of both Western and Chinese philosophical dispositions and proclivities, our response to it should do likewise. Just as we seek to reset one side, the other side, which does the resetting, must also, in the process, be reset as well. Such, is the nature of dialogical congress. Therefore, as far as my own engagement with Slote is concerned, two reciprocating rewards ensue. First, it reinforces my conviction that Confucian *qing*-ism is a resource for further thinking about moral sentimentalism. Second, sentimentalism's deontological questioning sharpens my construal of the logical structures of emotions in Confucian moral psychology.

Notes

1 In *From Enlightenment to Receptivity: Rethinking our Values* (2013), Slote continues to interrogate Enlightenment thinking and its modern extensions in terms of its over-emphasis on rational action at the expense of empathy, offering this time around an account of the importance of receptivity, an expression of commonsense morality that leads to open-mindedness and fair-mindedness.
2 For a substantive engagement with this work, see Huang 2015.
3 Cf. Burke 2005. For a view on the Chinese side of things, see Davis 2008.
4 A classic definition of emotions as subjective intrapersonal experiences is the one furnished by William James and Carl Lange. To them, emotions are feelings or

perceptions of bodily disturbances that are individually felt. See James and Lange 1967: 12–17. Mary Backover gives a succinct critique of the James-Lange thesis in particular and of the subjective-objective dichotomy in general in Backover 1994: 161–3. See also Hansen 1994: 184–6 for his argument that the primacy of the Euclidean paradigm yielded the Greek elevation of reason, that is, the construction of axioms as the principal locus of reality. The Western notion of the mind, as a result, perforce would deprecate emotions because of their indeterminate nature in terms of the sentential (word-based) model of truth. On the apotheosis on reason and deprecation of emotion in the Western traditions, see Mazi 1993.
5   For a discussion on the major approaches to the question of emotions in contemporary Western thought, see Marks 1994.
6   It is appropriate to acknowledge here the contributions of Owen Flanagan (see Flanagan 2014).

References

Analects (1960), in *The Chinese Classics,* with a translation, critical and exegetical notes, prolegomena, and copious indexes by James Legge. Hong Kong: Hong Kong University Press.

Backover, Mary (1994), "The Concept of Emotion Revisited: A Critical Synthesis of Western and Confucian Thought," in Joel Marks and Roger Ames (eds), *Emotions in Asian Thought,* Albany: SUNY Press.

Boucher, David (1989), *The Social and Political Thought of R. G. Collingwood,* Cambridge and New York: Cambridge University Press.

Burke, Peter (2005), "Is There a Cultural History of the Emotions?" in Penelope Gouk and Helen Mills (eds), *Representing Emotions: New Connections in the Histories of Art, Music and Medicine,* Burlington, VT: Ashgate.

Chan, Wing-tsit, ed. and trans. (1963), *Source Book of Chinese Philosophy,* Princeton: Princeton University Press.

Chan, Wing-tsit, trans. (1967), *Reflections on Things at Hand,* New York: Columbia University Press.

Dallmayr, Fred (2003), "Confucianism and the Public Sphere: Five Relationships Plus One," *Dao: A Journal of Comparative Philosophy,* 2 (2): 193–212.

Davis, Gloria (2008), "Moral Emotions and Chinese Thought," *Michigan Quarterly Review,* 47 (2): 221–44.

Er Cheng yishu (Survived works of the two Chengs). Sibu beiyao edition.

de Bary, Wm. Theodore and Irene Bloom, comp. *Sources of Chinese Tradition.* Volume One. 2nd ed. New York: Columbia University Press, 1999.

de Sousa, Ronald (1987), *The Rationality of Emotion,* Cambridge, MA: The MIT Press.

Flanagan, Owen (2014), *Moral Sprouts and Natural Teleologies: 21st Century Moral Psychology Meets Classical Chinese Philosophy,* The Aquinas Lecture, Milwaukee: Marquette University Press.

Goldie, Peter (2000), *The Emotions: A Philosophical Exploration,* Oxford: Clarendon Press.

Grahm, A. C. (1989), *Studies in Chinese Philosophy and Philosophical Literature*, Albany: SUNY Press.

Harbsmeier, Christoph (2004), "The Semantics of *Qing* in Pre-Buddhist Chinese," in Eifring Halvor (ed.), *Love and Emotions in Traditional Chinese Literature*, Leiden: Brill.

Hansen, Chad (1994), "Qing in Pre-Buddhist Chinese Thought," in Joel Marks and Roger Ames (eds), *Emotions in Asian Thought*, Albany: SUNY Press.

Henan Chengshi cuiyen (Essential words of the Chengs of Henan). Sibu beiyao.

Huang, Yong (2015), "[Review of Michael Slote's] *A Sentimentalist Theory of Mind*,." *Dao: A Journal in Comparative Philosophy*, 14: 307–13.

James, William and Carl Lange ([1922] 1967), *The Emotions* New York: Hafner.

Lau, D. C., trans (1970), *Mencius*, London: Penguin Books.

Knoblock, John ([1988] 1994), *Xunzi: A Translation and Study of the Complete Works*, 3 vols, Stanford: Stanford University Press.

Marks, Joel (1994), "Emotions in Western Thought," in Joel Marks and Roger Ames (eds), *Emotions in Asian Thought*. Albany: SUNY Press.

Mazi, Glen (1993), *Emotion and Embodiment*, New York: Peter Lang.

Mingdao wenji (Collected writings of Cheng Hao). Sibu beiyao edition.

Nivison, David S. (1996), "Motivation and Moral Action in Mencius," in Bryan W. Van Norden (ed. and introduction), *The Ways of Confucianism: Investigations in Chinese Philosophy*, La Salle, IL: Open Court.

Nussbaum, Martha (1988), "Narrative Emotions: Beckett's Genealogy of Love," *Ethics* 98: 225–54.

Santangelo, Paolo (2010), *Materials for an Anatomy of Personality in Late Imperial China*, Leiden: Brill.

Slote, Michael (2001), *Morals from Motives*, Oxford: Oxford University Press.

Slote, Michael (2007), *Ethics of Care and Empathy*, London and New York: Routledge.

Slote, Michael (2010a), *Moral Sentimentalism*, Oxford: Oxford University Press.

Slote, Michael (2011), *The Impossibility of Perfection: Aristotle, Feminism, and the Complexities of Ethics*, New York: Oxford University Press, 2011.

Slote, Michael (2013), *From Enlightenment to Receptivity: Rethinking our Values*, New York: Oxford University Press.

Slote, Michael (2014), *A Sentimentalist Theory of Mind*, Oxford: Oxford University Press.

Slote, Michael (2015), "The Philosophical Reset Button: A Manifesto," *Dao: A Journal of Comparative Philosophy*, 14: 1–11.

Slote, Michael (2018), *The Philosophy of Yin and Yang* (Chinese and English bilingual edition), Beijing: Shangwu Yingshuguan.

Shisanching jinzhu jinyi (Contemporary Annotations to and Translations of the Thirteen Classics). 1994. Changsha: Yuelu.

Solomon, Robert C. (2004), "Emotions, Thoughts, and Feelings: Emotions as Entanglements with the World," in Robert C. Solomon (ed.), *Thinking and Feeling: Contemporary Philosophies on Emotions*, Oxford: Oxford University Press.

Taylor, Charles (1999), "Conditions are for an Unforced Consensus on Human Rights," in Joanne Bauer and Daniel A. Bell (eds), *The East Asian Challenge for Human Rights*, Cambridge: Cambridge University Press.

Virag, Curie (2007), "Emotions and Human Agency in the Thought of Zhu Xi," *Journal of Song-Yuan-Ming Studies,* 37: 49–88.
Wang, Yangming (1963), *Instructions for Practical Living and Other Neo-Confucian Writings,* trans. with notes by Wing-tsit Chan New York: Columbia University Press.
Wong, David B. (1991), "Is there a Distinction between Reason and Emotion in Mencius?" *Philosophy East and West,* 41 (1) (Jan. 1991): 31–44.
Yichuan wenji (Collected writings of Cheng Yi). Sibu beiyao edition.

11

Striving for the Impossible

Early Confucians on Perfect Virtue in an Imperfect World

Aaron Stalnaker
Indiana University, United States

1 Introduction

Michael Slote's stimulating book *The Impossibility of Perfection* (2011) argues that it is not possible for any one person to possess perfect virtue, in the sense of a unified and harmonious collection of all the virtues, because some virtues are incompatible with each other, and so cannot in principle be combined. In the book he presents his argument as a critique of Aristotle's and Aristotelian ethics, but he could have (and has) made analogous arguments against various Ruist 儒 or "Confucian" thinkers, who, like Aristotle, think perfect virtue is possible, and is something we should strive for. The early Confucian Xunzi provides one clear example of such a thinker advocating the pursuit of perfect virtue. Interestingly, some others, including perhaps Confucius/Kongzi himself, think perfect virtue is probably not possible in many cases, but should nevertheless be sought anyway, even though it may well be impossible. Slote does explicitly address some of these differences with Ruist thinkers in a recent short essay (Slote 2013). But because his fullest arguments are in the book, I concentrate here on that account.

This chapter explores some of these disagreements between early Confucians and Slote about the possibility of perfection in virtue and happiness (since Slote addresses both), and the advisability of seeking such perfection. I argue that from certain early Confucian points of view, one of Slote's central examples to show intrinsic conflicts between virtues does not convince, because "frankness" is not actually a virtue, whereas "tact," understood as a component of ritual propriety (*li* 禮), is. Thus, if there is a conflict between frankness and tact, tact should win; nevertheless, benevolence will also direct the ends for which one is tactful or polite, and suggests different possible responses to Slote's hypothetical conflict. Reflecting on the ambiguities of these examples of value conflicts points to the limitations of Slote's argument in its current form. To forecast a bit, I am more convinced by his arguments for the impossibility of perfect happiness because of conflicts between various goods, than by the argument that partial and intrinsically mutually antagonistic virtues are a pervasive and serious problem. And the early Confucians appear to think that perfect virtue and even perfect happiness are possible, even if all too frequently not attained in practice, for reasons I briefly explore.

More deeply, early Confucians like Kongzi and Xunzi suggest that when we cannot harmoniously realize multiple values or virtues in some situation, this is often ultimately due to a failure of social justice, in the sense of a failure of what ought to be wise and benevolent leadership from those in charge of overseeing the community; or it may be due to the inexplicable workings of fate in an imperfect world. Examining Confucian views of the connections between personal virtue cultivation and the pursuit of good social order suggests that the "impossibility of perfection" is much more frequently a social problem than a logical one. And so even if it seems impossible to achieve, we should not despair, or rest content with badly flawed social arrangements, but instead strive to attain perfect virtue and act rightly, even in difficult situations, striving to order the world so that the Confucian Way prevails more broadly.

To put some of these points in a slightly different way, drawing on important recent work by my Indiana colleague Michael Ing (2017), I argue there is a diversity of views in early Confucian texts about whether perfect virtue and happiness are possible. Some, like Xunzi, and many modern Western interpreters summarizing the tradition as a whole, propound what Ing calls the "harmony thesis," that all goods can be harmonized in a state of quasi-divine order, and that perfect virtue is both possible and the appropriate standard for human beings—although even here they do not explicitly argue for the "unity of the virtues" thesis Slote is keen to critique. But many other early Ruist texts have a more conflicted or even tragic view of life: while virtues, and especially social obligations, do not *necessarily* conflict (contra Slote), they can conflict, sometimes disastrously. But despite this, the predominant early Confucian view is that perfect virtue and perfect social order should be sought anyway, whether one succeeds or fails in one's attempts to attain either. This suggests a relatively lower estimation of the value of "happiness" than Slote (and most contemporary people) have, as well as of personal freedom and autonomy, and a higher estimation of the value of moral striving. This appears also to represent a differential assessment of the appropriateness of anxiety, dissatisfaction, and even resentment, at least when focused on ethically appropriate objects. While this partly reflects the real differences between ancient and contemporary contexts, as Slote suggests (2011: 61, 129), it also bespeaks a different kind of view of what is most valuable in life.

2   Value Pluralism, Conflict, and Harmony with regard to Virtue

In *The Impossibility of Perfection*, Slote builds his analysis on fundamental insights from the intellectual historian and political theorist Isaiah Berlin, who asserts that values and goods are plural and conflicting, and thus cannot be perfectly harmonized in one overarching rational system, as many Enlightenment thinkers contend (2011: 40, 100–01). Slote shares Berlin's intuitions on these points, and wants to extend them to ethical virtues. Slote argues that at least some virtues are intrinsically one-sided, and rule out other virtues that oppose them in important respects.

One of his favorite examples is the conflict between "tact" and "frankness," which he contends are both virtues, albeit partial and opposed ones. To demonstrate this, he constructs a scenario designed to show an inevitable conflict case where, no matter what one might do, one will have failed to exhibit either one or the other of these paired virtues (29–31; also 41, 57–8, etc.). In this case, the reader is to imagine having a friend prone to picking out abusive romantic partners, who has shrugged off all previous counsel that he chooses poorly and tolerates (or even subconsciously welcomes) such abuse, and instead insists he is merely unlucky. After yet another breakup with an unsuitable partner, he begs you to tell him why this keeps happening to him. If one is frank, one will tell him yet again, pointlessly and perhaps cruelly, that he is attracted to and chooses such people, and therefore must reconsider his taste in women—knowing all the while that this attempt will most likely end like the previous ones. If one is tactful, one will lament his "bad luck" with women and sympathize, thereby caring for him as a wounded friend but failing to honor his explicit request, and also failing to do anything constructive that might lead him to change his behavior. Slote thinks these two options are the only reasonable possibilities, and both are equally mixed in their value: ethically praiseworthy to some degree, but still importantly lacking, because in either case the goods represented by the other possibility are sacrificed. He argues that "neither frankness nor tact can count univocally and unqualifiedly as a virtue" (2011: 31); they are "both partial virtues and, therefore, partial values, for these two qualities are paired opposites, and in some situations where they clash, acting on either one of them will be ethically less than ideal" (31).

Slote provides one further example of intrinsically conflicting partial virtues: prudence, in the contemporary sense of appropriate caution aimed at securing one's safety, and adventurousness (15ff., 22, 45, 62ff.). Again, Slote considers these to be intrinsically partial virtues and goods, which cannot be combined in any overarching virtue, nor can the goods sought be *perfectly* harmonized over time or at once in a given person's life, even if we each must work out the proper balance of these goals for ourselves in practice. There are, in other words, inevitable tradeoffs between security and adventure, however we choose to live. This case is revealing, I think, because it shows how Slote's interest in psychological dispositions to seek certain good ends, which is a reasonable way of thinking about virtues and vices, connects with reflection on the compatibility of those good ends themselves. In another resonant example of the incompatibility of highly desirable goods, he contends that it is impossible to combine fully and perfectly a commitment to career and work success with a flourishing family life (65–70).

On the basis of these arguments, Slote argues against a number of familiar ethical theses often associated with Aristotelian virtue ethics. First, he explicitly denies the common thesis of the "unity of the virtues" (e.g., 40–3). That thesis, commonly attributed to Aristotle, is the claim that to truly have any one virtue requires having them all, at least to some sufficient degree. So, for example, courage without wisdom is not really courage, because it can so easily contribute to wrong action and feeling. And second, Slote denies the possibility of perfection in either ethical character or happiness, because he thinks there are paired goods and virtues that are "partial," by which he means intrinsically opposed to each other, and which thus cannot be combined in one life. So, for example, he writes: "The ideal of having all the virtues and the ideal of ethical perfection… are in fact absolutely unrealizable" (40). And also: "imperfection—whether of virtue or of happiness—is inevitable" (40).

There are various ways one might criticize Slote's treatment of these cases, and the implications he draws from them. One might challenge the tact/frankness dilemma itself, and insist that other choices might be possible besides these two. Or one might insist that some of the purported virtues are not in fact virtues, and so are not relevant to the question of the unity of the virtues, or to the possibility of ethical perfection. Or, with regard to happiness, one might argue for the possibility of harmonizing the various seemingly conflicting goods involved in some optimal, truly harmonious way. Various Western reviewers of the book have explored some of these options, but none of them have engaged these questions seriously in dialogue with Confucian thought, which is what I propose to do here.

Let me begin with the unity of the virtues. While this idea *per se* was not an object of serious controversy in early China, I think we can still discern an early Confucian position on the question. The predominant view seems to be that people can possess some virtues while lacking others, which presents a real ethical problem; the solution to that problem is to seek a more properly balanced perfection in virtue, which they generally take to be possible, at least in principle.[1] So, for example, the Kongzi of the *Analects* explicitly discusses what happens when someone has one or more virtues but lacks others. In 17.8, the master talks about several virtues, including major ones like humaneness (*rén* 仁) and courage (*yǒng* 勇), which need to be combined with a love of learning in order to be truly good; this suggests they are sometimes found in ignorant or unpracticed people in a destructive form. Courage in particular seems vulnerable to the possibility of being cultivated without other, complementary or restraining virtues, or of being undone by other faults; so, for example, Kongzi claims that "a person who is fond of courage but despises poverty will become rebellious" (8.10; see also 14.4). He also warns his hot-headed, overzealous disciple Zilu against this danger repeatedly, as for example in 17.23, where Zilu asks about courage, and the master cautions him: "The gentleman admires rightness above all. A gentleman who possessed courage but lacked a sense of rightness would create political disorder, while a common person who possessed courage but lacked a sense of rightness would become a bandit" (17.23; see also 5.7,

7.11). This passage suggests that Kongzi thinks people may possess particular virtues while lacking others, which contradicts the unity of the virtues thesis.

Indeed, like Slote (104–22), the Kongzi of the *Analects* discusses the issue that drives most people to assert the unity of the virtues, but in different terms. They both suggest that some virtues may depend on others for their full possession or proper operation. Kongzi repeatedly insists that lesser virtues such as trustworthiness only function properly when directed by the overarching virtue of humaneness; those lesser virtues, in other words, depend on humaneness to actually work as virtues (e.g., 17.6; see also 13.19, 13.20, 13.27, 14.4). Nevertheless, Kongzi does not seem to deny that these lesser qualities are virtues, but he insists they are far from sufficient on their own for truly good or right action. The goal is to cultivate oneself sufficiently to become a "complete" or "perfect" person (*chéngrén* 成人), with all the various excellences harmoniously blended together (14.12).

Perhaps this position is some sort of artifact of the mostly non-theoretical character of the *Analects* as a text? This seems not to be the case. Similar remarks may be found in the *Mengzi* and the *Xunzi*, at the very least, and these are probably the most systematic, theoretically integrated early Confucian texts.[2] Mengzi, for example discusses how various virtues and practices can and should fit together in a unified and mutually supportive way (4A27), and clearly regards four virtues as primary or "cardinal" virtues (2A6, 6A6), without which one will often fail to act rightly, even if one possesses lesser virtues like courage or trustworthiness. This again suggests the possibility of perfect virtue, as well as the lamentable possibility of uneven, partial cultivation of virtues—or in other words, a denial of the unity thesis. And Xunzi builds an entire theory of error around the possible over-development of partial truths or excellences, which leave out other necessary values, because one has become "fixated" or "obsessed" by some values at the cost of others (*Xunzi*, Chapter 21). And he at least at times explicitly discusses having some virtues while lacking others (e.g., 21.390–1, 23.338–63). Nevertheless, Xunzi insists on perfection as the proper standard for both conduct and character, in a quite uncompromising way:

> One who misses a single shot out of a hundred does not deserve to be called good at archery. One who falls short of going a thousand *li* by the distance of even a half-step does not deserve to be called good at chariot-driving. One who … is not single-minded in pursuit of *ren* [benevolence] and *yi* [righteousness] does not deserve to be called good at learning.
>
> 1.206–11; see also 1.217–31

These positions thus seem to be widely shared in early Confucian ethical thought.

Slote and the early Ru thus clearly part company when it comes to the possibility of perfection, especially with regard to virtue, but also, seemingly, with regard to happiness. To begin to grapple with this disagreement, let us first explore how early

Confucians might respond to Slote's arguments about partial and conflicting virtues, beginning with the conflict between tact and frankness.

The first thing to note is a certain discrepancy between explicit statements about the virtues of good speech, which tend to emphasize caution and ritual propriety, and the actual behavior of sagely heroes like Kongzi and Mengzi, who give themselves the latitude to be frank at times, often when criticizing students, or remonstrating with leaders. For example, the Kongzi of the *Analects* suggests that "very few go astray who comport themselves with restraint" (4.23), and "the gentleman wishes to be slow to speak, but quick to act" (4.24), because he "is ashamed to have his words exceed his actions" (14.27). The gentleman is "scrupulous in behavior and careful in speech, drawing near to those who possess the Way in order to be set straight by them" (1.14). And Xunzi similarly suggests the gentleman is "respectful and cautious yet congenial" (3.52). He also quotes Ode #195 to express what truly respectful behavior requires: "Be careful, be cautious, as if you were approaching an abyss, as if you were treading on thin ice" (cf. 13.198–200). (It is worth noting that these sorts of cautionary suggestions are most numerous in the *Analects*, less so in the *Xunzi* and the *Liji* (*Record of Ritual*) and basically absent in the *Mengzi*.)

Despite these repeated paeans to caution when speaking, Kongzi is notably direct, even at times caustic, with some of his students. He blasts his most lazy disciple Zaiwo, likening him to "rotten wood" and a "wall of dung" who will not respond to reprimands (5.10). And more poignantly, as Amy Olberding fruitfully explores (2012: 155–61), Kongzi and his disciple Zilu frequently are very frank with each other, especially regarding criticisms and questions (e.g., 6.28, 11.26, 13.3, 15.2), and seem to appreciate the forthrightness in their relationship.

Mengzi, for his part, is repeatedly frank in his discussions with political leaders, both in his assertions of their moral capability, and in criticisms of their misrule. He even dares to discuss deposing or killing tyrannical leaders while at the King of Qi's court (1B8), and implies to the same king on a different occasion that he ought to resign if he cannot do better at ruling (1B6). He even articulates a rationale for this sort of demanding speech, centered around expressing respect via ritually appropriate action.

Mengzi distinguishes between moral authority on the one hand, and political or executive authority on the other, and argues that each sort of authority deserves a different kind of deference and respect (5B3). "Honoring the worthy" (*zūn xián* 尊賢) requires strict concern for protocol, and attentive and respectful listening to those whose moral authority and wisdom outstrips one's own, regardless of one's social position. "Treating the eminent as eminent" (*guì guì* 貴貴), on the other hand, also requires ritualized performances of respect, but does not entail anything resembling toadying, even when ritual might seem to require it. For example, Mengzi presents one of his heroes, an earlier Confucian named Zisi, as refusing to accept repeated gifts from a duke because properly accepting such gifts required kowtowing to the duke's messenger, the repetition of which seemed demeaning to

Zisi (5B6). Indeed, Mengzi clearly thinks that appropriately honoring those in high social positions not only allows but *requires* chastising leaders when they fail to fulfill their obligations (e.g., 1B6). It also requires presenting them with a clear and compelling account of the true Way of benevolence, righteousness, and ritual propriety, even though this might seem like too demanding a standard for particular rulers; anything less is a form of serious disrespect (e.g., 2B2).

How might we make sense of this somewhat mixed record, and bring it into conversation with Slote's ideas? One might begin with the obvious point that they do not analyze such questions in terms of a conflict between the two purported virtues of tact and frankness. Early Confucian texts do not explicitly regard frankness *per se* as a virtue or even a value, although as noted above, they occasionally seem to recommend speaking frankly, by representing scenarios in which Confucian masters remonstrate with or criticize others. The most relevant virtues from their points of view seem instead to be ritual propriety (lǐ 禮), and perhaps to a lesser extent, righteousness (yì 義), which might also be understood as a commitment to honor social obligations of all kinds. Thus, as I suggested in the introduction, "tact" seems closer to the recognizably Confucian virtue of ritual propriety, which governs all forms of situationally appropriate conduct and speech, as well as more specific ceremonial duties. But "frankness" is not in any sense an explicit virtue or value for early Confucians, and so any possible conflicts between frankness and ritual propriety (in lieu of tact) are irrelevant to the question of possible conflicts between virtues, from their points of view.

I agree with the implied position about frankness I am attributing to the early Confucians. Frankness seems to be a possible characteristic of speech or other communication that is sometimes good, and sometimes bad, depending on the context. There are numerous scenarios in which frankness is obviously bad, such as diplomatic negotiations or legal contests between adversaries or their representatives, interrogations by corrupt or racist police asking for information which could be used to harass or persecute the innocent, parents deciding how much to say to small children about difficult or disturbing events they are not mature enough to understand, and social gatherings with extended family in which strong religious or political disagreements threaten to create permanent breaches if repeatedly rehearsed. The real virtue in question in such cases seems to be something like excellence in speech or, more broadly, communication (and in some cases excellence in teaching). Whether frankness, tact, humor, irony, directness or indirectness, or any other possible characteristics of speech are called for in some situation depend on higher order considerations of effective communication or persuasion, as well as basic ethical norms governing human relationships. Furthermore, these qualities of speech seem unusually prone to cultural relativity, based on prevailing mores and norms.[3] Those of us who have been habituated into American norms favoring plain or even blunt speech thus have some reason to distrust our intuitions in this area. The key point, however, is that because frankness is not always good or right in itself as a characteristic of speech acts, we should be skeptical of saying it is a virtue or value that we should in every case seek to protect and further, which Slote's conflict case requires.

The specific case of the romantically misguided friend that Slote imagines seems closer to the master/disciple relations depicted in the *Analects* (and in some other texts) than to the court-centered interactions with political leaders in the *Mengzi*. Thus it would appear that a relatively high degree of freedom in expression might be appropriate, although the overarching motivation for whatever a Confucian might say to such a friend in this scenario would likely be benevolent concern for the friend, and would at least not contravene ritual propriety.[4] The challenge would be to arrive at some type of speech, however surprising and effective, that would actually awaken the friend to his true situation, and the defects of his past choices, and of his past and present desires. Whatever this might turn out to be, whether a uniquely incisive *bon mot* that "transforms him like timely rain" on parched earth (*Mengzi* 7A40), or some more reticent refusal that instructs precisely by refusing to engage and explicitly give advice (Mengzi 6B16; see also *Analects* 7.8), it would stem from a fundamentally different analysis of the situation. To put this differently, it seems to me a mistake to speculate extensively about what an early Confucian master might say to such a friend, because the conventions and expectations around sex and marriage are so vastly different between contemporary contexts and ancient China. But whatever they would do, they would not analyze the situation in the way Slote has, in terms of a dilemma where the considerations are equally poised between the virtues/goods of tact and frankness.

This lack of correspondence between analyses raises a fundamental problem with at least this example, which Slote does not consider (at least in this book): how to individuate and fully specify the virtues, and decide which ones are most relevant to a given situation. Slote, like many contemporary virtue ethicists, including many who are to some extent neo-Aristotelian in their approach, appears content to let a more or less infinite number of virtuous flowers bloom. Indeed, this suits his purposes, since he is trying to articulate cases of ineradicable conflict between virtues, and so the more virtues there are, the more likely that perplexing conflicts might arise.

But this is in an important sense to stack the deck in favor of Slote's own conclusions, and against any carefully articulated "comprehensive conception" of the human good, to use Rawlsian language, whether that be Confucian, Aristotelian, or some other vision of the good. The philosopher Daniel Russell provides an incisive analysis of these problems, in the course of articulating and defending what he calls "hard virtue ethics," which is a contemporary form of neo-Aristotelian virtue ethics centered on the over-arching virtue of practical reasoning (2009: 145–236). Fully canvassing his arguments would take us too far afield for present purposes, but his central point is that the "enumeration problem" of having a potentially infinite proliferation of virtues is a very serious problem, one which would jeopardize any form of virtue ethics. (This is so because, if virtues proliferate infinitely, virtue ethics could never give an account of right action, since those actions would be in accord with an infinite, unspecifiable set of values (2009: 145)). The two theoretical maneuvers Russell recommends to combat the enumeration problem come from the Stoics, by way of Aquinas: the idea of cardinal virtues, and the subordination of some virtues to others (such as treating "magnificence" as a subordinate of the more general virtue of "generosity" (2009: 212–36)).

Russell's arguments relate to the issues at hand because they directly address the question of which virtues are most relevant to any given practical problem, and how to rank and relate virtues, including what Slote calls "dependent" virtues.[5] One aspect of Mengzi's greatness as a thinker is his specification of four cardinal virtues, i.e., benevolence, righteousness, ritual propriety, and wisdom, which govern the operations of others, such as courage or trustworthiness. Indeed, it appears that benevolence and righteousness together govern the exercise of ritual propriety, the virtuous love of music, and even wisdom (4A27). Admittedly, Mengzi—and also Xunzi—do not treat these problems in anything like the systematic manner of Aquinas or even the Roman Stoics, and thus leave a number of open questions about the ways in which some virtues, such as wisdom, might depend or rely on other, higher ranking virtues, such as benevolence and righteousness. I do not propose to get any further into this weed patch for present purposes, but I think it does bear on the dispute with Slote over conflicts between tact and frankness.

Whereas an Aristotelian would probably analyze the case in terms of practical wisdom, Confucians would analyze the problem of advising the misguided friend in terms of cardinal virtues like benevolence, righteousness, and ritual propriety, as well as specific obligations related to the relationship in question, i.e., friendship. There are many qualities of human speech and action that they do not thematize as particularly important or valuable, including frankness, authenticity, and even honesty, which have a lot to do with the cultural history of the modern West.[6] They thus would be unmoved by Slote's supposed conflict, and would be much more concerned with thinking up some novel way to get the friend to see the error of his ways.

Slote might in turn be unmoved by worries about the multifaceted moral heritage of the contemporary West, which he fully accepts and argues is illuminating of the human situation in all its complexity. But I would submit that he should be more concerned with the question of enumerating and ranking values and virtues, because these issues do bear directly on the significance and prevalence of virtue conflicts. If, despite my skeptical arguments about frankness above, we accept that tact and frankness are partial virtues, it still seems that they are quite minor virtues, intrinsically dependent on higher order values. If that were true, then virtue conflicts might turn out to be rare and not very momentous, which undercuts this aspect of his argument for the impossibility of perfection, since near-perfection would still be possible.

I think the conflict between the supposed virtues of prudent caution and adventurousness is vulnerable to similar objections. Confucians appear to the think that prudence in this limited sense is a part of the virtue of wisdom (*zhì* 智), as for example in Mengzi 5A9.[7] And they do not appear to think adventurousness *per se* is a virtue at all; the only thing remotely similar would be the familiar virtue of courage. To the extent that the topic comes up, early Ruist texts tend to view adventurousness negatively, as in Kongzi's counsel: "While your parents are alive, you should not travel far, and when you do travel you must keep to a fixed itinerary" (4A19). Or in other words, do not do anything risky that might agitate or alarm your parents, since that would be unfilial. My own view is similar, if somewhat less constrained: wisdom and courage are both very important virtues, and caution/prudence is a minor part of wisdom, whereas adventurousness is fundamentally just a common human tendency most visible in the young. It is valuable, to the extent that it is, in the same way that any other appetite is, but that means that, as Mengzi says, it is a constituent element of the "lesser part" of our natures as human beings, not the "greater" or "more important" part (6A15), and when it comes into conflict with a real virtue, like wisdom, it should simply give way as a subordinate consideration. Adventure is often fun, and safety can be comforting, but that does not make seeking either of them a virtue.

3 Accidental and/or Tragic Conflicts among Values

Although I have expressed some skepticism about conflicts between virtues, on behalf of the early Confucians and for myself, I think Slote's arguments about the broader issue of the plurality of goods and values are more successful. To focus on one example Slote discusses at some length, there appears to be an intrinsic conflict between devotion to career (and creative work generally) and devotion to intimate personal relationships, including family relationships (32, 65–71). Slote discusses the common attempt to somehow balance these goods in one life, and comments "we would normally characterize such a life as involving a compromise between career/creative values and affiliative ones, and that very term, once again, suggests or even entails that such a life isn't ideally good or happy (even if it is on the whole reasonably satisfactory)" (69). He goes on to argue that many people think the difficulty of balancing career and family "is an artifact of the way social life is currently organized"—but in fact it is "conceptually, metaphysically, inevitable" (69–70). In this section I explore these more general conflicts of values in more detail.

One influential early philosophical reading of the *Analects* suggested that Kongzi teaches a "way without a crossroads" (Fingarette 1972). One counterintuitive aspect of Fingarette's reading was his suggestion that choice between alternatives was not an issue that early Confucianism recognized, much less analyzed (1972: 23). It is now clear that Fingarette's view is wrong, at least in this respect. Many early Confucian texts address choices, including ones in which obligations or other values conflict, and one must discern the right choice among seemingly problematic alternatives.

One locus classicus for this in the tradition is *Mengzi* 4A17. In this passage, Mengzi is debating with a critic who tries to put him in a bind by asking how he would handle a case when his sister-in-law is drowning. The problem is that ritual propriety requires men and women to refrain from touching when in public, but here that stricture seems to jeopardize a family member's life. Mengzi responds scornfully, suggesting this is a brainlessly obvious case, not a true dilemma: saving the sister-in-law's life takes precedence over the ritual obligation. He explains this in terms of the metaphor of "weighing" (*quán* 權) different goods or values against each other in a scale. Whichever consideration is "heavier" or more important should take precedence (see 6B1 and 7A26 for further discussion).

Michael Ing has written an illuminating recent study of these issues that draws on commentaries from several centuries of Confucian tradition (2017). As Ing shows, Confucians develop a sophisticated discourse regarding moral judgment in varying circumstances. Most of life may be handled through reliance on what they came to call "standard" (*jīng* 經) judgments, which track typical situations where normal ethical considerations are reasonably clear and do not conflict, and so one may confidently follow the usual ritual prescriptions, for example, without worry. But occasionally unusual situations arise, in which important values conflict, and so the morally cultivated person will need to "weigh" (*quán* 權) these various factors in order to discern the proper course of action. Capable moral agency requires the ability to do both, and above all to know when a resort to weighing will count as the morally required exceptional action (e.g., *Mengzi* 4A26), and when it will count as negligent or misguided action that corrupts ethical requirements by "bending the foot to straighten the yard," which is really just a veiled form of selling out moral principle in favor of expediency (*Mengzi* 3B1). One clear dividing line between such cases is whether the unusual action is taken in order to help or especially save others, or instead to gain some advantage or convenience for oneself, which is not allowed (Ing 2017: 35).

Many contemporary interpreters have argued that, by means of this sort of distinction between "standard" (*jīng* 經) and "exigent" or "discretionary" action (*quán* 權), Confucians think all moral difficulties can be resolved, at least by sufficiently wise and cultivated people. This view, which Ing calls the "harmony thesis" (2017: 52), suggests that value conflicts are in an important sense only epistemic, and only apparent. If one is truly wise, one will be able to discern in any challenging situation a "situation-specific harmonization of all values in a manner that honors the importance of each distinct value."[8]

Ing's truly outstanding contribution is to analyze the strengths of and warrants for the "harmony thesis" interpretation in some Confucian texts at various points in the tradition, and also to show the weaknesses of this view, and to explore at length countervailing tendencies in Confucian texts, especially in early China. Because of its direct relevance to the comparison with Slote, I will briefly discuss Ing's analysis and conclusions.

The harmony-centered reading of Confucian thought suggests that in situations of value conflict, a sage will be able to see some "situation-specific harmonization" of the relevant values in that situation, such that the resulting course of action will have a pleasing rightness that honors all the relevant considerations in an appropriate way. This is not a claim that a sage can maximize *all* values in *any* situation, but rather that even in seemingly very problematic conflict cases, some resolution will be possible that at least preserves and honors all the relevant values, in a sufficiently satisfying way that one can affirm it as morally admirable and even right, given the extreme situation. One case that Angle and Ing discuss is a story from Mengzi 5A3, in which Mengzi affirms the sage king Shun's deviant action in enfeoffing his morally corrupt brother Xiang as a ruler of a minor territory (Ing 2017: 53ff.). This seemingly bizarre action supposedly saves the relevant values, because Xiang was not given effective executive power in his territory, and so Shun's act was both loving and appropriately punitive, and protected the people of the kingdom. With respect to Slote's case of the misguided friend unlucky in love, were the man lucky enough to have a Confucian sage as his friend, that sagacious person would presumably figure out some surprising, revelatory way of both showing his deep love and concern for his friend, while also illuminating his destructive proclivities in some charming, probably humorous way, so that the man could begin to achieve better self-understanding and start down the road to changing his ways.[9] In contrast, regular, less than perfectly insightful people will be baffled by the value conflict and see no way out of the dilemma. Thus, metaphysically, on this reading all values can be harmonized, and the world is not deeply riven by conflict, although many of us will be unable to see this in particular situations.

As Michael Puett and Ing both explain, the "harmony thesis" reading of Confucianism has an old pedigree in the West, with versions of it propounded by Voltaire, Leibniz, Hegel, and Max Weber, as well as more recent scholars like Derk Bodde, David Keightley, K. C. Chang, Herbert Fingarette, and Henry Rosemont.[10] Nevertheless, despite the many strands of Confucian thought that propound this sort of faith in the deep harmony of all values in the order of the world, discernible by those with eyes to see, other strands of the tradition see a more conflicted and tragic situation.

Ing titles his recent book *The Vulnerability of Integrity in Early Confucian Thought*, and explores in fascinating detail the rich literature of ethical dilemmas in early Confucian texts. These dilemmas often concern a seemingly irresolvable conflict between duties to family, especially parents, and duties to one's political superiors. In a startling number of such cases, the protagonist chooses some forced action that jeopardizes a value he or she holds dear, and then attempts to recoup the situation, and his or her honor, by committing suicide in some dramatic way at the end of the story. These cases sometimes seem like early Chinese versions of the "Sophie's Choice" case Slote discusses, in which Nazis force a woman to choose only one of her two children to be saved from the death camps (Slote, 75ff.), complete with hostages taken by hostile powers.

Consider the following case, which Ing introduces as follows:

The *Han Shi Waizhuan* ... tells of Shen Ming 申鳴 (*fl.* 480 BCE), who was known for his filial piety and his ability to manage government affairs. After declining several requests to serve in the government, his father encouraged him to accept a position. He accepts, and excels at, his new role as a leader of the state of Chu's 楚 military forces. When a competing state learns that Shen Ming is a leader of the Chu army, however, they capture his father and threaten to kill him unless Shen Ming defects from Chu and joins forces with them. Shen Ming weeps bitterly before commanding the Chu forces to destroy their enemies. As a result of his choice, his father is killed. While the ruler of Chu rewards Shen Ming for the victory, Shen Ming laments that he could not be both loyal (*zhong* 忠) to the state of Chu and filial (*xiao* 孝) to his father. Shen Ming sorrows over the fact that his actions could not fulfill both values (*xing buliangquan* 行不兩全), and then he kills himself. The narrator of the story (Han Ying 韓嬰 *c.* 200 BCE–*c.*130 BCE) concludes with a quote from the *Shijing* «詩經»: 'Whether advancing or retreating, there is only obstruction' 進退惟谷."

Ing 2017: 71; see also 146–51 for discussion, a full translation
of the passage, and further source citations

Here we have a moral hero who is put in an impossible situation, where no harmonious way of saving the conflicting values is possible. In particular, he cannot fulfill two conflicting virtues, along with their accompanying relation-specific obligations: loyalty to one's lord, and filial reverence for one's father. All three forms of goods are compromised: virtues, obligations, and relationships. And as Ing notes, this is not an isolated case, but one of many from early Chinese literature. His integrity is so sullied, in his own eyes, that he commits suicide.

This case, and others like it, are early Chinese versions of extreme conflict between the goods of familial affiliation and the goods of public career (not to mention public goods). There is a crucial difference, however. These early Confucian cases are at the metaphysical level accidental, generated by dreadful collisions of circumstance that create the distinctive, insoluble conflicts between values. They typically involve major breakdowns in social order, such as wars, as in the preceding example, or at least garden-variety problems, such as misrule by benighted political leaders. Thus even these early Confucians, alert to the *possibility* of tragedy, appear to think that both individual people and communal social order could be ethically perfect, if events were well-ordered.

We thus have a real disagreement about exactly how far value pluralism, and value conflict, go. The early Confucians appear to be reasonably confident that in normal circumstances it is possible, and certainly desirable, at least for males, to pursue the goods of familial affiliation and flourishing on the one hand, and career (creative work in the public service) on the other. They generally do not extend these views to women, although this is partly because they view the work of family cultivation and management as a profoundly important good for society, as well as for particular family lineages. Insuring that households are well-run is thus of the highest public importance, from a Confucian point of view.[11] Nevertheless, there is no disputing that from a contemporary point of view, the restriction of most women's agency to the "inner" realm of family and household management, would be a deeply unjust restriction on women's autonomy and agency.

This is worth debating, at least very briefly, because it is possible the early Ru figures assume family and work can generally be harmonized for the primary population in question, i.e., elite males, only because there will be ample staffing available to actually do the day to day work of raising the children. Settling this question is beyond the scope of this paper, but it seems clear to me that at least some major early texts, such as the *Mengzi*, presume fathers will not be absentee parents, but rather that they will be actively involved in child-rearing, at least as children emerge from the nursery and pursue education. As Mengzi reportedly argues in 4A18, gentlemen teach *each other's* sons, rather than their own, because this demanding process is liable to lead to resentment of one's teacher, which should not be allowed to damage the loving relationship between fathers and sons (see also 4B30). But this is still a serious commitment of time and energy to the raising of the next generation, albeit restricted to sons.

Setting aside the thorny question of how we ought to morally evaluate the sexist presumptions of early texts such as the *Mengzi* (see, for example, 3B2), I think we can still discern a real challenge here, even to ethicists like Slote who espouse contemporary feminist conceptions of proper gender roles. Early Confucians seem to think that serious conflicts between family and public goods, including one's loyalty to the state or to one's job, are a symptom of social disorder. In other words, it would be quite possible in principle to arrange society in such a way that people could effectively harmonize these goods and pursue them both with sufficient fullness to avoid Slote's predicted conflict. When this fails to happen, it is fundamentally due to a failure of political leadership.

As I argue in the next section, this position challenges one aspect of Slote's position, i.e., the intrinsic impossibility of perfect happiness. It also suggests an alternative sort of feminist approach to these issues, which would probably be of interest to Slote, given his laudable commitment to gender justice.

4 Striving, Happiness, and Despair

As I argued in the last section, Ing argues that the "harmony thesis" reflects only part of the story in early Confucianism (Ing 2017). In contrast to a lengthy history of Western interpretation that sees Chinese culture as grounded in a harmonious conception of human life and the world, in which every person and thing has its rightful place and stays there, Ing shows that early Confucian texts repeatedly dramatize conflicts between crucial values, some of which are unresolvable. These conflicts tend to be generated by the demands of different relationships, which, in a chaotic world, sometimes come into irreconcilable opposition. These frequently take the form of conflicts between responsibilities to family and to public occupation, but not always. Some of the most dramatic concern the failure of even great sages like Confucius to attain political power, which they both merit and desire. In other words, Ing shows that early Confucians do not presume the world to be basically orderly and harmonious, but instead find it to be frequently deeply conflicted and disordered.

Ing shows that many agents found themselves unable to grapple with the conflicts they faced, often taking refuge in suicide to express their shame and despair. Even sages, who by definition in these texts were aiming at the greater good, were sometimes unable to attain their ends by morally pure means—thereby risking not only the transgression of important boundaries (such as protecting the innocent in war), but also their own moral integrity. Sometimes, in the words of the texts, a morally serious person needs to get "wet" or even "muddy" to save those who are "drowning." Such transgressions are sometimes the only way to successfully remove tyrants, as in the paradigmatic case of King Wu overthrowing the last Shang king; or to make a forbidden literary contribution to pass on the Way to later readers who might put it into practice, as with Confucius, tempted to usurp a status as official historian he deserves but does not possess, as represented in the common early belief that he created the *Chunqiu* chronicle (Ing 2017: 176–231).

All of this echoes other important themes in early texts, which insist that one should continue striving for moral perfection regardless of worldly rewards, or appropriate recognition and "success" in finding a suitable position. This can be a challenging proposition—as Zengzi suggests in *Analects* 8.7, for an aspiring Confucian, "the burden is heavy and the way is long." And while early Ru texts commonly represent self-cultivation as something that can be attained through sufficient effort and commitment, they do not promise appropriate worldly recognition. Indeed, Kongzi himself is something of a paradigmatic figure in this regard. He passionately wishes to put his learning to good use, serving in the government of his home state of Lu, but is repeatedly thwarted in this aspiration (e.g., 9.9, 9.13–14). The times are not propitious, because the leaders of Lu are villainous usurpers, profaning sacred rituals and pretending to a status and a degree of virtue they do not rightfully possess.

What does Confucius do about this? He continues to pursue the Way, to the point that others are by turns shocked and impressed. In *Analects* 3.24, a border guard admonishes the disciples, "why should you be concerned about your Master's loss of office? The world has been without the Way for a long time now, and Heaven intends to use your Master like the wooden clapper for a bell." Other figures are less sympathetic, and urge Kongzi to "just give up if no one understands him" [i.e., "recognizes" him as suitable for office], due to the perilously dangerous times they live in (14.39; see also 18.5). We can deduce from these and similar passages that Kongzi was indeed a figure "who knows that what he does is impossible and yet persists anyway" (14.38).

Later tradition presents Kongzi as the "uncrowned king," with virtue sufficient to rule the whole known world—and yet he held no significant office. Instead, his frustration at his political failures spurred him to gather and teach disciples, as "recorded" in the *Analects*, and reportedly also to compose a chronicle of the state of Lu, the text known to us as the *Chunqiu*.[12] This was a significant transgression of his status as a commoner, even if it was suitable to his abilities.

The sheer difficulty of Kongzi's struggles leads him at times to lament his fate, and dream about running off to live among the barbarians (9.14), or even setting sail on the open ocean on a raft, in hopes of escape (5.7). As Amy Olberding has insightfully discussed, Kongzi's laments over his life pursuing virtue suggest that his life was far from perfectly happy (2013). And while Kongzi is only one figure, albeit an important one for the tradition, his struggles were recorded and passed down in part because they resonated with the frustrating experiences of many later followers who sought to follow the Way, but found it hard going, less than perfectly joyful.

All of this implies two fundamental rejoinders to Slote's arguments in *The Impossibility of Perfection*. First, we should vigorously pursue social reform (i.e., strive to "put the Way into practice" broadly in our community), in order to make it more possible for average people to pursue the most important goods, including both family life and meaningful work, even if this might seem impossible during our lifetime. Deciding prematurely that we have run up against a logical or metaphysical impossibility threatens to further entrench bad versions of a social status quo that might make even more moderate degrees of happiness and flourishing unnecessarily difficult to achieve. To put this differently, it is far from clear where to draw any metaphysical lines that would tell us that any further attempts at social reform were pointless, because they try to do the impossible.

I would argue that this is actually a more thorough-going feminist position than the one Slote proposes, because it aims to learn from both "masculine" and "feminine" lists of objective human goods, and tries to imagine ways to instantiate them all harmoniously. Even if this turns out to be impossible in some absolute sense because of the limits imposed by human mortality, ignorance, and frailty, it could very well lead to much more satisfying "compromises" among these goods than previously possible, or than possible in disordered present circumstances.

And second, early Confucian thinkers' emphasis on ethical striving provides one kind of very basic objection to excessively focused pursuit of happiness as the ultimate goal of life. In other words, on their accounts, perfect virtue is the right goal, even if that turns out to be impossible to achieve in one's lifetime, and even if that may jeopardize our individual happiness in important ways. It is, in other words, categorically better to be an admirable person, and to take what joy one can in that pursuit, even if one has the misfortune of living in disordered times that make happiness impossible, or badly flawed.

While this is a demanding message, Confucians are hardly alone in placing morality or ethical virtue above the pursuit of happiness in the ranking of human goods. And in contrast to some versions of this sort of stance, they clearly relish many of the good and enjoyable things in life, such as family togetherness, music, good food and drink, poetry and other literature, and the pleasures of (married) sexuality. Such things simply need to be enjoyed when they are attained in a manner that does not contravene the Confucian Way as a whole.

Early Confucians appear to think that dissatisfaction, yearning, anxiety, and resentment of evil and injustice, or even of simple bad luck, are all worthy prices to pay if one is willing to pursue virtue. As Mengzi puts it, the gentleman "certainly has what concerns him: 'Shun was a person; I, too, am a person. Shun was a model for the world that could be passed down to future generations. Yet I am still nothing more than an ordinary person.' This is something to be concerned about" (4B28). But while this and similar passages can easily be read as a celebration of the joys of self-cultivation, such as they are, that process still points outward in many ways, and is in turn shaped by the struggle to reform and order the world, which cannot be put aside, according to these early Confucians.

Even the struggle can be of value. Mengzi, in a fit of metaphysical optimism, puts it this way:

> When Heaven is about to bestow a great responsibility on a particular person, it will always first subject one's heart and resolution to bitterness, belabor one's muscles and bones, starve one's body and flesh, deprive one's person, and thwart and bring chaos to what one does. By means of these things it perturbs one's heart, toughens one's nature, and provides those things of which one is incapable. One must often make mistakes, and only then can one improve. One must be troubled in one's heart and vexed in one's deliberations, and only then rise up.... Only in these ways do we know that we live through adversity but die through ease.
>
> 6B15

While bitter struggles may be necessary to achieve greatness, they can for long stretches come at the cost of ease and happiness, at least as these are generally understood. As Kongzi puts it in 6.12, "Someone whose strength is genuinely insufficient collapses somewhere along the Way. As for you, [Ran Qiu,] you deliberately draw the line" (see also 4.6, 9.18).

All of this suggests that perhaps we should not experience comfort or relief, as Slote hopes we might (70), when we contemplate the possibility that goods we pursue may be fundamentally incompatible, as he argues they are. If we more easily accept such conflicts as inevitable, we may "settle" and stop striving for goodness, "drawing the line" prematurely. Whether we should struggle and strive for perfection even if it is impossible, which we can hardly know for sure, on their premises, is the question the early Confucians put to Slote, and to us.

Notes

1. Slote recognizes the possibility of this position, but does not discuss it in depth (43).
2. I am focusing on pre-Qin and Western Han texts in part because these are the Confucian texts I know best, and in part also because later "neo-Confucian" writings from the Song and later, at least until Dai Zhen, often presuppose a robust metaphysical scheme that strongly implies the harmony of all values. For a recent overview of these issues, see Ivanhoe 2016. For ease of reference I am referring to the English translations of the *Analects* by Slingerland, of the *Mengzi* by Van Norden, and of the *Xunzi* by Hutton.
3. I agree with Slote (2011: 50; and 2013: 91–2) that cultural relativism about ethics is a profoundly flawed philosophical position, and we should resist it in general. But what is appropriate in terms of dress and behavior does vary in some important respects across cultures, and proper norms for speech also vary in these ways. Americans, I would suggest, are particularly prone to valuing plain, frank speech, and tend to regard this more highly than indirect, tactful communication of the sort more common in some East Asian and (most notably) Persian cultures. Analytic philosophers in particular place a high value on frank criticism of opposing views, even when this might give offense, or fail to actually conduce to finding the truth in some area.
4. One might think another virtue, "trustworthiness" or "faithfulness" (*xin* 信), which Mengzi suggests is the distinctive virtue of friends (3A4), would be relevant. Perhaps it is, but this virtue seems most often to refer to an ability to live up to one's spoken commitments, such as promises, and so does not track particularly well with the issues Slote raises in his case.
5. Slote addresses the issue of how different virtues relate to each other at some length in chapter six of the book, "Relational Profiles of Goods and Virtues" (2011: 104–22). He explores the ways some values and virtues seem to depend on others, although he does not discuss Aquinas or the Stoics on any overarching systematic hierarchy to virtue, nor the issues of cardinality or "parts" of virtues as Russell does.
6. For one insightful overview of these issues that traces modern Western developments back to early modern disputes over the legacy of Augustine on the supposedly "splendid vices" that were pagan virtues, see Herdt 2008. Comparing early Confucian accounts of *cheng* 誠, often translated as "sincerity" or "integrity," with modern Western views of authenticity, is beyond the scope of this paper. And despite their emphasis on friends being dependably true to their word (*xin* 信), early Confucian masters at times seem remarkably nonchalant about lying to non-friends (e.g., *Analects* 17.20).
7. For discussion, see Shun 1997: 66–71, and Van Norden 2007: 273–77.
8. This is Steve Angle's way of describing his own interpretation, which is admittedly centered on twelfth- to sixteenth-century neo-Confucian thinkers. See Angle 2008: 35–6 for the quotation, and also Angle 2009: 93–111. Ing discusses Angle and other scholars' similar interpretations in Ing 2017: 52–72, and throughout.
9. This scenario is admittedly unlikely, because of the particulars of the friend Slote describes, and his resistance to change. The early Ru are realistic enough to

suggest that sages with this kind of creative communicative ability are exceedingly rare. The real issue I am trying to suggest with this "sagely communication" image is that the conflict between tact and frankness is not the most challenging and interesting issue raised by Slote's case. This sort of case dramatizes the extreme challenges posed by communicating salvific (or even just therapeutically valuable) knowledge to another person, especially if that person is resistant to the ideas in question. As far as I am aware, the thinker who has explored these issues most fully is Søren Kierkegaard, especially in his (pseudonymous) account of the need for "indirect communication" of religious knowledge in the *Concluding Unscientific Postscript* (1992). Kierkegaard's use of irony and humor throughout his authorship is one aspect of his attempt to grapple with the challenges of communicating salvific knowledge to those who need but do not want to hear and understand it. In this he draws on Plato's Socrates, the original ironic communicator.

10 See Puett 2001: 1–15; Ing 2017; 142–6; and also Li 2014, for further discussion of the basis of this view in the Confucian tradition.
11 I realize this is a controversial and complicated view. Fully arguing for this interpretation is beyond the scope of this paper, unfortunately. For an early text that makes these linkages clear, see the "Great Learning" chapter of the *Liji*. For some recent scholarship that shows just how seriously early Confucians took child-rearing as a public matter, see Cline 2015.
12 For insightful discussion, see Ing 2016.

References

Angle, Stephen C. (2008), "No Supreme Principle: Confucianism's Harmonization of Multiple Values," *Dao: A Journal of Comparative Philosophy* 7.1 (2008): 35–40.
Angle, Stephen C. (2009), *Sagehood: The Contemporary Significance of Neo-Confucian Philosophy*, New York: Oxford University Press.
Cline, Erin M. (2015), *Families of Virtue: Confucian and Western Views on Childhood Development,* New York: Columbia University Press.
Fingarette, Herbert (1972), *Confucius: The Secular as Sacred,* New York: Harper Torchbooks.
Herdt, Jennifer (2008), *Putting on Virtue: The Legacy of the Splendid Vices,* Chicago: University of Chicago Press.
Ing, Michael D. K. (2017), *The Vulnerability of Integrity in Early Confucian Thought,* New York: Oxford University Press.
Ing, Michael D. K. (2016), "Born of Resentment: Yuan 怨 in Early Confucian Thought," *Dao: A Journal of Comparative Philosophy,* 15 (1): 19–33.
Ivanhoe, Philip J. (2016), *Three Streams: Confucian Reflections on Learning and the Moral Heart-Mind in China, Korea, and Japan,* New York: Oxford University Press.
Kierkegaard, Søren (1992), *Concluding Unscientific Postscript to Philosophical Fragments,* trans. Howard V. and Edna H. Hong, 2 vols, Princeton, NJ: Princeton University Press.
Li, Chenyang (2014), *The Confucian Philosophy of Harmony,* New York: Routledge.

Olberding, Amy (2012) *Moral Exemplars in the Analects: The Good Person is That*, New York: Routledge.

Olberding, Amy (2013), "Confucius' Complaints and the *Analects*' Account of the Good Life," *Dao: A Journal of Comparative Philosophy*, 12 (4): 417–40.

Puett, Michael J. (2001), *The Ambivalence of Creation: Debates Concerning Innovation and Artifice in Early China*, Stanford, CA: Stanford University Press.

Russell, Daniel C. (2009), *Practical Intelligence and the Virtues*, New York: Oxford University Press.

Shun, Kwong-loi (1997), *Mencius and Early Chinese Thought*, Stanford, CA: Stanford University Press.

Slote, Michael (2011), *The Impossibility of Perfection: Aristotle, Feminism, and the Complexities of Ethics*, New York: Oxford University Press.

Slote, Michael (2013), "The Impossibility of Perfection," in Stephen C. Angle and Michael Slote (eds), *Virtue Ethics and Confucianism*, 83–93. New York: Routledge.

Van Norden, Bryan (2007), *Virtue Ethics and Consequentialism in Early Chinese Philosophy*, New York: Cambridge University Press.

12

Virtue Ethics, Symmetry, and Confucian Harmonious Appropriation of Self with Others

Qingjie James Wang
University of Macau, Macau

1 Introduction

In the history of both Western and Eastern philosophical cultures and thought, morality has been understood often as a reflective way of thinking about—as well as a practical way of dealing with—the relationship between the self and others in our social and political life. In his early works, especially his book *From Morality to Virtue* (Slote 1992) and his essay on "Virtue Ethics, Utilitarianism and Symmetry" (Slote 1996), Professor Michael Slote examines mainly the symmetric nature of his so-called "commonsense virtue ethics." He compares it with act-utilitarianism and act-consequentialism on the one hand, and with Kantian ethical deontology and commonsense moral views on the other hand. According to Slote, act-utilitarianism as one of the ruling theories in contemporary ethics distinguishes itself from other major theories such as Kantian ethical deontology by its feature of the self-other symmetry, while the latter, together with commonsense moral views, take morality essentially as a self-other asymmetrical morality. Slote argues that his commonsense virtue ethics shares with act-utilitarianism and act-consequentialism in self-other symmetric feature of morality. Nevertheless, it is also substantially different from them. Commonsense virtue ethics does neither neglect the well-being or the happiness of oneself as the agent involved in a moral action, nor is it agent-neutral, as observed in act-utilitarianism or act-consequentialism.

In this chapter I would like to argue, first of all, that it might be "categorically" inappropriate here to use the schema of "self-other symmetry / asymmetry" in description and evaluation of the different types of moral theories such as utilitarianism, Kantian deontological morality as well as virtues ethics. The common goal of these major moral theories is very similar and all these theories are in fact more or less seeking for some kinds of moral "symmetry" between self and others. I then try to go a step further and argue, in light of my philosophical analysis of a cardinal virtue of Confucian ethics, i.e., the virtue of *xiao* (filial piety) of a virtuous adult child to his or her aged parents, that the Confucian virtue ethics is not a "self-other asymmetrical" morality as it looks at the first glance. It is rather a "self-other symmetrical," but not in an ordinary sense which is either the "interest-oriented symmetry of self and others" (act-utilitarianism), or the "rights-oriented symmetry of self and others" (Kantian ethics). More accurately speaking, it is even neither "symmetrical" nor "asymmetrical." It is rather a virtue ethics of "harmonious appropriation of self with others."

2 Slote's Idea of the Symmetric Nature of Commonsense Virtue Ethics

According to Slote's understanding and interpretation, his commonsense virtue morality has advantages in comparing with both commonsense intuitive moral views and Kantian deontological moral views. For example, Slote claims that Kantian moral views are essentially self-other asymmetric because in Kantian deontological moral theory "there is no fundamental duty or obligation to secure one's own happiness or well-being, but such a duty or obligation toward others does exist"; therefore, "corresponding moral judgments about the agent's own happiness lack a Kantian basis" (Slote 1996: 101) However, in commonsense virtue ethics, "When we look at the whole range of traits commonly regarded as virtue and actions we admire, we observe a fair or rough balance between other-regarding and self-regarding considerations." (Slote 1996: 102) It is thus a self-other symmetric view of morality. Similar to Kantian deontological morality, our ordinary thinking about morals, or commonsense moral intuitive morality, says Slote, is also "highly" self-other asymmetric because "Neglecting the well-being of another person can sometimes intuitively seen wrong in a way or to a degree that it does not seem wrong – though it may be foolish or eccentric—to neglect oneself, and similar points apply from the standpoint of commonsense to issues of harming others vs. harming oneself. Furthermore, ordinary moral thinking would tend to regard it as morally better to choose the lesser good of another rather than secure one's own greater good" (Slote 1996: 100).

Assuming that we accept Slote's distinction between the self-other symmetry and asymmetry as one of the major distinctions between Kantian moral theory and his own commonsense virtue ethics, we still need to ask: what is the problem with a self-other asymmetric morality? Slote points out that there are mainly two problems. First, a self-other asymmetric morality may lead us to "get very odd, and even in some sense incoherent results" (1996: 107). I cannot imagine, for example, how a self-other asymmetric Kantian or an intuitive self-other asymmetric moralist could consistently and coherently think and argue why, if all other things are equal, the well-being of any other individual being should weigh more than mine, i.e., the well-being of the agent himself of an particular action. Moreover, the second problem mentioned by Slote is that this kind of the self-other asymmetric morality, especially the commonsense morality could face "the by-now familiar problem of moral luck" (1996: 107). For example, if it is morally unjustified in praising or blaming one's action merely on the basis of things which are totally outside his or her control and subject to pure luck, e.g., one's looks, genius, calm or easy-going temperament, etc., why should we take those morally accidental positions in our moral judgment? We cannot simply say that a moral action depends solely on a simple fact that the action will benefit the non-agent other rather than the agent himself. Therefore, Slote says correctly that "The person who not only shows a great concern for others, but who, in addition, seems to deprecate or ignore his own needs whenever there is slightly good he can do for others, would typically be thought to have something wrong" (1996: 103). Following this reasoning and criticism, Slote comes to his conclusion that "we can plausibly deny that either selfishness or selflessness is a virtue." Instead, his "commonsense virtue ethics espouses an ideal of (some degree of) balance between self-regarding and other-regarding concerns: one is not admirable and is open to criticism if one does not have and act upon both self-regarding and other-regarding concerns, if one is not concerned both with oneself and with others" (1996: 103).

Another advantage of the commonsense virtue ethics, according to Slote, can be seen from its comparison with act-utilitarianism or act-consequentialism. Different from Kantian morality and Commonsense moral views discussed above, act-utilitarianism and act-consequentialism are neither other-favoring nor self-neglecting moral theory. They are essentially agent-neutral and thus self-other symmetric morality. Although act-utilitarianism and act-consequentialism share Slote's commonsense virtue ethics in their understanding of the self-other symmetric nature of morality, there are still substantial differences between these two types of moral theories. A utilitarian self-other symmetry insists that the welfare or preferences of every individual should weigh equally in the reckoning of the goodness of results and this equality should constitute the basis for its claims about moral obligation and moral rightness. However, at the same time, Slote points out, "this equality of weight and concern cuts across the difference between self and the other, as well as that between different others, in regard to the evaluation of any given agent's activities" (1996: 104). In other words, a utilitarian self-other symmetry only asks and cares about *a quantitative symmetry* among different ones, while a genuine idea of the self-other symmetry of morality must concern further and deeper on the real and *qualitative self-other symmetry* in our moral consideration and evaluation.

Then, how can a moral theory really concern both self-regarding and other-regarding aspects and reach a balance between them, and at the same time, care both sides equally and substantially, i.e., not only quantitatively but also qualitatively? Slote has suggested a very unique and different way of solving or dissolving the problem, and clearly, this solution indicates the advantages of Slote's theory of the commonsense virtue ethics.

Briefly, Slote suggests that we pay attention to the problem of self-other symmetry and asymmetry from a perspective of virtue ethics rather than from that of rule ethics. As we know, virtue ethics focuses more on the formation of the virtuous characters of a good being such as a good person or a good community while rule ethics focuses on the prescriptive or normative rules directing or regulating good actions of moral agents. Therefore, we are suggested to make a substantial switching," *a switching from symmetric calculations of the possible, action-based consequential and beneficial effects to anyone involved in that action, toward a "symmetric balance" between different virtues possessed by the agent-self.* Among these virtues we can distinguish those with self-regarding aspects such as "prudence," "sagacity," "circumspection," "discretion," "fortitude," etc., those with other-regarding aspects such as "justice," "kindness," "probity," "generosity," etc., and those "admired both for what they do for their exemplifiers and for what they lead their exemplifiers to do in regard to other people" such as "notably, self-control, courage, etc" (Slote 1996: 102). This switching, according to Slote, does not only help the commonsense virtues ethics to solve the problem hidden in self-other asymmetric moral theories such as commonsense moral views or Kantian deontological morality, but also the problem of the "neutral agent" hidden in the self-other symmetric morality such as in utilitarianism. It is symmetric without a "neutral agent" because it could not only reach a general "symmetric" balance between the virtues, but also allow some kinds of preferences towards either the self-regarding concerns or the other-regarding concerns in different life situations of morality. Following this way of thinking, Slote says further that "Someone whose self-regarding and other-regarding concerns are in some kind of (rough) balance may be more concerned with some other people than with others, and a commonsense ethics of virtue will presumably consider it less than admirable if one is no more concerned with particular friends or family members than with given individuals one hardly knows" (1996: 104).

3 Possible Problems with Slote's Position

Slote's solution to the problem of self-other symmetry not only provides us with a different perspective of seeing the traditional philosophical controversy, but also gives us a way to explore further, together with his taking the sentimentalist concept of empathy, a new and thought-provoking way to understand the very nature of human moralities. Although I find myself very sympathetic to Slote's commonsense ethics of virtue, especially his sentimentalist approach to it developed in recent years, I shall not accept his position and his arguments without hesitation and questioning.

One of the possible problems is about the legitimacy of the "switching" from rule ethics to virtue ethics when using the same concept of the "self-other symmetry." It seems to me that there are two different meanings of the concept involved here. When Slote uses the concept of the "self-other symmetry" in the discussion of utilitarianism and Kantian morality, he uses it in a sense of the "consequential symmetry of interests" which are benefiting or affecting the agent and the others involved in a moral action or moral actions. For example, he adopted Phillipa Foot's view that "if a trait of character does not benefit or serve the needs of its possessor, the trait cannot properly be regarded as a virtue" (Slote 1992: 8). However, when he uses the concept in the discussion of his own commonsense virtue ethics, the meaning is changed to be "distributive symmetry of virtue" in classifying and balancing different types of virtues possessed by a moral being. Thus, we can easily see the advantage of a virtue ethics when it deals with such a problem like "symmetric" or "asymmetric" distribution because now the question is not about the distribution of beneficial interests but that of virtues. The former deals directly with quantitative interests or qualitative rights of each individual like the self and the other, while the latter deals only with virtues within one specific being, i.e., the possessor of the virtues. Therefore, we can say that Slote's solution to the problem is not really a solution. The problem is simply "escaped" through a way of the "switching," but the switching itself might not be "categorically" appropriate because first, we can easily imagine that a virtue ethicist, like a Confucian virtue ethicist, holds both a "consequential interests-asymmetric" and a distributive "virtue-symmetric" moral position at the same time without any problem or contradiction. Second, in regard to virtue distribution, we should say that any moral theory of virtue ethics, must be "symmetric" or "balanced" because it is required by the "middle way" (*zhong dao* 中道) nature of the very concept of virtue itself, whether it is defined or viewed by an Aristotelian, a Confucian, or other virtue ethicists.

However, when Slote talks about the symmetric nature of his commonsense virtue ethics, he does not seem to use the concept consistently or he swings back and forth between the above two different meanings. Sometimes he uses the "self-other symmetry" in the sense of the "consequential symmetry" of beneficial interests gained by the agent and the other rather than the "distributive symmetry" between different types of virtues. Moreover, he uses the concept in an "indirect" sense rather than a "direct" sense when he uses it to describe the "symmetric" nature of utilitarianism. There seem to be two steps here. First, the "self-other symmetry" of the commonsense virtue ethics occurs between the different aspects of different virtues, self-regarding, other-regarding or both-regarding. They are balanced or symmetric on this level. Second, through a balanced way of practicing of these different virtues, the interest of the agent-self and that of the others are also getting "balanced," symmetrically and consequently. In light of this understanding, we could "classify" our virtues basically into two balanced "groups," the self-concern" and "the others-concern." Slote then says: "We can clarify the difference between the symmetries involved in virtue ethics and in utilitarianism by saying that our ordinary understanding of what is admirable and counts as a virtue embodies roughly balanced equal, or symmetrical concern for self and others" (1996: 104).

Here we need more and further discussions and explorations. The first is about the concept of "others." To Slote, this "others" does not refer to any separate or individual other, but a "class" or a "category" of "others" in contrast to another "class" which is the agent himself. It is in this way that we can reach a balance or "symmetry."

However, we have to notice that this balance or symmetry can only be made when it is among distributions of virtues, not among the beneficial interests as we have seen it for discussion of the self-other symmetry in utilitarianism. As Slote points out, this "others" must be understood *in sensu composito* rather than *in sensu diviso*, as defined in utilitarian ethics. On the basis of this "classification," Slote leads us to his second step and asks, what then makes a virtue to be counted as a virtue or to be admirable? The answer is: a virtue is a virtue because it "embodies roughly balanced equal or symmetrical concern for self and others" (1996: 104). Now Slote leads us to complete the "transition" again from the "distributive symmetry of virtue" back to the "consequential symmetry of beneficial interests" and thus he has "legitimized" his commonsense virtue ethics through this new concept of the "self-other symmetry."

If my reconstruction of Slote's reasoning and argument is correct, we will then find that there are some further problems. One is about the nature of Slote's commonsense virtue ethics. A virtue ethics says a being or a life of human being is good because it is a virtuous life or it is full of virtues. Then we would ask what makes a virtue to be a virtue? Slote answers the question in saying that a virtue is good because it brings us a greatest balance or "symmetry" of the beneficial interests between the agent-self as one "class" and all the others as another "class." If this is the case, Slote's virtue ethics might not be called as a virtue ethics but a new type of and an indirect way of consequentialism. Different from both act-consequentialism and rule-consequentialism, we might call it the virtue-consequentialism because symmetric or asymmetric *consequences* will determine a virtue to be a virtue. However, we will have a similar problem of the act- utilitarianism. Someone, say a contemporary virtue ethicist influenced by Kant or Confucius, may argue that a virtue's being a virtue does not depend on any consequences of carrying out of the virtue, but on the virtuosity or the virtue itself, no matter to whom it benefits consequently. Another is about the divisions between the self-regarding and others-regarding aspects of a virtue. I am a little reluctant to classify all of our moral virtues in this way. For example, one could classify "fortitude" as a self-regarding aspect of virtue, but for another, it may look more like a virtue which would manifest itself through some agent's self-neglecting or even self-denying activities. Moreover, why do we divide virtues through self-regarding aspect and others-regarding aspect? Why don't we classify it, for example, through a division between body and spirit, or like Aristotle did, between reflective wisdom and practical action? Is this distinction or division necessary or only accidental?

4 An Analysis of a Confucian Cardinal Virtue of *Xiao* 孝 (*Yang* 養) as Taking Respectful Care of One's Elderly Parents

An analysis of the very nature of Confucian morality may lead us to think more and deeper about the problem raised by Slote. Confucian theory of morality is obviously one of the most important and influential virtue ethics in human history of thought. It teaches what a virtuously good person—as well as a virtuously just society—is. It also shows the ways one becomes a good person and how we build up a just society. We do this via virtues such as moral love (*renai* 仁愛) and learning (*haoxue* 好學), as practicing a government of humanity (*renzheng* 仁政) and justice (*yi* 義) etc.. In what follows I would like to use a Confucian virtue of *xiao* 孝 or "filial piety" as an example of how a Confucian son would develop and culture this most important moral trait or character in himself and reach a "harmony"(*he* 和) between him and others, as well as with the surrounding world when practicing the virtue of "filial piety."

The virtue of filial piety, which primarily defines children's moral duty to their parents, has been understood in the Confucian tradition as the "root" of morality in China (*Analects* 1:2).[1] Generally speaking, there should be at least three important meanings of Confucius' term "*xiao*" in the *Analects* (Roetz 1993: 53–66). First, it means *yang* 養, i.e., adult children's willing and being able to take respectful care of their aged parents (*Analects*, 1:7; 2:6; 2:7; 2:8; 4:9; 4:21; 17:21). Second, it means *wu wei* 無違, i.e., one's compliance with the way of, and never disobedience of the will of, one's father because father should be seen as a symbol of authority in the familial community and in the tradition (*Analects* 1:11; 2:5; 4:18; 4:20; 13:18; 19:18). Third, it means "*shi yu you zheng*" 施於有政. That is to extend one's exercise of filial piety from family life to public and governmental service (*Analects*, 1:2; 2:20; 2:21). To simplify my argument, I would like to focus on the first meaning of *xiao*, i.e., *yang* 養, as an example of my analysis of the Confucian virtue ethics. In the *Analects*, Confucius' term "*yang*," as taking respectful care of one's parents in their later life, may be interpreted as: (1) taking care of one's parents' lives (*yang kou ti* 養口體); (2) taking care of one's parents' mental needs and making them happy (*yang zhi* 養志); and (3) taking care of one's parents' spirits after they have died (*yang ling* 養靈). On the one hand, Confucius thought that taking care of one's parents' lives is the fundamental virtue of a filial son. For example, he said that a filial son should "undertake the hard work when anything has to be done and let the elder enjoy wine and food when these are available" (*Analects* 2:8). He also taught that a filial son ought to "try his best to serve his parents" (*Analects* 1:7), to "worry about his parents' health" (*Analects* 2:6) and "old age" (*Analects* 4:21), and that he ought not to travel far away from his parents while they are alive (*Analects* 4:19). On the other hand, Confucius emphasized that a true filial son ought not only to satisfy his parents' physical needs by providing them with fine food, clothes, and shelter, but more importantly to satisfy their mental needs and to enable them to live a happy life. Therefore, the care for parents must be accompanied by a genuine respect, which Confucius called "reverence" (*jing* 敬). In the *Analects*, when Confucius was asked once by his disciple about being filial, he said: "Nowadays for a man to be filial means no more than that he is able to provide his parents with food. Even dogs and horses are, in some way, provided with food. If a man shows no reverence, where is the difference?" (*Analects* 2:7). In the *Mencius*, we are given examples of Zeng Shen's caring for his father Zeng Xi and of Zeng Yuan's caring for his father Zeng Shen to show the difference between care with full virtue of respect and that without the fully realized virtue (*Mencius* 4A:19).

Confucius' emphasis on *xiao, yang,* and *jing* as adult children's taking respectful care of their aged parents, had a tremendous influence in shaping the Chinese understanding of the Confucian virtue as well as the very nature of morality. Looking after one's parents is thus not only seen as a cardinal virtue of a superior moral person (*jun zi* 君子), but also of being a good citizen. According to Confucius and other Confucians, one cannot be seen as a good citizen without being a filial son first (*Analects* 1:2; 1:6; 1:7; 2:20). Mencius also said that the most important feature of *ren* 仁 (humanity) is "loving and caring for one's parents" (*Mencius* 4A:27; 13:15). Thus, that all aged parents and the elderly received good care from their children in the last years of their lives was taken in Chinese tradition as proof of a good society and a good government. Mencius praised King Wen, the founder of the Zhou Dynasty, as a sage monarch and his government as a government of humanity, partially because of his policy of taking good care of the aged (*Mencius* 7A:22). Mencius said that in a good society "a son and a younger brother should be taught virtues of taking good care of their parents during their later years. The people with grey hair should not be seen carrying burdens on the street" (*Mencius* 1A:7). Otherwise, it would be a matter of shame for the children of those elderly persons as well as for the government.

This Confucian tradition of seeing one's taking good care of his or her aged parents as a moral virtue and even a duty (*ben fen* 本分) was also reflected in the very earliest Chinese laws. For example, according to the laws of the Tang Dynasty, a man should be acquitted from fighting with another if his parents or grandparents have been attacked by the other; and an official must resign from his official position and return home during the mourning period for his dead parents. During the Qing Dynasty, a serious penalty could be reduced, and even a death penalty could be changed, if the criminal happened to be the only son in the household and his parents or grandparents would not be properly cared for if he were to be imprisoned for life or executed. Today, according to the Chinese Marriage Law, adult children's legal duty of taking respectful care of their parents is defined as "Children have an obligation to support and to assist their parents. . . . . When children fail in such duty, parents who cannot work or who have difficulty with their living have a right to demand alimony from their children."[2]

5 Confucian Virtue Ethics: A Symmetrical Morality between Self and Others or a Harmonious Morality of Self with Others?

It goes without saying that taking respectful care of one's elderly parents is one of the most important moral virtues of an adult child in Confucian China, as well as in all East Asian societies. Very few people would deny this. However, the virtues of *xiao, yang,* and *jing* in Confucian virtue ethics look like, if we borrow Slote's words, very "self-other asymmetric" and not "symmetric." Can we simply and rightly say that Confucianism as a virtue ethics is different than Slote's commonsense virtue ethics and advocates instead "self-other asymmetric" virtues?

Norman Daniels, a Rawlsian liberal philosopher and once a US president advisor on public health policies, made a criticism when considering the issue of adult children's obligation for caring of their aged parents in our modern society. In his view, there is a "basic asymmetry between parental and the filial obligations" (Daniels 1988: 29). The parental obligation of caring for their young children, says Daniels, is a "self-imposed" duty, while the so-called children's obligation of caring for their elderly parents is "non-self-imposed" and thus cannot be morally justified and required. In contrast to act-utilitarian "interest oriented self-other symmetry" and to Slote's "virtue oriented self-other symmetry," Daniel's symmetry might be called as the "rights oriented self-other symmetry." All of them are against the self-other asymmetry in morality.

I once developed two arguments in answering Daniels' challenge (Wang 2016: 152–4). First, I claimed that his criticism misunderstood the very nature of the children-parents relationship from its very beginning. It should not be a self-other relation which deals with the rights possessed by children on the one side and by parents on the other. Daniels insists that there is no consensual commitment by children in establishing such kind of filial relation from the beginning. Because one does not choose to be the son or the daughter of one's parents, the so-called filial relation is asymmetrical. But is it really asymmetrical? It might be true that children do not give their consent in establishing the parent/child relationship. But it is also true that they do not give their consent not to establish such a relationship. Therefore, whether a child gives consent to being brought into the world, or to establish a parent/child relationship, is actually a fake or a misleading question. A child as a moral agent in such a relationship does not exist at all. Moreover, even if such a child does exist, it would be impossible for her either to give or to refuse to give consent in the first place. Thus understood, the right question should not be whether a child actually gives consent, but whether a child *would give* consent if the child were a "fully fledged human person." If we agree that life itself is the most valuable thing we have in the world and that most children would have a normal family life, i.e., they receive adequate care and love from their parents,[3] we should say that a child would give consent to or "impose" him/herself into the filial relation, and thus make it "symmetrical."

The second argument for the Confucian moral virtue of "filial duty" against Daniels' criticism is based on the Confucian concept of "justice as appropriation" which includes not only the inter-subjective relations but also the inter-generational ones in a Confucian community and society. Daniels' bias may lead him to claim that a request for adult children's moral virtue of taking respectful care of aged parents must be an unfair one for the younger generation, because it asks the younger generation to make sacrifices for the well-being of the older generation. (Daniels 1988: 34). But if we, as a Confucian often does, take human life as an organic whole and a dynamic process of birth, growing, flourishing, declining, and dying, then the rationale behind the Confucian concept of filial virtue as *yang* 養 will become clearer. Nothing seems more natural and fair than, having received care from our parents when we were young, reciprocating this care by taking care of our parents when they are old.[4] Therefore, the charge of "asymmetry," or unfairness and inequality of Confucian filial virtue, can only make sense on the assumption that the individuals in our social and communal life must be seen as undifferentiated, colorless, and isolated social atoms. But for Confucian ethics, this assumption itself is questionable and unacceptable.

Therefore, it seems to me that this traditional idea of the "self-other symmetry/asymmetry" must be based on a self-other dichotomy ontologically. If a comprehensive moral theory such as virtue ethics does not presuppose this dichotomy, the problem of the self-other symmetry might then not bother us as it does to utilitarianism, or in a moral consequentialism, and liberal moral theory. My above discussions and arguments may indicate that a virtue ethics such as Confucian moral theory would claim that aretaic characters of a morally superior person (*junzi* 君子) should have a deeper ontological ground than that of the self-other dichotomy which belongs essentially still to a philosophical subjectivism and a monistic individualism. Because of this, I should call it the "self-others harmony" rather than the "self-other symmetry."

The Confucian concept of "harmony" (*he* 和) has a much broader sense than the concept of "self-other symmetry" which is used by Slote in his early works of commonsense virtue ethics. Ontologically it goes together with other Chinese philosophical categories such as *qi* 氣 (vital energy), *yin yang* 陰陽, *tai ji* 太極 (the Ultimate), *tian dao* 天道 (way of heaven), *cheng* 誠 (sincerity and completeness), as well as *zhong yong* 中庸/中道 (middle way). It is also morally and politically associated with those cardinal and primary Confucian virtues such as *ren* 仁 (benevolence as love and care), *li* 禮 (ceremony as social rituals) and *yi* 義 (justice as appropriation). Ontologically as well as morally, Confucian virtue ethics may not accept any *a priori* or metaphysical priority of individual rights, dignity and interest of self and other on which the so-called self-other symmetry could be established or acknowledged. However, if we say that individual rights, dignity, and interests, as well as all the virtues associated with them, can be derived, identified, respected, and protected "symmetrically", this "symmetry" must depend ontologically on a deep level of "harmony." This is an ontological as well as a psychological harmony among different but interactive tendencies (*shi* 勢) such as *tian di* 天地 (sky and Earth), female and male, old and young, strong and week, the positive and the negative, one and the many, the individual and community, etc.

6 Conclusion

Let me conclude this essay by analyzing again a social and political virtue of "justice" as "appropriation" (*yi* 義) in Confucian virtue ethics and politics. I'll try to explore why and how a virtue in Confucian virtue ethics comes out of a conceptually much broader and ontologically much deeper notion of "harmony" rather than, as Slote once showed, merely out of a concept of the "self-other symmetry." The Confucian virtue of the moral, social and political justice (*yi* 義) comes out of multiple intra- and interactive relations of self with the other or others. However, here the "other" is defined neither as any quantitative one as we find in utilitarianism nor as a single rationalized and thus dignified individual person as we find in Kantian deontology. Instead, I would like to stress that it is a relation of myself *with* others rather than a relation *between* the self and the other. From the relation of "with" we come to the concept of "harmony" or "discord" while from the concept of "between" we have the concept of "symmetry" or "asymmetry." Moreover, a Confucian would further understand the "other" with whom he or she co-exists primarily as *qun* 群, i.e., different family life "circles," communities and the surrounding natural environment such as animal worlds and natural worlds out of which I myself get at least partially identified as well as cultivated through ways of emotionally loving and caring, and that of being cared. Along with this way of self-identification and self-cultivation a Confucian virtue of justice / righteousness (*yi* 義) and vice of injustice/non-righteousness (*bu yi* 不義) get established and understood in the traditional Confucian virtue ethics. That is also why early Confucian philosophers such as Dong Zhong Shu 董仲舒 (*c*.179 BCE–*c*.104 BCE.) defined the meaning of the Chinese character *yi* 義 (justice/righteousness) from its two constituent parts as the "personal self" (*wo* 我) and my surrounding social, historical, and natural communities. Dong also interpreted this Confucian virtue of "justice/righteousness" (*yi* 義) philosophically from its homophone, of "appropriation" (*yi* 宜) in the following passage:

> *Yi* 義 means *yi* 宜 (appropriation) to one's own person. Only once one is appropriate to his own person can this be called *yi* 義 (righteousness). Thus, the expression *yi* 義 combines the notions of "appropriateness" (*yi* 宜) and "personal self" (*wo* 我) in one term. If we hold on to this insight, *yi* as an expression refers to personal self. Thus it is said that to realize *yi* 義 in one's actions is called attaining it in oneself (*zi de* 自得); to neglect *yi* 義 in one's actions is called self-negligence (*zi shi* 自失).[5]

According to Dong and other Confucians during his time, *yi* 義 should be defined in term of *yi* 宜, which means "right, proper, appropriate, suitable." In both classical and modern Chinese, the word *yi* 宜 often refers to one's making oneself over to become harmoniously appropriate to one's surrounding environments, e.g., one's familial, social, and natural communities. It refers also to making one's surrounding environments harmoniously appropriate for one's self-attainment or self-accomplishment. Therefore, Dong's interpretation of *yi* 義 in terms of *yi* 宜 indicates an interplay or a dialectical interaction of *yi* 義 with *yi* 宜, of the personal self (wo 我) with my contextual and communal environments out of which my individual personhood reaches my identity, realization, and accomplishment. Based on this conception of *yi* 義 as justice and righteousness and as a harmonious and caring interplay of my individual self with my surrounding communities, Confucians think that fulfilling one's virtues, such as being a lovely parent and taking good care of my young children, and/or being a filial son/daughter by taking respectful care of my parents when the parents are old, is simply part of the way of self-realization and of self-accomplishment. Failure to do this will be called *bu yi* 不義 (non-righteousness). Our natural and innermost moral feelings of *xiu* 羞 (shame) and *wu* 惡 (dislike) or *bu an* 不安 (an uneasy mind), according to Confucians (see *Mencius* 3A:5), are simply signals of both internal and social disapproval of these non-righteous actions, and thus mark the beginning of the development of righteousness and justice. That said, the harmonious interplay of *yi* 義 with *yi* 宜 not only asks a yielding or a sacrifice of my personal self to my environmental communities in the way of appropriation, but also affirms my uniqueness in such an appropriation. That not only includes my duties but also my privileges and rights, which are due to my specific situation in my surrounding communities. Thus understood, the Confucian virtues of moral and social justice and righteousness are not against the idea of equality and fairness among the members of the society. They are rather an affirmation of it if we consider them within a larger social and historical context.*

Notes

* The research project is supported by University of Macau (File no. SRG2019-00176-FAH).
1 For English translations of the *Analects*, see Lau 1973 or Waley 1989.
2 *The Chinese Marriage Law*, Section 3, Article 15 (the English translation is mine).
3 My discussion of adult children's filial obligation will exclude the case of abusive parents. A parent's abuse of his or her child can be seen as a case of the parent's failure to fulfil his her parental obligations and is condemned in most moral traditions.
4 Here it is nothing to do with "owing" or "paying debts," as we found from reading Jane English's (Sommers and Sommers 1993: 761–3) article.
5 See Dong Zhong Shu, 8/8b; I use Hall and Ames' translation here. See Hall and Ames 1987: 92.

References

Confucius (1973), *Analects*, trans. D.C. Lau, London: Penguin Classics.
Daniels, N. (1988), *Am I My Parents' Keeper?: An Essay on Justice between the Young and the Old,* Oxford: Oxford University Press.

Hall, D. and R. Ames (1987), *Thinking Through Confucius,* Albany, NY: SUNY Press.
Mencius (1979), *Mencius,* trans. D. C. Lau. London: Penguin Classics.
Slote, Michael (1992), *From Morality to Virtue,* New York and Oxford: Oxford University Press.
Slote, Michael (1996), "Virtue Ethics, Utilitarianism, and Symmetry,", in Roger Crisp (ed.), *How Should One Live? Essays on the Virtues*, Oxford: Oxford University Press.
Sommers, C. and F. Sommers, eds (1993), *Vice and Virtue in Everyday Life,* Fort Worth, TX: Harcourt.
Roetz, H. (1993), *Confucian Ethics of the Axial Age,* Albany: SUNY Press.
Waley, A. trans. (1989), *The Analects of* Confucius, New York: Vintage Books.
Wang, Q. (2016), *A Confucian Exemplary Ethics of Virtue,* Beijing: Peking University Press.

13

Replies to Commentators

Michael Slote
University of Miami, United States

1 Introduction

Before I respond to the comments and criticisms made by the philosophers who attended the conference that focused on my encounter (and engagement) with Chinese philosophy, let me make some general remarks that may help put the comments/criticisms and my replies to them into perspective. A philosopher whose work has been developing and continues to develop has to make a choice. They can delay publishing till all possible development has ceased or they can issue progress reports in the form of articles and even books. I have chosen the latter course, and that much is evident from the way different commentators in this volume have chosen to focus on different periods or stages of my work. That being said, though, I would like to offer you a brief picture of what I am currently doing and intending that can help put the commentaries of this volume and my replies to them into a useful larger perspective.

In a well-known op-ed piece in the *New York Times* in May 2011 (available at Google), Jay Garfield and Bryan Van Norden argued that American and other analytic philosophy departments ought to diversify so as to include philosophers teaching courses on Asian/Chinese philosophy and researching that area as well. But they never considered what an analytic philosopher could say in criticism of their call for diversity. The analytic philosopher can say that, as far as they can tell, Chinese philosophy is full of antiquated or confused ideas and that where Chinese philosophy seems at all on the right track, its ideas are already anticipated in Western philosophy. What need, then, to diversify except on grounds of sheer historical coverage rather than anything important to philosophy itself?

This potential (and, in the minds of many analytic philosophers who read the op-ed piece, actual) reply was never considered much less countered by Garfield and Van Norden, and yet it has to be if a good case for change on the part of Western departments and Western philosophy is going to be made. This, I believe, is where my own work comes in. In many recent publications I have sought to show that Western philosophy is fundamentally misguided and that Chinese thought is not only not misguided, but can also point the West toward new and plausible ways of handling and answering what it considers to be important philosophical questions. One has to make such a case in order to properly answer the reply to Garfield and Van Norden I have attributed *in pectore* to Western analytic philosophers (a couple of prominent analytic philosophers have actually made that reply to me). So we have to show what is deeply wrong with Western thought and indicate how Chinese thought can help with problems that the West is preoccupied with if we are to make the case for taking Chinese philosophy seriously to Western/analytic philosophers. Beyond that, we need to show both China and the West how their separate traditions can be validly integrated at the most fundamental philosophical level.

Most of my recent work is in the service of these aims—especially the book *The Philosophy of Yin and Yang: A Contemporary Approach* (2018, with parallel English language and Chinese language texts); the short article "*Yin-Yang* and the Heart-Mind" (2018); and the new book *A Larger Yin/Yang Philosophy: From Mind to Cosmic Harmony* (now being translated into Chinese by Professor Li Jialian for eventual publication with dual-language texts). But let me try to put all of that into a larger perspective. I was recently interviewed in Beijing by two major cultural news outlets and in one of the interviews was asked what I thought was the most central idea of Chinese philosophy. I came up with two, but subsequent reflection showed me a way to combine them into one putative central thesis of Chinese philosophy. But having done as much, I began to wonder whether and how something similar could be done with Western philosophy, and I have now come up with something that, together with what can be said about Chinese philosophy on the whole, allows us not only to capture the essential difference between the two philosophical traditions but also to point toward the way or ways in which the West needs to learn from China and China itself needs to understand how much it has to offer present-day philosophy.

I realize that what I am about to say represents an extremely bold claim, but I think the claim is in fact plausible and can usefully be made. In my view, the main or most basic thesis or theme or tenet of Western philosophy is: Reason, in the absence of emotion, can all on its own or in conjunction with experience enable us to know and understand the world. (Notice how this accommodates both empiricism and rationalism.) I believe that my own work shows this basic thesis to be mistaken, but let's be clear. That criticism is perfectly consistent with acknowledging that Western and especially analytic philosophy has made great contributions to our understanding of issues in philosophy of science (e. g., Hempel on the paradoxes of confirmation), in logic (e. g., modern symbolic logic), in philosophy of language (e. g., Austin's speech act theory), in ethics (e. g., Kant's distinction between categorical and hypothetical imperatives), in epistemology (e. g., the problem of *a priori* knowledge), in metaphysics (e. g., the problem of free will), and in philosophy of mind (e. g., Davidson's account of reasons for action). What the mistakenness of the basic thesis does entail, however, is that Western philosophy is in need of a major course correction. If, as my work argues at length, emotion cannot be separated from reasoning and cognition, then the above-stated thesis is mistaken, and we need a philosophy that can allow us at one and the same time to recognize the conceptual connections between reason/cognition and emotion and to make progress in ethics, epistemology, philosophy of mind, etc., within the ambit of such thinking. Chinese thought, in contrast with the Western (even Hume), does assume a deep connection between thought and emotion and to that extent is much more on the right track. But let me now mention what I have come up with as constituting the fundamental thesis of Chinese philosophy.

I believe that thesis is: Properly guided and cultivated emotion is the basis for all human virtue. This thesis is far from the standard assumption of Western ethical rationalism that emotion plays no essential role in morality or moral virtue and it in part reflects the Chinese idea that reason/cognition and emotion cannot be separated. To that extent too, Western ethical rationalism is a non-starter if reason and emotion cannot be separated in the way it assumes. There is no such thing as pure practical reason and, more generally, there is no such thing as pure reason. This is a lot to have follow out of the acknowledgment of one philosophical error, but I think it shows how central that error is to Western thinking (this is not just some "butterfly effect"). And we can go much further. China thinks we need emotion as basic to virtue, but has never seen the constructive (and plausible) role one of its own most distinctive concepts can play in understanding and justifying virtue, the concept or complementary concept pair of *yin* and *yang*. Mencius and Wang Yangming helped us to a deeper understanding of virtue in relation to emotion, but neither saw that the concept of empathy can help us better understand the grounds, the justification, for what they were talking about; and, then too, neither of them recognized how empathy itself can be more deeply understood in terms of *yin* and *yang*. (Compassion involves *yin*-receptive empathy with the feelings of another person and *yang*-directed and purposeful motivation to help them. But that just summarizes a lengthy philosophical explication.)

Yin and *yang* can not only be of service to Chinese philosophy's historical attempts to understand virtues like compassion, but would also help anyone who is *today* interested in understanding these things better. Further, in the book now being translated and going beyond what I take to be the main thesis of Chinese/Confucian philosophy, I indicate how *yin* and *yang* can help us toward a better metaphysical understanding of the way the natural universe is and works. That *yin/yang* understanding is not only consistent with modern science but, as I argue, actually grows out of modern science. If this is on the right track, then even outside of ethics and in ways that have not previously been anticipated, Chinese ideas can be philosophically useful to us Western philosophers.

However, it is not just Western philosophers who have to learn this lesson. Chinese philosophers nowadays have to a certain alarming extent given up on their own traditions in favor of a purely Western approach to philosophy. But this need not happen and should not continue to happen. If one can point to important ways in which Western philosophy has much to learn from China, this is a lesson both Chinese and Western philosophers need to learn. It would be nice to see Chinese philosophy show more pride in itself than it has recently shown, and I hope my recent and future work will help toward such a benign development. I also hope that it will lead toward the major course correction that I have said Western philosophy stands in need of and, ultimately, toward a fundamental integration of what Chinese philosophy and Western philosophy have to teach us.

What I say in response to my commentators in what follows should be viewed in the light of what I have just been saying, and it is now time for me to directly consider the various sets of comments that have appeared in this volume. As a group, they raise important philosophical issues that need attending to. This volume is overall supposed to be about my encounter with Chinese philosophy, and that encounter began only a dozen years ago. So I shall begin with those commentators who have focused on my more recent work.

2 Reply to Karyn Lai

Karyn Lai holds that the notion of responsiveness is relevant to what I have said in *The Philosophy of Yin and Yang* (PYY) and elsewhere about *yin* as receptivity and *yang* as directed purpose. (In a *yin/yang* philosophy of nature, directed purpose is generalized to the notion of impulsion.) I agree with her about the relevance but disagree with her contention that without that additional notion a philosophy of *yin* and *yang* is inadequate to the issues it takes on. Lai says that if one doesn't spell out the connection between *yang* motivation/purpose and actual action, "the connection between motivation and action remains tenuous." But surely this is an overstatement. Since Davidson, the connection between motivation and action hasn't seemed all that mysterious or tenuous, and I have assumed that motivation together with other factors can explain actions or, often, the absence of a given action, as when a strong motive is undercut or outweighed by an even stronger one.

Lai correctly assumes that if empathy motivates us to help another person, that motivation may not lead to action if some other motive, e. g., self-defense, becomes relevant in the given situation. In such a case, the person is in some familiar sense not responsive to the suffering or needs of the other person, but there is no moral failing, presumably, and no failure of *yin/yang*. Should Lai then respond that there has to be responsive action if we are to have genuine *yang*, I would remind her that *yin* and *yang* are *mutually necessary* complements according to my revived or purified usage of those concepts.

Yin and *yang* have often been seen as opposites or contraries, but there is also a Chinese tradition of seeing them as friendly or non-opposed complements—as when Heaven (Tian) is seen as *yang* and Earth (Di) as *yin*. The familiar depiction of *yin* and *yang* as curvy half circles within a larger circle each of which contains an element of the other illustrates this complementarity understanding, and if we understand *yin* and receptivity and *yang* as directed purpose (or impulsion) we get just such a complementarity. If, as Lai suggests, we make actual response/action necessary to *yang*, we destroy the mutually necessitating complementarity because, in the familiar case of compassion, the receptivity of empathy doesn't entail helpful action but only motivation to help. Of course, in many or most cases, where there is motivation to help, the person actually does help, so responsiveness is a *normal accompaniment* of *yin/yang* empathic compassion. But we shouldn't regard it as essential to the *yin/yang* complementarity in such cases and others; and if I don't discuss the actual dynamics of action, that is because I am assuming *something like* the Davidson model of how motivation causally explains action. (I am also assuming for the moment that empathy with suffering *necessarily involves* motivation to help. I will defend that idea in responding to Yao and Zhang below.)

I say "*something like* the Davidson model" because Davidson rigidly separates belief and emotion/motivation in a way I have argued against in many places. In brief, when we believe a proposition, we favor it over others incompatible with it, and there is no reason to think this use of "favor" is just some metaphor. My dictionary says confidence is strong belief; and since this puts belief and confidence on a single scale and confidence is clearly an epistemic emotion, there is reason to conclude that belief too is or involves an epistemic emotion: one that is just a bit less (strongly) positive than confidence. (Certitude is on the same scale of epistemic emotions and entails an even more positive epistemic attitude than confidence, much less belief, does.) Of course, one can believe something but wish it weren't so, but that just means that one can epistemically favor what one would not practically want to make or allow to happen. But even if belief and emotion interpenetrate, there is no reason to think that beliefs and emotionally-laden motivations cannot bring about actions, and I see no reason for a philosophy of *yin* and *yang* to have to say more than that.

Lai concludes her comments with a discussion of some of the criticisms Daoism has made of Ruism/Confucianism. And some of those criticisms hit home. There is an awful lot of emphasis on ritual and convention in Ruism that Daoism is properly wary of, but a *yin/yang* philosophy doesn't have to emphasize ritual and convention, and my PYY strongly indicates as much. It is also very critical of Daoism as a total philosophy, but Lai says nothing to overcome that overall critical attitude.

Lai also suggests that we need to bring inter-relationality more into a *yin/yang* account of the moral life, but I very much wonder what aspect of the account of morality and politics in PYY needs more focus on inter-relationality. Our relations with others help to define who we are, and that is actually a theme in some of my most recent work (see *A Larger Yin/Yang Philosophy*—LYYP). But that doesn't mean that that metaphysical fact about our identities has to enter into a valid *yin/yang* account of individual or social morality. If it does, Lai needs to do more to explain why.

Moreover, even if most moral virtue is instantiated in the context of our inter-relations or interactions with others, what counts as virtuous action doesn't essentially depend on what others do in interactive response to such action. I try to help someone who is in a state of distress, but (for reasons I had no way of anticipating) they are insouciant or ungrateful in a way that makes our overall interaction less than satisfactory. My empathically caring responsiveness is not met with morally appropriate responsiveness on their part, but even if the (inter-)relationship between us is far from desirable, my empathically-based attempt to help fully realizes both *yin* and *yang* and counts as morally good on that sole basis. And let me now say a bit more about responsiveness in particular.

Lai very graciously says she wishes to use the concept of responsiveness to supplement and enrich rather than replace my *yin/yang* account of moral virtue. But as I see it, responsiveness is a desirable *emergent feature* of situations of moral choice, rather than serving to explain and justify what we think about virtue. If I feel empathic compassion for someone who needs help, I may end up not helping them if at the same time someone comes at me with a knife and makes me think of defending myself rather than helping the person who needs help. But in such a circumstance my desire to help exemplifies moral virtue even if it doesn't eventuate in helpful action. Any virtue ethics will presumably agree, and I don't think Lai opposes virtue ethics at this critical juncture. In that case, although responsiveness and actual response are (usually) good features of a person and of their interactions with others, a *yin/yang* account of what virtue involves will do the trick without having to supplement itself by references to responsiveness, even if responsiveness needs to enter any picture of what is desirable in human life.

Finally, let me speak of moral self-cultivation. At one point, Lai applauds my skepticism about the central Chinese idea of moral self-cultivation, but during the course of her comments she seems to think she has rescued the notion from my criticisms using both Ruist and Daoist ideas. Now it is true that she rather sketchily suggests ways in which individual self-cultivation can occur, but I think she gives us no clear or even putative examples of how *substantial moral change* in an individual can occur through their own efforts, and she also doesn't respond to my worry (in the article she cites) about why or how individuals who are, say, already benevolent should want to become more benevolent, more morally virtuous. (The sinologist David Nivison also used to worry about this.) Western philosophers like Aristotle and Kant also believe in moral self-cultivation, but in my skeptical article reasons/arguments are offered for thinking that these traditions of thinking about and recommending moral self-cultivation are psychologically naïve and unrealistic.

3 Reply to Vincent Shen

I am grateful to Vincent Shen for his appreciative remarks about my recent work, but I think some clarifications are needed concerning his comments on my work.

Shen indicates that *yin* and *yang* are both complementary and different, and he says this in a way that strongly suggests I don't appreciate the difference between them. I am mystified by this: PYY is full of discriminations between the *yin* and the *yang* of things. Although in my view they necessarily go together, they present very different images of the realities they instantiate or apply to. Shen goes on to say that *yin* and *yang* as a difference/complementarity needs to be integrated into a dynamic process, and this shows me more of where he is coming from. In one main tradition of Chinese thinking about *yin* and *yang*, those two are in dynamic relationship: where there is too much *yin*, *yang* comes in, and vice versa. This views *yin* and *yang* as opposed but as necessarily and dynamically operating with or against one another, but *my interpretation of yin and yang avoids viewing them as causally interacting contraries*. On my view, and it is a view that I think yields plausible philosophical results that the oppositional view of *yin* and *yang* never has, *yin* and *yang* are not parts of any process, but rather fully characterize orderly states of mind at one and the same time. And I seek to show that if one is present, the other has to be.

This means that one cannot causally explain processes in nature in terms of some sort of opposition between *yin* and *yang*, but I think we should be quite happy with such a limitation. *Yin* and *yang* were traditionally used to offer proto-scientific explanations of natural phenomena, but we nowadays have better explanations of such phenomena, and *yin* and *yang* are widely regarded (at least among Chinese academics) as having no explanatory role to play in science. I agree with all this, but have offered a philosophical account of *yin* and *yang* which, at the same time it avoids involving them in causal explanations, allows them to offer a metaphysically structural account of what is involved in moral and intellectual virtue and in the mind's or *xin*'s basic functionality. For example, the intellectual or epistemic virtue of curiosity involves *yin* receptivity to what is going on around one but also *yang* attentiveness to or focus on one's surroundings. This *yin* and this *yang* are metaphysically/structurally built into curiosity, they help constitute curiosity, but they don't causally explain why human beings are curious or how quickly or reliably curiosity leads to actual knowledge. *Yin* and *yang* are thus necessary and mutually dependent constituents of orderly human reality, but are not asked to do the kind of causal explaining they no longer seem relevant to. They do philosophical (but not scientific) work for us, and this modesty of purpose makes PYY more plausible than more inclusive or overreaching views of *yin* and *yang*.

Shen notes that my structural, as opposed to dynamic, emphasis marks my work as very different from much traditional Chinese thinking about *yin* and *yang*. But in these modern times I think that is actually an advantage of my approach, and in fact (as I have already indicated and shall explain a bit further in my reply below to Robin Wang), my non-oppositional structural *yin/yang* has more of a basis in traditional Chinese thought than Shen seems to suppose. I hope all this will make Chinese or other thinkers who don't give much intellectual credit to the notions of *yin* and *yang* think again about the philosophical value of these notions.

Shen fascinatingly introduces the work of Fang Yizhi into his comments, and speaks of the ways he sought to integrate thinking about *yin/yang*, *dao*, and *qi* into a larger whole. But Fang's approach was, again, dynamic, and so the most interesting question to ask is whether the just-mentioned notions have a role to play in a *yin/yang* philosophy that has been updated to rule out questionable causal hypotheses and to concentrate on (*a priori*) metaphysical structure or constitution. The answer, I am happy to suggest, is definitely yes—at least if my own approach is on the right track. PYY seeks to integrate *dao* and *tiandi* into its *yin/yang* picture of things, and the soon to be published LYYP extends that integration to *qi* and even *taiji*. I think of *taiji* as the supreme ultimate, but it is a metaphysical (necessary) ultimate, not a "big bang" of causal explanation the way it is, for example, in Zhou Dunyi's *taijitu shuo*, which was the source of some of Fang Yizhi's most basic philosophical views.

Zhou was in my opinion right to believe in a *taiji*, a supreme ultimate in the universe. But I think he gave it a causal/explanatory role that is superseded by current science (and the idea of a big bang), whereas I believe its greatest significance, a significance that not only is compatible with modern science, but also, as LYYP seeks to show, *grows out of modern science*, lies in its metaphysical status as underlying and constituting all processes in any possible world. Zhou also held that *taiji* brought forth the five elements of water, wood, fire, metal, and soil, but we know that water is not an element and that there are more than a hundred elements, not five, so again, it seems a mistake to use *taiji* or (derivatively as in Zhou's *taijitu shuo*) *yin* and *yang* to explain the elements there are. Rather, again, it makes more modern sense to employ *yin* and *yang* as constituting the metaphysical structure of whatever elements there turn out to be in the universe.

Now Shen notes that in PYY I seem to make *yin* and *yang* the most ultimate metaphysical factors in the universe, and he questions this in the light of what Zhou Dunyi says. Well, I now agree that we need to go deeper than *yin* and *yang*, and my discussion of *qi* and *taiji* in LYYP acknowledges that earlier limitation. But at the same time it calls for a halt on using these deeper concepts in competition with modern science. That, in my opinion, is the best way to honor them today. If we emphasize conceptual/structural over dynamic/causal uses of *yin* and *yang*, we get something that makes sense in contemporary terms, so I reject Shen's insistence on a dynamic *yin* and *yang*. That is not, in my opinion, the right way for us now to go.

More explicitly and in very partial anticipation of what I say in LYYP, my idea of *qi* arises out of my present belief that we find *yin* receptivity and *yang* purpose or (better) impulsion in both *xin* and nature. I argue that since *yin* and *yang* are traditionally viewed as forms of *qi*, it makes sense to explore the possibility of a *qi* that also pervades *xin* and nature, and I argue further that there is an abstract sense of motion (which in Newtonian terms includes rest) that can fill that role. *Qi* is vital energy conceived as a kind of motion, but also can be viewed, as it traditionally was, as a stuff that is more ethereal than the five elements of Chinese thought (not to mention the more than one hundred elements of Western science). As I see it, then, *qi* is a kind of matter/energy that exists in *yin/yang* form in any conceivable orderly world, a matter/energy that is less specific and more metaphysically necessary than the matter/energy today's physicists talk about. Their matter/energy obeys Einstein's law of $e=mc^2$. But in other conceivable worlds, that law doesn't hold but, as I argue, there will still be *qi*, still be the more abstract matter/energy that traditional Chinese philosophy hints and more than hints at. Chinese thought to that extent anticipates modern physics but in a more abstract way that doesn't force it to compete with modern physics.

Then *taiji* can come into the picture because *qi*, as I view it, is more basic, more metaphysically necessary, more pervasive of every aspect of reality, than anything else we can think of as a factor in our or any universe. I think this qualifies *qi* to count as *taiji*, the supreme ultimate, even if such *taiji* is no longer regarded as causally initiating the world. But let me return to Shen's comments.

Shen brings in the Hegelian dialectic at one point, but this is a dangerous move. The movement of dialectic is similar to the dynamic movement Shen sees in *yin* and *yang* conceived as opposites. But if we see *yin* as receptivity and *yang* as directed purpose or impulsion, the two are instantiated together at one and the same time and are not part or stages of any process. This allows one to eschew the kind of causal explanations that Shen wants to accept and that Hegel also believes in (such as that the French Revolution caused the Reign of Terror). As I have already indicated, I think we today know better than that. Dialectic and *yin/yang* dynamism cannot really compete with modern science, and my more modest (though hardly in itself modest) deployment of *yin* and *yang* is simply more relevant in today's philosophical world.

Shen ends with an idea I very much agree with. He takes my philosophy as part of what one can hope to be an internationalizing or globalizing trend in philosophy. I share those hopes, and let me mention a concept that derives from the twentieth-century Chinese philosopher Feng Qi and has been further promulgated by his student, *Yang* Guorong. Feng explicitly proposed the idea of a world philosophy that was not limited to one or even two philosophical traditions, and this seems very much in keeping with what Shen says. Let me just add that I think a genuinely responsive world philosophy must go beyond China and the West to at least include the other great original tradition of philosophy on this planet: Indian philosophy. Although it may seem repetitive or even self-aggrandizing for me to say this, my most recent thinking has focused on the idea of world philosophy and has grappled with how India (and Buddhism) can be brought into fruitful critical interaction with the Chinese and Western philosophical traditions. This takes us well beyond the tasks and goals I mentioned in my introduction to these replies.

Let me just ruminate a bit more on the subject of nomenclature. World philosophy is very much of a piece with what is called New Confucianism. Just as neo-Confucianism sought to stem the tide of the externally derived Buddhist influence in China and to revive ancient endogenous Chinese philosophical thinking, the New Confucians sought to integrate ancient Chinese thought with the forcefully felt external influence of Western philosophy. The most notable New Confucian Mou Zongsan was influenced, for example, by Kant, but sought to rework Kant's philosophy by fitting it into Chinese ideas, most specifically into what Mencius had to say about our immediate moral sense of alarm when seeing someone (a child) face danger. This, together with Feng Qi's notion of world philosophy, brought Chinese thought into serious relationship with Western philosophy. Since, in addition, Mou attempted to integrate Buddhism into his overall philosophy, he was also doing world philosophy in the sense indicated above; and my own advocacy of a fruitful interaction among Indian, Chinese, and Western thought is of course very much in keeping with the idea of doing world philosophy. Consequently, if the New Confucians were either implicitly or explicitly advocating world philosophy, my own approach can perhaps also be labeled a form of New Confucianism, a New Confucianism coming, for the first time, *from the West*. I have no objection to such labeling as long as it is understood that it can be subsumed under the larger idea and goal of a world philosophy, one that in my work is also, for the first time, coming from the West.

4 Reply to JeeLoo Liu

JeeLoo Liu seeks to "refute" my account of the unity of the mind or *xin*. She does so by bringing in ideas about how the mind/*xin should* be unified that she considers to go beyond my sheer descriptive theory of the mind. In doing so, she relies on the assumption made by Mencius and many others following him that we or our minds are essentially good rather than bad, and of course she knows that other Chinese philosophers have either denied or avoided saying that we humans are basically good: e. g., Confucius and Xunzi.

Unfortunately, Liu's account of my views on the emotional nature of all psychological functioning relies principally on what I said in the book *A Sentimentalist Theory of the Mind* (2014), but the discussion there is superseded by what I say on this topic in PYY. Liu considers the later discussion to be inferior to what was said, without benefit of *yin* and *yang*, in the earlier book, but her criticisms of what I say about unity and direction of fit in the earlier book in any event fall short of the mark because those specific ideas are *replaced* by *yin/yang* explanation in the later book.

Liu complains that my arguments that all cognition involves emotion require empirical backup that I don't supply, but the argument for that conclusion in PYY is fully *a priori*. The argument I briefly gave (in replying to Karen Lai) for the conclusion that belief involves emotion was strictly *a priori*. But arguably every cognitive process in a functioning mind involves belief. Reasoning involves believing that certain premises entail or justify certain conclusions; and, similarly, criticism, planning, intending, "seeing as," intuiting, and every other cognitive function one can think of involve believing *something*. So it seems *a priori* that all functioning cognition involves belief and given the *a priori* argument I offer for holding that all belief involves emotion, my conclusion that all cognition involves emotion can be reached by *a priori* argument and doesn't pace Liu call for empirical backup. If she wants to disagree with me, she needs to show what is wrong with the *a priori* argument, and this is something she never does. All in all, there is too much emphasis in her comments on my earlier views and not enough on my present ones. (We philosophers are allowed to develop, aren't we?)

Liu goes on to discuss Zhang Zai's view of the mind, a view that, with its foundational emphasis on emotion, clearly anticipates my own. She evidently thinks that my view of the mind or *xin* differs from Zhang's because it focuses only on how the mind actually functions, not on how it ought to function. In saying this, however, she shows she hasn't read or at least taken seriously what I say toward the end of PYY. The earlier parts describe how a functioning mind must exemplify *yin* and *yang* as necessary complements, but this arguably leaves open the question: why is such *yin/yang* functioning desirable, and how can it constitute, as PYY argues, both moral and epistemic virtue? The answer to that question I offer late in PYY picks out a feature of *yin* and a feature of *yang* that are relevant to that issue. I argue that receptivity/*yin* is a desirable feature of the mind and that directed purpose is also something desirable. I point out, moreover, that *yin/yang* unity between such desirable factors represents a further desirable or valuable feature of situations where *yin* and *yang* are both present and mutually dependent. All of that represents a *yin/yang* account or explanation not just of how functioning minds operate but of what is desirable and thus virtuous (or rational) in such operations.

But everyone knows that the mind doesn't always work in a functional way. Rage and panic, for example, constitute non-functional states of mind, but since these states also fail to exemplify *yin* and *yang* (a panicky person isn't receptive to what is going on around them and cannot act in a strong purposeful way), my *yin/yang* account of functionality also explains what happens when *xin* is not functional. Given my view that *yin*, *yang*, and unified *yin/yang* are all desirable, the mind is arguably not functioning as it desirably, virtuously, or rationally should when these elements are absent. Thus *yin* and *yang* can explain both what is desirable (virtuous and/or rational) and what is undesirable about mental processes, and to that extent they offer us a way to *justify* the value claims we tend to make about such processes. So where is the disagreement with Zhang Zai and with Liu?

Ultimately, it seems to consist in my unwillingness to posit the basic goodness of human beings. But those who do posit this offer a hostage to intellectual fortune that we should be wary of. Chinese thought may tend toward the idea that we are all basically good, but does empirical evidence really favor such a view? Children may have an empathic tendency toward helping others, but they are also often very self-centered and inconsiderate. Is one of these tendencies more basic than the other? I think it is better not to commit oneself on this point, and that is why I favor my own account of how the mind (desirably) functions over the kind of picture Zhang offers and Liu endorses. Zhang and Zhu Xi may also want to speak of our basic goodness as due to our "heavenly endowed" nature or principles, but is such a view philosophically respectable at this point in time?

At the end of her comments, Liu claims that my view of *yin* and *yang* is superficial. And I welcome that characterization even though it was not intended as a compliment. My use of *yin* and *yang* avoids reference to Heaven or God and doesn't treat *yin* and *yang* as causal factors in the universe, the way much original *yin/yang* thinking did. As I have previously mentioned, such thinking is outmoded in the light of present-day science, and that is one of the reasons why, over the recent centuries, Chinese thinkers have steered clear of *yin* and *yang*. I am trying to show that they needn't and shouldn't do that. *Yin* and *yang* have much to teach us about the necessary metaphysical structure of the mind and nature, but they can acceptably do that only if they avoid going "deeper" into actual facts about scientific causality and about the nature of the elements, that they are ill-equipped to deal with.

Liu says she cannot "fathom what explanatory advantages Slote's *yin yang* could possibly give us in our understanding of the nature of emotion or the nature of belief." But some of the explanatory advantages I believe *yin/yang* to offer are conceptual/philosophical ones. The very fact, as PYY argues, that in functioning minds both belief and emotion have inextricably connected *yin* and *yang* sides is surely a conceptual fact worth knowing. Liu refers to my specific view that empathy is the *yin* side and motivation to help the *yang* side of compassion, but the idea that compassion (or *ren*) can be analyzed in *yin/yang* terms is a new one and surely, again, philosophically worth learning about. Does Liu really want to be so hostile to *a priori* metaphysics and to foundational conceptual analysis? But then, of course, there are also the justificatory advantages of *yin* and *yang* that I mentioned just above. In understanding belief, emotion, and the functioning mind/*xin* generally in terms of a *yin/yang* that embodies deep values, we allow ourselves to go beyond conceptual truths to an understanding and explanation of the conditions under which rationality and virtue are manifested in our lives.

I should also mention Liu's (presumably conceptual) claim that I conflate the affective and cognitive functions of the mind. But far from it, I simply insist that and explain why all mental functioning contains both elements. Cognition involves belief, which has an emotional side to it, and our emotions are always based in our cognitive receptivity to factors that underlie such emotions. And I also allow that desire and belief, though not the same thing, involve both *yin* and *yang* factors. However, when we *speak* of beliefs, *yin* receptivity is foregrounded in our minds, and when we *speak* of desires, *yang* purpose is in the foreground our thinking. But that needn't prevent emotion from being present in both beliefs and desires. Liu says "belief is *truth-apt* while emotion is not," but some emotions definitely *are* truth-apt. The epistemic emotion of confidence in the truth of some proposition is clearly truth-apt, and if (as I argued earlier) belief constitutes a less strong epistemic emotion than confidence, then belief is another example of a truth-apt emotion. Might not happiness that one has received a promotion also count as a truth-apt emotion? Liu in a surprisingly Western way seems to want to make more rigid distinctions in the mind than we have good reason to believe exist, and a *yin/yang* philosophy can help make it clear why those distinctions don't obtain.

Finally, Liu claims that I hold that there is no unity of the intellectual and the emotional "since the two were never separated to begin with." But this is a non-sequitur. What I have said in fact is that the Chinese take the non-division or unity of the intellectual and the emotional completely for granted and have never explicitly argued against the Western assumption that the intellectual/cognitive *can* be separated from the emotional. I have speculated that this may be due to excessive deference to the West and to a consequent tendency to implicitly assume that there is some mere ambiguity of language underlying what seem to be major differences between Western and Chinese views of the mind. By contrast, I have argued, as a native English-speaker, that the Western view of beliefs and of cognitive functioning is just plain mistaken. Intellect/belief/cognition cannot be separated from emotion, and the West has simply (or not so simply) mistheorized its own concepts. If the arguments I have given succeed, then they vindicate implicit Chinese thought as against Western thinking in a way that the Chinese themselves never thought to do.

5 Reply to Xinzhong Yao and Yan Zhang

At the beginning of their comments, Xinzhong Yao and Yan Zhang say that my view that belief involves and may even be an emotion "risks dissolving intellect in emotion." But although I believe that all reasoning and cognition involve belief, and although I have argued that all belief involves emotion, I don't see why this means that I am dissolving these mental factors. I am offering a *reductive* account of reason(ing) and belief in terms of emotion, and this in no way entails *eliminating* these categories or the entities they apply to. Moreover, as I shall explicitly argue in replying to Yong Huang, my idea that belief is an emotional state doesn't pace Yao and Zhang make it difficult for me to explain how belief can be rationally justified.

Yao and Zhang go on to say that in highlighting emotion, my *yin/yang* approach may end up dissolving *yang* into *yin*. They also say that *yin* is more fundamental for me than *yang*, but all this is a big mistake. They identify the emotional with the *yin* receptive but I never imply such an identification. Rather, I hold that when we have emotions we are both receptive in a *yin* way and motivated in *yang* fashion to act. Yao and Zhang themselves eventually note that I consider *yin* and *yang* to both involve emotion(ality), so how does my emphasis on emotion put *yin* in the driver's seat and dissolve *yang*?

Yao and Zhang also accuse me of holding that Chinese philosophers are unable to distinguish intellect from sentiment because the term *xin* doesn't draw a rigid distinction between them, but Chinese thinkers have no problem deliberately talking of intellectual matters without referring to feelings or sentiments. Unlike most Western philosophers, however, they don't think these areas can be sharply or deeply separated. As far as I know, no Chinese thinker has ever explicitly claimed that the West is mistaken on this point, but I have been more than prepared to argue for that conclusion *on behalf* of Chinese thought and philosophy.

Returning to the issue of the supposed predominance of *yin* over *yang* in my philosophy, Yao and Zhang say I hold that it is only in *yin* receptivity that we can justify our beliefs, motives, and actions. But, again, this is a mistaken interpretation. I attempt to show that the moral justification of motives/actions and the epistemic justification of beliefs are best anchored in a *yin/yang* foundation. Instances of moral or epistemic virtue and justification have to instantiate both *yin* and *yang*, and *yin* is given no precedence in all this. Thus I hold that in order to have rationally justified beliefs about the world, we must *yang* focus on the world around us and be *yin* receptive to what, for example, our senses tell us about it.

Yao and Zhang don't understand how one can view belief as emotional in nature while at the same time maintaining that we ought to only hold rational beliefs, but *yin/yang* marks the difference between rational beliefs involving emotion and irrational or unreasonable beliefs involving emotion that we would criticize as based in wishful thinking, paranoia, panic, laziness, or what have you. And remember (a point I made in replying to Liu) that *yin/yang* is a good feature of mental states and its absence an undesirable feature of such states. This would explain the value we place on rational belief and the value that is built into the concept of rationality itself, in a way completely compatible with viewing beliefs as emotions and using *yin/yang* as a general philosophical technique of metaphysical and axiological analysis.

However, Yao and Zhang very correctly point out that Wang Yangming is more of a monist than I am. We both highlight emotion within the mind or *xin*, but Wang accepts a form of metaphysical idealism that makes no essential distinction between the mind and the world it knows. For all-too-obvious reasons, I don't go in for the kind of unity you get by claiming that everything is in the mind. Wang also says that Heaven is the source of our nature, and I give an entirely secular picture of these matters. What I say about emotion and mental unity is thus more geared to present-day intellectual circumstances than what Wang has to tell us. Yao and Zhang go on to say that on my view, unlike Wang's, the heart-mind is primarily an epistemic entity, and since it is natural to think of the epistemic process of acquiring beliefs as involving *yin* receptivity to the world around one, they are in effect once again saying that I prioritize *yin* over *yang*. But this is a mistake, at the very least, of interpretation.

My PYY argues that the acquisition of new beliefs about the world involves *yang* purpose every bit as much as it involves *yin* receptivity. If the world is to seem more than a blooming, buzzing confusion, then we have to focus on and pay attention to things around us, and although such mental actions are often not self-conscious, they do exhibit purpose. When we focus or pay attention we want to know what is happening, say, over there to the left. Learning about the world thus involves a certain amount of curiosity, and curiosity is more evidently *yang* than *yin*, so, again, I treat *yin* and *yang* co-equally with respect to epistemic processes and, perhaps more importantly, I say nothing to suggest that epistemic processes are more important to our minds than any other mental function. Nothing in PYY even begins to suggest that learning about the world is more important than acting virtuously.

But let me, finally, suggest another possible explanation of why they think I prioritize the epistemic and *yin* over moral virtue and *yang*. They say that on my view the mind proceeds from receptivity to directed purpose in cases of moral virtue: we receptively *yin* empathize with the suffering of another and only thereafter are motivated to help, have the *yang* purpose of helping, the other. But that is actually not how I conceive the matter. PYY argues that when we empathize, we take in another's feeling *as directed toward a given intentional object*. So when I compassionately empathize with someone's distress at the pain in their arm, I too am distressed by that pain, and distress by its very definition involves a desire to eliminate or lessen what one is distressed about. So *yin* receptive empathy isn't causally prior to the *yang* desire to help (purpose of helping)—it *includes* such desire/purpose within itself, and the connection in cases of compassion between empathy and altruistic motivation is thus a necessary one, rather than a contingent and causal one.

This is exactly analogous with what Wang Yangming says about knowing and loving a beautiful thing. The knowledge doesn't cause the love but already includes love. So *pace* Yao and Zhang, I don't have to say that *yin* or receptivity is prior to *yang*, and there is no reason therefore to think that the *yin* is more important than the *yang* in cases of compassion. Better still for my purposes, the example of curiosity shows that our *yin/yang* thinking doesn't have to start with *yin* and proceed to *yang*. As I have already mentioned, the *yang* aspect of curiosity is more initially obvious than its *yin* aspect, and the focusing and attention curiosity involves are hardly derivative from the receptivity to the world that also has to be there. Rather, if they are there at all, these things are of necessity all there together.

At the end of their comments, Yao and Zhang state that my views on cognition and emotion "break away from the modern or scientific way of thinking." But in fact many present-day neuroscientists (most famously, Antonio Damasio) think that cognition/rationality and emotion cannot be separated, and I should also note that my *yin/yang* approach doesn't compete with or in any way go against modern science. My just-finished *A Larger Yin/Yang Philosophy* extends the *yin/yang* analysis to processes in the natural world outside the human *xin*, but that analysis doesn't offer causal explanations of natural events that might contradict what scientists have to say. Rather, it offers a conceptual/metaphysical framework that applies and applies of necessity to any processes or situations that occur in an orderly natural world and to any that occur in a functioning mind as well. I see my work as offering, therefore, an *a priori* structural framework into which the results of science, whatever they may be, fit rather neatly.

6 Reply to Yong Huang

Before I reply to Yong Huang's comments, let me thank him for editing this volume and organizing the conference on which it is largely based. Let me also thank those who attended the conference and/or have contributed to the present volume. I think we have all had a good opportunity to learn from one other.

Huang's comments focus almost exclusively on my 2014 OUP book *A Sentimentalist Theory of the Mind* (STM). Although this allows him to discuss and develop some themes and arguments that are of interest to himself (and also many others), his focus on the earlier work leaves out of account the ways in which my thinking especially about *yin* and *yang* has advanced beyond the confines of the earlier thinking. Huang is critical of what I claim about direction of fit, "besire," and the unity of the mind in STM, but he doesn't tell the reader that my subsequent *yin/yang* philosophy in no way depends on using or applying those specific views. I think some of the things he says in questioning those earlier concepts are insightful, but that very point usefully underscores the conclusion or suggestion that it makes more sense for me now to leave STM behind and focus my philosophical efforts on *yin/yang*.

I don't, therefore, propose to examine what Huang says about Wang Yangming's implicit use of the notion of besire or what he says on behalf of his own views on besire and mental function generally. But I do want to question what he or others might take to be the implications of his discussion for a philosophy of *yin* and *yang*. At the end of his comments, for example, he claims that I hold the implausible view that all beliefs are (also) desires, but I think a philosophy of *yin* and *yang* can rob such a view of its initial implausibility. Earlier in my replies I sketched the argument I have given in PYY and elsewhere for saying that all beliefs involve emotion, and it is difficult to think of any emotion that doesn't at least involve desire. Now involving is different from being, but in the case, say, of the belief that one is seeing a tree, that belief is tantamount to epistemically favoring the proposition or hypothesis that one is seeing a tree. There is, moreover, no reason (I have argued) for thinking this talk of favoring is metaphorical, and I then ask the reader to consider what beyond such epistemic favoring is involved in belief.

I don't think there is any such further element, but then someone might say that if beliefs are (just) emotions, they cannot be epistemically justified because the justification of an emotion has to rest on the justification of something that doesn't involve emotion and beliefs are the most basic object or seat of epistemic justification. This is an assumption that seems universally agreed on within analytic philosophy, but I believe it is mistaken. When I see a tree and am confident that there is a tree over there that I am seeing, that justified confidence doesn't rest on any belief but at most *includes* belief. But by universal agreement (no?) confidence is an epistemic emotion, and so at least this emotion can be rationally justified without resting on a justified something that doesn't involve emotion. If that is possible for confidence, it should also be possible for beliefs, even if beliefs are emotions. (Once again, we understand belief better by understanding the nature of confidence.)

So we have reason to say that belief is an emotion, an epistemic one, and if all emotion involves desire, it is but a short step to saying that beliefs *are* desires. Does that then mean that there is no distinction between beliefs and desires? In a sense it does, but it is important to recognize that this doesn't mean that the *concept* of belief is the same as the *concept* of desire. When we speak or think of belief, *yin* epistemic receptivity to the world is foregrounded in our minds, and when we speak or think of desire, *yang* practical purpose or motivation is in the foreground of our minds. So the concepts are different, but PYY gives us reason to think that they are co-instantiated in every instance. If one goes through the arguments, I think the idea that beliefs are desires becomes much more philosophically acceptable.

Huang emphasizes propositional knowledge in his discussion of Wang Yangming's views, knowledge, for example, *that* a given thing is beautiful. But Wang also—and more primordially—talks of thoroughly knowing a beautiful *thing*, and this at least on the face of it involves knowledge by acquaintance, not propositional knowledge by description (which latter is always *based in* some sort of acquaintance). That fact takes us beyond the usual domain of discussions of besires and relates, rather, to the ideas of *yin* and *yang*. When we become thoroughly acquainted with a beautiful thing, we exemplify a *yin* receptivity in its direction, and if Wang is right that such acquaintance automatically includes loving and cherishing the thing, then the *yin* knowledge by acquaintance is tightly tied to *yang* motivation. I think Wang's example here nicely illustrates the way in which *yin* and *yang* can be metaphysically inseparable, but Wang himself never uses the concepts of *yin* and *yang* except in reference to natural phenomena. I want to say, then, that a *yin/yang* analysis of what is happening when knowledge involves emotion and (desire for) action allows us to deepen and further justify Wang's view of these matters. So even if, as Huang maintains, the concept of besire can usefully be attributed to Wang or his account of knowledge and action, I believe we can go further and conceptually deeper if we bring in *yin* and *yang*.

7 Reply to Robin Wang

Robin Wang has written extensively on *yin* and *yang*, but her ideas about them come out of the tradition that sees them as opposites or opposed: like *yin* darkness, wetness, and cold and *yang* brightness, dryness, and warmth. As I noted earlier, that tradition historically used such oppositional notions to causally explain various natural phenomena, but (as I have also already said) most Chinese academics avoid talk about *yin* and *yang* precisely because it leads to explanations that are out of keeping with a modern scientific understanding of the natural world. Wang has no such hesitations, however. She thinks *yin* and *yang* can be used for "dynamic" explanations of natural events and processes, and she applies this idea to what happens when the sun shines and then sets.

Like so many others, I reject this way of thinking, and I believe what Wang says about dynamic processes is not only superseded by present-day science but beset with internal obscurity and unclarity. There is an impasse obviously between us, but I should in any event mention that even if her use of oppositional *yin* and *yang* for dynamic explanatory purposes were somehow acceptable, that would not impugn the validity of what I say using mutually complementary and friendly notions of *yin* and *yang*. To be sure, the most salient Chinese thinking about *yin* and *yang* treats these as opposites: not just dark and light, cold and warm, and wet and dry, but also acid and alkaline. Still, the idea of *yin* and *yang* as mutually necessitating complements is visible in the standard diagram of *yin* and *yang* as curvy half circles that each contain an element of the other. One can also recognize it in what has historically been said about the relationship between *yang* Heaven (Tian) and *yin* Earth (Di). These are not seen as contrary but in rather subtle ways are thought of as working harmoniously together.

So there is historical precedent in my thinking about *yin* and *yang*, and the most important question, then, is whether that thinking gives us interesting or plausible results regarding virtue, reason, and the nature of the mind or *xin*. PYY is devoted to showing that it does, and nothing comparable has been forthcoming from the tradition that sees *yin* and *yang* as dynamically interrelated opposites. In fact, Chinese thought has neglected *yin* and *yang* for hundreds of years, and my work on *yin* and *yang* seeks to persuade not only Western philosophers but the Chinese themselves that there is philosophically more to *yin* and *yang* than anyone has thought. The reader will have to read PYY if they want to determine whether such a conclusion is true. And although Robin Wang makes various brief attempts to question what I say about rational choice and rational belief in the book, I think the book itself answers her objections if one reads it with sufficient care.

8 Reply to R. A. H. King

In the Introduction to my 2010 OUP book *Moral Sentimentalism* (MS), I said that Mencius seems to have had the idea of empathy all those centuries ago. But I now have doubts about that conclusion and would like to share or start sharing some of them with the reader. R. A. H. King thinks something like the concept of empathy is operative in the *Mencius,* and he supports that contention through discussion of the Chinese term *buren,* roughly translatable as being unable to bear some situation. But he hesitates to say outright that *buren* is tantamount to empathy, and I think he is right so to hesitate. It is not obvious that when one is unable to bear, say, the suffering of another person or animal, that has to be because one is feeling or sharing their suffering. Perhaps one remembers oneself suffering in a similar situation and it is that memory and its unpleasantness that make one unwilling to tolerate or accept the situation or state of the present sufferer. However, King also says that if we translate *ren* as benevolence, that suggests that Mencius is concerned with empathy, but we have to be careful here. Benevolence may in fact involve empathy, but that doesn't mean that those who talk about benevolence recognize that supposed fact. Mencius may be concerned with phenomena that involve empathy but not be making use of empathy as a concept.

King goes on to describe what I say in MS about the role of empathy in moral approval and disapproval, but he misinterprets my views on that subject. He seems to regard me as holding that approval and disapproval are the first function of empathy, but on my view moral approval and disapproval constitute second-order empathy of a kind that presupposes the first-order empathy that occurs when an agent has empathy with another's suffering and tries to do something about it. Young children can have first-order empathy for others without possessing moral concepts or (even) experiencing second-order empathy with those who have or lack first-order empathy. So approval and disapproval in no way constitute the first function of empathy.

9 Reply to Tao Jiang

Unlike King, Tao Jiang thinks Mencius clearly has and makes use of the concept of empathy. Much of his discussion focuses on the ways in which Mencius deals with rulers and attempts to make them better rulers and better people; and he pays considerable attention to Mencius's claim that he is good at using the words of those he speaks with to interpret or know what is really going on in their minds. But I should point out straight off that this claim isn't at all tantamount to any claim about, or making use of, the concept of empathy. The so-called theory theory of psychological understanding can easily say that Mencius is just good at framing plausible hypotheses about what someone is thinking and feeling on the basis of the words they use. Mencius never says that he can feel what the ruler or anyone else feels, so the explicit idea of empathy doesn't come into this aspect of Mencius's text.

Mencius also speaks of the particular ruler who takes pity on an ox that he sees going in a terrified manner toward the kitchen where it is going to be slaughtered. The ruler prefers to substitute a lamb he doesn't see for the ox whose terror he does see, and that, indeed, is how empathy in fact works. It makes us partial to the interests and problems of those we see as opposed to those we only know about. But that just means that Mencius is talking about a phenomenon that involves empathy, and it hardly follows that he knows about empathy as a mechanism that influences our emotions and actions. Compassion too arguably involves empathy with someone in distress or trouble, but those who talk about compassion don't have to know or believe that it specifically involves empathy. (Let me just add that the passage 7a4 in the *Mencius* where it is said that "ten thousand things are within me" may hint at empathy but is also thought to have possibly been interpolated into the text at a later time.)

So far, then, I see little or no evidence that Mencius is aware of or makes use of the concept of empathy. Even the celebrated passage where Mencius talks of the universal human tendency to feel alarm and distress when we witness a child about to fall into a well doesn't bring in the concept of empathy. Mencius never says that the observer feels what the child feels or that s/he emotionally identifies with what the child is or will be going through. Alarm and distress (like being unable to bear something) can occur because one knows what the child will suffer and doesn't want to see that happen. But the knowledge here needn't be empathic knowledge, so again, and pace Jiang's discussion, I see no evidence that Mencius really understands or recognizes our concept of empathy.

To that extent, what I have been doing in my work on empathy and on its *yin/yang* basis serves to deepen and perhaps partly justify what Mencius thinks about the case of the child. He thinks it is a sign of virtue that one is distressed by what one takes will happen or is happening to the child, but in my opinion, not Mencius's, such distress involves us in feeling what the child is feeling or (through empathic imagination) what the child will feel. Empathy is involved in the well case even if Mencius doesn't see that it is, and one can reason further that the empathy is tied to what is virtuous in typical human responses to such cases. A psychopath who can't empathize with the actual or potential feelings of others will not feel distress or alarm in such cases and may even be pleased that the child is going to suffer. Their lack of virtue reflects, arguably, their lack of empathy and of the altruistic motives that arise in connection with empathy.

So much my moral sentimentalism would tell us, and to that extent it can be said to deepen or extend the account of virtue and human feeling/motivation that Mencius offers via the well case. But then one can go further. PYY argues that cases of compassion can be analyzed in terms of *yin* receptivity and *yang* motivational purpose, and I have already briefly made the case for that conclusion earlier in these replies. *Yin* and *yang* offer us the structure, the psychological structure, that is of necessity instantiated in any case of compassion; and PYY uses similar *yin/yang* analysis to limn the structure of a whole range of moral (and prudential) cases. So I think of my *yin/yang* philosophy as in this area supplementing and conceptually deepening what Mencius says and in no way denying its validity.

Jiang discusses a number of different aspects of Mencius's ethical thought and my own, but I would like now to focus on his critical view of what I say about social justice. He quotes from Virginia Held at some length, and Held has argued that empathy cannot serve to fully understand justice because patriarchy is unjust but women in patriarchal circumstances don't recognize the injustice and aren't discontented with their lot in the family and society. If they are contented with their position, then according to Held empathy with them will not mandate any change in their situation, and the injustice of that situation will continue. Held then takes this to undermine my sentimentalist account of social justice as based in empathy.

I am surprised that Held should have written this way, given her presumed familiarity with what Carol Gilligan says about the traditional treatment of women and their reactions to such treatment, in her famous book *In a Different Voice* (1982). But let me put this in my own terms. Under patriarchy, little girls often express a desire for a professional career or even just to go to university (which wasn't possible through much of the nineteenth century). If the girl tells her mother or father that she wants to be a doctor, she will typically be told something like: you don't really want to be a doctor, dear; you'd be much happier as a nurse or (stay-at-home) mother. This throws cold water on what the little girl expresses about her hopes and desires, and it doesn't even fully recognize that she has the desire or aspiration that her words taken literally refer to. Something similar would likely happen in the nineteenth century if a girl expressed a desire to go to university/college like her brother.

As Gilligan points out, such responses on the part of parents tend to make girls start to doubt their own thoughts and their own aspirations. But does this make the original aspirations go away or does it just push them underground and leave them open to reexamination and revival through the kind of consciousness raising that occurs within the women's movement? Patriarchy is far from empathic when it treats girls in the way I have just described: the parent who says "you don't really want that, dear" is in fact refusing to empathize with their daughter's point of view at the time. So an ethics of empathic caring like my own can in fact account for what is unjust about the sexist denial of careers or a college education to women. Sexist parents and societies frequently don't listen (in Gilligan's terminology) to the voice of little girls, and that translates into a lack of empathy for half of the very people society should be most (empathically) concerned about: its children. Moreover, if many women who have had their aspirations suppressed retain such aspirations at some level but cannot access or acknowledge them (before the women's movement starts helping them to do just that), then only a superficial sense and instantiation of empathy would treat the situation as totally unproblematic. No, pace Jiang and Held, and very much in line with Gilligan's views, an ethics of empathic caring is very capable of explaining what is unjust about the situation of women and girls under patriarchy.

More generally, a sentimentalism based in empathic caring can account for social/legal justice in terms of empathy operating at a social level. This differs interestingly from what my famous sentimentalist predecessor Mencius says about the nature or origin of justice. Mencius says there are four independent sprouts/beginnings (*duan*) of morality, and justice (*yi*) constitutes the full realization of just one of them. For Mencius, justice is at least to some extent independent of *ren* or benevolence, and this differs from my view, which treats justice as entirely derivative from the same empathy that is manifested at the individual level in compassion or benevolence. Interestingly too, Mencius treats approval and disapproval as original sentiments that, again, are independent of the other *duan*, whereas I argue that approval and disapproval are just second-order forms or instantiations of empathy. On my view moral approval of an agent's empathic warm helpfulness toward another person is constituted by the approver's empathically feeling warmed by that agent's warm-heartedness. Disapproval, then, is being empathically chilled by some agent's cold attitude and/or actions toward some third party or parties. So both benevolence and approval/disapproval can be understood in terms of empathy, but the former involves first-order empathy and the second involves second-order empathy.

This means that an empathy-based account of morality can operate with a single basic notion, empathy, and this then makes for a more unified or simpler overall account of morality than Mencius offers us. But what about the fourth sprout/*duan* and its realization in ritual propriety or *li*? This has a less central role in morality because many rituals are simply not geared to moral purposes. When they are, I would maintain that they exemplify and embody empathic concern(s). So, again, the empathy-based account of morality is desirably simpler and more unified than what Mencius offers us, *but Mencius shows us sentimentalists the way.* The account of social justice offered by empathy-based sentimentalism is totally different from what Kantian/liberal ethical rationalists want to say about justice, but PYY argues at length that the sentimentalist view of justice is (with regard to ranges of actual moral cases) superior to the rationalist view despite the initial oddness of relating justice to sentiment.

Finally, I should also (predictably) mention that PYY shows us how to reduce and undergird general moral sentimentalism with the categories of *yin* and *yang*. Since it accounts for empathy in *yin/yang* terms, this means that on my view both social justice and individual moral virtue can ultimately be conceptualized—and justified (remember my reply to Liu)—in *yin/yang* terms.

10 Reply to On-cho Ng

On-cho Ng begins his comments by reviewing four books of mine that preceded my recent interest in and focus on *yin* and *yang*. He usefully points out that my sentimentalist approach is thoroughly naturalistic, a point the other commentators of this volume have not paid much attention to. One objection to naturalism that has been voiced—most forcefully by Sharon Street—in recent years is that it doesn't allow us to account for normativity. This may be true of the naturalistic approaches she mentions and/or is familiar with, but it doesn't hold for an approach like mine that makes fundamental use of empathy. Empathy neatly bridges the supposedly unbridgeable gap between factual knowledge and motivation/reasons to act. The example of compassion mentioned earlier in these replies can serve as an example. When we empathize with the distress or suffering of another, we are acquainted rather directly with their distress and suffering. We *know* what they are going through, and that constitutes knowledge of something real and existentially independent of ourselves. But as I have already pointed out, such knowledge, such acquaintance, necessarily includes motivation to help the other person. So here knowledge of what really and in one sense objectively exists is necessarily tied to motivation, and when normativity is understood in terms of motivation, this means that empathic knowledge of what is outside of us has an automatic normativity.

But normativity is also frequently understood in terms of reasons for action, and I have argued that my naturalistic account of morality also allows our empathic knowledge to give us reasons for action. If someone is in a burning building and is pushing from the inside on the only door that would allow them to escape, they clearly have a practical reason to try to get through that door. But in PYY and in related articles I have pointed out that a morally decent and caring outside observer who can see or hear that someone inside a burning building wants very badly to get through a given door will empathize with the desire to escape of the person inside the building. However, I think we can also say that they empathize with that person's reason for wanting to escape. If empathy can pick up on desires and emotions. I think it can also pick up on the practical reasons that are constituted by those desires and emotions.

Now this move depends on seeing reasons as based in and constituted by emotion-laden desires in many instances, and it has been part of my philosophical program to argue that self-interested or prudential reasons or rationality can be reductively understood in sentimental/emotional terms. This goes against rationalistic views of reasons for action of the sort one finds in the work of Derek Parfit and T. M. Scanlon, but sentimentalism can view reasons very differently from the way such authors view them. The overall approach I take in PYY sees belief, virtue, epistemic justification, and, yes, also practical reasons in a uniformly sentimentalist way, and that wide-ranging uniformity represents a theoretical advantage of the approach. In the case of the fire, then, it can say that the person outside can through empathy pick up on and feel both the inside person's emotion-laden desires *and* their reasons for wanting to get through a particular door and, more generally, to escape the fire inside. So once again my naturalistic sentimentalist theory can account for the reason-giving normativity that of necessity arises out of empathy in relevant circumstances. (I should also perhaps mention that the semi-Kripkean reference-fixing account of moral semantics offered in *Moral Sentimentalism* helps explain how moral *judgments* can refer to natural realities independent of the speaker/thinker making the judgment.)

Ng also speaks of our "increasingly globalized world," a world in which Chinese philosophy can be brought to bear on topics that have long engaged Western philosophers. Nowadays, and as my reply to Vincent Shen made clear, I like to speak of the prospects of a genuine "world philosophy." I believe that an increased attention to the role of emotion and to the way *yin/yang* underlies emotional states and processes can help us toward such a philosophy and work as a corrective to the Western emphasis on pure rationality and to the standard Western assumption that our reasons and the cognitive processes we engage in are metaphysically separate from our emotions. Ng refers to what he calls *qing*-ism and points out that Chinese philosophy, by making emotion central to the life of the mind or *xin*, is a prime example of *qing*-ism. Well, I am a *qing*ist too. Like Zhang Zai long before me, I think of emotion as the cornerstone of our psychology and the basis of what we need to say about epistemic and moral virtue/rationality. But unlike Zhang and other Chinese thinkers, I think *qing*-ism can be based in and justified in terms of a philosophy of *yin* and *yang*. That is what my book PYY seeks to accomplish.

Ng notes that if one makes emotion philosophically central, one has to deal with the problem of how it can allow for or lead to objective knowledge of the world and the problem of how virtue can flourish while emotion is capable of derailing us from virtuous action. My PYY seeks to answer these questions. It holds, for example, that the fact that confidence is an epistemic emotion doesn't undercut the fact that when we (say) see a tree, our confidence that there really is a tree there may represent, not some aberrant interference with knowledge of the world, but an instance of our knowing the objective world validly and well. Similarly, although emotions like fear and anger can get in the way of rational and/or virtuous action, that interference can be conceptualized in terms of *yin* and *yang*. When rage or panic interferes with rational or virtuous action, that very fact can be explained in terms of *yin* and *yang* or, rather, their absence. As I mentioned earlier, panic (for example) makes us less than *yin* receptive to what is actually happening around us and interferes with our capacity for *yang* directed purposeful action. By the same token when, as with the example of the burning building, fear leads to effective instrumental action, e. g., attempts to leave by the only door available, we have both *yin* and *yang*. The person in question is being *yin* receptive to what is happening around them and to their own needs in the situation; and they are motivated in a *yang* directed way to do what they need to do in order to escape. So the philosophy of *yin* and *yang* can allow emotion to be foundational to its account of virtue and rationality while at the same time allowing that emotion can sometimes undercut our virtue or rationality.

I believe that what I am saying here should be congenial to Ng's *qing*-ism. He notes that emotion or *qing* can or perhaps has to epistemically register facts about oneself or one's environment, but this is quite compatible with a view like my own that treats emotional desiderative *yang* states as always having a *yin* receptive cognitive side. So, yes, as I understand it, emotion is basically geared to reality.

Ng devotes a great deal of space to reviewing what Chinese thinkers have notably said about emotion and the emotions, but the concept of *yin*/*yang* is absent from those discussions, and I believe my own intended contribution to our understanding of the basicness of emotion is promising in great part because it brings *yin* and *yang* into the discussion. Toward the end of his comments, Ng notes my most recent involvement with the concepts of *yin* and *yang*, but he also brings in the concept of *qi*. That notion is absent in my PYY, but (as already mentioned) in my most recent work on *yin* and *yang*, *qi* enters decisively into the discussion. That recent work applies *yin* and *yang* both to *xin* and to nature outside of *xin*, and

I argue that *qi* constitutes the unity that lies behind or is manifested in both psychological and external *yin* and *yang*. This is very Chinese, yes, but unlike earlier Chinese discussions of *qi* and as I mentioned in my reply to Shen, what I have to say about *qi* is entirely consistent with the results of modern science. In fact, surprisingly enough, my view of *qi* (and subsequently of *taiji*) grows out of modern scientific thinking (in particular, what modern science says about the laws of motion). But the reader who is interested in this development will have to look at this new work to see whether it makes good on these stated philosophical ambitions.

11 Reply to Aaron Stalnaker

Aaron Stalnaker's comments are devoted to work of mine on the impossibility of perfection that only partially intersects with my interest in sentimentalism and in the concepts of *yin* and *yang*. He mainly draws on my 2011 OUP book *The Impossibility of Perfection* (IP), which addresses issues about perfection in virtue or happiness as they have been discussed in the West, but he notes an article of mine in which those same issues are addressed in relation to Chinese thought, and much of what he has to say in criticism of my views in fact arises from Chinese modes of thinking. Thus he questions what I say in IP about the supposed clash between tact(fulness) and frankness by denying that frankness is a virtue, and indeed Chinese thought doesn't attribute as much value to frankness as we tend to do in the West. This makes him question one of my prime examples of the inevitable clash of virtues in a way that Westerners not familiar with the Chinese ethical tradition(s) would perhaps be less inclined to do. Stalnaker (consequently) thinks that my arguments for the impossibility of perfect happiness have greater force than those for the impossibility of perfect virtue, but let us see.

Stalnaker notes that some Confucian thought advocates striving after perfect virtue even when and where there is no (empirical) chance of success, and nothing I have written absolutely contradicts this idea. My focus is on what is impossible and my views don't entail that we shouldn't strive after what we in fact can never achieve. But Stalnaker directly addresses the situation of choice between tact and frankness that I use to advocate the impossibility of perfection in that moral area. I am not going to repeat the details of what I and now Stalnaker have said about the details of that situation. But I do want to consider the main reason he offers for considering frankness not to be a virtue. That reason seems to be the fact that frankness is inappropriate or worse in many situations. But if this sort of fact undermines virtue status, then a lot of supposed virtues will also not really be virtues. There are times when courage is out of place (e. g., when one is prudently fleeing from an overpowering personal or national enemy or when one is seated in the dentist's chair) but that hardly makes us think that courage isn't a virtue. Similarly, there are times when it is more appropriate to be magnanimous and merciful rather than strictly just in one's treatment of some individual or group. Most of us know this, but this doesn't make us conclude that justice isn't a virtue. Finally, fidelity to one's promises is universally considered a moral virtue, but everyone knows that there are many times when it is appropriate and even morally necessary to break a promise. Virtue status thus allows for exceptions in many cases, so I don't see that Stalnaker gives us any good reason to think that frankness is not a virtue. (This doesn't mean and I have never said that it is a moral virtue.)

Stalnaker also worries about the "proliferation" of virtues that pluralistic views of virtue seem especially prone to, and he recommends making a distinction between cardinal and other virtues and subordinating particular virtues to others as a way of counteracting that tendency. But the main reason he gives (following Daniel Russell) for the worry about proliferation is the difficulty of having an explicit general account of right action where proliferation is allowed to occur (or be accepted). I don't very much see this as a problem for proliferation, but to return to the example of tact vs. frankness with an unfortunate friend, Stalnaker's claim that Confucians would be unwilling or unlikely to accept what I say about that example isn't directly relevant to my own arguments re that example. Does he really have any philosophical justification for denying my view of the case?

Not that he makes at all apparent. What we get instead is an insistence that both frankness and tact may count as minor virtues, so that the necessary virtue imperfection that follows in the wake of such cases needn't disturb us very much. Virtue perfection might be impossible, but "near-perfection" might still be eminently possible. I agree with this and have never denied it. Nor, to speak more radically, have I ever said that the impossibility of virtue perfection means that no one can be really or admirably virtuous. My impossibility of perfection thesis is limited in its implications and doesn't in any way count as a form of ethical skepticism, but still many thinkers both East and West have held that perfection is possible and it is very much worth considering whether they have been correct about this.

More particularly, and as IP points out, many women lament their inability or failure to perfectly balance career and family, and it might make women feel less bad about this if they realized that the inability or failure is totally inevitable. However, Stalnaker thinks that even if a perfect balance between career and family is impossible, it makes sense to attempt to pursue it and for society to encourage that pursuit because this could well result in better compromises between the goods available from family relationships and those that arise from careers. I am not sure he is mistaken about this, but it seems to me on the face of it rather blithe and insensitive to recommend sustained striving after perfection when, as we see from women's reactions to present-day circumstances, this tends to leave women frustrated by what is happening or has happened in their lives.

Finally, Stalnaker also questions whether either adventurousness or a prudent regard for one's own safety is any kind of virtue, partial or otherwise. But I don't find any argument for denying virtue status to either of them, and more generally

I think he doesn't offer any persuasive reason for denying IP's main conclusions about virtue or about happiness.

12 Reply to Qingjie James Wang

Qingjie James Wang discusses the views about self-other symmetry I defend in my 1992 OUP book *From Morality to Virtue* (FMTV). He notes that in that book I regard such symmetry as a desirable feature of any account of morality and fault commonsense morality for asymmetrically emphasizing our obligations to others at the expense of any clear notion or understanding of our moral obligations to ourselves. We know that symmetry is considered a desirable feature and is a sought-after feature of scientific theories, and I assumed and in fact still assume that such symmetry is desirable for moral theory as such. FMTV deliberately parted ways with those like Bernard Williams who hold that the practical goals of morality are not well served by thinking of morality in theoretic terms analogous with the way theories are regarded in science. Theorizing leads us toward simplifying our basic assumptions, and Williams believes we need more ideas rather than fewer in our ethical responses to people and the world.

FMTV doesn't confront this negative attitude toward moral theorizing head on, but rather seeks to develop and deploy moral theorizing in the most satisfactory way possible. And doing so at least *prima facie* means preferring symmetry to asymmetry. That led me to leave ordinary moral thinking behind and develop a symmetrical form of virtue ethics (as per the title of the book); but I now think there are countervailing reasons to be less intolerant of the asymmetry of ordinary moral thought.

The main countervailing reason has to do with empathy. At the time I wrote FMTV I was pretty much unaware of the potential relevance of (the concept of) empathy to moral theory. But once I become aware of that possible relevance, my philosophical attitude toward commonsense morality began to change. It slowly started occurring to me that the self-other asymmetry of commonsense or ordinary morality might be due to the self-other asymmetry of empathy and to the fact that empathy is (somehow) built into moral concepts like rightness, wrongness, and moral goodness. Once one has got this far, one is tempted to conclude that self-other asymmetry is built into the very concept of morality, in which case it cannot be an objection to ordinary asymmetrical moral judgments that they are and necessarily are asymmetrical. They have to be asymmetrical on purely conceptual grounds, assuming only that we have empathy with others and not with our ongoing selves.

My unwillingness in FMTV to countenance ordinary morality's self-other asymmetry was in some part due to my inability at the time the book was published to see any good reason why our ordinary moral thinking *should be* asymmetrical. (I was aware of this at the time the book was written.) And my subsequent recognition of the potential role of empathy in moral thought and action gave me precisely such a reason. So I have now and for a long time backed off from my earlier insistence on the need for symmetry in our theorizing about morality/ethics and have instead (as in my 2010 *Moral Sentimentalism*) attempted to work out a theoretical view of moral virtue and more thinking that gives empathy a central and foundational place.

Wang undertakes a thoroughgoing and highly accurate review of the main arguments of FMTV, emphasizing in particular how it argues for the advantages of commonsense virtue ethics over other symmetrical theories like utilitarianism. In fact, he ingeniously construes my argument in a way that makes it seem more forceful than it might appear from reading the book itself. Pointing out that utilitarianism advocates symmetrically regarding and caring for the welfare of every individual as an individual, he points out that my virtue ethics stresses symmetry and balance between virtues rather than *vis-à-vis* individuals. The virtue of benevolence is thus to be balanced against virtuous prudential self-concern as virtues, and this allows that, contrary to utilitarianism, it is acceptable and good to have greater concern for one's own welfare than for the welfare of particular other individuals. Someone with that greater concern can still be said to be balancing symmetrically between prudence and benevolence, and this allows the defender of FMTV's commonsense virtue ethics to argue 1) that such a symmetry of virtues is more in keeping with commonsense intuitive thinking than utilitarianism's symmetry in regard to individuals and 2) that this virtue-ethical kind of balance is just as much a balance, just as symmetrical, as the balance and symmetry we find in utilitarianism.

As I have indicated, I never myself make this specific argument in FMTV (though I come close). What Wang has suggested bolsters the case for the kind of commonsense virtue ethics defended in that book, but as I have also indicated, there are reasons to be happier with self-other asymmetry that I wasn't aware of at the time I wrote FMTV. That is why I no longer accept commonsense symmetrical virtue ethics and defend, instead, an arguably commonsensical asymmetrical virtue ethics based in empathy. In his comments, Wang also makes some interesting criticisms of the commonsense virtue ethics defended in FMTV, but since I no longer accept that approach, I hope I may be excused from examining those criticisms and either arguing against them or admitting their force and validity.

13 Conclusion

Before I leave you, let me just say a bit of something to those analytic and non-sinologist philosophers who may be reading this volume. The idea of *yin/yang* is totally out of left field from your standpoint, and it may be very tempting to ignore the whole idea of a philosophy based on that complementarity. But the *yin/yang* philosophy emerged originally from two criticisms I have made of Western thinking: first, of the almost universal assumption that belief/cognition/reasoning can occur in the absence of all emotion and, second, of the assumption, standardly made by both Western psychologists and Western philosophers, that empathy with suffering can exist in the absence of any motivation to alleviate that suffering. I have given brief versions of those criticisms in the replies I have made to the commentators of this volume, and elsewhere I have given them at length. I ask the analytic philosophy reader to look at those criticisms. If they find them difficult to refute, then they may want to look at the overall *yin/yang* philosophy that can be developed, via analytic argument, once one accepts them. I assume there will be resistance to all this, but it is my hope that as China takes an increasingly large place in the world, its ideas will be taken more seriously than they are at present. And perhaps some of you analytic philosophers will be willing, as against everything that is philosophically familiar and has been accepted as a matter of course, to make the journey even now with *yin* and *yang*.

By way of conclusion let me once again express my gratitude to those who have contributed to this volume. Your criticisms, observations, and suggestions about my work have given me much to think about, and I can only hope that my replies here will give *each of you* something to think about. Let's now all go and do some "world philosophy."

Index

The letter *f* following an entry indicates a page that includes a figure.

absolute, the 37, 38
act-consequentialism 199, 201
act-utilitarianism 199, 201
action 20, 84, 216
    capacity for 121
    circumstances of 22
    Davidson, Donald 81–2, 217
    empathy 124
    knowledge, unity with 72–3, 89–91
    normativity 235
    responsiveness 25–9
    Scanlon, Thomas 84
    terms 117–18
    Williams, Bernard 82–3
adventurousness 181, 187–8
agency 23–5
    Zhuangzi 28
Altham, J. E. J. 85, 86
Ames, Roger 100
Analects of Confucius 193, 194
    choice 188
    filial piety 204, 205, 206
    frankness/tact 184
    jing 205, 206
    qing 160
    unity of virtues 182–3
    xiao 204–6
    xin 69
    yang 205
analytic philosophy 213–14
Angle, Steve 190
Anscombe, G. E. M. 83, 91
anti-Humeanism 81 *see also* besire
approval 123–4, 130, 148–9, 231, 233–4
Aristotelian ethics 2, 144, 182
authority 184–5 *see also* government
autonomy
    yin-yang 8

baptism (terms) 118
bao 102
baoyang 102–3
belief 4–5, 58, 84, 217 *see also* besire
    Anscombe, G. E. M. 83
    desire 229
    emotion 48–51, 63–5, 66, 68–9, 222–3, 226, 229–30
    Humean belief-desire model 81–5, 90
    non-normative 92, 93
    normative 91–2, 93, 94, 96
    Plato 66
    Platts, Mark 83
    Scanlon, Thomas 84
    Socrates 66
    truth-apt 51, 224–5
    yin/yang 68–9, 224
benevolence 118, 231 see also *ren*
Berlin, Isaiah 180–1
besire 81, 83–8, 95
    Wang Yangming 88–94, 95
Book of Mencius (Mencius). See *Mencius*
buren 118, 119, 123, 130, 230–1

capacity 121, 122
cardinal virtues 187
care
    children 207–8, 210
    elderly parents 129, 199–200, 204–8, 210
care, ethics of 156, 157, 170–1 *see also* empathy
    self-other symmetry/asymmetry 199–204, 207–9, 239–40
    social justice 146–8, 170, 180, 232–4, 238
career/family balance 181, 188, 191–2, 194, 238

Index

centralities 38
change 35, 103, 107–8
Cheng Hao 6, 164–6, 172–3
Cheng Yi 163–5
Cheng-Zhu school 70
children 207–8, 210
Chinese Marriage Law 206
Chinese philosophy 5–8, 15, 213–16
choices 188–91
Chunqiu (Confucius) 193, 194
cognition 224
Collected Commentaries on the Doctrine of the Mean (Zhu Xi) 70
"Comments on Bryan van Norden's *Virtue Ethics and Consequentialism in Early Chinese Philosophy*" (Slote, Michael) 5–6
commonsense virtue ethics 200–4, 240
communication 185–6
comparative philosophy 43, 44
compassion 20, 67, 215, 231, 232 *see also* empathy
    Mencius 120–1, 122
complementarity 19, 34–5f, 41, 219
confidence 217
Confucianism *see also* Confucius *and* Song Confucianism
    adventurousness 188
    care ethics 170
    career/family balance 191–2
    emotion 169
    filial piety 210
    harmony 180, 189–90, 192, 208, 209
    justice as appropriation 207–8, 209, 210
    moral judgement 188–91
    morality 133–4, 204–5
    perfection 179–80
    prudence 188
    qing-ism 158–74
    unity of the virtues 182–3
    unrest 22
    virtue 183–6, 194–5
    Zhou Dunyi 38–9
Confucius 5 *see also* Confucianism?
    adventurousness 188
    Analects of Confucius. See *Analects of Confucius*
    Chunqiu 193, 194
    emotion 160–1

empathy 170
filial piety 204, 205, 206
Great Learning 72–3
jing 205, 206, 207
moral perfection 193
qing 160
unrest 22
virtue 180, 182–3, 184, 188, 194
xiao 204–7
yang 205, 206, 207
consequentialism 2, 5–6
contrast 40–2, 43
courage 182, 188, 237
cultivation 28–9 *see also* self-cultivation
curiosity 219

Daniels, Norman 207–8
dao xin 70
Daodejing (Laozi) 35, 102–3
Daoism 217
    responsiveness 21–5
Davidson, Donald 51, 216, 217
    Humean belief-desire model 81–2
decisiveness 68
definition (terms) 118
deontological morality 199–200
desire 55–7, 84, 92, 224 *see also* besire
    Anscombe, G. E. M. 83, 91
    belief 229
    Humean belief-desire model 81–5, 90
    passages of problematic desires (PPDs) 136–9, 142–3
    Platts, Mark 83
    Zhu Xi 167
dialectic 41, 221
difference 35f, 41, 219
directed active purpose 20
disapproval 123–4, 130, 148–9, 231, 233–4
Discourse on the natural theology of the Chinese (Leibniz, Gottfried Wilhelm) 34
"Doctrine of the Four Axioms" (Wang Yangming) 75
Doctrine of the Mean (Zhongyong) (Zisi) 163
Dong Zhong Shu 209–10
dynamic contrast 41–2

"Early Confucian Ethics and Moral
    Sentimentalism" (Luo, Shirong) 5
East/West contrast 37–8
elderly parents 129, 199–200, 204–8, 210
emotion 4, 5, 47, 157–8, 166, 222–3 see also
    heart-mind
  belief 48–51, 63–5, 66, 68–9, 222–3,
    226, 229–30
  buren 118, 119, 123, 130, 230–1
  Cheng brothers 163–6
  Confucianism 169
  Confucius 160–1
  controlling 165, 166–7
  definitions 175 n. 4
  empirical 74
  intellect, dissolving in 63, 67, 225
  intellect, separation from 47, 59–60, 65,
    225
  moral emotions 171–2
  qing-ism 158–74
  seven feelings 74
  truth-apt 51, 224–5
  Wang Yangming 74
  yin/yang 68, 224, 236
  Zhu Xi 54–5, 166–9
emotional unity 49, 51
empathy 3–5, 77, 115–17, 123–30, 227,
    230–1, 230–5 see also *xin*
  cognition 125
  Confucius 170
  epistemic rationality 48–9
  epistemic virtue 66
  first-order 4, 145–8, 150, 231, 234
  government 119–22, 133–4, 136–43,
    150
  human-heartedness 71–2
  Mencius 118–24, 145–51, 230–4
  Mencius 118–24, 230–1
  morality 123, 124, 125, 156
  motives 124
  music 138
  normativity 235
  obligation 124–5, 126
  patriarchy 146, 232–3
  reason 215
  relationships 128–9
  ren 118–19, 122–3, 129, 170–1, 231
  second-order 4, 145, 148–9, 150, 231,
    233–4

  self-other asymmetry 239–40
  sympathy, comparison with 144–5, 150
  terms 117, 126
  Wang Yangming 6
  yin/yang 8, 66, 215
Empiricism 52
*Entretien d'un philosophe chrétien et d'un
    philosophe chinois sur l'existence et
    la nature de Dieu* (Malebranche,
    Nicolas) 34
epistemic rationality 48–9
"Epistemology of Yin and Yang" (Slote,
    Michael) 68
Equalizing East and West (Fang Yizhi) 35
equilibrium 163, 167
Essays on the History of Ethics (Slote,
    Michael) 156, 157
ethical deontology 199
ethics 1, 157 see also virtue ethics
  of care 156, 157 see also empathy
  ethical dilemmas 190
  rule ethics 201–2
Ethics of Care and Empathy (ECE) (Slote,
    Michael) 126, 156
evil 167
evil/good 55, 56, 75
examples (terms) 118
*Explanation of the Diagram of the Great
    Ultimate* (*Taiji Tushuo*) (Zhou
    Dunyi) 39–40

family balance/career 181, 188, 191–2, 194,
    238
Fang Yizhi 36–8, 220
  centralities 38
  East/West contrast 37–8
  Equalizing East and West 35
  Humble Knowledge of Physics 36, 37
  Yaodi Paozhunag (*Fang Yizhi's
    Processed Commentaries on the
    Zhuangzi*) 37
feminism 194 see also gender equality
Feng Qi 221
fidelity 238
filial piety 129, 199–200, 204–8, 210
Finagrette, Herbert 188
first-order empathy 4, 145–8, 150, 231, 234
Flanagan, Owen 93–4
fortitude 204

four moral sprouts 53, 55, 161, 164, 233
frankness 179, 181, 184–7, 237–8
From Enlightenment to Receptivity (Slote, Michael) 6
From Morality to Virtue (FMTV) (Slote, Michael) 199, 239
fu 102
fuyin 102–3

Garfield, Jay/van Norden, Bryan
  "If Philosophy Won't Diversity, Let's Call It What It Really Is" 15, 213–14
gender equality 146–7, 157, 191–2, 232–3
Gilligan, Carol
  In a Different Voice 233
Global Maps (Ricci, Matteo) 38
globalization 43, 221
good 126
good/evil 55, 56, 75, 172
goodness 223–4
government 119–22, 133–4, 136–43, 150, 184–5
  elderly, the 206
  conflicting values 190–1
Graham A. C. 159, 160, 161
Great Learning 72–3, 89
Great Ultimate concept 38–9, 41 see also *taiji*
Gu Dongqiao 90
Gui Guzi (*The Master of Spirit Valley*) 106

Han Shi Waizhuan (Han Ying) 191
Hanfeizi (Han Fei) 105
Hansen, Chad 159
happiness 194–5 see also perfection
hard virtue ethics 186–7
harmony 180, 189–90, 192, 208, 209
He Guanzi (*Pheasant Cape Master*) 107–8
heartmind 133, 135–6 see also *xin*
heart-mind 7–8, 47, 59–60, 63 see also *xin*
  Cheng Yi 164
  heartmind 133, 135–6
  Mencius 161–2, 169
  Wang Yangming 63–4
  yin-yang 66–9
  Zhu Xi 166–9
heavenly principle 55–6
Hegel, Georg Wilhelm Friedrich 109

Hegelian thesis-antithesis-synthesis method 109–10
Hegelianism 41, 221
Held, Virginia 146–7, 232–3
historicity 41
Huang, Yong 228–9
Huangdi Neijing 101, 108
hubu 107
huhan 106
human body 101
human-heartedness 71–2
human nature
  Cheng brothers 163–5, 172–3
  dual nature 192–3
  Mencius 53, 89–90, 169
  Mencius, four moral sprouts 53, 55, 161, 164, 233
  nature 159–60
  neo-Confucianism 172
  "Records of Music" (*Yueji*) 159–60
  Wang Fuzhi 173
  Zhang Zai 172
  Zhu Xi 54–5, 56–7, 166–9
humanization 40
Humble Knowledge of Physics (Fang Yizhi) 36, 37
Hume, David 115, 144
Humean belief-desire model 81–5, 90

"If Philosophy Won't Diversity, Let's Call It What It Really Is" (Garfield, Jay/van Norden, Bryan) 15, 213–14
Impossibility of Perfection: Aristotle, Feminism, and the Complexities of Ethics, The (Slote, Michael) 156, 157, 179, 180, 194, 237
In a Different Voice (Gilligan, Carol) 233
incommensurability 43–4
Indian philosophy 221, 222
Infinite, the 39–40
Ing, Michael 180, 189–91, 192–3
  Vulnerability of Integrity in Early Confucian Thought, The 190
innatism 48, 52–3
  xin 74–5
intellect
  emotion, dissolving in 63, 67, 225
  emotion, separation from 47, 59–60, 65, 225

inter-relationality 217–18
intercultural philosophy 43, 44
irrationality 51

Jiang, Tao 231–4
jiaogan 106–7
jing 205, 206, 207
judgement 188–91
justice 209–10 *see also* social justice
justice as appropriation 207–8, 209, 210

Kant, Immanuel 50, 93, 94,
    deontological morality 199–200
Kierkegaard, Søren 197 n. 5
King, R. A. H. 230–1
knowing, way of 100
knowledge 88–9, 229
    action, unity with 72–3, 89–91
kokoro 7
Kongzi. *See* Confucius
Kripke, Saul
    Naming and Necessity 118

Lai, Karyn 216–18
language 44, 60, 65, 225 *see also* terms
    holism of meaning 110–11
Laozi 40–1
    Daodejing 35
Large Philosophy of Yin and Yang, The
    (Slote, Michael) 10, 14
Larger Yin/Yang Philosophy: From Mind to
    Cosmic Harmony, A (LYYP) (Slote,
    Michael) 214, 217, 220, 227
laws 206
Leibniz, Gottfried Wilhelm
    Discourse on the natural theology of the
    Chinese 34
    Novissima Sinica 34
Liang Qichao 102
Liji (Record of Ritual) 184
Liu, JeeLoo 222–5
Lu Jiuyuan 71
Lü Kun 173
Luo, Shirong
    "Early Confucian Ethics and Moral
    Sentimentalism" 5
Lüshi Chunqiu (*The Annals of Lü Buwei*)
    107

Malebranche, Nicolas
    Entretien d'un philosophe chrétien et
    d'un philosophe chinois sur
    l'existence et la nature de Dieu 34
"Mandate of Empathy, The" (Slote,
    Michael) 6
maodun 105
maum 7
meaning, holism of 110–11
medicine 105, 107
Mencius 5–6 see also *Mencius*
    adventurousness 188
    Book of Mencius. See *Mencius*
    cardinal virtues 187
    empathy 118–24, 145–51, 230–4
    four moral sprouts 53, 55, 129, 161, 164, 233
    frankness/tact 184–5
    government 119–22, 133–4, 136–43, 150, 184–5, 206
    human nature 53, 89–90, 169
    justice 147–8, 233
    Mencius see *Mencius*
    moral persuasion 133–5, 144, 151
    moral script 138–41, 143, 144
    moral therapy 134–6, 141–3, 144, 147, 151
Nivison, David 161
qing 161, 169
tranquillity 161–2
virtue 183, 195, 215
xin 69–70
Mencius (Mencius) 6, 116, 127 *see also*
    Mencius
    buren 118–23
    caution 184
    empathy 118–24, 230–1
    examples, use of 118
    filial piety 129, 205–6
    four moral sprouts 129
    government 119–22, 133, 136–43
    judgement 189, 190
    moral persuasion 133
    moral/profit script 139–41
    parenting 192
    passages of problematic desires (PPDs) 136–9, 142–3
    passion 130
    ren 119

rules 126–7
virtue 128, 129, 183
xin 69
Meng Peiyuan 54, 55
Mengzi. *See* Mencius
Mengzi. See *Mencius*
mercy 238
metaethics 4, 156, 157
metaphysics 37
mind, the 5, 7 *see also* heart-mind
   cognition 224
   divided theory 51
   neo-Confucian unified theory 48, 52–60
   rationalism of 48
   sentimentalist theory 47–52, 58–60
   sentimentalist unity 64–6
   unified theory 47–52, 63
   yin/yang 223
   Zhang Zai 47, 48, 52–4, 58, 59
   Zhu Xi 47, 48, 54–5, 57–8, 59
mind-heart. *See* heart-mind
moral emotions 171–2
moral persuasion 133–5, 144, 151
moral realism 94
moral script 138–41, 143, 144
Moral Sentimentalism (MS) (Slote, Michael) 63, 117, 156, 230, 235
moral therapy 134–6, 141–3, 144, 147, 151
morality 96 n. 2 *see also* self-other symmetry/asymmetry
   approval 123–4, 130, 148–9, 231, 233–4
   commonsense 200–4
   Confucian 133–4, 204–5
   deontological 199–200
   disapproval 123–4, 130, 148–9, 231, 233–4
   empathy 123, 124, 125, 156
   filial piety 129, 199–200, 204–8, 210
   Flanagan, Owen 93–4
   Humean belief-desire model 81–5
   inter-relationality 217–18
   judgements 189
   Mencius 118–24, 230–1
   Mencius, four moral sprouts 53, 55, 161, 164, 233
   moral persuasion 133–5, 144, 151

   moral realism 94
   moral therapy 134–6, 141–3, 144, 147, 151
   neo-Confucian unified theory of the mind 59
   perfection 193
   qing-ism 158–74
   self-cultivation 25, 28–9, 218
   Williams, Bernard 239
   yin-yang 19–20
   Zhang Zai 53, 59
   Zhu Xi 55, 56–7, 59
   Zhuangzi 27
Morals and Motives (Slote, Michael) 156
motivation 20, 96 n. 2, 216–17, 235
   Davidson, Donald 217
   Humean belief-desire model 81–5, 90
   Scanlon, Thomas 84
Mou Zongsan 222
Mozi 5–6
music 136–8

Naming and Necessity (Kripke, Saul) 118
"Natural Autonomy, Dual Virtue, and Yin-Yang" (Slote, Michael) 8
natural world, the 101, 102
naturalism 101, 122, 234–5
neo-Confucianism 38–9, 221–2
   qi 172
   unified theory of the mind 48, 52–60
   xin 70
Ng, On-cho 234–7
Nivison, David 161
normativity 234–5
Novissima Sinica (Leibniz, Gottfried Wilhelm) 34

obligation 124–5, 126, 128
opposites 37, 40–1, 42, 229–30 see also *maodun* and *xiangyi*
others 203, 209

parents 129, 199–200, 204–8, 210
partial care 3
passages of problematic desires (PPDs) 136–9, 142–3
passion 130
passion-nature 127
patriarchy 146, 157, 232–3

perfection 179, 183, 193 *see also* happiness
   harmony thesis 180
   impossibility of 179–80, 182, 194, 237–8
"Philosophical Reset Button: A Manifesto, The" (Slote, Michael) 7, 174
philosophy 213–14
   analytic philosophy 213–14
   Chinese philosophy 5–8, 15, 213–16
   Western philosophy 15, 213–15
Philosophy of Yin and Yang, The (PYY) (Slote, Michael) 8, 25, 33–4, 214, 216–7, 219, 230
   belief 58, 172, 222–3, 226–7
   compassion 232
   complementarity 19–20, 219
   development of 6
   emotion 58, 172, 222–3, 236
   mind, the 222–3
   responsiveness 19–20, 216
Plato 66
   Republic 64
Platts, Mark 83
political philosophy 4
process cosmology 100
profit script 139–41
prudence 181, 187–8
purposiveness 20

qi 39, 45 n. 5, 172, 220–1, 236–7
qing 155, 159–61
Qing Dynasty, laws of 206
qing-ism 158–74, 236

rationalism 5, 64 *see also* heart-mind
   belief 84–5
   Kant, Immanuel 50
   yin/yang 8
rationality 43, 157 *see also* epistemic rationality
Rawls, John 93
reason 214–15 *see also* rationalism *and* rationality
receptivity 5, 6, 27, 68
   yin 68, 101–2
   Zhuangzi 26–7
"Records of Music" (*Yueji*) 159–60
Records of Rites (*Liji*) 159
relationality 20, 27–8

relationships 128–9, 138, 140
ren 118–19, 122–3, 129, 170–1, 206, 231
ren xin 70
Republic (Plato) 64
responsiveness 19, 20, 216–18
   agency 25–9
   Zhuangzi 21–5
reversal 107
Ricci, Matteo
   Global Maps 38
   True Meaning of Lord of Heaven 34
right 126
rituals 234
rule ethics 201–2
Russell, Daniel 186–7

sages 57, 75
Scanlon, Thomas 84
science
   classification 36
   Fang Yizhi 36–7
   taiji 220
   yin-yang 219
second-order empathy 4, 145, 148–9, 150, 231, 233–4
self-cultivation 25, 28–9, 218
self-other symmetry/asymmetry 199–204, 207–9, 239–40
   utilitarian 201
self-others harmony 208
sentimentalism 3–5, 72, 76, 155–8
   empathy 145–51
   Hume, David 144
   unity of the mind 47–52, 58–60, 64–6
   Wang Yangming 76
Sentimentalist Theory of Mind, A (STM) (Slote, Michael) 5, 47, 49, 63, 157–8, 228
seven feelings 74
shame 136, 191, 193
Shen, Vincent 218–22
shi yu you zheng 205
Sima Qian 111
Slote, Michael 1–5, 213–14
   Chinese philosophy 5–8, 15, 213–16
   "Comments on Bryan van Norden's *Virtue Ethics and Consequentialism in Early Chinese Philosophy*" 5–6
   "Epistemology of Yin and Yang" 68

Essays on the History of Ethics 156, 157
Ethics of Care and Empathy (ECE) 126, 156
From Enlightenment to Receptivity 6
From Morality to Virtue (FMTV) 199, 239
Impossibility of Perfection: Aristotle, Feminism, and the Complexities of Ethics, The 156, 157, 179, 180, 194, 237
Large Philosophy of Yin and Yang, The 10, 14
Larger Yin/Yang Philosophy: From Mind to Cosmic Harmony, A (LYYP) 214, 217, 220, 227
"Mandate of Empathy, The" 6
Moral Sentimentalism (MS) 63, 117, 156, 230, 235
Morals and Motives 156
"Natural Autonomy, Dual Virtue, and Yin-Yang" 8
"Philosophical Reset Button: A Manifesto, The" 7, 174
Philosophy of Yin and Yang, The (PYY). See *Philosophy of Yin and Yang, The*
Sentimentalist Theory of Mind, A (STM) 5, 47, 49, 63, 157–8, 228
"Updating Yin and Yang" 6–7
"Virtue Ethics, Utilitarianism, and Symmetry" 199
"Virtue's Turn and Return" 7
Western philosophy 15, 214–15
"Yin-Yang and the Heart Mind" 7, 214
Small, Christopher 138
Smith, Michael 85, 86
social justice 146–8, 170, 180, 232–4, 238
social reform 194
society 192
Socrates 66
Song Confucianism 163
"Sophie's Choice" case 190
soul, unity of the 64
Stalnaker, Aaron 237–9
strangification 44
Street, Sharon 234
structural contrast 41, 42
structuralism 41, 42
suicide 191, 193
sumpatheia 127

sumpnoia mia 127
sympathy 64–5, 144–5, 150
  epistemic virtue 66
  yin/yang 66

tact 179, 181, 184–7, 237, 238
taiji 35f, 220, 221 *see also* Great Ultimate concept
Taipingjing (*Classic of Great Peace*) 106–7
Tang Chün-I 52
Tang Dynasty, laws of 206
Taylor, Charles 110–11, 160
terms 117–18, 126
tong 54
tranquillity 161–2, 167
transformation 103, 107–8
transgression 193
True Meaning of Lord of Heaven (Ricci, Matteo) 34

unity of the virtues 182–3
universal benevolence 3
"Updating Yin and Yang" (Slote, Michael) 6–7
utilitarianism 201, 240

van Norden, Bryan 5–6, 144–5
van Norden, Bryan/ Garfield, Jay
  "If Philosophy Won't Diversity, Let's Call It What It Really Is" 15, 213–14
virtue 116, 121, 127–8, 186, 194–5 *see also* perfection *and* virtue ethics
  adventurousness 181, 187–8
  appropriateness 237–8
  cardinal virtues 187
  career/family balance 181, 188, 191–2, 238
  communication 185–6
  conflict 180–1, 184–92
  courage 182, 188, 237
  definitions 16 n. 1, 203, 204
  emotion 215
  fidelity 237
  filial piety 129, 199–200, 204–8, 210
  fortitude 204
  frankness 179, 181, 184–7, 237–8
  mercy 238

obligations 128
other-regarding 202–4
others-concern 203
partial 181, 182, 183, 184
pluralism 180–1, 188
proliferation 186–7, 238
prudence 181, 187–8
ranking 187
self-concern 203
self-regarding 202–4
tact 179, 181, 184–7, 237, 238
unity of the virtues 182–3
Watson, Gary 16 n. 1
wisdom 188
xiao 199–200
yin-yang 8, 215
virtue-consequentialism 204
virtue ethics 2–5, 204 *see also* morality
 commonsense 200–4, 240
 hard virtue ethics 186–7
 revival 7
 self-other symmetry/asymmetry 201–4, 207–9, 239–40
 Watson, Gary 16 n. 1
"Virtue Ethics, Utilitarianism, and Symmetry" (Slote, Michael) 199
"Virtue's Turn and Return" (Slote, Michael) 7
volition 57
Vulnerability of Integrity in Early Confucian Thought, The (Ing, Michael) 190

Wang, Qingjie James 239–40
Wang, Robin 229–30
Wang Fuzhi 36–7, 173
Wang Yangming 6, 63–4, 71–8, 226, 227
 besire 88–94, 95
 "Doctrine of the Four Axioms" 75
 knowledge 88–9, 229
 knowledge/action unity 72–3, 89–91
 moral realism 94
 ren/empathy 170–1
 virtue 215
Watson, Gary 16 n. 1
West/East contrast 37–8
Western philosophy 15, 213–14
Williams, Bernard 82–3, 239
wisdom 188

women's equality 146–7, 157, 191–2, 232–3, 238
world philosophy 43, 221–2, 235
wu wei 205
wuji zhefa 112 n. 4
wuwei 21, 22–3

xiangyi 105–6
xiao 199–200, 204–7
xin 7, 54, 59–60, 64–5, 223 *see also* heart-mind *and* heartmind
 Cheng-Zhu school 70
 innatism 74–5
 Lu Jiuyuan 71
 Mencius 69–70
 monism 73
 neo-Confucianism 70
 translation 151 n. 1
 unity of 69–78
 Wang Yangming 63–4, 71–8
 Zhu Xi 70–1
xing 161 *see also* human nature
Xunzi 162, 183, 184
 Xunzi 162, 183, 184
Xunzi (Xunzi) 162, 183, 184

yang 20, 29 n. 1, 67–8, 172, 225, 226–7
 baoyang 102–3
 care of parents 205, 206, 207, 208
 change 107–8
 medicine 107
 mutual support 107
 yin, interaction with 106
 yin, interdependence with 105
 yin, mutual inclusion with 106
Yao, Xinzhong 225–7
Yaodi Paozhunag (*Fang Yizhi's Processed Commentaries on the Zhuangzi*) (Fang Yizhi) 37
yi 209–10
Yijing (*The Book of Changes*) 35, 37, 106
yin 20, 67–8, 172, 225, 226–7
 change 107–8
 Daodejing 103
 fuyin 102–3
 medicine 107
 mutual support 107
 as receptivity 101–3
 yang, interaction with 106

yang, interdependence with 105
yang, mutual inclusion with 106
yin/yang 6–8, 33–4, 58–9, 108–9, 226–7, 240–1 see also *yinyang* clusters
  belief 224
  belief/desire 229
  compassion 232
  complementarity 19, 34–5f, 41, 104, 216–17, 219, 230
  contrast 40–2
  cultivation 28–9
  curiosity 219
  Daodejing 102–3
  diagram 35f, 216–17, 230
  difference 35f, 41, 219
  dissolving *yang* in *yin* 67–8, 225
  emotion 68, 224, 236
  empathy 8, 66, 215
  Great Ultimate concept 38–9
  Hegelian thesis-antithesis-synthesis comparison 109–10
  Huangdi Neijing 101
  Infinite, the 39–40
  knowledge 229
  Lü Kun 173
  meaning, holism of 110
  mind, the 223
  morality 19–20
  mutual restraint 103–4
  opposites 37, 40–1, 42, 105, 229–30
  origins 100–1
  pattern 108
  qi 172, 220–1, 236–7
  qing-ism 172–4, 236
  relationships 111
  responsiveness 21–9, 216–18
  science 219, 220
  superficiality 58, 224
  taiji 35f
  unity of the heart-mind 66–9
  virtue 8, 215
  Wang Fuzhi 173
  Wang Yangming 229
  Yijing (*The Book of Changes*) 35, 37
  Zhuangzi 21
  "Yin-Yang and the Heart Mind" (Slote, Michael) 7, 214
  ying 20, 27–8 see also responsiveness
  Zhuangzi 21–5
yinyang clusters 99–100, 104–9, 110–11

Zhang, Yan 225–7
Zhang Zai 47, 48, 52–4, 58, 59, 223, 224
  mind-heart 169
  qing-ism 172
Zhu Xi 47, 48, 54–8, 59, 224
  emotion 54–5, 166–9
  ren 170
  human nature 54–5, 56–7, 166–9
  Great Learning 72–3
  Collected Commentaries on the Doctrine of the Mean 70
  xin 70–1
Zhuangzi (Zhuangzi)
  receptivity 26–7
  responsiveness 21–9
  flexibility 22–3
Zhuangzi
  Zhuangzi see Zhuangzi
zhuanhua 107–8
Zhou Dunyi 38–40, 220
  Explanation of the Diagram of the Great Ultimate (*Taiji Tushuo*) 39–40
Zhouli (*The Rites of Zhou*) 107

www.ingramcontent.com/pod-product-compliance
Lightning Source LLC
Chambersburg PA
CBHW072139290426
44111CB00012B/1919